Bryant Julstrom

Object-Oriented Compiler Construction

Jim Holmes
Bethel College, MN

Prentice Hall
Englewood Cliffs, NJ 07632

Library of Congress Cataloging-in-Publication Data

Holmes, Jim
    Object-oriented compiler construction / Jim Holmes.
        p.   cm.
    Includes bibliographical references and index.
    ISBN 0-13-630740-X
    1. Object-oriented programming. 2. Compilers (Computer programs)
    I. Title.
    QA76.76.C65H64   1995
    005.4'53--dc20
                                                      94-33320
                                                      CIP

Acquisitions Editor: Bill Zobrist
Production Editor: Joe Scordato
Cover Designer: Wendy Alling Judy
Buyer: Lori Bulwin
Editorial Assistant: Phyllis Morgan

 ©1995 by Prentice-Hall, Inc.
A Simon & Schuster Company
Englewood Cliffs, New Jersey 07632

The author and publisher of this book have used their best efforts in preparing this book. These efforts
include the development, research, and testing of the theories and programs to determine their effectiveness.
The author and publisher make no warranty of any kind, expressed or implied, with regard to these programs
or the documentation contained in this book. The author and publisher shall not be liable in any event for
incidental or consequential damages in connection with, or arising out of, the furnishing, performance, or use
of these programs.

Printed in the United States of America

10 9 8 7 6 5 4 3 2 1

ISBN 0-13-630740-X

Prentice-Hall International (UK) Limited, London
Prentice-Hall of Australia Pty. Limited, Sydney
Prentice-Hall Canada Inc., Toronto
Prentice-Hall Hispanoamericana, S.A., Mexico
Prentice-Hall of India Private Limited, New Delhi
Prentice-Hall of Japan, Inc., Tokyo
Simon & Schuster Asia Pte. Ltd., Singapore
Editora Prentice-Hall do Brasil, Ltda., Rio de Janeiro

Contents

Preface

0.1 About This Text

An elementary text.   This is an entry-level text about concepts and methods used
to construct interpreters and compilers. More precisely, this is a book about the
construction of a particular compiler, a Pascal compiler. Though probably not
the language of choice for any of us, Pascal does have the advantages of familiarity,
simplicity and yet nontriviality. Focusing on the implementation of a single compiler
for a relatively simple language enables a compiler tyro to see the big picture as
well as to master the details of the various components.

An introduction to object-oriented techniques.   This is also a book about using
object-oriented analysis, design, and C++ coding techniques to build interpreters or
compilers. Compiler construction is a mature subject, containing some interesting
theory and a number of standard tools. We spend some time (Chapters 5 and 6)
looking at how these standard components work, how to build them, and how to
encapsulate them so that they can be conveniently used in an system designed and
implemented using object-oriented methodologies. However the major focus of the
text (Chapters 8 and 9) is the definition of special objects which are used to build
an important tree structure. Since these objects, in addition to storing program
information, can also exhibit behavior, the tree itself can be used to replace several
complex procedures normally used for interpreting and producing code.

Preparation for building user interfaces.   Few of us have either sufficient time or
interest to build a complete compiler for a modern programming language. Even
fewer will have opportunity to build compilers professionally. However, many of
the ideas in this text can also be used in applications programming, particularly if
the application contains a nontrivial user interface supporting both interactive and
batch input. The design of an interface language involves many of the same issues
confronting the designer of a programming language. Moreover, communication
between the interface and the application can often be efficiently implemented as
essentially the interpreting of a program representing the user's dialog with the
interface.

0.2   Prerequisites

Language prerequisites. Previous Pascal experience will be an obvious aid in understanding the language structures described or illustrated here. No prior knowledge of C++ is assumed, though any C experience, will prove helpful, especially in terms of syntax. There are a number of excellent introductory C++ texts (e.g., Graham [6]) presently available. Lippman's primer [12] actually has become a favorite C++ reference book. Appendix A of this text provides a very brief overview of the C++ language and describes the specific features that are used most often in the construction of the Pascal compiler.

Computer Science prerequisites. You should have seen standard data structures such as linked-lists and hash tables. You should also have had some experience with the standard sort, search, and hash algorithms. These topics can be found in almost any text written for the traditional CS 2 course in the computer science major.

0.3   Ancillary Documents

Many readers have found it useful to have more detailed information available as they construct their own versions of the ideas in this text. A project text, *Building Your Own Compiler with C++* [7] has been designed specifically for this purpose. The project chapters are directly correlated with those in this text and a complete program for a tiny compiler is contained in and appendix.

A fairly complete instructor's manual is also available. In addition to the standard fare of exercise answers, topics of relevance or importance which have been omitted in this text are often discussed at some length in the manual.

The following systems are available by anonymous ftp from *ftp.bethel.edu* in the directory *pub/epc*. They are compressed tar files.

- *epc.tar.Z* The complete example compiler described in the project text.

- *txt_epc.tar.Z* The example compiler described in this text.

Both of these systems are undergoing constant revision by students and faculty and so are provided "as is" and without any expressed or implied warranties.

0.4   Acknowledgements

I am grateful to all who reviewed the text and provided feedback, especially the following: Brian Beuning, Duane Olawsky, Andrew Perrie, Ralph Johnson, and Timothy Budd. Also, special thanks to the excellent people at Prentice Hall. Their encouragement and expertise have vastly increased the quality of this text. Professors J. Kenneth Shultis and Richard Paul blazed trails through the LaTeXforest and generously shared their information with those of us using the system to prepare our texts.

Chapter 1

Compiler Structure

Topics:

- Background
- Compiler components
  - Scanner
  - Parser
  - Symbol tables
  - Error handlers
  - Intermediate representations
  - Optimizers
  - Code generators

Computers process information according to a collection of instructions, called a **program**. Such programs are stored and then executed by means of integrated sets of algorithms and data structures. When these algorithms and structures are implemented or constructed from electronic components, the computer is called a **hardware computer** [16, page 14]. A hardware computer can be programmed by placing the sequence of instructions along with the data directly into computer memory. In this case the format of the information will necessarily be entered in machine-recognizable code. Since such code is often hard for humans to accurately read and write, programming at this level usually is a very difficult task. Clearly, what is needed is a way of specifying computer instructions in a format more suitable for the human eye. Such specifications, called **programming languages**, can essentially contain mnemonic equivalents of the existing machine instructions, or they can look very much like a natural language containing a rich collection of control and data structures.

Of course, the next problem is to make the instructions in the programming language accessible to the computer. One way do accomplish this is to use a program called a **compiler** to translate the programming language into machine instructions. Another method is to modify the computer by writing a program called an **interpreter**, whose machine instructions are those of the programming

1

language. In the first case, the programming language instructions are modified into a form that can be executed on an existing computer; in the second case, the interpreter and the computer are combined into a **virtual** computer that takes the high-level language instructions and simulates them on the hardware computer.

Common wisdom indicates that interpreting a program is not as efficient as the execution of corresponding code produced by a compiler. Actually, this was not quite the way it was originally. Early computers were often used for scientific applications that required extensive floating-point calculations. Since the machines of that era usually had hardware implementations for only integer data, floating-point operations required software emulation. So much computation was spent on this floating-point emulation that compiled applications were not significantly more efficient than interpreted versions. Though it seems strange to us now, early scientific programmers often chose to develop their systems in an interpreter environment which provided efficient system development and convenient debugging (Backus [2]).

In 1954 IBM introduced its 704 system, which had *hardware* floating-point operations. That same year the FORmula TRANslating System was announced as a high-level language whose compiler produced machine code as efficient as that written by human programmers. It is interesting that the new FORTRAN language was so much easier to use than machine language that the compiler writers decided not to retain the facilities for syntax checking and program debugging that had been developed earlier for the machine language environments. The important point, however, is that humanlike languages had now been machine translated into very efficient target programs.

In the late 1950s and early 1960s languages began to be proposed that were increasingly rich in new symbols, operations, and concepts. Algol 58 and the even more influential Algol 60 introduced important issues such as block structure (with corresponding scope rules) and special mechanisms for subprogram parameter passing. The COBOL language demonstrated that computer programs written in pseudo-English could be effectively compiled. That compiler also introduced the important ideas of MACRO and the data division. Later versions of FORTRAN introduced independent compilation of subroutines and new control structures such as the logical IF construct. Quite naturally, the role of the compiler was necessarily expanded to include extensive checking of the source code for conformity to an increasingly complex set of language specifications.

During the 1960s and 70s a great deal of research was aimed at the problems of defining and compiling higher level programming languages. The result of this extensive work is a well-defined theory of compiler structure and fundamental algorithms that are now often viewed as the components in Figure 1.1.

1.1   The Scanner

Programming language specifications usually begin by describing the collection of valid characters, often called the **alphabet** of the language. Strings of correct

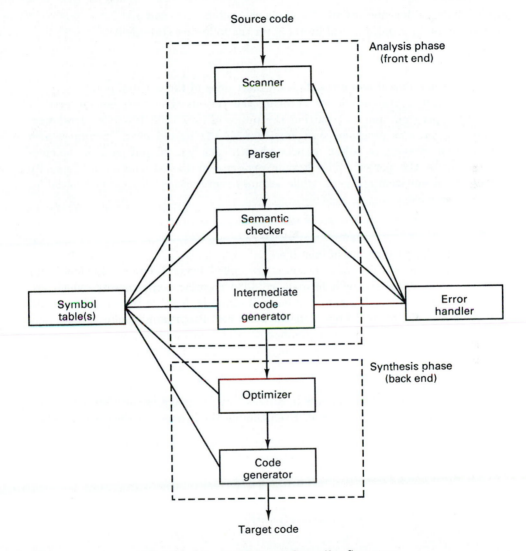

Figure 1.1. Traditional Compiler Structure

characters can be constructed to make valid words or **lexemes** in the language. For example, the words `program` and `Simple` in the following string

```
program Simple(input,output);
```

are valid Pascal lexemes, as are the single characters (,), and ;.

On the other hand, the real literal `3.` in the following statement

```
x := 3.
```

is invalid, since Pascal requires a digit on both sides of the decimal point.

A **scanner** is responsible for checking the various characters encountered in the source program and to partition the program into valid lexemes. Irrelevant characters, such as program comments, are simply passed over. Scanners also determine a category or **token** associated with each lexeme and pass the lexeme-token pair to the parser. The lexeme `program` in Pascal source code usually belongs to a one-item category, while lexemes representing user-defined variables in statements like

```
i := 123
```

are part of a larger category of identifiers.

Rules used to specify valid lexemes are called **lexical rules**. Lexical rules are most often expressed by a formalism called **regular expressions**, which are described in Chapter 5. Scanners can be built either by hand or by using a program that generates the scanner from a specification file. Programming effort, code size, and scanner performance are not significantly different for either method.

1.2   The Parser

Part of the meaning of a sentence in almost any language is the *order* in which the lexemes occur in that sentence. Even though the lexemes in the Pascal phrase below

```
Sample program(input);
```

are all valid, the following order

```
program Sample(input);
```

is required.

Rules that specify lexeme order are called **syntax rules**.[1] The set of all syntax rules is called a **grammar**. **Parsers** enforce a language's syntax rules notifying the programmer of errors detected and indicating possible causes of the errors.

---

[1] Actually, syntax rules specify the order of the *tokens* or lexeme categories.

Chapter 6 describes the process of constructing a parser that enforces a collection of syntax rules. Appendix E contains a complete set of such rules for Pascal.

The output from a parser is a special graph that faithfully represents the original source program. This graph is actually a rooted tree, called a **parse tree**. The nodes of the tree are often "decorated" with data that the compiler is able to derive from the source program during the various semantic checks imposed by the parser.

There are two kinds of parsers presently in wide use, **recursive descent** and **shift/reduce** parsers. Recursive descent parsers build the parse tree in a natural top-down manner; shift/reduce parsers build the tree bottom-up, i.e., starting at the leaves and ending with the root. Recursive descent parsers can often be efficiently constructed by hand. The more powerful shift/reduce parsers are much more difficult to code and are popular today primarily because they can be constructed by automated parser generators.

1.3 Semantic Checkers

Programming languages have many rules dealing with requirements far beyond lexical or syntax rules. These additional language requirements are called **semantic rules**. Semantic rules that can be checked during compilation are called **static**. A Pascal example of a static rule is the requirement that both sides of an assignment statement have compatible types. Semantic requirements that can only be enforced at runtime, such as checking that an array index remains inside the index bounds, are called **dynamic** rules.

1.4 Symbol Tables and Error Handlers

Figure 1.1 contains two components that play much different roles from those found on the main data stream. Both interact with a number of different parts of the compiler, and neither actually processes the source program as it passes through the various compiler components.

The first of these is a **symbol table**. The main purpose of these tables is to store the names or identifiers encountered in a source program and relevant identifier information or **attributes**.

The second item is an **error handler**. A good compiler must do more than shut down after gleefully pointing to the first programming error it can find. Each compiler component must report program errors as they are encountered and then try to recover sufficiently from the problem so that the compilation process can (at least partially) continue with an eye toward locating additional errors in the program.

1.5 Intermediate Code Generator

The data structure passed between the analysis and synthesis phases (See Figure 1.1) of a compiler is called the **intermediate representation** of the source program, or **IR**. It contains all the information that the compiler is able to collect or infer during the analysis phase, as well as additional instructions inserted by the compiler to implement certain dynamic semantic checks.

Specifications for source languages have a way of being changed by standards committees. Modifying a compiler front end to incorporate such changes or to add language enhancements should have minimal impact on the back end. Similarly, modifying the compiler's back end to produce code for a new target machine should not require extensive modifications to the front end. A well-designed intermediate representation contributes greatly to efficient maintenance and continued development by facilitating a high degree of independence of the front- and back-end phases.

There are two kinds of intermediate representations in primary use today: instructions resembling assembly language and tree representations. The assembly-like representation has received a lot of attention over the years, especially in compilers for systems having only modest amounts of internal memory, or for compilers where the source language may need to be regularly modified or even replaced at a later date. The modern trend seems to be toward tree representations of the program, with languages like Ada even specifying a required format for the tree.

1.6   Code Optimizer

Target code generated by a compiler can be very bad, especially if the code generator has been constructed in either a naive or an ad hoc manner. Modifications can be made to the IR before code generation begins. This greatly improves the quality of the target code. The term used to describe this process is **optimization**, though no one would argue that optimized code is necessarily optimum in terms of either size or speed.

Program speed and code size are often improved *after* a first effort at producing target code has been made, especially if the host machine has special instructions for efficiently executing frequently encountered operations. **Peephole optimizers** are constructed that scan small segments of the target code for standard replacement patterns of the inefficient instructions.

1.7   Code Generator

The **code generator**'s task is to translate the intermediate representation of the source program into the native code of the target machine. There are several approaches to this problem, each having its own advantages and liabilities. At one extreme is the production of actual machine-executable code, like a number of student FORTRAN compilers that were in such widespread use on large mainframes during the 1960s and 1970s. The other extreme is the translator that outputs a standard high-level language. The early AT&T C++ translators are examples of systems emitting C code which must then be further compiled and linked. Compilers that output machine instructions are necessarily not as portable as compilers outputting a language that is widely available on many different platforms. However, the former efficiently produces quality code, while the latter takes numerous additional steps before an executable module is produced.

The compiler example in this text uses a fairly popular compromise of emitting assembly language code for a specific target machine. The code is then converted into executable code by the target machine's own assembler and linker. Assembly languages are often identical across families of target machines so that at least a degree of portability is achieved for the compiler. Furthermore, the actual amount of additional computer resources required for assembling and linking is really quite reasonable.

Producing low-level target code requires at least some familiarity with many machine-level issues such as data handling and machine instruction syntax. How are variables allocated? What is the usual program layout in memory? Where do instructions and data go? Which instructions are fast and which ones are slow? Are there special areas of memory that can be used for high-speed calculations?

1.8 Exercises

1. Consider the following Pascal program.

```
program Sample(input,output);
var
     IntVar: integer;
begin {Sample}
     readln(IntVar);
     IntVar := IntVar + 1;
     writeln(IntVar)
end {Sample}.
```

(a) List the lexemes found in the Pascal program.

(b) Specify categories or tokens describing the various lexemes in Exercise 1a, above.

(c) Rewrite each phrase in the Pascal program as a sequence of the categories you have constructed.

2. (**CLIP** Project)

   CLIP[2] is an acronym for a *Command Language Interpreter Package*. This language will allow users to create or input sets of integer or real data and then to perform various algebraic operations on the sets of data and to submit the data to a small collection of statistical routines.

   (a) Modify Figure 1.1 to represent a system having the features described above.

---

[2] This exercise is the first in an ongoing series of exercises aimed at building a simple system using the main ideas from the various chapters.

(b) Give examples of the kinds of numerical data that would be typically used in a statistical analysis package. What kind of data would typically be placed in a single set for statistical analysis?

(c) Specify operations that could be used on sets of numeric data.

(d) List three or four standard statistical procedures that would be present in any statistical package.

Chapter 2

Object-Oriented Methods

Topics:

- Object-oriented concepts
- Object-oriented life cycle
- Applications to compilers

2.1 Fundamental Ideas

Traditional procedurally oriented programming languages such as Pascal, C or Ada allow a programmer to construct various data structures and the subprograms designed to manipulate those structures. In object-oriented programming the data structures and the subprograms acting on those structures can be placed together into a single **object**.[1] Programs then consist of instructions for creating these objects and for allowing them to modify their own structures or to send messages[2] requesting similar activity from other objects.

As is the case with any programming methodology, object-oriented programming has a number of characteristic features that impact the application of that methodology. Of the seven or eight features most often cited, the following four emerge as the most relevant to compiler problems.

- Abstraction

- Encapsulation

- Hierarchy

- Typing

---

[1] Actually, most object-oriented languages view the data as being a part of the object while the procedures or functions are associated with the *class* to which the object belongs.

[2] Object *A* **sends a message** to object *B* when *A* requests that one of *B*'s member functions is executed.

2.1.1 Abstraction

Generally, an abstraction consists of the *essential characteristics* of a system that distinguish it from other systems and provide sufficient functionality for understanding or utilizing the system. In visual art, an abstraction of a particular landscape may consist of strong sweeping strokes representing the main features of the original view. In mathematics, an abstraction of points in three-dimensional space can be a list of axioms, called a vector space. In programming, an abstraction consists of an interface that specifies only the essential structures and behaviors of a particular structure. Such abstractions often take the form of a well-documented interface or a definition module for an abstract data type. The task of specifying abstractions that are appropriate for a given application is the central design problem in object-oriented programming methodology.

2.1.2 Encapsulation

It is important to hide from clients any details that are not part of an object's abstraction. Restriction of access to implementation detail allows program changes to be made reliably and economically.

2.1.3 Hierarchy

The application of object-oriented techniques for any nontrivial problem results in the creation and management of a very large number of objects. One natural way to deal with this kind of complexity is to *classify* the objects. Similar objects are placed together in a **class**. Objects that are not closely related are placed in different classes. When this is done the *structures* and *behaviors* of the objects in a given class can then be thought of as belonging to that class. These class structures and behaviors actually become the abstractions for the objects. Class specifications are therefore just abstractions of the objects being represented by that class.

   Within a group of objects forming a class, there may be a subset of objects that have additional common features. It may be that this collection should be placed in a **subclass** of the original one. If so, we can establish a ranking or **hierarchy** among various classes of objects in a given problem domain. Obviously a specification for a particular subclass would consist of the specification of the original parent class, together with additional distinguishing structures or behaviors for the subclass. Object-oriented programming environments allow such subclass specifications to simply reference the parent class and then list the additional structures or behaviors. In this case we say that the subclass has **inherited** the structures and behaviors of the parent class.

2.1.4 Typing

The notion of a type in traditional programming languages is essentially the same thing as the idea of a class in object-oriented languages. But the impact of applying the type or class idea is quite different in these environments. Typing in an object-oriented environment can be the normal **static typing** that enforces type compatibility in expressions or assignment statements. But the combination of the concept of **dynamic** or **late** binding and the notion of class hierarchy provides a powerful tool that can drastically reduce the complexity of implementation code control structures. This is most frequently achieved by declaring variables to be of a general or parent class. If during execution a subclass object is actually assigned to the general variable, a call to a given parent behavior can result in the corresponding behavior of the *subclass* being executed. Selection control structures such as

<pre>
         if youra thing1 then
                 doa thing1_procedure
         else if youra thing2 then
                 doa thing2_procedure
         else if . . .
</pre>

are then no longer needed.

2.2   Object-Oriented Software Life Cycle

2.2.1   Analysis

The analysis of any system begins with a problem statement or **requirements definition**, which is written from the *user's* point of view. It contains information about what the system is to do, how it will interact with the user, specific equipment required, and so on. It probably isn't complete or even consistent. Rumbaugh et al. [17] suggest that the statement should not be seen as a final, unchangeable document. It should instead serve as the basis for refining the real requirements.

Traditional software engineering methods augment and clarify the requirements definition with the **requirements specification**, a rigorous and consistent document intended for system designers and programmers. Object-oriented analysis sharpens the requirements definition a different way. Instead of a rigorous document specifying what the system must *do*, a document, called a **list of things**, is produced that views the problem domain from the perspective of what *constitutes* the system and how these constituents are related to each other. The list-of-things may contain diagrams of objects or classes that indicate the various relationships between the various items.

2.2.2   Object-Oriented Design

Design begins to move from the specification of a list of the various players in the game to a description of the relationships of the players. This is neither a simple nor linear task. However, it does involve the following recognizable activities.

Specifying class meaning.   Once the top-level classes have been named and described we need to establish the *meaning* of the various classes. It must be emphasized that initially we are viewing these classes from the outside. This is where decisions are made about how the various objects communicate with each other. The decisions about object interaction are actually made in terms of *class behaviors*. The set of all the operations that can be used to effect class behavior is called class **protocol**. We are therefore trying to design the exterior properties of each class presently under consideration.

Specifying class relationships.   This step documents how classes and objects interact within the system. Some objects will be related in a client-provider relationship. At other times, the relationship is more that of inheritance. And whatever the interconnections, issues of visibility must be resolved at this level.

Designing the inside of classes.   This is the last stage of class design, though usually not the final design activity. Here we look inside each class at the present level of abstraction and decide how the behavior for each class should be implemented. As we think about what the various members of the classes should be and what algorithms are appropriate for each method, we often find existing classes requiring significant changes to their definitions or even additional classes that still need to be invented. This inside design activity can therefore send us scurrying back to the low level classes for modifications or even redefinition.

Arranging classes into modules.   Having decided on the various high-level classes, their protocols, and their internal representations, we now need to think about how we are going to package these classes for efficient development of the Pascal compiler. Groups of classes are called **modules**. Our goal is to produce modules that consist of highly similar classes (**cohesive**) and do not send lots of messages to classes in other modules (**uncoupled**).

The process for deciding how to form modules is quite similar to the way classes are abstracted from objects. Some grouping is done strictly by logical class arrangement. Some grouping is done by common action or behavior. Other modules contain special-purpose items.

Modules most often come in pairs: **definition** and **implementation** modules.[3] Class definitions and relevant enumerated constants are placed in a definition module. Code for class functions is placed in the implementation modules. In C++, definition modules are placed in files having the ".h" extension, which is so familiar in standard C include files; implementation modules are files having a ".C" extension. There are times when one definition module corresponds to a number of (partial) implementation modules.

2.3   Application to Compiler Construction

Object-oriented compiler constructions methods are different from traditional techniques in a number of ways.

- Standard compiler components can be encapsulated.

---

[3] Wirth's module terminology seems to more accurately describe the design approach taken in this text.

- Parse tree nodes can be objects that encapsulate source program data.

- Semantic checkers, interpreters, and code generators can be replaced with corresponding parse tree behaviors.

2.3.1 Encapsulating Components

There are widely used techniques for generating a compiler's scanner and parser components. These techniques often produce C code, making extensive use of global data structures. Software engineering principles indicate that such global structures can be rather dangerous, even within a particular module or file. For example, if a compiler needs to scan or parse in several different ways during a normal session, we might want to utilize several scanners or parsers configured in slightly different ways. Including multiple copies of generated procedures, each of which utilizes the same global identifiers, would clearly result in unacceptable redefinition of the globals. However, encapsulating these scanners and/or parsers into an object converts the globals to an object's local data. Multiple copies of scanner or parser objects are then easily maintained in a given module.

2.3.2 Parse Tree Nodes Are Objects

Object-oriented compiler construction methods focus on the classification of parse tree nodes illustrated in Figure 2.1. These nodes can usually be grouped into five or six major classes, each of which has its own required information data structure. Within each class, there may be a number of subclasses having additional data storage requirements. Since subclasses can inherit parent class structures, subclass structures can be specified by referencing the parent class and then listing only the information relevant for that particular subclass. The result is that data structures associated with the different phrases of a programming language are considerably less complex to specify and to use.

2.3.3 Behaviors Replace Complex Procedures

Of even more significance than encapsulation of important data structures is the association of specific procedures or behaviors with the various classes of parse tree nodes. The traditional semantic checker, interpreter and code generator (Figure 1.1) can be replaced with corresponding parse tree behaviors (Figure 2.1).

- **Semantic checks.** Contextual information for a well-designed, modern computer language is almost always *available* to the parser at the time a particular phrase is being recognized. The problem is that this semantic information is just not *detectable* by a parser based upon a context-free grammar. Since the ability to display timely error messages depends upon using this information as soon as it becomes available, testing contextual constraints should therefore be performed at the same time the corresponding phrase is being recognized.

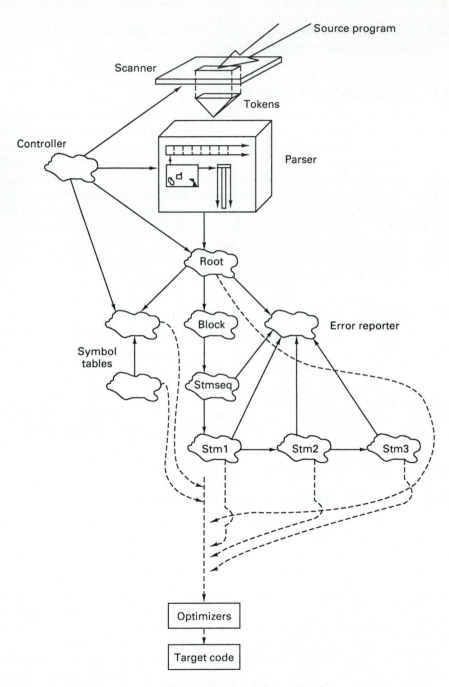

Figure 2.1. Object-Oriented Compiler Structure

This can be systematically achieved by coordinating the actual contextual testing with the construction of the parse tree node, especially since the parser activity that universally occurs after the recognizing of each phrase is the creation of the parse tree node representing that phrase.

Object-oriented languages provide special manager functions that are called during normal object handling activities. One of the most important is the **constructor** function that is automatically called each time any object is **instantiated**, i.e., dynamically created. Contextual constraints can therefore be uniformly and automatically applied in an object-oriented environment by placing the required semantic tests for each phrase inside the constructor for the corresponding parse tree node. The emphasis is therefore shifted from designing a single semantic checker to the implementation of accurate contextual constraints for each parse tree class.

- **Interpreter activity.** Traditional interpreters usually take a parse tree or some equivalent form of the original source program as input data. They then "execute" the program by traversing the tree and performing the instructions as they are encountered. Required tree traversal is not easily programmed nor efficiently implemented, since these trees do not necessarily have predictable n-ary structures.

  If object-oriented techniques are used, it is possible to replace the concept of a tree-traversing interpreter with a tree that knows how to execute itself. Since objects can have their own behaviors, it is possible to build into each object the ability to perform its part of the required interpreting of the program. Execute behavior for a high-level object, such as a block of code, amounts to sending *execute()* messages to its own list of instructions. Each instruction object can send *evaluate()* messages to any of its expressions and then perform the specific task associated with that instruction.

- **Final code production.** Rather than producing target code by traversing the parse tree, each class of parse tree node can be given specific behavior to emit the code required for that particular construct. Essentially, this amounts to providing a 'template' or standard set of target code instructions that, when executed on the target machine, will perform the tasks specified for that particular node.

A frequently asked question at this point in the discussion is "How do you become skilled in *picking* the objects?" The usual response "experience is the best teacher" is only partially correct. Chapters 3 and 8 contain a number of suggestions and examples of the process of locating and defining the objects used in compiler construction.

2.4   Exercises

For the exercises in this chapter, choose one of the following systems based on your personal knowledge or interest.

- A place of employment

- A computer system

- A source of specific service

- A civic or religious group

List objects responsible for various forms of communication in the system. Then select an important cluster or class of similar objects.

1. (Abstraction)

   > An abstraction denotes the essential characteristics of an object that distinguish it from all other kinds of objects and thus provide crisply defined conceptual boundaries, relative to the perspective of the viewer.
   >
   > Booch [3, page 39]

   (a) Specify the essential characteristics of the class of objects.

   (b) Specify essential behaviors of the objects.

2. (Encapsulation)

   > Encapsulation is the process of hiding all of the details of an object that do not contribute to its essential characteristics.
   >
   > Booch [3, page 46].

   Specify characteristics or behaviors of the class that may be important to the internal structure of the objects but not relevant or appropriate use by other, outside objects.

3. (Hierarchy)

   > Hierarchy is a ranking or ordering of abstractions.
   >
   > Booch [3, page 54].

   (a) Describe two separate subclasses of objects.

   (b) What distinguishes the objects in each subclass from other objects in the original cluster of objects?

4. (Typing)

> Typing is the enforcement of the class of an object, such that objects
> of different types may not be interchanged, or at the most, they may
> be interchanged only in very restricted ways.
>
> Booch [3, page 59].

The following format is similar to the typing mechanisms used in many object-oriented programming languages.

```
class  <ClassName>  Derived from: <ParentClassName>
     visible characteristics:
          <Char1>
          <Char2>
     hidden characteristics:
          <Char3>
          <Char3>
```

Any irrelevant portion of the specification is simply omitted.

(a) Use the above specification format to collect all relevant information about the largest cluster of objects.

(b) Use the format to specify each of the derived classes.

Chapter 3

Analysis

Topics:

- Requirements definition for example
- "List of things"

It is difficult to convey a dynamic process using a static medium. Animation succeeds, of course, by rapidly superimposing models of the process, each one representing the system at successive time intervals. Lacking equipment or ability to describe a process quickly and repetitively, we must choose a single representation and then describe in words the system's previous or subsequent changes.

Object-oriented analysis and design is certainly a dynamic process, not readily admitting an animated description. Displaying a "final" state often gives the learner a false expectation of being right on the first try; showing a first attempt presents an incompletely or even erroneously understood system. In this chapter we have chosen to share work from a very early stage, risking the possibility of giving a beginning reader a few misconceptions about what the system will ultimately become. In much the same way that programmers abuse program syntax while thinking about an algorithm, we will also abuse the acceptable notations for object-oriented analysis and design. It is a very useful exercise to work up your own analysis document after you have had time to understand the project. There are a number of excellent formalisms (see [3] and [17]) for precisely specifying your work.

3.1   Requirements Definition

This section describes the Pascal compiler, which will be the central example for this text.

- **General description.**

  - **Who will use the system as a compiler?** The system to be constructed must be suitable for use by programmers who are learning Pascal. It should therefore have most of the student-oriented features found in the classic Berkeley Pascal compiler written by W. Joy et al.:

19

ease of use, graceful recovery from user input errors, and timely output of meaningful error messages. The compiler should not include error *correction* capabilities, since such recoveries do not assist student mastery of the programming language.

- **Another use of the compiler.** This compiler should also be a suitable example of compiler construction for advanced undergraduate computer science students. It should contain the fundamental structures and algorithms that are in common use today. It is to be constructed using object-oriented design and program techniques.

- **Characteristics.** The characteristics of the compiler are as follows:

  - It will accept as input, a file containing a Pascal program and various switches or options to indicate requested compiler activity such as listing, optimizations, and so on. Editors used to create or modify input files will not be considered a part of this system.

  - It will produce as output:

    * To the terminal: a line-numbered program listing, if requested by the user.
    * To the terminal: relevant error messages, indicating what the errors are and where in the source file the errors occurred.
    * To a disk file: a reasonably small and efficient executable file. The file will be produced by using the SUN-4 ™ SPARC ®[1] assembler and linker to translate SPARC ® assembly language target code.

  - The compiler will perform the following analysis of the source code:

    * Enforce the standard Pascal lexical requirements.
    * Check the syntax and report syntax and lexical errors at the earliest possible stage of compilation.
    * Enforce static semantic checks during the compilation process and insert target code to provide dynamic semantic checks, which are part of standard Pascal.

  - The compiler should execute efficiently. Since it is probable that many users will be using the compiler simultaneously on a particular platform, the compiler must be implemented in a language that provides the necessary object-oriented facilities without the execution overhead often attributed to object-oriented languages.

  - It may be desirable to use the system on other platforms. The system should therefore contain a Pascal interpreter that can be built and executed on a number of different machines.

---

[1] SUN-4 ™, SPARC ® and SPARCStation are registered trademarks of SUN Microsystems, Inc.

- **Main Platform.** The compiler is to be executed on a SUN SPARCStation.

- **Availability.** The compiler source code is to be public domain and made available through normal free-software exchange channels.

3.2   List of Things

The following is a first effort at listing the major objects that comprise a compiler. These possible objects have been obtained by a common practice of scanning the nouns occuring in the problem domain (Chapters 1 and 2). Booch [3, page 191] calls such a collection of potential objects and classes a **list of things**.

- **Controller.** Since our focus is on who the players are and not what they do, coordinating the creation of these objects and the timing of their various activities is usually accomplished by a special controller object.

- **Scanner-parser.** Though the scanner and parser do not have object attributes, each certainly exhibits behavior. In fact the coupling between these two subsystems is so tight that they probably should be modeled as a single object.

- **Lexeme-token object.** This object encapsulates all the important information associated with the various valid lexemes encountered by the scanner. Here we are concerned more with the attributes of this object than on any of its behaviors. Contextual information (line number, name of file, ...) and even corresponding token information can be collected into such a LexTok object and conveniently accessed at such a time as that information might be needed for error reporting or parse tree decoration.

- **Symbol tables.** Even traditional symbol tables have numerous attributes. One important variable is the size of the table, which can be dynamically increased to facilitate table growth when hashing collisions become highly probable. Symbol tables also have a number of behaviors relating to the entering and viewing of table information. Tables also can be made responsible for outputting target code that allocate resources required for their identifiers.

- **Parse tree nodes.** The nodes of the parse tree for a traditional compiler have a variety of associated attributes. Some nodes have attributes pointing to various other parse tree nodes. Other nodes contain specialized information about type information or expression values. There are a large number of parse tree node objects.

    - **Program node.** This could actually serve as the root of the parse tree.
    - **Declaration nodes.**
        * Constant definition nodes.
        * Type definition nodes.

* Variable declaration nodes.

* Procedure-function declaration nodes.

– **Statement nodes.**

– **Expression nodes.**

• **Error handler.** Error handlers display various kinds of behavior, depending
  on the nature of the error encountered. Warning messages are sent when an
  abnormality or possible problem is encountered. But production of target
  code is allowed, even in the presence of warnings. Actual (Pascal) errors
  result in various kinds of messages being sent to the user and the suppression
  of target code generation. Internal compiler errors that often occur during the
  development of the system should result in an informative message, followed
  by a decisive system halt.

A diagram of the top-level objects for the Pascal compiler is displayed in Figure 3.1. The controller object calls the scanner-parser, which performs internal
communication by LexTok objects and reports syntax errors through error objects.
The controller also communicates directly with the parse tree. The tree is asked to
either execute itself or to perform optional optimization and then emit assembler
code. Tree nodes, especially those representing various identifiers, make numerous
references to symbol tables.

Objects that are essentially the same are then collected into tentative boxes
that eventually are given names and become the high-level classes. The set of all
the different parse tree nodes, for example, are collected into a common box that
eventually becomes a class called PTreeNodeCls. The various LexTok objects are
enclosed in a box that eventually becomes the class LexTokCls. Figure 3.1 contains
the resulting diagram where the various objects have been replaced by class boxes
and where the object links are now represented as class associations. This diagram
is called a **class diagram** and is extremely useful as a means of organizing the
various pieces of design information throughout the entire project.

We now summarize this in a tentative list of classes.

• **ControllerCls.** There is only one instance of this class created during the
  compilation process. Its task is to coordinate the creation and activities of
  the compiler objects during the compilation process.

• **ScanParseCls.** The close coupling of behavior and (global) variables shared
  by the scanner and parser suggests that these two compiler filters might best
  be made member functions a single class.

• **LexTokCls.** This class defines objects that facilitate scanner/parser communication.

• **SymtabCls.** This single class will have many symbol table instances during
  the course of the compiling process. Symbol tables are used to store information about source program identifiers.

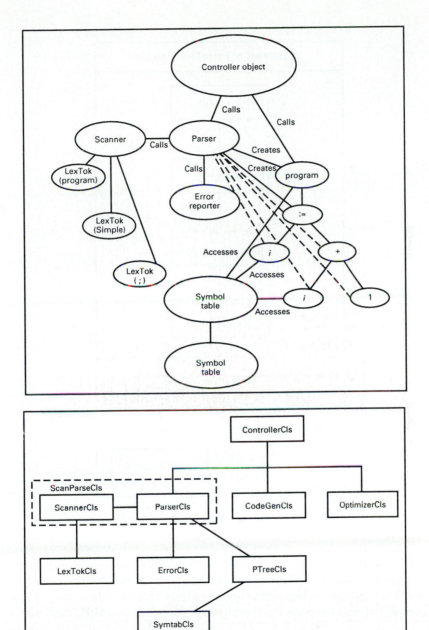

Figure 3.1. Preliminary Top-Level Object and Class Diagrams

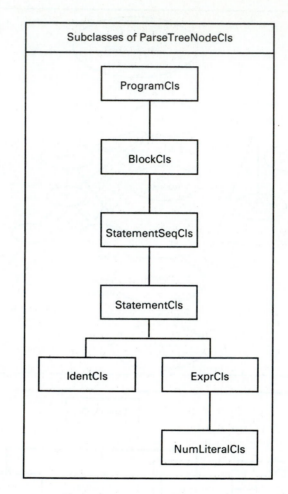

Figure 3.2. Preliminary Class Diagram for Tree Nodes

- **PTreeNodeCls.** All the different kinds of parse tree node objects will be classified as subclasses of this general class. This will be the major area in which we will use the important object-oriented idea of inheritance. Figure 3.2 contains a class diagram for the higher level subclasses of PTreeNodeCls.

- **ErrorCls.** Warnings could be instances of this class. You might make a separate WarningCls if you felt that the compiler warnings and errors were sufficiently different behaviors. Another approach would be to make ErrorCls and WarningCls subclasses of some superclass like MessageCls.

3.3   Exercises

1. Test your understanding of the details of the Pascal compiler's analysis and design by carefully writing a paragraph describing each of the following.

   (a) LexTok object

   (b) ScanParse object

   (c) SymtabEntryCls

   (d) ParseTreeNodeCls

2. Write a requirements definition for a Pascal compiler to be used on a reasonably small PC or Mac. Be sure to discuss the following items:

   - What compiler features would you want? Which ones are feasible on this sized machine?

   - Would you prefer a compiler or an interpreter? Explain your answer, especially in terms of hardware speed, etc.

3. Suppose that you are going to design and implement a window system to run on your PC.

   (a) Make a list of key abstractions for this project. You may want to restrict your list to the highest level of abstractions.

   (b) Produce a class diagram showing possible class associations.

4. Could any of the following items be considered a key abstraction for the Pascal compiler? Explain your answer.

   (a) Pascal source file

   (b) Scanner

   (c) Parser

   (d) Token

   (e) Assembly language code

5. (**CLIP** Project)

   (a) Write several scenarios that would be representative of the use of the **CLIP** language. Pay special attention to the features of the language that may be useful to the user:

      - Declaration of special data sets. Would these sets of data be assigned to variables? If so, would they possibly have different types? Would these types be upward compatible?

      - Control structures: selection and repetition.

      - Interactive use of the system.

- Special syntax for calling statistical procedures.

You are essentially defining the **CLIP** by example at this point. Think about the implication of the various constructs you are proposing for your language.

(b) Are there any special options that could be selected when **CLIP** is executed?

(c) Construct a list of objects to be used in the **CLIP** interpreter.

(d) Design a set of high-level classes for **CLIP**. Store the class information in a class diagram.

(e) Specify a tentative module arrangement for the **CLIP** interpreter.

Chapter 4

Controller

Topics:
- Definition of *OptionCls* and *ControllerCls*
- Implementation of *OptionCls* and *ControllerCls*

The controller module consists of the required C++ function *main()* as well as the definition and implementation details of *OptionCls* and *ControllerCls*. The module consists of two files, as illustrated in Figure 4.1. The declarations of the classes are

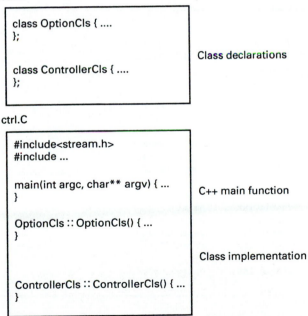

ctrl.h

```
class OptionCls { ....
};

class ControllerCls { ....
};
```
Class declarations

ctrl.C

```
#include<stream.h>
#include ...

main(int argc, char** argv) { ...
}

OptionCls :: OptionCls() { ...
}


ControllerCls :: ControllerCls() { ...
}
```
C++ main function

Class implementation

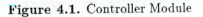

Figure 4.1. Controller Module

found in *ctrl.h*. The required C++ function *main()* and the implementation details
of the various class functions are in *ctrl.C*

4.1   Class Definitions

C++, like C makes a very careful distinction between *definition* and *declaration* for
variables. A variable is **defined** when storage is allocated. It is **declared** by an
`extern` statement that indicates that the storage has indeed been allocated, but in
some other module.

The same distinction of the two terms for classes cannot exist, since classes
are the object-oriented equivalent of types. The normal term for specifying a C++
class is **definition**, even though storage is not usually allocated for types. We
therefore use Wirth's Modula-2 term **definition module** for any ".h" file containing
collections of class definitions and occasional variable declarations. Files containing the code for the corresponding member functions are called **implementation
modules**. These are given the ".C" extension.

4.1.1   OptionCls

Our first task is to define a class, *OptionCls*, encapsulating the idea of user-selected
options.

```
 ctrl.h

    5 typedef class OptionCls *POptionCls;
    6 class OptionCls {
    7    public:
    8         OptionCls();
    9         void            set_no_back_end();
   10         void            set_list();
   11         void            set_emit();
   12         void            set_optimize();
   13         void            set_peephole();
   14         void            set_format();
   15         static int      no_back_end();
   16         static int      list();
   17         static int      emit();
   18         static int      optimize();
   19         static int      peephole();
   20         static int      format();
   21    private:
   22         static int      option_val;
   23 };
```

The listing of this definition contains a `typedef` type specifier *POptionCls*
adapted to the task of specifying a pointer to an object of that particular class. The
`typedef` is then followed by a class definition that specifies the member functions
and a data member *option_val*.

A file name is indicated in the top-left corner of the listing. The line numbers have been added for reference purposes only and should not be considered normal output from any C++ compiler.

The `virtual` reporter functions are class functions and so can be directly accessed through the class *OptionCls*.

The various options are to be represented by bits in the single data member, *option_val*. This member is designated `static` so that all *OptionCls* objects have access to a single location storing the option information.

All compiler objects who know about *OptionCls* have been given access to the various member functions, since they have been declared `public`. A more extensive explanation of the notion of public class members can be found in Appendix A. There are two kinds of member functions: those that set the options and those that report back on the contents of *option_val*. Some degree of safety is provided, since compiler objects must use an *OptionCls* object to access a *set* function.

4.1.2   ControllerCls

Object-oriented development focuses on specifying and designing the classes which comprise a system. Deciding *when* the various classes should do their thing is usually the responsibility of some *ControllerCls* object. Since a compiler is essentially a linear collection of procedures, the task of coordinating object construction and message passing is really quite simple.

```
ctrl.h

29 typedef class ControllerCls *PControllerCls;
30 class ControllerCls {
31    public:
32         ControllerCls(int ArgC, char** ArgV);
33         void            print();
34    private:
35         int             argc;
36         char**          argv;
37         char*           source_file;
38         SymtabCls        *std_table;
39         PTreeCls         *parse_tree;
40
41         int             init();
42         int             set_options();
43         int             open_file();
44 };
```

Other compiler objects should clearly not be able to force a change in the state of the controller by sending any messages. With the exception of the constructor for *ControllerCls* and a left-over debugging function *print()*, all data members and member functions are therefore declared `private`.

There are a number of data members for the controller.

- **argc.** The number of user input arguments to the compiler.

- **argv.** The actual input string.

- **source_file.** The name of the Pascal source file being compiled.

- **std_table.** A symbol table containing all the Pascal standard identifiers.

- **parse_tree.** The parse tree of objects representing the Pascal program.

In fact *std_table* and *parse_tree* are pointers, since they represent an association (see Rumbaugh et al. [17, page 27]) between classes.

4.2   Class Implementation

Files containing the implementation code for member functions of a collection of classes are called **implementation modules**. The compiler's control implementation module contains the following items.

4.2.1   Imports of Other Definition Modules

The first set of `includes` in the following code imports information from system libraries.

```
Header (ctrl.C)

  8 #include <stream.h>
  9 #include <string.h>
 10
 11 #include "../utilities/lstbld.h"
 12 #include "../utilities/string.h"
 13 #include "../utilities/value.h"
 14 #include "../scanparse/scanparse.h"
 15 #include "../p_tree/p_tree.h"
 16 #include "../symtab/symtab.h"
 17 #include "../error/error.h"
 18
 19 #include "ctrl.h"
 20
```

The remaining ones import class name information from the compiler's definition modules which are needed by either *OptionCls* or *ControllerCls* member functions. Descriptions of *lstbld.h*, *string.h*, *value.h* and *error.h* can be found in Appendix C. Chapter 6 contains a description of most of *scanparse.h*. The contents of *symtab.h* and *p_tree.h* can be found in Chapters 7 and 8, respectively.

4.2.2 main() (ctrl.C)

The code for the compiler's main function is quite simple.

```
main()

24 main(int argc, char** argv) {
25      //cout << " Educational Pascal compiler" << endl;
26
27      PControllerCls ctl = new ControllerCls(argc,argv);
28      return 0;
29 }
30
```

It just creates a (pointer to a) controller object and returns the value 0 indicating successful termination of compilation. A more complete version of the compiler would return a non-zero value if compilation terminated due to programming errors in the source code.

The code illustrates several important ideas.

Command line arguments. Users often initially communicate with a program by setting options or specifying a file name after invoking the program. An example of this *command line* communication is the following:

$$epc - l \quad prog.p$$

where the $-l$ requests a listing of the source program. In a UNIX environment these extra pieces of information are made available to the function *main()* through the two arguments *argc* and *argv*, the first indicating the number of command line strings available for access by *main()* and the second an array of strings containing the actual commands. These two arguments are then passed to the constructor for the ControllerCls object, which then modifies the behavior of the compiler, based upon the contents of the arguments.

Comments. C++ has two forms of comments.

- The usual C-like /* ... */.

- The line-restricted version, //, which comes from C's predecessor BCPL.

4.2.3 OptionCls

The next major section of the controller module deals with *OptionCls* member functions. The simple *OptionCls* constructor is implemented first.

Setting options (ctrl.C)

```
33 OptionCls :: OptionCls() {
34     //cout << "OptionCls() " << endl;
35     option_val = 0;
36 }
37
38 void OptionCls :: set_no_back_end() {
39     //cout << "OptionCls::set_no_backend()" << endl;
40     option_val = option_val | 0x01;
41 }
42
43 void OptionCls :: set_list() {
44     //cout << "OptionCls::set_list()" << endl;
45     option_val = option_val | 0x02;
46 }
47
48 void OptionCls :: set_emit() {
```

Then several of the *OptionCls set*-functions are listed. Note that set commands return no value, so their return type is listed as void. Note also the standard use of the usual bitwise "or" operator | to set values of various bits.

The next section of the controller module contains those *OptionCls* functions which return option information. The bitwise "and" operator & and usual masks are used to decide when a bit is on.

Checking options (ctrl.C)

```
69 int OptionCls :: no_back_end() {
70     return (0x01 & option_val);
71 }
72
73 int OptionCls :: list() {
74     return (0x02 & option_val);
75 }
76
77 int OptionCls :: emit() {
78     return (0x04 & option_val);
79 }
80
81 int OptionCls :: optimize() {
```

4.2.4   ControllerCls

In the code, below, the first part of the constructor just initializes the controller's *argc* and *argv* data members.

Then an object containing all the Pascal standard types is requested to initialize itself. The declaration for this object is in the parse tree module definition file, *p_tree.h*, as is the class definition. The implementation is in the module *type.C*.

The compiler maintains a linked-list of symbol tables. *Std_table*, the outermost table in the list, contains all the entries for all the Pascal standard identifiers.

ControllerCls Constructor (ctrl.C)

```
 96 ControllerCls :: ControllerCls(int ArgC, char** ArgV) {
 97     //cout << "ControllerCls() " << endl;
 98
 99     argc = ArgC;
100     argv = ArgV;
101
102     std_type.init();
103     std_table = new SymtabCls;
104     ScopeCls::set_vista(std_table); //static member
105
106     PSymtabCls globals = new SymtabCls(std_table);
107     ScopeCls::set_vista(globals);
108
109     if (argc <= 1) {
110         cout <<
111             "   Usage:  epc [-leopf] <filename>.p" << endl;
112         return;
113
114         this -> source_file = new char[80];
115         this -> set_options();
116
117         if (this -> open_file()) {
118             //Call the scanner/parser
119             PScanParseCls sp = new ScanParseCls;
120             this -> parse_tree = sp -> parse_tree;
121             //fdopen(stdin,0);
122
123             //Then decorate the tree.
124             this -> parse_tree -> decorate();
125
126             //Now the back-end
127             if (!OptionCls::no_back_end()) {
128                 if (OptionCls::emit()) {
129                     if (OptionCls::optimize()) {
130                         this -> parse_tree -> optimize();
131                         this -> parse_tree -> emit();
132                         this -> parse_tree -> peephole();
133                     } else {
134                         this -> parse_tree -> emit();
135                     }
136                 } else {
137                     this -> parse_tree -> execute();
138                 }
139             }
140         }
141     }
142 }
```

Identifiers have **scope**, the part of a program in which they are visible. Source

programs have **vistas**, the collection of all identifiers visible at any given location
in the program. *ScopeCls* is responsible for maintaining the vista information. The
set_vista() function is another example of a static function, whose access doesn't
require the construction of a *ScopeCls* object.

Another symbol table is created for the global variables declared in the main
program of the Pascal source program. The *std_table* argument for the constructor
just makes the *globals* table point to *std_table*, so that any vista will also include
the standard identifiers.

```
setopt() (ctrl.C)

145 int ControllerCls :: set_options() {
146      //cout << "ControllerCls::set_options" << endl;
147      POptionCls opt = new OptionCls;
148
149      for (int i = 1; i < argc; i++) {
150          if (*argv[i] == '-') {
151              while (*++argv[i]) {
152                  switch(*argv[i]) {
153                  case 'l':
154                      opt -> set_list();
155                      continue;
156
157                  case 'e':
158                      opt -> set_emit();
159                      continue;
160
161                  case 'o':
162                      opt -> set_optimize();
163                      continue;
164
165                  case 'p':
166                      opt -> set_peephole();
167                      continue;
168
169                  case 'f':
170                      opt -> set_format();
171                      continue;
172
173                  default:
174                      soft.err("Unknown option ");
175                      soft.err_cont(argv[i]);
176                      return 0;
177                  }
178              }
179          } else {
180          source_file = argv[i];
181          return 1;
182          }
183      }
184 }
```

The controller's member *setopt()* member function, listed above, creates an

OptionCls object which can then be used to call the appropriate *set_opt()* functions.

The subsequent loop just walks through the various pieces of information which have been entered at the command line. Anticipating the various ways a user will enter a dash and some option is not a trivial task. Perhaps, we should even build a very simple scanner for this task using the concepts of Chapter 5.

The following code for the *open_file()* member function contains a few nonstandard ideas.

---

open_file() (ctrl.C)

```
186 int  ControllerCls :: open_file() {
187     //cout << "ControllerCls::open_file()" << endl;
188     int length = strlen(source_file);
189     //Check for  .p  extension
190     if ((length > 1) && ((source_file[length -2] == '.') &&
191                          (source_file[length -1] == 'p')  )) {
192         if (!freopen(source_file, "r", stdin)) {
193             soft.err("File does not seem to exist -- Sorry ");
194             return 0;
195         } else {
196             ios::sync_with_stdio();
197             return 1;
198         }
199     } else if (length == 0) {
200         soft.err("No file specified");
201         return 0;
202     } else {
203         soft.err("File must have a  .p  extension");
204         return 0;
205     }
206 }
```

- Freopen() is a system call available on most C systems which opens up a file and then associates it with a stream. In this case, the file is associated with the standard input stream.

- Since C++ input/output objects do not normally use C's input or output functions in *stdio.h*, the two systems must be rather carefully coordinated. The function *ios::sync_with_stdio()* is required to synchronize the C++ stream output with the input obtained from the scanner input using *stdio.h*. While invoking this function does create significant overhead for the compiler, it does not seem to degrade performance to an unacceptable level.

The *ScanParseCls* constructor calls the scanner/parser and then constructs the parse tree. Since the particular scanner used in this text expects input from standard input, we also require that *open_file()* redirect input to the source file.

4.3   Exercises

1. Modify the definition of *OptionCls* in Section 4.1.1 so that only *ControllerCls* has the ability to set the options.

2. Which objects can call the various member functions of *ControllerCls*?

   Hint: The *ControllerCls* definition in Section 4.1.2 contains no friends! Why would this be appropriate for a controller?

3. In the implementation of the compiler's *main()* function, one argument is typed *char ***. What kind of data would this be representing?

4. Describe the compiler's flow of control as specified by the *ControllerCls* constructor. Compare this with that specified in Figure 1.1 of Chapter 1.

5. Explain the purpose of each of the following instructions.

   (a)   `option_val = option_val ! 0x01;`

   (b)   `return (0x02 & option_val);`

6. (**CLIP** Project)

   Design, implement, and test a controller for **CLIP**. The options specified in Exercise 3.5 should be operational in this version of the controller.

Chapter 5

Scanner

Scanners are that first "compiler filter" (Figure 2.1), that is responsible for breaking the source file stream into lexemes. Scanners also determine the basic category or token into which each lexeme falls and then send the corresponding token to the parser for syntax checking. This chapter contains theoretical information about scanners and rather detailed suggestions for their construction and verification.

5.1   Theory of Scanning

Lexical rules determine the valid characters and lexemes in a programming language. These rules are usually specified by a formalization called **regular expressions**. Such sets of regular expressions can be used to construct a finite-state machine that then recognizes precisely the set of lexemes specified by those expressions.

5.1.1   Regular Expressions

Before we actually begin a formal development of regular expressions, we will look at ways in which these expressions rather naturally arise in the process of trying to describe Pascal lexemes.

We will let V represent the set of all valid characters occurring in a Pascal source program. As a first task we would like to specify the valid (numeric) digits in V. Naturally, we could write an expression like

$$\{0, 1, 2, 3, 4, 5, 6, 7, 8, 9\}$$

or, more formally the following **selection**

$$[0 \vee 1 \vee 2 \vee 3 \vee 4 \vee 5 \vee 6 \vee 7 \vee 8 \vee 9]$$

of the indicated characters to express a valid digit. However, a moment's thought about doing the same thing for valid letters convinces us of the need for another symbolism that doesn't depend strictly on listing. Since V is actually linearly ordered it is reasonable to specify Pascal digits as the set of all elements in V that are between "0" and "9" (inclusive). A suggestive notation for this is the expression

$$[0 - 9]$$

that uses the **range operator** "−", representing an **interval**. Similarly, a valid capital letter in Pascal source is represented by the expression

$$[A - Z]$$

while the expression

$$[a - z]$$

clearly denotes a valid lower-case letter. These two expressions could be combined using the selection operator to produce an expression

$$[A - Z] \vee [a - z]$$

representing a valid letter in Pascal. This kind of expression occurs so often that we often use an equivalent, abbreviated expression, like $[A - Za - z]$.

A valid Pascal identifier consists of a letter *followed* by any number of letters or digits. To specify these, we obviously need some way to indicate the **juxtaposition** and **repetition** of characters. The natural way to indicate that one letter follows another is just to place the second one behind the first one. For example

$$[A - Z][0 - 9]$$

represents a capital letter followed by a digit. Repetitions are indicated by the **Kleene star operator** "*". The expression

$$[A - Z]^*$$

represents a (possibly empty) string of capital letters. The following expression

$$[A - Za - z][0 - 9A - Za - z]^*$$

therefore represents a valid Pascal identifier since it represents any string of letters or digits beginning with a letter.

Expressions of normal arithmetic operations involve the use of operator precedence to remove ambiguities. An expression like $3 + 4 * 5$, is unambiguous, since "*" has a higher precedence than "+". This same kind use of precedence exists for regular expressions. The highest precedence is given to the star operator "$*$"; concatenation comes next; selection is lowest. In the identifier regular expression above, the "$*$" repeat operation will be first applied to the number-or-character expression $0 - 9A - Za - z$. However, the range operator "$-$", since it is merely selection, will have lower precedence than catenation. Since we want the selection operation within this expression and the preceding $A - Za - z$ to take place before catenation, we enclose these expressions using the pairs of brackets.

We are now ready to try to make precise the above ideas. **Regular expressions** over the set V of valid input symbols are defined recursively by the following rules.

1. The set of no characters and the string having no characters are regular expressions.

2. Each valid input character is a regular expression.

3. If A and B are regular expressions, then so are each of the following:

   - The selection or union $A \vee B$ of A and B
   - The juxtaposition or concatenation AB of A and B
   - The string A^* of (possibly zero) repetitions of A

4. Nothing else is a regular expression.

Regular expressions can often involve other "short-hand" or "simplifying" operators. An example of this is the regular expression representing the Pascal unsigned integer lexeme, that is defined as a sequence of digits. The regular expression

$$[0 - 9]^*$$

isn't quite correct, since this expression will represent the *empty* string of digits as well as the valid sequences. The corrected expression

$$[0 - 9][0 - 9]^*$$

is such a common structure in regular expressions that the alternate expression

$$[0 - 9]+$$

is used instead.

5.1.2 Specifying Lexemes by Regular Expressions

Regular expressions are of interest to us primarily because they can be used to prescribe a corresponding set of words over an alphabet.

The collection of all words in a language satisfying a regular expression[1] is called the **language defined by the regular expression.**

---

[1] The language defined by a collection $\{r_1, r_2, \ldots\}$ of regular expressions is the same as the set of words defined by the single expression $r_1 \vee r_2 \vee \ldots$.

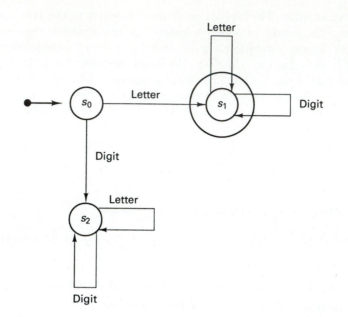

Figure 5.1. Transition Diagram for Identifier Recognizer

5.1.3   Scanners: Lexeme Recognizers

Language recognized by finite-state machines.   Recall that a finite-state machine consists of a collection of states and a mechanism for moving between those states, based up the nature of various input values.[2]

One important use of finite-state machines is that of recognizing the valid lexemes of a programming language. A finite-state machine is first placed in its initial state and then allowed to change states based on the input. If, after a sequence of characters, the machine is in a "good," or **accepting** state, we declare the string of characters to be a valid lexeme. Any string leaving the machine in a nonaccepting state is lexically invalid.

Finite state machines are therefore called **recognizers** when they have the following features.

A **language recognizer** $\mathcal{M}$ consists of

- A finite set $\mathcal{S}$ of machine states.

- A finite set $\mathcal{I}$ of input messages to the machine.

- A finite set $\mathcal{O}$ of output messages from the machine.

---

[2]Appendix B contains a brief review of the definition of finite-state machines and the use of transition diagrams to assist in their description.

- A "next-state" function f that tells us which state $f(s,i)$ to go to, given that we are in a present state s and have just received a particular input message $i \epsilon \mathcal{I}$.

- An "output" function g that produces an output message $g(s,i) \epsilon \mathcal{O}$ as the machine switches from a state s to state $f(s,i)$.

- An initial state s_0. In a transition diagram, an **initial arrow** (having no source state) often points to this state.

- A collection of the states that are designated as **final** or **accepting** states. The transition diagram notation for accepting states is a state enclosed in a circle.

The recognizer with transition diagram illustrated in Figure 5.1 represents a finite-state machine that will accept any sequence of letters and digits so long as the first one is a letter. This finite-state recognizer therefore accepts valid Pascal identifiers.

We will say that a set of words over an alphabet is **defined** or **accepted** by a finite-state recognizer if the set consists precisely of the words that leave the finite-state machine in an accepting state.

The following theorem states that if you have any collection of regular expressions over an alphabet, there is some finite-state recognizer that will recognize the language defined by those expressions and only that language.

Theorem 5.1 (Kleene). *The language defined by a regular expression can also be recognized by a finite-state recognizer.*

Proof: The discussion in this section contains a *constructive* proof from Cohen [4]. It proves the theorem by actually specifying how to build the machine. Understanding how the corresponding machine is constructed often provides ideas of alternative expressions that may do an even better job of recognition.

Recall that the steps involved in specifying the language associated with regular expressions are the following.

1. The language consisting of the empty word Λ is associated with the empty regular expression.

2. The language consisting of a one-letter word is associated with the regular expression that specifies that letter.

3. If L_0 is the language defined by the regular expression r_0 and L_1 is defined by r_1, then the language defined by the union $r_0 \vee r_1$ is the language

$$L_0 \vee L_1$$

consisting of all words in L_0 or in L_1.

4. If L_0 is the language defined by the regular expression r_0 and L_1 is defined by r_1, then the language defined by the catenation $r_0 r_1$ is the language

$$L_0 \, L_1$$

consisting all combinations of a word in L_0 catenated with a word in L_1.

5. If L is the language defined by the regular expression r, then the language defined by the Kleene star r^* of r is the set L^* of catenations of any subset of words in L.[3]

Since each of the five steps above are used to prescribe the language defined by a regular expression, proving each of the following assertions would therefore constructively demonstrate that there is a finite-state recognizer that would recognize precisely that same language.

1. There is a finite-state recognizer that accepts the empty word.

2. There is a finite-state recognizer that accepts a particular letter of an alphabet.

3. If FSR_0 is a finite-state recognizer that accepts the language defined by the regular expression r_0 and if FSR_1 accepts the language defined by r_1, then there is a finite-state recognizer $FSR_0 \vee FSR_1$, called the **union** of FSR_0 and FSR_1, that accepts the language generated by the union $r_0 \vee r_1$ of r_0 and r_1.

4. If FSR_0 is a finite-state recognizer that accepts the language defined by the regular expression r_0 and if FSR_1 accepts the language defined by r_1, then there is a finite-state recognizer $FSR_0 FSR_1$, called the **product** of FSR_0 and FSR_1, that accepts the language generated by the catenation $r_0 r_1$ of r_0 and r_1.

5. If FSR is a finite-state recognizer that accepts the language defined by the regular expression r, then there is a finite-state recognizer FSR^*, called the **Kleene closure** of FSR, that accepts the language generated by the Kleene star r^* of r.

Let's therefore begin working on the proofs of the following five lemmas.

Lemma 5.1. *There is a finite-state recognizer that accepts the empty word.*

Proof: The finite-state recognizer whose transition diagram is displayed in Figure 5.2 accepts only the empty word.

Lemma 5.2. *There is a finite-state recognizer that accepts a particular letter of the alphabet.*

Proof: The finite-state recognizer in Figure 5.3 accepts only the word consisting of the specific letter x.

---

[3] L^* is called the **Kleene closure** of L.

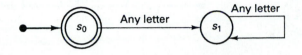

Figure 5.2. Empty Word Recognizer

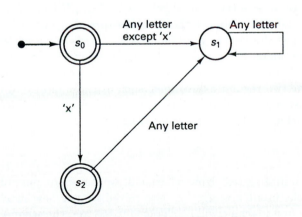

Figure 5.3. Recognizer for Single Letter

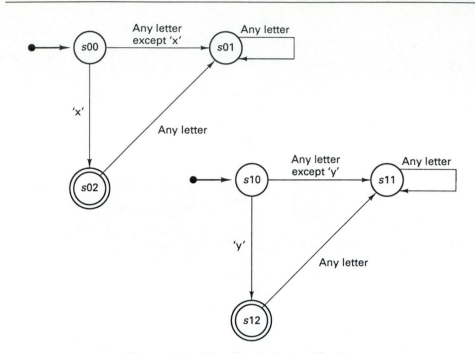

Figure 5.4. Two Single-Letter Machines

Lemma 5.3. *If FSR_0 is a finite-state recognizer that accepts the language defined by the regular expression r_0 and if FSR_1 accepts the language defined by r_1, then there is a finite-state recognizer that accepts the language generated by the union $r_0 \vee r_1$ of r_0 and r_1.*

Proof: Before we give the general rule for building $FSR_0 \vee FSR_1$, let's consider a very simple example. Suppose the regular expression r_0 is just the single letter "x" and that r_1 is the letter "y". Our task is to produce a finite-state recognizer that accepts the union of r_0 and r_1, that is, it recognizes either the letter "x" or the letter "y". Moreover, we must build this new machine from existing machines representing the two regular expressions, such as those indicated in Figure 5.4 We do this by constructing ordered pairs of the various states. Naturally, the initial state of the machine would be the ordered pair

$$(s_{00}, s_{10})$$

of each of the initial states. Now what shall we do about possible "next" states? Suppose that the input message "x" is received by our new machine. The initial state s_{00} of the first machine will be changed to s_{02} and the second machine's initial state s_{10} changes to s_{11} so that the new machines initial (pair) state changes to the following state.

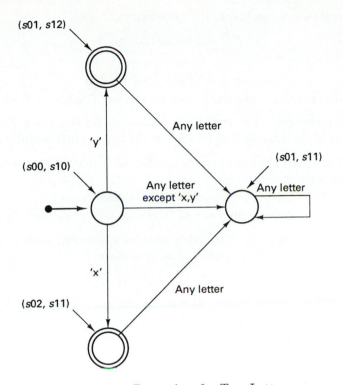

Figure 5.5. Recognizer for Two Letters

$$(s_{02}, s_{11}) \qquad\qquad (5.1)$$

Similarly the new machine, when receiving the input message "y" will switch to this state.

$$(s_{01}, s_{12}) \qquad\qquad (5.2)$$

If any other letter is encountered the machine will switch to the following "black hole" state.

$$(s_{01}, s_{11})$$

Next question: what shall we take for accepting or terminal states? This is where the notion of a union makes sense: any (pair) state is an accepting state for the new machine if an accepting state from the first machine or from the second machine occurs in the pair. So states 5.1 and 5.2 are accepting. This example is summarized in Figure 5.5.

The general case is handled in the following way.[4] Let

$$S^{(0)} = \{s_{00}, s_{01}, \ldots, s_{0m}\}$$

and

$$S^{(1)} = \{s_{10}, s_{11}, \ldots, s_{1n}\}$$

be the respective states of the finite-state recognizers FSR_0 and FSR_1.

- **Input messages.** The set of input messages for the union $FSR_0 \vee FSR_1$ machine is the same as it is for each of the two original machines.

- **Set of states.** The set of states for the union machine is the subset of the ordered pairs

$$(s_{0j}, s_{1k})$$

of states that are actually reached by the following *next-state* function.

- **Next-state function.** The union machine's function, upon receiving input message i, switches from state (s_{0j}, s_{1k}) to state

$$(f^0(s_{0j}, i), f^1(s_{1k}, i))$$

where $f^{(0)}$ is the next-state function for the first machine, and $f^{(1)}$ belongs to the second machine).

- **Accepting states.** Any pair

$$(s_i^{(1)}, s_j^{(2)})$$

is an accepting state for the union machine if either of the component states are accepting states for their respective machines.

Can you see that we are finished with the proof? Why are there only a finite-number of states for the union machine? Is it possible that the union machine states might be a *proper* subset of all possible ordered pairs?

Lemma 5.4. *If FSR_0 is a finite-state recognizer that accepts the language defined by the regular expression r_0 and if FSR_1 accepts the language defined by r_1, then there is a finite-state recognizer that accepts the language generated by the catenation $r_0 r_1$ of r_0 and r_1.*

Proof: Let's again illustrate the proof's construction process with examples before trying to specify the algorithm in a general manner.

The product of two character recognizers. One rather reasonable strategy would be to make the new catenated machine start where FSR_0 starts. The next state for the catenated function could be determined by the first machine until an accepting state is reached and then use the next-state rules from the second machine FSR_1 until (hopefully) an accepting state is reached there. This idea is illustrated in Figure 5.6. The dotted line in the box indicates the switching to the second machine.

---

[4]Since we are using finite-state recognizer for accepting lexemes, we will not worry about defining the output messages or the output function for the new machine.

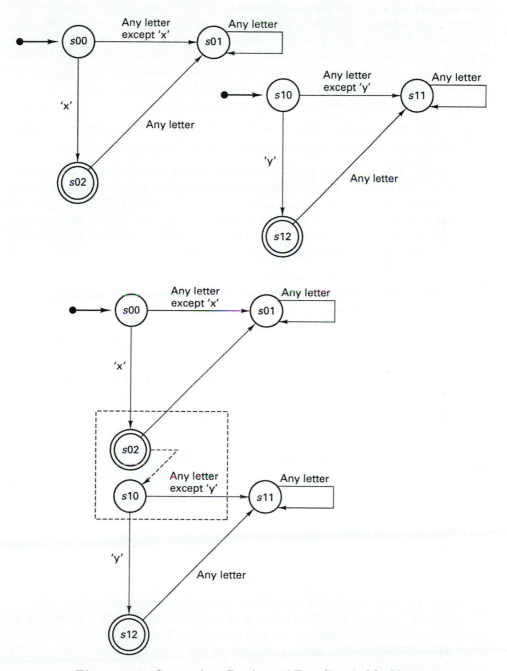

Figure 5.6. Catenation: Product of Two Simple Machines

The product of more complex recognizers.   Actually, the above simple example doesn't quite indicate where the major difficulty can occur. To observe the difficulty, let's modify FSR_0 so that it accepts *any word* beginning with an "x" and leave FSR_1 accepting only a "y" as illustrated in Figure 5.7. The lower transition diagram in the figure contains a first attempt at building the catenated machine. Again, the little box is a state where the machine switching takes place.

Now let's check this new machine on various strings.

- ("xy") The machine works perfectly on this one, switching from the initial state to the box state to the accepting state of the second machine.

- ("xay") The first input message sends the machine to the box state, the "a" keeps the machine at the same state and the "y" again moves us to the accepting state of the second machine. That works just fine—or does it? What happens if the "x" sends us to the accepting state for the first machine and we make the (legal) jump to the second machine only to bump into the unacceptable "a", forcing us to reject the word?

We saw in the last lemma that we could encapsulate the selection uncertainty in a pair of states. That same idea can be used in this situation also. Replace the box state of Figure 5.7 with the pair

$$(s_{02}, s_{10})$$

representing the possible selection of one or the other of the states.

Now let's see how this pair-state will change, based upon various input. Suppose the input is an "x". If we happened to be on FSR_0 we could either remain at state s_{02} or we could switch to the initial state s_{10} of FSR_1. On the other hand, if we were already on machine FSR_1, we would then have to go to the black-hole state s_{11}. So the pair (s_{02}, s_{10}) would have the *triple*

$$((s_{02}, s_{10}), s_{11}) = (s_{02}, s_{10}, s_{11})$$

as next state, given an input of "x". In fact for any character except "y," the pair (s_{02}, s_{10}) has the triple (s_{02}, s_{10}, s_{11}) as next state. (Verify this!)

What is the next state for (s_{02}, s_{10}) when receiving a "y" input? If we were still on FSR_0, we could either remain at s_{02} or switch to the initial state s_{10} as before. But if we were already on FSR_1, we would move to s_{12}. So the pair (s_{02}, s_{10}) would have the triple

$$(s_{02}, s_{10}, s_{12})$$

as next state, given an input of "y". These ideas are illustrated in Figure 5.8.

In exactly the same manner the next states can be calculated for the two triples just produced. Not surprisingly, a 4-tuple turns out to be one next state. This work is illustrated in Figures 5.9 and 5.10. The next states for the 4-tuple are similarly derived in Figure 5.11.

When we place these various states on a single transition diagram, the resulting machine looks like the one in Figure 5.12. Note what this machine does with the

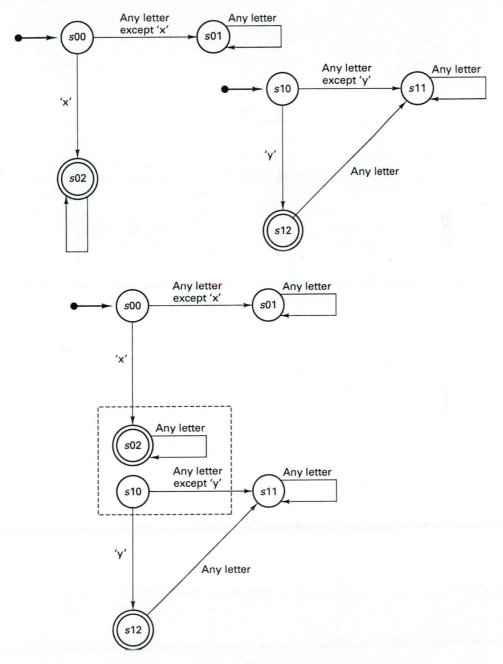

Figure 5.7. Product of More Complex Machines

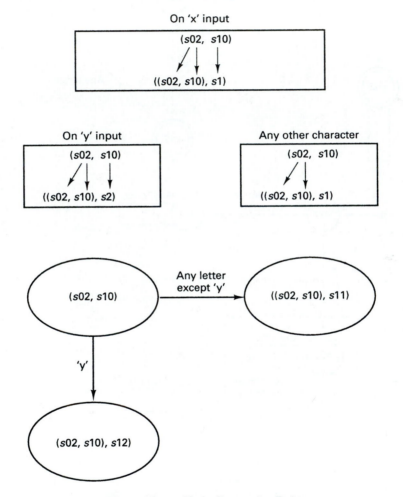

Figure 5.8. Next States for Pair

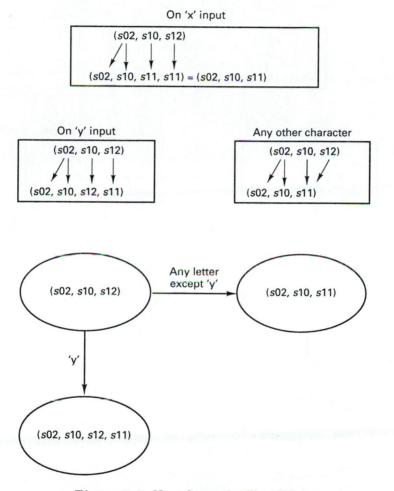

Figure 5.9. Next States for First Triple

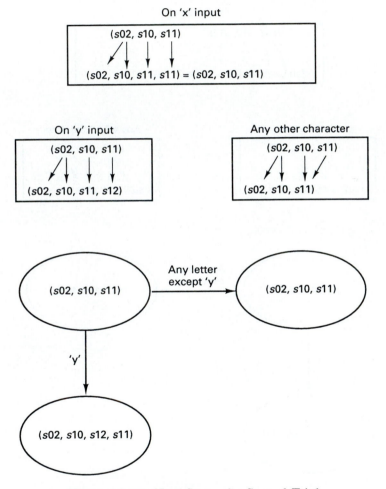

Figure 5.10. Next States for Second Triple

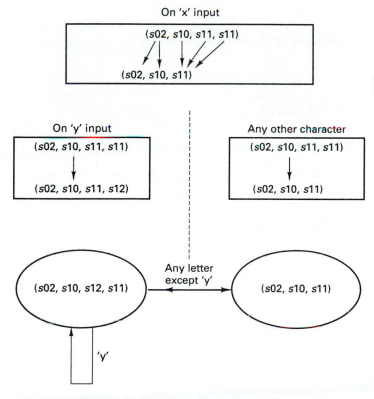

Figure 5.11. Next States for 4-Tuple

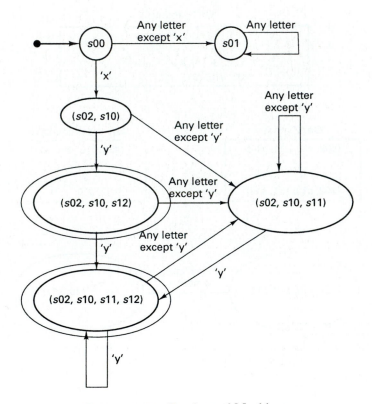

Figure 5.12. Product of Machines

input string "xy". The machine terminates in state $((s_{02}, s_{10}), s_{12})$ so we should definitely call this state an accepting state of the new machine. Since the machine terminates in state

$$(((s_{02}, s_{10}), s_{11}), s_{12})$$

after processing the correct string "xay", we should also call this an accepting state. Strings not starting with "x" and ending with "y"' always end in states that do not include *both* accepting states s_{02} and s_{12} of FSR_0 and FSR_1.

The pattern is now sufficiently clear that we can state the general construction process. Let

$$S^{(0)} = \{s_{00}, s_{01}, \ldots, s_{0m}\}$$

and

$$S^{(1)} = \{s_{10}, s_{11}, \ldots, s_{1n}\}$$

be the respective states of the finite-state recognizers FSR_0 and FSR_1. Let N^0 be the nonaccepting states in FSR_0.

- **Input Messages.** The set of input messages for the catenation FSR_0 FSR_1 machine is the same as it is for each of the two original machines.

- **Set of States.** The set of states for the catenation machine is the set of all states in N_0 together the pairs

$$(s_{0,j}, s_{1,k})$$

  where the first component is an accepting state of the first machine and the second is the initial state of the second and all other pairs, triples or n-tuples of states that are actually reached by the following *next-state* function.

- **Next-state Function.** The catenation machine, upon reading an input message i switches from state $(s_{0,j}, s_{1,k})$ to state

$$(f^0(s_{0,j}, i), f^1(s_{1,k}, i))$$

  where $f^{(0)}$ is the next-state function for the first machine, and $f^{(1)}$ belongs to the second machine. A similar pattern is used for any triples. In the event that two states of a triple are the same, the triple is replaced with the obvious corresponding pair.

- **Accepting States.** Any tuple of states

$$(s_{0,j}, s_{1,k}, \ldots)$$

  is an accepting state for if it contains accepting states from both FSR_0 and FSR_1.

Lemma 5.5. *If FSR is a finite-state recognizer that accepts the language defined by the regular expression r, then there is a finite-state recognizer FSR^* that accepts the language generated by the Kleene star r^* of r.*

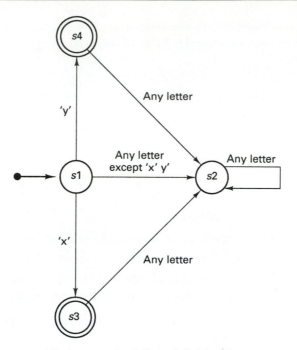

Figure 5.13. "x" or "y" Machine

Proof: This time let's use an example finite-state recognizer that accepts either an "x" or a "y", illustrated in Figure 5.13. The required Kleene finite-state machine must accept any number of repetitions of the single letters "x' and "y' that are recognized by FSR. Obviously, the new machine will start off at the initial state of the initial machine and will contain all nonaccepting states that can be reached by the machine's next-state function. But what happens when we come to an accepting state? If there are more input characters, we can either keep trucking along from that accepting state, or we can go back to the beginning state and start to recognize another string. When do we switch back to the beginning? We don't really know. We therefore place the uncertainty in a pair as we have done before. A single accepting state of FSR will thus be replaced by a pair consisting of that accepting state and the initial state. The next states for this pair are again pairs, which may convert to triples if an accepting state of the original FSR occurs as a component, and so on. At first this looks like big trouble—as if there will not be a finite number of states. But notice that the tuples are really unordered and therefore never contain more elements than there are total states in the original finite-state recognizer.

Figure 5.14 contains the transition diagram for the Kleene machine FSR^* corresponding to FSR. To see this, first note that the initial state s_1^* of the new machine

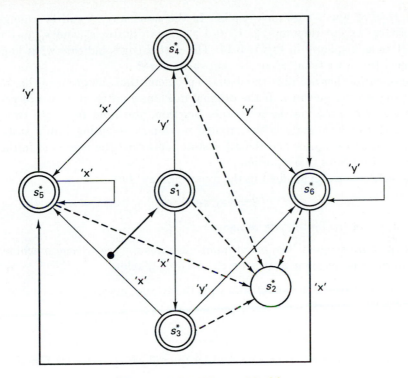

Figure 5.14. Kleene Machine

can be the initial state s_1 of the original machine.[5] The next-state function can map this initial state to the following states.

1. (Input message x) $s_3^* = (s_3, s_1)$

2. (Input not x or y) $s_2^* = (s_2, s_2)$

3. (Input message y) $s_4^* = (s_4, s_1)$

Notice that s_3^* and s_4^* are both pairs, since they are associated with accepting states of the original machine. Now s_3^* can also be changed to the following states.

1. (Input message x) $s_5^* = (s_2, s_3, s_1)$

2. (Input not x or y) $s_2^* = (s_2, s_2, s_2)$

3. (Input message y) $s_6^* = (s_2, s_4, s_1)$

---

[5] By the way, the Kleene closure always contains the empty string. That is why the initial state of the Kleene machine in Figure 5.14 is illustrated as an accepting state, even though it wasn't accepting in the original.

Notice that s_5^* and s_6^* are now triples. In the same way s_4^* can be changed into three states, except they are s_5^*, s_2^* and s_6^* again. States s_5^* and s_6^* just map to themselves as displayed in Figure 5.14. The dotted edges indicate what happens if any character other than "x" or "y" are encountered.

This example has not illustrated all the problems that can occur in the construction of the Kleene machine. If the original machine's initial state is not accepting but can be reentered via the next-state function, you need to create two Kleene machine states: One state is the original machine's accepting initial state as we have done in our example and the other state represents the reentered initial state. Exercise 5.4 explores this situation.

The general case is handled in the following way. Let

$$S = \{s_0, s_1, \ldots, s_m\}$$

be the states of the finite-state recognizer *FSR*.

- **Input messages.** The set of input messages for the Kleene machine FSR^* machine is the same as it is for the original machine.

- **Set of states.** The set of states for the Kleene machine is the subset of the unordered tuples

$$(s_j, s_k, \ldots)$$

of states that are actually reached by the following *next-state* function.

- **Next-state function.** The Kleene machine's function switches from state (s_j, s_k) to state
$$(f(s_j, i), f(s_k, i), \ldots)$$
except that a pair may convert into a triple if an accepting state of the original machine is encountered, and so on.

- **Accepting states.** A tuple
$$(s_j, s_k, \ldots)$$
is an accepting state for the Kleene machine if any of the component states is an accepting state for the original machine.

These five lemmas have constructively verified an important result: Any regular expression can be recognized by a finite-state machine.

5.2   Generating Scanners

Building finite-state recognizers from scratch obviously would be a time-consuming and error-prone task. Fortunately, we can use a **scanner generator** to produce such a recognizer. In this section we illustrate this by using the scanner generator *lex* to produce a recognizer for the Pascal programming language. This is accomplished by performing the following steps.

- Specifying the tokens that the scanner will pass to the parser

- Constructing a scanner specification file

- Generating the scanner function, using *lex*

- Compiling the scanner function

5.2.1 Specifying Tokens

The tokens used for scanner/parser communication are listed in the following table.

```
┌─────────────────────────────────────────────────────────────────────┐
│ ┌──────────────────────────────┐                                    │
│ │ Pascal Tokens (parser.gram)  │                                    │
│ └──────────────────────────────┘                                    │
│                                                                      │
│    18    %token PROGRAMTK        57   %token NILTK                   │
│    19   %token LABELTK           58                                  │
│    20   %token CONSTTK           59   %token UNSIGNEDINTTK           │
│    21   %token TYPETK            60   %token UNSIGNEDREALTK          │
│    22   %token PROCEDURETK       61   %token STRINGTK                │
│    23   %token FUNCTIONTK        62   %token BADSTRINGTK             │
│    24   %token VARTK             63   %token IDENTIFIERTK            │
│    25   %token BEGINTK           64                                  │
│    26   %token ENDTK             65   %token PLUSTK      '+'         │
│    27   %token DIVTK             66   %token MINUSTK     '-'         │
│    28   %token MODTK             67   %token ASTERTK     '*'         │
│    29   %token ANDTK             68   %token SLASHTK     '/'         │
│    30   %token NOTTK             69   %token DOTTK       '.'         │
│    31   %token ORTK              70   %token COMMATK     ','         │
│    32   %token INTK              71   %token LPARENTK    '('         │
│    33   %token ARRAYTK           72   %token LBRACKTK    '['         │
│    34   %token FILETK            73   %token LBRACETK    '{'         │
│    35   %token RECORDTK          74   %token UPARROWTK   '^'         │
│    36   %token SETTK             75   %token COLONTK     ':'         │
│    37   %token PACKEDTK          76   %token RPARENTK    '('         │
│    38   %token CASETK            77   %token RBRACKTK    ']'         │
│    39   %token OFTK              78   %token RBRACETK    '}'         │
│    40   %token FORTK             79                                  │
│    41   %token FORWARDTK         80   %token EQTK   /* =  */         │
│    42   %token TOTK              81   %token NETK   /* <> */         │
│    43   %token DOWNTOTK          82   %token LTTK   /* <  */         │
│    44   %token DOTK              83   %token LETK   /* <= */         │
│    45   %token IFTK              84   %token GTTK   /* >  */         │
│    46   %token THENTK            85   %token GETK   /* >= */         │
│    47   %token ELSETK            86   %token ASGTK  /* := */         │
│    48   %token REPEATTK          87   %token DDTK   /* .. */         │
│    49   %token UNTILTK           88   %token SCTK   /* ;  */         │
│    50   %token WHILETK           89                                  │
│    51   %token WITHTK            90   %left PLUSTK MINUSTK           │
│    52   %token READTK            91   %left ASTERTK MODTK            │
│    53   %token READLNTK          92   %left SLASHTK DIVTK            │
│    54   %token WRITETK           93   %right ORTK                    │
│    55   %token WRITELNTK         94   %right ANDTK '&'               │
│    56   %token GOTOTK                                                │
└─────────────────────────────────────────────────────────────────────┘
```

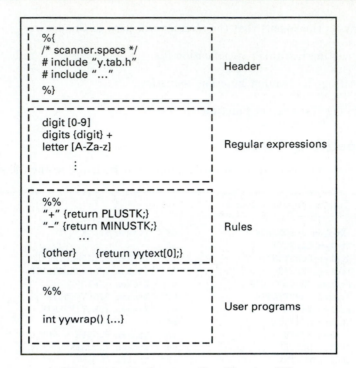

Figure 5.15. Scanner Specification File

This list is a part of a file, *parser.gram* that will be used to generate the parser using a parser generator called *yacc*. The -d option on the command

$$yacc - d\ parser.gram$$

produces the file *y.tab.h* that contains the definitions of the tokens as special integer values. These can then be included in the code for the scanner function. See Chapter 6 and the student workbook [7] for more specific information.

5.2.2   Constructing Scanner Specification File

A scanner specification file consists of up to four major parts, as illustrated in Figure 5.15.

Header.   The first section of the scanner specification file can contain user-defined globals and supporting functions.

```
┌─────────────────────────────────────────────────────────┐
│┌──────────────────────────────────────────┐             │
││ Scanner Specification Header (scanner.specs)│           │
│└──────────────────────────────────────────┘             │
│                                                         │
│   6 #include <ctype.h>  //for isupper and tolower        │
│   7 #include "y.tab.h"  //for the tokens                 │
│   8                                                      │
│   9 #include "../ctrl/ctrl.h"                            │
│  10 PLexTokCls lex_tok; //global definition              │
│  11                                                      │
│  12 #include "scanner.fcts"                              │
│                                                         │
└─────────────────────────────────────────────────────────┘
```

Regular expressions.   The table below contains a summary of the particular regular expression syntax used by our scanner generator, *lex*.

[xz]	The same thing as x or z
[x - z]	The same thing as x, y, or z.
[^x]	Any character except x.
.	Any character except the end-of-line character.
^x	An x at the beginning of a line
x$	An x at the end of a line
x?	An optional x
x*	0,1,2, ... instances of x
x+	1,2,3, ... instances of x
x|y	x or y
(x)	The same thing as x.
x/y	x only if followed by y
x{m,n}	m through n occurrences of x

One detail not included in the table is the catenation of two expressions which is denoted by writing the two component expressions side by side.

- [ab] represents a single character.

- [a] [b] represents two.

Most of the items in the table are clear.

- [ ] represents the blank character

- [\t] represents the tab character. The \ indicates that the character which follows is a special character, in this case representing a tab rather than the letter *t*.

- [\n] represents the newline character.

- [\t\n]. Therefore represents a space, tab, or newline. We call any such character a **white space**.

- [^}] represents any character except a right brace.

- [a-z] represents any lower-case letter.

- [a-z][a-z0-9]* represents any collection of lower-case letters and digits having a lower-case letter as an initial character.

- [a-z][a-z0-9]{0,7} represents the same thing, except that its total length cannot exceed 8.

- [0-7][0-7]*/[B] represents any string of digits 0–7, but only if preceded by a capital B. You may recognize this as the specification of a Modula-2 octal literal.

A set of regular expressions that describe the various Pascal lexemes is listed below.

```
┌─────────────────────────────────────────────────────────────────────────┐
│ Scanner Regular Expressions (scanner.specs)                              │
├─────────────────────────────────────────────────────────────────────────┘
│                                                                          │
│   16 digit     [0-9]                                                     │
│   17 digits    {digit}+                                                  │
│   18 letter    [A-Za-z]                                                  │
│   19 l_or_d    ({letter}|{digit})                                       │
│   20 sign      [+\-]                                                     │
│   21 dtdgts    {dot}{digits}                                            │
│   22 exponent  [Ee]{sign}?{digits}                                      │
│   23 real      {digits}({dtdgts}|{exponent}|{dtdgts}{exponent})         │
│   24 ident     {letter}{l_or_d}*                                        │
│   25 newline   [\n]                                                      │
│   26 quote     [\"]                                                      │
│   27 whitespace [ \t]                                                    │
│   28 comment   ("{"[^}]*"}"|"(*"("*([^*)]|[^*])")"|"*"[^)])*"*"*"*)")   │
│   29 string    \'([^'\n]|\'\')+\'                                        │
│   30 badstring {quote}[^"]*{quote}                                      │
│   31 dotdot    ".."                                                      │
│   32 dot       "."                                                       │
│   33 other     .                                                         │
│                                                                          │
└─────────────────────────────────────────────────────────────────────────┘
```

The following items are most noteworthy in the preceding collection of regular expressions.

- A digit is any character 0 through 9; *digit*s represents any string of one or more digits.

- Letters are either upper or lower case, and *l_or_d* illustrates the "or" regular expression format.

- The "\" is used in the expression for *sign* to protect the "-" so that *lex* won't think that it represents a range of values.

- An exponent consists of a required "E" and then a signed integer. Pascal signed integers need not include the sign.

- A real number can look like 1.2, 1e2, or 1.2e3.

- A white space consists of either a space " ", a tab or a new-line character. These will be ignored by the scanner.

- Pascal comments can be specified by regular expressions.[6] The regular expression used here has been gleaned from Schreiner [18]. The first specification "{"[^}]*"}" is quite easy to understand. It just says that a comment must start with a { and then be followed by any number of non-} characters that is, in turn, followed by the closing }. The second expression is explained Exercise 5.6.

- A Pascal string must start and end with an apostrophe. In between these delimiters must exist at least one character that cannot be an apostrophe (unless there are two of them) or a new-line character (strings can't span across lines).

Rules. The next section of the scanner specification file contains the rules specifying the action the scanner is to perform when the various lexemes are recognized.

The Pascal language really has an amazingly simple structure for a full-fledged language. There are only some 20 single or double character lexemes that the scanner must recognize. We have chosen to use A separate token for each of these lexemes, though you could place such special symbols directly in the grammar if you found the scanner was not performing its task efficiently. The first listing below describes scanner rules for the these special symbols. The scanner action calls the function *ckout()* that produces the source listing if selected by the *-l* option, and then returns the appropriate token value.

---

[6] Scanners for languages that allow nested comments have to recognize comments differently. Often what is done is to recognize the start of a comment and then pass control to a special comment-eating function.

```
Scanner Rules for Symbols (scanner.specs)

  36   {newline}            {ckout();}
  37   {whitespace}         {if (! at_margin || !OptionCls::format())
  38                             {ckout();}}
  39   "+"                  {ckout(); return PLUSTK;}
  40   "-"                  {ckout(); return MINUSTK;}
  41   "*"                  {ckout(); return ASTERTK;}
  42   "/"                  {ckout(); return SLASHTK;}
  43   "["                  {ckout(); return LBRACKTK;}
  44   "]"                  {ckout(); return RBRACKTK;}
  45   {dot}                {ckout(); return DOTTK;}
  46   ","                  {ckout(); return COMMATK;}
  47   ":"                  {ckout(); return COLONTK;}
  48   ";"                  {ckout(); return SCTK;}
  49   "^"                  {ckout(); return UPARROWTK;}
  50   "("                  {ckout(); return LPARENTK;}
  51   ")"                  {ckout(); return RPARENTK;}
  52   "="                  {ckout(); return EQTK;}
  53   "<>"                 {ckout(); return NETK;}
  54   "<"                  {ckout(); return LTTK;}
  55   "<="                 {ckout(); return LETK;}
  56   ">"                  {ckout(); return GTTK;}
  57   ">="                 {ckout(); return GETK;}
  58   ":="                 {ckout(); return ASGTK;}
  59   {dotdot}             {ckout(); return DDTK;}
```

The next listing contains rules for the non-trivial categories of lexemes. Here, many different lexemes must be associated with the single representing token.

- In each of the first four categories, the lexeme (stored in *yytext*) and corresponding line number are first stored in a special *LexTokCls* object and then the token value returned.

- The rule for {ident} is an example of a more complex rule. Since Pascal is supposed to be case insensitive, recognized identifier lexemes are modified to lower case prior to the search through the (lower case) reserved word list by *ck_reserved_wd()*.

- No token is returned for a comment.

- Any unrecognizable lexeme is represented with a zero token value. This will generate the necessary parsing error since all other token values are automatically given values greater than 256.

Scanner Rules for More Complex Lexemes (scanner.specs)

```
61 {digits} {ckout();
62     lex_tok = new LexTokCls(yylineno, UNSIGNEDINTTK, yytext);
63     return UNSIGNEDINTTK;}
64
65 {real}   {ckout();
66     lex_tok = new LexTokCls(yylineno, UNSIGNEDREALTK, yytext);
67     return UNSIGNEDREALTK;}
68
69 {string} {ckout();
70     lex_tok = new LexTokCls(yylineno, STRINGTK, yytext);
71     return STRINGTK;}
72
73 {badstring} {ckout();
74     lex_tok = new LexTokCls(yylineno, BADSTRINGTK, yytext);
75     return BADSTRINGTK;}
76
77 {ident}  {
78     char lc_text[256]; //Assuming no identifier is longer!
79     strcpy(lc_text,yytext);
80     for(int i=0; i<yyleng; i++)  {
81     if (isupper(lc_text[i])) lc_text[i] = tolower(lc_text[i]);
82     }
83     int actual_tk = ck_reserved_wd(lc_text);
84     lex_tok = new LexTokCls(yylineno, actual_tk, lc_text);
85     ckout();
86     return actual_tk;}
87
88 {comment} {ckout();}
89
90 {other}  {ckout();
91     return yytext[0];}
92
```

The scanner's supporting functions. The last major section of the scanner specification file is an optional collection of user-supplied functions. In the example Pascal compiler, we have chosen to place these in a separate, included file, *scanner.fcts*. Actually, placing user functions in the scanner specification file has the rather negative implication of requiring the scanner to be regenerated each time a change to the functions is desired.

It is required that the user provide at least a simple version of a program *yywrap()* describing the scanner's behavior upon completing the input stream.

Scanner wrap-up function (scanner.fcts)

```
 9     int yywrap() {
10         return 1;
11     }
```

```
                 Scanner function ckout() (scanner.fcts)

 20  void ckout() {
 21      //cout << "ckout(): text: " << yytext << endl;
 22      strcpy(temp,yytext);
 23      char *tmp = temp;
 24      while (*tmp != '\0') {
 25          if (OptionCls::list()) {
 26              if (at_margin) {
 27                  cout << "[";
 28                  cout.width(5);
 29                  cout << line_no << "]     ";
 30                  at_margin = 0;
 31              }
 32              if (*tmp == '\t') {
 33                  for (int j=1; j<TAB_WIDTH; j++) {
 34                      cout << " ";
 35                  }
 36              } else {
 37                  cout << *tmp;
 38              }
 39          } else if (OptionCls::format()) {
 40              if (at_margin) {
 41                  for (int i=0; i< indent_level ; i++) {
 42                      for (int j=1; j<= INDENT_WIDTH ; j++) {
 43                          cout << " " ;
 44                      }
 45                  }
 46                  at_margin = 0;
 47              }
 48              cout << *tmp;
 49          }
 50          //Since line numbers are used for error messages...
 51          //    do each time.
 52          if(*tmp++ == '\n') {
 53              line_no++;
 54              at_margin = 1;
 55          }
 56          if (indent_after) {
 57              indent_after = 0;
 58              indent_level++;
 59          }
 60      }
 61  }
```

Recall that *ckout()* is required to output the content of the lexeme presently being examined if the list option has been set by the user. Since Pascal comments can span multiple lines, source listing line numbers can printed out in a rather strange manner. This version of *ckout()* therefore maintains its own count of line numbers and outputs the line header if a new-line character \n is encountered. It also has the ability to create its own left margin in support of the formatting option described in Chapter 6.

The following code defines the reserved word table that is used by *ck_reserved_wd()*.

```
    Scanner's Reserved Words (scanner.fcts)

    64 struct rwtable_str {
    65     char *rw_name;        /* lexeme */
    66     int  rw_yylex;        /* token  */
    67 };
    68
    69 rwtable_str rwtable[] = {
    70     "",               IDENTIFIERTK,
    71     "and",            ANDTK,
    72     "array",          ARRAYTK,
    73     "begin",          BEGINTK,
    74     "case",           CASETK,
    75     "const",          CONSTTK,
    76     "div",            DIVTK,
    77     "do",             DOTK,
    78     "downto",         DOWNTOTK,
    79     "else",           ELSETK,
    80     "end",            ENDTK,
    81     "file",           FILETK,
    82     "for",            FORTK,
    83     "forward",        FORWARDTK,
    84     "function",       FUNCTIONTK,
    85     "goto",           GOTOTK,
    86     "if",             IFTK,
    87     "in",             INTK,
    88     "label",          LABELTK,
    89     "mod",            MODTK,
    90     "nil",            NILTK,
    91     "not",            NOTTK,
    92     "of",             OFTK,
    93     "or",             ORTK,
    94     "packed",         PACKEDTK,
    95     "procedure",      PROCEDURETK,
    96     "program",        PROGRAMTK,
    97     "read",           READTK,
    98     "readln",         READLNTK,
    99     "record",         RECORDTK,
   100     "repeat",         REPEATTK,
   101     "set",            SETTK,
   102     "then",           THENTK,
   103     "to",             TOTK,
   104     "type",           TYPETK,
   105     "until",          UNTILTK,
   106     "var",            VARTK,
   107     "while",          WHILETK,
   108     "with",           WITHTK,
   109     "write",          WRITETK,
   110     "writeln",        WRITELNTK
   111 };
```

Since the checker uses a binary search algorithm it is important that the reserved table be arranged alphabetically. The table just contains the Pascal reserved words that must be differentiated from user defined identifiers.

```
     ┌─────────────────────────────────────────────┐
     │ Reserved Word Checker (scanner.fcts)         │
     └─────────────────────────────────────────────┘

 172 #define LEN(x)            (sizeof(x)/sizeof((x)[0]))
 173 #define ENDTABLE(v)       (v - 1 + LEN(v))
 174
 175 int ck_reserved_wd(char* yytext) {
 176     //cout << "ck_reserved_wd()" << endl;
 177     rwtable_str *low = rwtable;
 178     rwtable_str *high = ENDTABLE(rwtable);
 179     rwtable_str *mid;
 180     int comp;
 181
 182     strcpy(temp,yytext); /* temp defined up top */
 183
 184     while (low <= high) {
 185         mid = low + (high-low)/2;
 186
 187         if ((comp=strcmp(mid->rw_name, temp)) == 0) {
 188             if (OptionCls::format()) {
 189                 ck_indent(mid -> rw_yylex);
 190             }
 191             return mid->rw_yylex;
 192         } else if (comp < 0) {
 193                 low = mid+1;
 194         } else {
 195                 high = mid-1;
 196         }
 197     }
 198     return rwtable->rw_yylex;  /* ie. token: IDENTIFIER! */
 199 }
```

5.2.3   Generating the Scanner

Scanner generators usually produce code for a scanner function or procedure. The command

```
lex scanner.specs
```

produces a C (integer-valued) function *yylex()*, that is placed in the file *lex.yy.c*. If a *main()* function has been included in the scanner specification file, as we illustrate in the section below, the scanner can be compiled, linked, and then tested directly.

5.2.4   Testing the Scanner

A scanner presents an interesting testing situation. Scanners need to behave predictably on the set of all valid lexemes for the given programming language. This set is a large collection of strings. Moreover, the corresponding set of tokens is therefore a large collection of computer-generated integer values, not exactly the most interesting form of reading you might find. However, the scope of the testing task is sufficiently small that this work really can be efficiently done by hand. Time spent trying to automate the test is usually not rewarded with any improvement in the scanner's performance.

Scanners must also handle erroneous lexical input with grace. In no case should the scanner halt or crash. The key to testing this side of the scanner is the creation of a collection of character strings, which are a faithful representation of all possible invalid scanner input. Often, ideas of quality error input occur in while you are actually trying to get the scanner to recognize a particular lexical structure.

We have found the following procedure to be a good way of testing the scanner as it is being created.

- Create a simple function *main()*, that calls the scanner. In our UNIX environment, this usually means working first in C, rather in C++. We usually place the scanner call *yylex()* in an infinite loop, assuming that the testing will continue until the program is terminated using $< ctrl > C$ or some shell command. It is also helpful to place the call to *yylex()* in a print statement so that the actual token value returned can be verified.

- Place the testing *main()* function in the user-defined supporting function section of the scanner specification file. Generate the scanner file as described in the section above, and verify that *main()* is working properly.

- Enter collections of regular expressions designed to recognize either a class of related lexemes or a particularly sensitive lexeme. At this time create or update two additional files.

  - An input file. Include valid forms of lexemes that the new regular expressions are to recognize. Also include strings that contain specific errors.

  - An expected output file. List the expected integers that should be generated by *main()* in response to the input file. Be sure to anticipate what proper scanner response to the error input.

The following order of lexical recognition should be helpful.

  - First, enter regular expressions for the various literals of the programming language. Integer literals are a good place to start. Don't forget string literals. Also decide how you will handle set literals if they are a part of the language.

  - Enter expressions that will recognize identifiers and reserved words. Be sure to include input that tests the various case sensitivity requirements of the language.

  - Add regular expressions that will recognize all single- and double-character lexemes. Be sure to test the scanner when single characters not in this list are entered.

— Add regular expressions associated with the source language comment structure.

Often information obtained in a later stage of development will suggest additional tests to be inserted in the test files for expressions developed earlier.

When the scanner has been thoroughly tested, we usually remove the trivial testing *main()* so that conflicts with other testing functions will not occur when testing the parser.

5.3   Exercises

1. Give *lex*-style regular expressions for each of the following.

    (a) A Pascal signed integer

    (b) A Pascal signed real

    (c) A FORTRAN string that is delimited by the " character

2. (a) Construct a machine FSR_0 recognizing either an "a" or "b".

    (b) Construct a machine FSR_1 recognizing a "c".

    (c) Construct the recognizer $FSR_0 \vee FSR_1$. What strings will this machine recognize?

    (d) Construct the recognizer $FSR_0 \ FSR_1^*$. What strings will this machine recognize?

    (e) Construct the recognizer $(FSR_0 \ FSR_1)^*$. What strings will this machine recognize?

3. Suppose that the set V of valid characters consists only of the letters a, b, c, and the digits $1, 2$.

    (a) Construct a regular expression that describes "Pascal" identifiers (start with a letter and then any number of letters or digits) over this alphabet.

    (b) Construct the corresponding finite-state recognizer that represents this expression.

4. The finite-state recognizer FSR in Figure 5.16 has an initial state s_0 that is not accepting and yet can be entered via the next-state function. Denote by s_0^* the accepting initial state for the Kleene machine corresponding to the starting role for s_0 and by s_1^* the state representing that same state when s_0 is entered from another location in FSR. Draw a transition digram that represents the Kleene machine FSR^*.

5. The example scanner in this chapter does not return a token when it encounters white spaces or comments. Explain what would happen if you defined and returned special tokens for these lexemes.

    Hint: How would the parser handle these tokens?

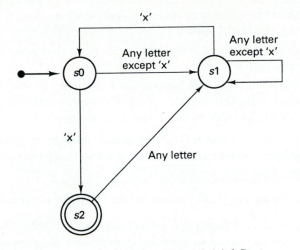

Figure 5.16. Nonaccepting Initial State

6. This exercise is designed to explore the regular expression

$$\text{"(*""("*([^*)]|[^*]")"|"*"[^)])*"*"*"*)"}$$

that represents the alternate form (* *) of a Pascal comment. Explain in words the meaning of each of the following regular expressions.

(a) `[^*)]`

(b) `[^*]")"`

(c) `"*"[^)]`

(d) `([^*)]|[^*]")"|"*"[^)])*`

(e) `"(*""("*`

(f) `"*"*"*)"`

(g) `"(*""("*([^*)]|[^*]")"|"*"[^)])*"*"*"*)"`

7. This exercise deals with the problem of recognizing comments in a language (such as Modula-2) that allows their nesting.

(a) Prove that no regular expression can be written that will recognize all such comments by working through the following steps.

- Assume there is such a finite-state recognizer. How many states would it have?

- Suppose you write a program having comments nested more deeply than the number of states in your machine (say, **n + 1**, where n is the number of states).

- Argue that there is necessarily one state that gets visited more than once (say **k** times).

- But then what will happen for a comment having $k + n + 1$ of the start delimiters and only $n+1$ of the terminating delimiters? Is that any kind of way to run a comment recognizer?

(b) Write a function that will eat characters until the proper end of comment delimiter is encountered. You may want to make your program recursive or just implement a stack directly.

8. (Testing the scanner) Write a scanner bench testing program:

   (a) Write a *main()* that calls *yylex()* until a zero value is returned. You may want to make a switch/case structure for the purpose of translating token values to a more readable form.

   (b) Generate *yylex*. Don't forget to include the scanner supporting functions necessary for your scanner, especially the simple *yywrap()* function, that should trivially just return a value of 1.

   (c) Link the pieces.

   (d) Check the scanner by selectively entering single lexemes followed by a `<ctrl D>`. Be especially tough with tests of the various forms of real literals and of strings.

   (e) Check the scanner on longer sequences of lexemes.

9. Produce a partial Pascal scanner that recognizes the following reserved words.

   - **var**
   - **for**
   - **to**
   - **do**
   - **if**
   - **then**
   - **else**

   Make suitable modifications to the token specifications in the grammar so that new scanner can be tested directly from your compiler.

10. (Exploration)

   (a) Write a complete scanner specification file for the C language.

(b) Use *lex* to generate a scanner for the C-lexemes.

(c) Thoroughly test the scanner.

11. (**CLIP** Project)

Design, implement, and test a scanner for **CLIP**.

Chapter 6

Parser

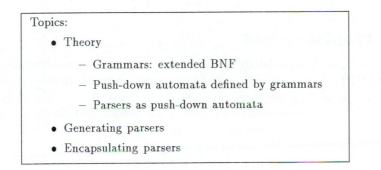

Topics:

- Theory

  - Grammars: extended BNF

  - Push-down automata defined by grammars

  - Parsers as push-down automata

- Generating parsers

- Encapsulating parsers

Parsers are the second major compiler component (Figure 2.1). They are responsible for checking the syntax or lexeme order of the incoming source program. Parsers also play a central role in the construction of the important parse tree data structure. This chapter contains theoretical background that aids in the understanding of how parsers work. Also included is a step-by-step description of how such parsers can be constructed and tested.

6.1   Theory of Parsing

In Chapter 5 we noted the following important facts.

- Any set of regular expressions uniquely determines a corresponding set or language of lexemes.

- The language defined by a set of regular expressions can be recognized by a finite-state machine.

- The finite-state machine recognizer can be constructed directly from the set of regular expressions by a scanner generator.

The regular expression rules for specifying valid source language lexemes are called lexical rules. Rules that specify the order of source code lexemes are called **syntax rules**. These rules are most often specified using a formalism called **BNF** and are usually called **productions**. A collection of productions is called

75

a **grammar**. The set of all strings satisfying every production in a grammar is called a **language defined by the grammar**. The main ideas in this chapter are the following.

- Any set of productions uniquely determines a corresponding language.

- The language defined by a set of (suitably nice) productions can be recognized by a special finite-state machine, called a **push-down automaton**.

- The push-down automaton recognizer can be constructed directly from the set of productions by a parser generator.

6.1.1   Productions: BNF

In response to the heated debates and creative activities surrounding the construction of ALGOL 58, John Backus devised an elegant notation to describe important ideas in the developing language. In 1960, Peter Naur began editing the *ALGOL Bulletin*. His activity necessitated a careful study the ALGOL 58 report by Backus. Naur decided that the Backus notation should be used to describe the results of the next major effort on ALGOL 60 and later wrote his description of the proposed new language in this notation. The formalism has since proved very useful for specifying the grammars of most modern programming languages and is now known as **Backus-Naur formalism** or **BNF**. Let's look at several examples of Pascal syntax rules or productions.

The first example contains productions specifying that a Pascal identifier will be recognized directly by the scanner and signaled by the IDENTIFIERTK token.

```
%token IDENTIFIERTK
%start Ident
%%
Ident: IDENTIFIERTK
     ;
```

The next example similarly specifies the recognition of Pascal numeric literals.

```
%token UNSIGNEDINTTK
%token UNSIGNEDREALTK

%start Unsigned_number:
%%
Unsigned_number: UNSIGNEDINTTK
    | UNSIGNEDREALTK
     ;
```

Note the use of the | symbol to indicate the presence of two productions for the unsigned numbers. For the sake of simplicity in the following examples, both of these tokens are represented by NUMTK.

The following example is the first of several leading to a simplified description of Pascal expressions. This first expression example is based upon only three tokens and consists of two productions.

```
%token       NUMTK
%token       LPARENTK
%token       RPARENTK

%start       Factor
%%
Factor: NUMTK
      | LPARENTK NUMTK RPARENTK
      ;
```

The first production specifies that the **nonterminal** Factor can be replaced by a numeric literal such as "1." In this case we say that "1," or more precisely, the token NUMTK, is **derived directly** from Factor and denote this by the following formalism.

$$Factor \Rightarrow \text{NUMTK}$$

The second production states that the nonterminal Factor could also consist of a numeric literal inside a pair of parentheses. The string " (1) " is therefore recognized using the second production, summarized as follows.

$$Factor \overset{2}{\Rightarrow} \quad \text{LPARENTK NUMTK RPARENTK}$$

The next example uses the same set of tokens and contains the same first production as the grammar above. Clearly, a single numeric literal will be recognized in exactly the same way as before.

```
%token       NUMTK
%token       LPARENTK
%token       RPARENTK

%start       Factor
%%
Factor: NUMTK
      | LPARENTK Factor RPARENTK
      ;
```

The second production is significantly different. It allows the nesting of a numeric literal inside arbitrarily many pairs of parentheses. A string like " ((2)) " will be recognized by the following sequence of productions.

$$ParenExpr \quad \overset{2}{\Rightarrow} \quad LPARENTK \; ParenExpr \; RPARENTK$$

$$\overset{2}{\Rightarrow} \quad LPARENTK \; LPARENTK \; ParenExpr$$
$$RPARENTK \; RPARENTK$$

$$\overset{1}{\Rightarrow} \quad LPARENTK \; LPARENTK \; NUMTK$$
$$RPARENTK \; RPARENTK$$

This sequence of derivations is often abbreviated by using the following notation.

$$Factor \overset{*}{\Rightarrow} \text{LPARENTK LPARENTK UNSIGNEDINTTK RPARENTK RPARENTK}$$

Of course, the string " ((2) " would not allow a complete reduction since the required last RPARENTK is missing.

For our final example, take all possible integers, together with the two operations " + "," · " and the usual parentheses " (" and ") " as the set of lexemes.

```
%token  NUMTK
%token  ADDOPTK
%token  MULOPTK
%token  LPARENTK
%token  RPARENTK
%start Expression

%%
/* 1,2 */ Expression:
                Term
                | Expression  ADDOPTK  Term
                ;
/* 3,4 */ Term:
                Factor
                | Term  MULOPTK  Factor
        ;
/* 5,6 */ Factor:
                NUMTK
                | LPARENTK  Expression  RPARENTK
                ;
```

This grammar is a simplified version of Pascal expressions. Let's see how a string like " 1 " would be recognized. Production 1 must try to recognize the " 1 " as a *Term*, since the string does not contain any *ADDOPTK*. Similarly, production 3 must recognize the " 1 " as a *Factor*. Finally, production 5 will recognize the " 1 " as an *NUMTK*, the token passed to the parser by the scanner.

$$Expression \; \overset{1}{\Rightarrow} \; Term$$
$$\overset{3}{\Rightarrow} \; Factor$$
$$\overset{5}{\Rightarrow} \; NUMTK$$

Consider the recognition of another string like " $1 + 2 * 3$." This time the expression grammar must use the second production since it encounters an *ADDOP*. The leading " 1 " must therefore first be recognized as an expression (using the same set of steps as in the above example) and the remaining " 2*3 " must be recognized as a *Term*. Since the fourth production indicates that a *Term* can contain a *MULOP*, the " 2 " and the " 3 " must therefore be recognized as a *Term* and a *Factor*, respectively. These last two recognized can then be done just as we did in our very first example.

$$Expression \; \overset{2}{\Rightarrow} \; Expression \; ADDOPTK \; Term$$
$$\overset{1}{\Rightarrow} \; Term \; ADDOPTK \; Term$$
$$\overset{3}{\Rightarrow} \; Factor \; ADDOPTK \; Term$$
$$\overset{5}{\Rightarrow} \; NUMTK \; ADDOPTK \; Term$$
$$\overset{4}{\Rightarrow} \; NUMTK \; ADDOPTK \; Term \; MULOPTK \; Factor$$
$$\overset{3}{\Rightarrow} \; NUMTK \; ADDOPTK \; Factor \; MULOPTK \; Factor$$
$$\overset{5}{\Rightarrow} \; NUMTK \; ADDOPTK \; NUMTK \; MULOPTK \; Factor$$
$$\overset{5}{\Rightarrow} \; NUMTK \; ADDOPTK \; NUMTK \; MULOPTK \; NUMTK$$

The above process recognizes the given lexemes as an expression, since it has been completely derived from the %*start* symbol.

Not all strings of integers and operations are valid expressions. Consider how the grammar reacts to the string " $+2 + 3$." This time a sequence of productions takes the form

$$Expression \; \overset{1}{\Rightarrow} \; Expression \; ADDOPTK \; Term$$
$$\overset{3}{\Rightarrow} \; error$$

since no production begins with an *ADDOPTK*.

6.1.2   Specifying Syntax by Grammars

A **grammar** is a 4-tuple $G = (T, N, S, \mathcal{P})$.

- T is the set of tokens.

- N is the set of nonterminals.

- S is the start symbol.

- $\mathcal{P}$ is the set of productions.

What we actually have in mind is a **context-free** grammar in which productions always contain a single nonterminal on the left side. A source program is valid syntactically if it can be derived from the start symbol by applying various productions in the grammar. The set of all source programs that can be so derived from the start symbol is called the **language generated** by the grammar G.

6.1.3   Parsers: Syntax Recognizers

Language Recognized by a Push-Down Automaton

In Chapter 5, we saw that an ordinary finite-state machine could be used to recognize any language defined by regular expressions. We also noted that language structures allowing arbitrarily deep nesting of matching tokens such as parentheses could not be recognized by a finite-state machine, at least not the simple machines described in the proof of the Kleene theorem and produced by scanner generators such as *lex*. Clearly what is needed is the specification of a more powerful machine that could be used to recognize structures such as those found in modern programming languages.

A natural place to gain insight into the structure of such a machine can be obtained by trying to build a recognizer for the example grammar on page 77, above, that allows for nesting of parentheses. One thing that comes to mind is that a stack might be used to store left parentheses as they are encountered. As parsing progressed we could pop a left parenthesis off every time we encountered a right parenthesis. Imagine the machine in Figure 6.1 to have such a stack and to be given two new operations *push* and *pop*. We also will imagine that there exists an input tape on which is stored the input string terminated by an end-of-file marker, here denoted by Δ. Let's see how this machine responds to various kinds of input. It certainly recognizes an input string consisting of a single integer value, since the first read state sees the token NUMTK, and the second read state will produce the Δ that, after a pop, leads to an accepting state. The machine will also recognize strings consisting of a numeric literal surrounded by any number of parenthesis pairs because each pushed RPARENTK must match a corresponding popped LPARENTK. Finally, note that if there are fewer left than right parentheses, the machine will move to the bottom reject state. If there are too many left parentheses, it will go to the top right reject state.

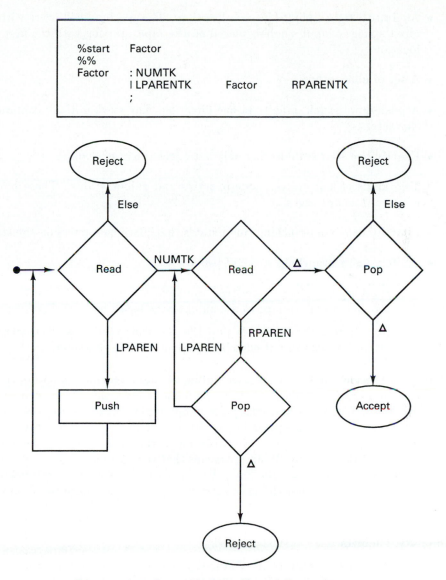

Figure 6.1. Recognizer for Nested Parentheses

The machine illustrated in Figure 6.1 is an example of a **push-down automaton**. More precisely, a push-down automaton, or **PDA** consists of the following things.

- A set of states that form a connected, directed graph.
- A set of input symbols.

- An **input tape**, infinite in one direction. The machine will start with the input string of input symbols placed on the tape, starting with the first tape location.

- A set of **characters**.

- A push-down **stack**, infinite in one direction. The stack initially contains no characters.

- Exactly one *start* state having only out-edges (no in-edges).

- Two kinds of halt states: **accept** states and **reject** states. These have *in* edges and no *out* edges.

- Finitely many nonbranching **push** states that place characters on the stack.

- Finitely many branching states of two kinds:

  - **read** states. These states read the next unused symbol from the input tape and then attempt to use an out-edge based upon the new symbol.

  - **pop** states. These states pop the top character from the stack and attempt to use an out-edge based upon the new character.

Running this machine on an sequence of input characters amounts to beginning at start and following all paths that are made possible by the various read, push, and pop states. If there is one such path ending at an accept state, the original string is declared to be **accepted** by the PDA. Landing in a reject state or any other nonaccept state does not necessarily mean that the character sequence is not accepted by the machine. It simply means that the particular path through the machine did not lead to an accept state. A sequence of input characters is **rejected** if all possible paths through the graph generated by the sequence terminate in a reject state.

Chomsky Theorem

Theorem 6.1 (Schützenberger, Chomsky, Evey). *Given a context-free grammar, there is a push-down automata that accepts precisely the language generated by the grammar.*

Proof: The complete proof of this theorem, though informative, constructive and certainly understandable, would take us too far afield from our compiler interests. There are several excellent texts that do go through the proof. The most precise is by Hopcroft and Ullman [9]. Cohen [4, pages 370–379] contains a very readable and informative discussion on the actual construction of the PDA.

You may find the following proof sketch to be interesting and reassuring.

1. Take the given context-free grammar and convert it to a special canonical form called Chomsky normal form, or CNF. A grammar is in CNF if all the productions look like

$$A :\ B\ C \tag{6.1}$$

where a nonterminal goes to two other nonterminal and the form

$$A :\ \text{TK} \tag{6.2}$$

that takes a nonterminal to a token. Almost all context-free grammars can be put in this form. Those that cannot are not significantly more complex and are often handled as a special case of a corresponding CNF grammar.

2. Build a machine that will recognize each production in the grammar. Essentially each production of type 6.1 corresponds to a graph that is a loop involving a rather simple collection of pops and pushes, while productions of type 6.2 are constructed by loops involving pops and reads.

Deterministic Recognizers: Shift/Reduce Parsers

The main problem with the Chomsky theorem is that the guaranteed PDA does not need to be a *deterministic* machine; that is, there may be several next-state choices for a particular input value at a given machine state. In fact, it can be shown that the language defined by the following palindrome context-free grammar

```
%start    Pal
%%
Pal: /* empty */
 | 'a'
 | 'b'
 | 'a' Pal 'a'
 | 'b' Pal 'b'
 ;
```

requires a PDA recognizer that is not deterministic. Naturally the construction or programming of such a recognizer would be a very difficult task.

If we are going to be able to build a deterministic machine that serves as a recognizer, we are therefore going to have to limit the scope of languages that it will be able to handle. Clearly we don't want to limit the set of recognizable languages to the point that most modern programming languages are excluded. Actually, the specification of recognizable languages has been handled a very practical way: Just find the most powerful recognizer possible and then say that the set of languages we are concerned with are those that can be recognized by this kind of machine. The machine we consider in this text is called a **shift/reduce recognizer**, and the set of recognizable languages are called **LR(1)**[1] languages, indicating the nature of the recognizer.

---

[1] The L refers to the source program being read from left to right. The R stands for *rightmost reductions in reverse*, a process we illustrate in this section. The 1 refers to the ability of our recognizer to look ahead one word in the input stream to help in the parsing process.

There are a number of terms that we can probably best introduce by means of the following grammar, a tiny subset of a Pascal grammar.

```
%start        Program
%%
Program: Program_heading SCTK Block DOTTK
    ;
Program_heading: PROGRAMTK Identifier Parameter_piece
    ;
Identifier: IDENTTK
    ;
Parameter_piece: /empty/
    | LPARENTK RPARENTK
    ;
Block: Statement_part
    | Statement_part
    ;
Statement_part: BEGINTK ENDTK
    ;
```

A program like the following

```
program VerySimple;
begin
end.
```

could be recognized as valid by tracing through the following set of grammar productions.

Prog	⇒	*Program_heading* SCTK *Block* DOTTK
	⇒	PROGRAMTK *Identifier Parameter_piece* SCTK *Block* DOTTK
	⇒	PROGRAMTK IDENTTK *Parameter_piece* SCTK *Block* DOTTK
	⇒	PROGRAMTK IDENTTK SCTK *Block* DOTTK
	⇒	PROGRAMTK IDENTTK SCTK *Statement_part* DOTTK
	⇒	PROGRAMTK IDENTTK SCTK BEGINTK *Statement_seq* ENDTK DOTTK
	⇒	PROGRAMTK IDENTTK SCTK BEGINTK *Statement* ENDTK DOTTK
	⇒	PROGRAMTK IDENTTK SCTK BEGINTK *Empty_stmt* ENDTK DOTTK
	⇒	PROGRAMTK IDENTTK SCTK BEGINTK ENDTK DOTTK

This process of going from the start symbol to the sequence of tokens is called **leftmost derivation.**

It turns out that the kind of parsers discussed in this text are better understood if we do our derivations from the *right* as illustrated below.

Prog	⇒	*Program_heading* SCTK *Block* DOTTK
	⇒	*Program_heading* SCTK *Statement_part* DOTTK
	⇒	*Program_heading* SCTK BEGINTK *Statement_seq* ENDTK DOTTK

$\Rightarrow$ *Program_heading* SCTK BEGINTK *Statement* ENDTK DOTTK

$\Rightarrow$ *Program_heading* SCTK BEGINTK *Empty_stmt* ENDTK DOTTK

$\Rightarrow$ *Program_heading* SCTK BEGINTK ENDTK DOTTK

$\Rightarrow$ PROGRAMTK *Identifier Parameter_piece* BEGINTK ENDTK DOTTK

$\Rightarrow$ PROGRAMTK *Identifier* SCTK BEGINTK ENDTK DOTTK

$\Rightarrow$ PROGRAMTK IDENTTK SCTK BEGINTK ENDTK DOTTK

To get a picture of how a shift/reduce parser might work, imagine flipping the above rightmost derivations over as indicated below.

$\Rightarrow$ PROGRAMTK IDENTTK SCTK BEGINTK ENDTK DOTTK

$\Rightarrow$ PROGRAMTK *Identifier* SCTK BEGINTK ENDTK DOTTK

$\Rightarrow$ PROGRAMTK *Identifier Parameter_piece*

       SCTK BEGINTK ENDTK DOTTK

$\Rightarrow$ *Prog_heading* SCTK BEGINTK ENDTK DOTTK

$\Rightarrow$ *Prog_heading* SCTK BEGINTK *Empty_stmt* ENDTK DOTTK

$\Rightarrow$ *Prog_heading* SCTK BEGINTK *Statement* ENDTK DOTTK

$\Rightarrow$ *Prog_heading* SCTK BEGINTK *Statementu_seq* ENDTK DOTTK

$\Rightarrow$ *Prog_heading* SCTK *Statement_part* DOTTK

Prog $\Rightarrow$ *Prog_heading* SCTK *Block* DOTTK

Parsing would then amount to going from the tokens down to the 'start' symbol. This 'bottom-up' parsing process that uses **rightmost derivations in reverse** is called **reduction**. The most popular machine that follows this bottom-up process is called a **shift/reduce PDA**. Such machines contain the following items.

- **Stack.** This stack will store *machine states* as well as the corresponding input values.

- **Input tape.** There are two kinds of tape access. One kind just inspects the contents of the current input value. The other inspects and then moves to the next value.

- **Operations.** There are five kinds of operations found in this machine's transition table.

  1. **accept.** This operation happens only if we encounter the end-of-file marker on the tape precisely when we are getting ready to successfully complete the recognition of the program.

  2. **error.** This operation is executed whenever the next value on the tape is not valid in the current state.

  3. **shift n.** This operation is executed when the next value on the tape is acceptable for the current state. In this case we push the new state

number n (and the corresponding input value) on the stack and then advance to the next input value.

4. **goto n.** This operation just places state n and a nonterminal (see below) on the stack.

5. **reduce m.** This operation indicates that the entire right-hand side of the mth production has just been recognized (and so is represented by the top entries of the stack). At this point we pop as many states off the stack as there are symbols in the right-hand side of production m. The uncovered state on the stack temporarily becomes our present state. That state, plus the nonterminal *left-hand* member of mth production will determine a *goto* operation that is then performed.

One way to gain familiarity with the above ideas is to examine shift/reduce PDA's that recognize the languages defined our previous example grammars.

```
%token          NUMTK
%start          Expression
%%
Expression: NUMTK
          ;
```

```
y.output

    0   $accept : Expression $end
    1   Expression : NUMTK
state 0 [$accept : . Expression $end   (0)]
    NUMTK  shift 1              Expression  goto 2
    . error

state 1 [Expression : NUMTK .   (1)]
        . reduce 1

state 2 [$accept : Expression . $end   (0)]
        $end  accept

3 terminals, 2 nonterminals
2 grammar rules, 3 states
```

Note that each state is labeled or named by at least one grammar production. On closer inspection, you will note that these productions contain a dot, " . ", that essentially indicates how far the recognition process has gone when this particular state is entered. Productions containing this here-is-dot are called **items**.

Another way to visualize the PDA is to place the operation information in a transition matrix, such as the one in Figure 6.2 that has been adapted from Aho [1, page 217]. Notice that the machine contains an input tape that is infinite "to the right," a stack for storing possibly infinitely many state/symbol pairs,

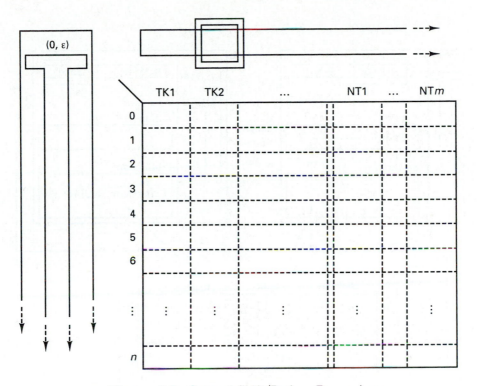

Figure 6.2. General Shift/Reduce Recognizer

and a transition matrix. The two-dimensional table is indexed on the left by the various possible states of the recognizer and on the top by all possible tokens and nonterminals. Note also that there are two sections of the matrix. The first is headed by all possible tokens; the second section is headed by left-hand sides (nonterminals) of the grammar productions. Shift and reduce operations will occur in the left section; these operations occur whenever the next input values (tokens) are valid. Goto operations are found in the right section; these are used during the last step of a reduction.

The transition matrix in Figure 6.3 contains the PDA operation information for the simple example grammar, above. Let's follow the machine's behavior as it attempts to recognize the valid sequence NUMTK end corresponding to an input string of a numeric constant.

1. (Shift state 1) The machine uses the state 0 action corresponding to window value NUMTK, i.e., *shift 1*. According to our description above, the state/symbol pair $(1, \text{NUMTK})$ is thus pushed onto the stack and the window is moved one position to the right.

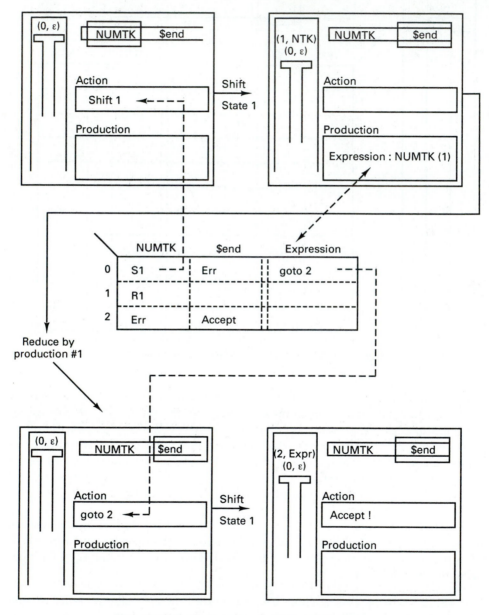

Figure 6.3. Recognizer for Trivial Grammar

2. (Reduce by production 1) The state 1 action indicates that the machine should reduce by production 1. Since production 1 has only one grammar symbol on its right side, the machine performs the following steps.

   (a) One pop. This leaves the pair $(0, \epsilon)$ on the top of the stack.

   (b) Determine new state. Since the machine is now (temporarily) in state 0, and since the left side of production 1 has the nonterminal *Expression*, the corresponding action is to goto(2).

   (c) One push. To goto(2) the machine needs only to push the pair $(2, Express)$, where the second member of the pair comes from the left side of the reducing production.

   (d) (Accept) The state 2 action and the $end value of the window variable determine a move to the accept state.

For our next example, let's look at the recognizer on page 89 for the somewhat more realistic expression grammar on page 78.

Recall that we examined the derivations of the expressions $1, 1+2*3$ and $+2+3$. Following the progress of this recognizer on each of these expressions, though a bit tedious, gives significant insight into the actual behavior of more complex parsers.

The PDA, illustrated below, traces the following sequence of steps for the trivial expression 1.

State	Stack	Next Input	Action
0	0	1	Shift 1
1	0,1	$end	Reduce by 5: 1 pop (Factor)
0	0	(Factor)	goto 5
5	0,5	$end	Reduce by 3: 1 pop (Term)
0	0	(Term)	goto 4
4	0,4	$end	Reduce by 1: 1 pop (Expression)
0	0	(Expression)	goto 3
3	0,3	$end	Accept!

The first action is to shift to state 1. The only action in this state is to reduce by production 5. The machine performs one pop, uncovering state 0. The left side of production is the nonterminal Factor, and so the corresponding action is to goto state 5. Here, we reduce by production 3, resulting in a goto 4. The existence of $end requires that we reduce by 1, for Expression. One pop takes us back to state 0, and then to state 3 where we accept the string.

```
state 0 [$accept : . Expression $end  (0)]
    NUMTK   shift1                    Expression  goto 3
    LPARENTK  shift 2                 Term  goto 4
    .  error                         Factor  goto 5

state 1 [Factor : NUMTK .  (5)]
    .  reduce 5

state 2 [Factor : LPARENTK . Expression RPARENTK  (6)]
    NUMTK  shift1                     Expression  goto 6
    LPARENTK  shift 2                 Term  goto 4
    .  error                         Factor  goto 5

state 3 [$accept : Expression . $end  (0)]
          [Expression : Expression . ADDOPTK Term  (2)]
    $end  accept
    ADDOPTK  shift 7
    .  error

state 4 [Expression : Term .  (1)]
          [Term : Term . MULOPTK Factor  (4)]
    MULOPTK  shift 8
    $end  reduce 1
    ADDOPTK  reduce 1
    RPARENTK  reduce 1

state 5 [Term : Factor .  (3)]
    .  reduce 3

state 6 [Expression : Expression . ADDOPTK Term  (2)]
          [Factor : LPARENTK Expression . RPARENTK  (6)]
    ADDOPTK  shift 7
    RPARENTK  shift 9
    .  error

state 7 [Expression : Expression ADDOPTK . Term  (2)]
    NUMTK  shift1                     Term  goto 10
    LPARENTK  shift 2                 Factor  goto 5
    .  error

state 8 [Term : Term MULOPTK . Factor  (4)]
    NUMTK  shift1                     Factor  goto 11
    LPARENTK  shift 2
    .  error

state 9 [Factor : LPARENTK Expression RPARENTK .  (6)]
    .  reduce 6

state 10 [Expression : Expression ADDOPTK Term .  (2)]
          [Term : Term . MULOPTK Factor  (4)]
    MULOPTK  shift 8
    $end  reduce 2
    ADDOPTK  reduce 2
    RPARENTK  reduce 2

state 11 [Term : Term MULOPTK Factor .  (4)]
    .  reduce 4
```

Things are a bit more interesting for $1 + 2 * 3$.

State	Stack	Next Input	Action
0	0	1	Shift 1
1	0,1	+	Reduce by 5: 1 pop (Factor)
0	0	(Factor)	goto 5
5	0,5	+	Reduce by 3: 1 pop (Term)
0	0	(Term)	goto 4
4	0,4	+	Reduce by 1: 1 pop (Expression)
0	0	(Expression)	goto 3
3	0,3	+	Shift 7
7	0,3,7	2	Shift 1
1	0,3,7,1	*	Reduce by 5: 1 pop (Factor)
7	0,3,7	(Factor)	goto 5
5	0,3,7,5	*	Reduce by 3: 1 pop (Term)
7	0,3,7	(Term)	goto 10
10	0,3,7,10	*	Shift 8
8	0,3,7,10,8	3	Shift 1
1	0,3,7,10,8,1	$end	Reduce by 5: 1 pop (Factor)
8	0,3,7,10,8	(Factor)	goto 11
11	0,3,7,10,8,11	$end	Reduce by 4: 3 pops (Term)
7	0,3,7	(Term)	goto 10
10	0,3,7,10	$end	Reduce by 2: 3 pops (Factor)
0	0	(Factor)	goto 5
5	0,5	$end	Reduce by 3: 1 pop (Term)
0	0	(Term)	goto 4
4	0,4	$end	Reduce by 1: 1 pop (Expression)
0	0	(Expression)	goto 3
3	0,3	$end	Accept!

Notice the machine's action just before the first major (3-pop) reduction.

State	Stack	Next Input	Action
7	0,3,7	(Term)	goto 10
10	0,3,7,10	*	Shift 8
8	0,3,7,10,8	3	Shift 1
1	0,3,7,10,8,1	$end	Reduce by 5: 1 pop (Factor)
8	0,3,7,10,8	(Factor)	goto 11
11	0,3,7,10,8,11	$end	Reduce by 4: 3 pops (Term)

At state 7, the nonterminal *Term* is placed on the stack. This is followed by the *Mulop* and then by the *Factor*, 3. At this point every item on the right side of production 4 has been placed on the stack (note the item representing state 11). This entire **handle** is then popped and replaced by the left side of production 4. So state 7 now represents the entire Term $2 * 3$. Going back up the machine's actions, we see the following.

State	Stack	Next Input	Action
0	0	1	Shift 1
1	0,1	+	Reduce by 5: 1 pop (Factor)
0	0	(Factor)	goto 5
5	0,5	+	Reduce by 3: 1 pop (Term)
0	0	(Term)	goto 4
4	0,4	+	Reduce by 1: 1 pop (Expression)
0	0	(Expression)	goto 3
3	0,3	+	Shift 7

State 3, therefore contains the addop and state 0 contains the 1, recognized as an expression. But this is precisely the right-hand side of production 2 (note the item representing state 10), and so this handle is removed from the PDA's stack and Factor is placed on the stack at state 0. From there on the machine behaves exactly as in the earlier example when it was just recognizing the expression 1.

The recognizer responds rather quickly to the erroneous input string, $+2+3$,

State	Stack	Next Input	Action
0	0	+	error

since the first input is neither an integer nor a left parenthesis.

PDA Problems: Conflicts and Worse

In the following, somewhat whimsical, tiny Pascal statement grammar, we are representing an entire boolean expression by *EXPRTK* and allowing only the empty statement and the **if** statement.

```
IfStatement: /* empty */
           | IFTK BEXPRTK THENTK
                   IfStatement
           | IFTK BEXPRTK THENTK
                   IfStatement
             ELSETK
                   IfStatement
           ;
```

But don't let the size fool you. Its few lines contain a major problem. Consider the following "program."

if true then if true then else

We can derive this string as indicated below.

$$
\begin{array}{ll}
\text{IfStatement} & \overset{2}{\Rightarrow} \quad \text{IFTK BEXPRTK THENTK IfStatement} \\
& \overset{3}{\Rightarrow} \quad \text{IFTK BEXPRTK THENTK} \\
& \qquad\qquad \text{IFTK BEXPRTK THENTK IfStatement} \\
& \qquad\qquad \text{ELSETK IfStatement} \\
& \overset{1}{\Rightarrow} \quad \text{IFTK BEXPRTK THENTK}
\end{array}
$$

```
                          IFTK BEXPRTK THENTK IfStatement

                          ELSETK

        1
        ⇒      IFTK BEXPRTK THENTK

               IFTK BEXPRTK THENTK

               ELSETK
```

On the other had we can use the following *different* set of rightmost derivations.

```
                          3
IfStatement    ⇒    IFTK EXPRTK THENTK IfStatement

                    ELSETK IfStatement

               1
               ⇒    IFTK EXPRTK THENTK IfStatement

                    ELSETK

               2
               ⇒    IFTK EXPRTK THENTK

                         IFTK EXPRTK THENTK IfStatement

                    ELSETK

               1
               ⇒    IFTK EXPRTK THENTK

                         IFTK EXPRTK THENTK

                    ELSETK
```

Grammars that allow the derivation of a string with different orders of productions are called *ambiguous*. We all know that this ambiguity is resolved, at least in languages like Pascal, by insisting that the *else* be associated with the closest *if*, as in the second set of derivations. Let's try to design a PDA so that this behavior is guaranteed by reversing the orders of the two sets of sentential forms.

```
IFTK BEXPRTK THENTK IFTK BEXPRTK THENTK ELSETK
IFTK BEXPRTK THENTK IFTK BEXPRTK THENTK IfStmt. ELSETK
IFTK BEXPRTK THENTK IfStmt ELSETK
IFTK BEXPRTK THENTK IfStmt ELSETK IfStmt
IfStmt
```

```
IFTK BEXPRTK THENTK IFTK BEXPRTK THENTK ELSETK
IFTK BEXPRTK THENTK IFTK BEXPRTK THENTK IfStmt. ELSETK
IFTK BEXPRTK THENTK IfStmt ELSETK
IFTK BEXPRTK THENTK IfStmt ELSETK IfStmt
IfStmt
```

Notice that both sets of reversed sentential forms are identical until the third line. The uncertainty or ambiguity occurs at the here-is-dot on the second line: In the first collection of forms, the *IfStatement* is used complete the inner *if* statement before working on the outer. In the second, the *IfStatement* is (correctly) associated with the subsequent *ELSETK*. In the first case, a reduction would occur, while in the second, a shift would be required. This kind of ambiguity is called a **shift/reduce conflict**. It therefore makes sense to require our PDA to choose the shift operation when such a conflict occurs. Indeed, that is exactly what the following description of the PDA specifies. Note especially the state function for state 5.

```
    0  $accept : IfStatement $end
    1  IfStatement :
    2               | IFTK BEXPRTK THENTK IfStatement
    3               | IFTK BEXPRTK THENTK IfStatement ELSETK IfStatement
state 0 [$accept : . IfStatement $end  (0)]
        [IfStatement : .  (1)]
    IFTK  shift 1                       IfStatement  goto 2
    $end  reduce 1

state 1 [IfStatement: IFTK . BEXPRTK THENTK IfStatement  (2)]
        [IfStatement: IFTK . BEXPRTK THENTK IfStatement ELSETK IfStatement (3)]
    BEXPRTK  shift 3
    .  error

state 2 [$accept : IfStatement . $end  (0)]
    $end  accept

state 3 [IfStatement: IFTK BEXPRTK . THENTK IfStatement  (2)]
        [IfStatement: IFTK BEXPRTK . THENTK IfStatement ELSETK IfStatement (3)]
    THENTK  shift 4
    .  error

state 4 [IfStatement: IFTK BEXPRTK THENTK . IfStatement  (2)]
        [IfStatement: IFTK BEXPRTK THENTK . IfStatement ELSETK IfStatement (3)]
        [IfStatement: .  (1)]

    IFTK  shift 1                       IfStatement  goto 5
    $end  reduce 1
    ELSETK  reduce 1

5: shift/reduce conflict (shift 6, reduce 2) on ELSETK
state 5 [IfStatement: IFTK BEXPRTK THENTK IfStatement .  (2)]
        [IfStatement: IFTK BEXPRTK THENTK IfStatement . ELSETK IfStatement (3)]
    ELSETK  shift 6
    $end  reduce 2

state 6 [IfStatement: IFTK BEXPRTK THENTK IfStatement ELSETK. IfStatement (3)]
        [IfStatement: .  (1)]
    IFTK  shift 1                       IfStatement  goto 7
    $end  reduce 1
    ELSETK  reduce 1

state 7 [IfStatement: IFTK BEXPRTK THENTK IfStatement ELSETK IfStatement . (3)]
    .  reduce 3

6 terminals, 2 nonterminals
4 grammar rules, 8 states
```

Shift/reduce conflicts do occur in grammars, particularly those representing developmental languages. Normally we try to rewrite the grammar to remove as many of them as possible. However, some language constructs, like the *if/else*, will require the existence of this kind of conflict.

There is another PDA conflict that is of a different ilk. Its presence almost always indicates an *error* in the specification of the grammar. In order to appreciate the origin of the problem, we need to spend a bit more time examining the construction of the PDA's, described above. A good place to start is the following slightly enhanced grammar of our first example on page 86.

```
%token        NUMTK
%token        LPARENTK
%token        RPARENTK

%start        Factor
%%
Factor: NUMTK
        | LPARENTK Factor RPARENTK
        ;
```

The corresponding PDA description is as follows.

```
   0   $accept : Factor $end
   1   Factor : NUMTK
   2          | LPARENTK Factor RPARENTK

state 0 [$accept : . Factor $end  (0)]
    NUMTK   shift 1              Factor   goto 3
    LPARENTK  shift 2
    .  error

state 1 [Factor : NUMTK .  (1)]
    .  reduce 1

state 2 [Factor : LPARENTK . Factor RPARENTK  (2)]
    NUMTK   shift 1              Factor   goto 4
    LPARENTK  shift 2
    .  error

state 3 [$accept : Factor . $end  (0)]
    $end   accept

state 4 [Factor : LPARENTK Factor . RPARENTK  (2)]
    RPARENTK  shift 5
    .  error

state 5 [Factor : LPARENTK Factor RPARENTK .  (2)]
    .  reduce 2

5 terminals, 2 nonterminals
3 grammar rules, 6 states
```

Notice that each state in this machine is labeled with a single item, that is, a single production containing a here-is-dot.

Now, let us increase the complexity of the grammar a bit.

```
%token  NUMTK
%token  MULOPTK
%token  LPARENTK
%token  RPARENTK
%start Term

%%
Term:
        Factor
    |  Term  MULOPTK  Factor
    ;
Factor:
        NUMTK
    |  LPARENTK  Term  RPARENTK
    ;

state 0 [$accept : . Term $end  (0)]
    NUMTK   shift 1                    Term   goto 3
    LPARENTK  shift 2                  Factor  goto 4
    .  error

state 1 [Factor : NUMTK .  (3)]
    .  reduce 3

state 2 [Factor : LPARENTK . Term RPARENTK  (4)]
    NUMTK   shift 1                    Term   goto 5
    LPARENTK  shift 2                  Factor  goto 4
    .  error

state 3 [$accept : Term . $end  (0)]
        [Term : Term . MULOPTK Factor  (2)]
    $end  accept
    MULOPTK  shift 6
    .  error

state 4 [Term : Factor .  (1)]
    .  reduce 1

state 5 [Term : Term . MULOPTK Factor  (2)]
        [Factor : LPARENTK Term . RPARENTK  (4)]
    MULOPTK  shift 6
    RPARENTK  shift 7
    .  error


    .
    .
    .
```

This time there are states that are labeled with *more than one item*. Why should there exist states that are representing more than one location in the parsing process? One reason is pretty clear. If there are several states represented by items having the same set of tokens and nonterminals before the here-is-dot, that is, having the same **core**, then we can simply merge the states and differentiate the machine's behavior based on the value of the next input symbol. State 3 on page 96 is an example of such a merged state.

Another reason for multiple items representing a state is slightly more involved. We need to include in a state all items that could possibly be reached during the recognition process just prior to entering that state. While the actual algorithms used to select this collection of reachable states is too complex for this text, we can still appreciate the reason such states must exist. In the case of state 2, page 96, after recognizing *Term*, we are sent to state 5. Looking at the grammar, notice that the only two items indicating that *Term* had just been recognized would be

$$\text{Term} \; : \; \text{Term} \; . \; \text{MULOPTK Factor} \quad (2)$$

and

$$\text{Factor} \; : \; \text{LPARENTK Term} \; . \; \text{RPARENTK} \quad (4)$$

that are precisely the items representing state 5.

If a state is represented by a collection of **incomplete** items, that is, items not terminating in a here-is-dot, then the corresponding machine operation would be a shift, based upon the value of the next input symbol. If a state contains a **complete** item, i.e., if the here-is-dot is at the end, then a reduction by the corresponding production is to be expected.

However, looking at state 5 on page 95, we can see that a shift/reduce conflict will occur for a state containing among its collection two items having the same core, one complete and one incomplete, since a shift would be indicated by the possibility of a new input symbol and a reduce would be possible before the new symbol was even read. As noted in our discussion of shift/reduce conflicts above, the PDA will always[2] choose the shift.

Parenthetically, we mention that shift/reduce conflicts also result from erroneous grammar specifications, as the following grammar will indicate.

---

[2] This is the case unless special instructions are given that specify a particular operator precedence.

```
    0   $accept : Term $end
    1   Term : Term
    2        | Term MULOPTK Factor

    3   Factor : NUMTK
    4          | LPARENTK Term RPARENTK

state 0 [$accept : . Term $end  (0)]
    Term   goto 1


1: shift/reduce conflict (shift 2, reduce 1) on MULOPTK
state 1 [$accept : Term . $end  (0)]
        [Term : Term .  (1)]
        [Term : Term . MULOPTK Factor  (2)]
    $end   accept
    MULOPTK   shift 2
    $end   reduce 1


    .
    .
    .


6: shift/reduce conflict (shift 2, reduce 1) on MULOPTK
6: shift/reduce conflict (shift 7, reduce 1) on RPARENTK
state 6 [Term : Term .  (1)]
        [Term : Term . MULOPTK Factor  (2)]
        [Factor : LPARENTK Term . RPARENTK  (4)]
    MULOPTK   shift 2
    RPARENTK   shift 7


    .
    .
    .
```

The presence of such conflicts should at least give reason to check the grammar.

A shift/reduce conflict can be produced by quite a different kind of problem. If the collection of items for a given state contains two complete items, a **reduce/reduce conflict** conflict has occurred. There is one kind of grammatical construct that, in fact, does require the valid existence of reduce/reduce conflicts. Almost any desk-top publishing or formatting package provides a facility for producing an arrangement of symbols like

$$A_i^j$$

of subscripts and superscripts. For example, LaTeX, which has been used to produce this text, will produce the above string from the instruction A_{i}^{j}. A grammar for (partially) recognizing such strings is listed below.

```
%token LBRACETK
%token RBRACETK
%token SUBTK
%token SUPTK
%token IDENTTK
%start Expr
%%
Expr: Expr SUBTK Expr SUPTK Expr
    ;
Expr: Expr SUBTK Expr
    ;
Expr: Expr SUPTK Expr
    ;
Expr: LBRACETK IDENTTK RBRACETK
    ;
```

The second and third productions recognize single subscript or superscript structures; the first production recognizes the double configuration. In addition to a number of shift/reduce conflicts, this grammar also produces the following reduce/reduce conflict.

```
    0   $accept : Expr $end
    1   Expr : Expr SUBTK Expr SUPTK Expr
    2        | Expr SUBTK Expr
    3        | Expr SUPTK Expr
    4        | LBRACETK IDENTTK RBRACETK

state 0 [$accept : . Expr $end  (0)]
    LBRACETK   shift 1                        Expr   goto 2


        .
        .
        .

state 10 [Expr : Expr . SUBTK Expr SUPTK Expr   (1)]
         [Expr : Expr SUBTK Expr SUPTK Expr .   (1)]
         [Expr : Expr . SUBTK Expr   (2)]
         [Expr : Expr . SUPTK Expr   (3)]
         [Expr : Expr SUPTK Expr .   (3)]
    Reduce/reduce conflict (reduce 1, reduce 3) on $end
    $end   reduce 1
```

Since we usually write our grammars in a top-down fashion a PDA, when confronted by a reduce/reduce conflict, will resolve the ambiguity by performing the reduction by the representative item coming from the lowest numbered production as illustrated in the PDA description.

Most of the time, however, reduce/reduce conflicts are the result of erroneous productions. Replacing a correct nonterminal by another incorrect one often produces this type of conflict. Even more frequently the problem is in the actual structure of the various productions. Look for structures like the following,

```
%token  NUMTK
%token  ADDOPTK
%token  MULOPTK
%token  LPARENTK
%token  RPARENTK
%start Expr


%%
Expr: Term
    | Factor
    ;
Term: NUMTK
    | Term  MULOPTK  Factor
    ;
Factor: NUMTK
     | LPARENTK  Expr  RPARENTK
     ;
```

where, both *Term* and *Factor* have productions beginning with a common collection of tokens/nonterminals.

6.2   Generating Parsers

Generating a parser is usually accomplished by performing the following steps.

1. Constructing a parser specification file

2. Generating the parser

3. Compiling the parser

Bottom-up parsers seem to be more suited to the object-oriented approach used in this text. The most accessible generator for such parsers is *yacc* or any of the more modern and somewhat improved relatives such as *byacc*, available via anonymous ftp from *okeefe.cs.berkeley.edu*, or *Gnu's bison*, from *aeneas.mit.edu*. There also is at least one system that generates C++ code, rather than the usual C code. These seem to be a mixed blessing, since they are often the work of an individual, and therefore experience revisions and corrections when the creator or collection of local devotees have sufficient time. Our approach has been to use a more standard generator and to modify the output C code so that it is acceptable for the particular C++ system being used for development.

6.2.1   Parser Specification File

A parser specification file consists of up to three major parts, as illustrated in Figure 6.4.

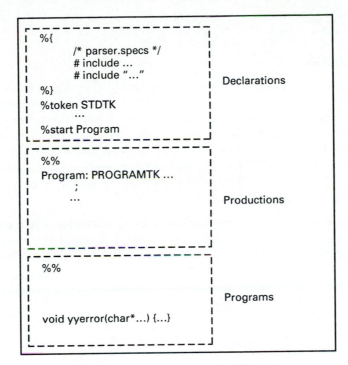

Figure 6.4. Parser Specification File

Declaration Section

As illustrated in the figure, this section contains the following items.

- Any C (or C++) initialization details that might be necessary for the parser's interface with the rest of the system. Typically, this amounts to including a number of definitions used by the parser as it builds its parse tree.

- The specification of the various language categories or tokens. These tokens are later defined as integer values to be used by the scanner, the parser, and even by user-created functions. The list of Pascal tokens was introduced in Section 5.2.

- The specification of the left-hand side of a particular production as the grammar's start symbol.

There are a number of other things that can be placed in this section. Some grammars, particularly of older languages dealing with arithmetic expressions are ambiguous. Certain **disambiguating** rules may be specified in this section. Since

Wirth has very carefully crafted nonambiguous grammars for his languages, Pascal does not require these rules.

Production Section

This part of the specification file contains a listing of Pascal grammar. Since any reduce/reduce conflicts are resolved by choosing the production of lowest number in the possible list of reductions for that given state, production order can be very important. We start with the highest level productions and work down in a kind of leftmost derivation approach. This allows the decomposition of the grammar into major categories that parallel the analysis and design of compiler objects in later chapters.

High-level productions.   The specification of the start symbol, `Program`, and productions for two of the three nonterminals `External_files` and `Block` are contained in the following listing.

```
High-level productions (parser.gram)

Program:
    PROGRAMTK Ident External_files SCTK Block DOTTK
    ;
External_files : /*empty*/
    | LPARENTK  Ident_1st RPARENTK
    ;
Block:
    Label_dec_part
    Const_def_part
    Type_def_part
    Var_dec_part
    Proc_fun_dec_part
    Statement_part
    ;
```

Pascal's rather rigid declaration order is reflected in the production for `Block`.

In compiling most languages, there are three major categories of structures that must be parsed: declarations, statements and expressions.

Productions for declaration of labels.   The fact that Pascal actually has a goto statement may be the best kept secret of the undergraduate computer science curriculum. Using this highly discouraged statement quite naturally requires a way of labeling the targeted statements. In Pascal, such labels are integers of no more than four digits and these labels must be declared prior to their use. The syntax for declaring a list of integers to be labels is listed below.

```
Label Declarations (parser.gram)

Label_dec_part: /* empty */
    | LABELTK Label_lst SCTK
    ;

    Label_lst: Label
        | Label_lst COMMATK Label
        ;

        Label: UNSIGNEDINTTK    /* 0 <= value <= 9999 */
            ;
```

Checking the actual number of digits in a label is in fact a *semantic* check and so is not part of the grammar. Chapter 8 contains a complete discussion of the Pascal semantic checks and the way they are implemented in a compiler built using object-oriented techniques.

Productions for declaration of constants. User-defined constants in Pascal are identifiers associated with literals of any standard type (except for boolean) and even of type string.

```
Constant Definitions (parser.gram)

Const_def_part: /* empty */
    | CONSTTK Const_def_lst SCTK
    ;
    Const_def_lst: Const_def
        | Const_def_lst SCTK Const_def
        ;
        Const_def: Ident EQTK Constant
            ;
            Constant: Unsigned_number
                | PLUSTK Unsigned_number
                | MINUSTK Unsigned_number
                | Ident    /*check that it is constant*/
                | PLUSTK Ident
                | MINUSTK Ident
                | STRINGTK      /*type is char if len=1*/
                | BADSTRINGTK
                ;
                Unsigned_number: UNSIGNEDINTTK
                    | UNSIGNEDREALTK
                    ;
```

Productions for declaration of types. One of the most important programming activities is the construction of special data types.

```
┌─────────────────────────────────────────────────────────────────────────┐
│  High-level type productions (parser.gram)                                │
│                                                                           │
│ Type_def_part: /* empty */                                                │
│     | TYPETK Type_def_lst SCTK                                            │
│     ;                                                                      │
│   Type_def_lst: Type_def                                                   │
│       | Type_def_lst SCTK Type_def                                         │
│       ;                                                                    │
│     Type_def: Ident EQTK Type                                              │
│         ;                                                                  │
│       Type: Simple_type                                                    │
│           | PACKEDTK Struct_type                                          │
│           | Struct_type                                                   │
│           | UPARROWTK IDENTIFIERTK    /*forward reference */              │
│           ;                                                               │
│           Simple_type: LPARENTK Ident_lst RPARENTK                        │
│               | Constant DDTK Constant                                    │
│               | Ident                                                     │
│               ;                                                           │
│           Struct_type: ARRAYTK                                            │
│                   LBRACKTK Index_t_lst RBRACKTK OFTK Type                 │
│               | RECORDTK /*a scope*/ Field_lst ENDTK                      │
│                                                                           │
│               | SETTK OFTK Simple_type                                    │
│               | FILETK OFTK Type                                          │
│                                                                           │
│               ;                                                           │
└─────────────────────────────────────────────────────────────────────────┘
```

Giving the programmer sufficient power to construct such structures requires that the language place minimal restrictions on the complexity of such declarations. The production for Type specifies that such types must be either a simple type, a structured type, or a pointer to another type. Doing the required semantic checks on this latter type inflicts some pain, since the IDENTIFIERTK need (cannot) always be declared prior to its use in the declaration of standard linked data structures. Details of this are found in Chapter 8. Simple types consist of enumerated types, subrange types, and references to previously declared types.

Arrays, records, sets, and files make up the structured types. The only nonterminal on the right side of the array production is the list of index types.

```
┌─────────────────────────────────────────────────────────────────────────┐
│  Index Productions (parser.gram)                                          │
│                                                                           │
│               Index_t_lst: Simple_type                                    │
│                   | Index_t_lst COMMATK Simple_type                        │
│                   ;                                                        │
└─────────────────────────────────────────────────────────────────────────┘
```

Records are rather complex structures built of fields and allowing variant parts that use tag fields of either specified or unspecified name. The following listing

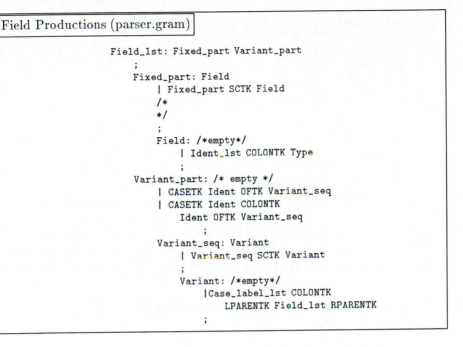

```
Field Productions (parser.gram)

                    Field_lst: Fixed_part Variant_part
                    ;
                 Fixed_part: Field
                      | Fixed_part SCTK Field
                      /*
                      */
                      ;
                    Field: /*empty*/
                         | Ident_lst COLONTK Type
                         ;
             Variant_part: /* empty */
                      | CASETK Ident OFTK Variant_seq
                      | CASETK Ident COLONTK
                         Ident OFTK Variant_seq
                         ;
                 Variant_seq: Variant
                      | Variant_seq SCTK Variant
                      ;
                  Variant: /*empty*/
                         |Case_label_lst COLONTK
                             LPARENTK Field_lst RPARENTK
                         ;
```

contains the rather extensive set of productions for these nonterminals.

Productions for the declaration of variables.   The productions specifying Pascal declaration of variables are next.

```
Variable declaration (parser.gram)

Var_dec_part: /* empty */
    | VARTK Var_dec_lst SCTK
    ;
Var_dec_lst: Var_dec
       | Var_dec_lst SCTK Var_dec
       ;
       Var_dec: Ident_lst COLONTK Type
           ;
```

Numerous grammar productions reference Ident and Ident_list. The productions for these are on page 112.

Productions for procedures and functions.   A major amount of compiler construction effort is spent in providing the facilities for parsing user-defined procedures and functions. Even more effort goes into outputting code or building interpreters that will implement these subprograms, including the construction of special data structures called stack frames for each subprogram. The following productions

```
Procedure and function declaration (parser.gram)

Proc_fun_dec_part: /* empty */
    |Proc_or_fun_dec_seq
    ;
  Proc_or_fun_dec_seq: Proc_or_fun_dec
    | Proc_or_fun_dec_seq /* SCTKs already there */ Proc_or_fun_dec
    ;
    Proc_or_fun_dec:
        Proc_heading SCTK
            Body SCTK    /*check if forward or fwd refd*/
        | Func_heading SCTK /*also func heading may be -type*/
            Body SCTK /*also func heading may be -type*/
        ;
```

are used to check the high-level syntax of such subprogram declaration.

Slight differences exist between the productions for procedures and functions, especially in the productions for a procedure `Block` and a function `Function_form`.

```
Procedure and function declaration (parser.gram)

        Proc_heading: PROCEDURETK
                Ident Formal_param_stuff
            ;
            /* result determined in block */
            ;
        Body: Block
            | FORWARDTK
            ;
        Func_heading: FUNCTIONTK
                Ident Function_form
            ;
        Function_form: /*empty*/    /*if forward referenced*/
            | Formal_param_stuff COLONTK Ident
            ;
```

Of course, one major part of a procedure/function declaration is the specification of the formal parameters. These are lists of `Formal_p_sections` consisting of the following.

- Value formal parameters

- Variable formal parameters

- Procedure or function parameters

```
Formal parameters (parser.gram)

              Formal_param_stuff: /*empty*/
                  | LPARENTK Formal_p_sect_lst RPARENTK
                  ;
              Formal_p_sect_lst: Formal_p_sect
                  | Formal_p_sect_lst SCTK Formal_p_sect
                  ;
              Formal_p_sect: Param_group
                  | VARTK Param_group
                  | Proc_heading
                  | Func_heading
                  ;
              Param_group: Ident_lst COLONTK Paramtype
                  ;
```

Parameter type specifiers can come in several flavors.

- An identifier specifying a type already declared

- Two forms of anonymous types

    - A possibly multiply-dimensioned array

    - A much simpler packed array

The unusual use of identifiers in the array index production is addressing the sticky issue of conformant arrays. A formal conformant array parameter includes read-only bound identifiers. These set the lower and upper limits of the conformant array's dimensions. Actually, this part of the language was not part of the original specification. It was added by an ISO standardization committee, after much debate. Some production Pascal compilers still do not support this feature.

```
Formal parameters, continued (parser.gram)

                  Paramtype: Ident
                      | ARRAYTK
                          LBRACKTK Index_spec_seq RBRACKTK
                                          OFTK Paramtype
                      | PACKEDTK
                          ARRAYTK LBRACKTK Index_spec RBRACKTK
                                          OFTK Ident
                      ;
                  Index_spec_seq: Index_spec
                      | Index_spec_seq SCTK Index_spec
                      ;
                  Index_spec:
                          Ident DDTK Ident COLONTK Ident
                          ;
```

```
High-level statements (parser.gram)

Statement_part: Compound_stmt
    /*
        */
    ;
    Compound_stmt: BEGINTK Statement_seq ENDTK
        ;
        Statement_seq: Statement
            | Statement_seq SCTK Statement
            ;
            Statement: /*empty*/
                | Assignment

                | IFTK Expr THENTK Statement
                | IFTK Expr THENTK Statement
                  ELSETK Statement  /*1  shift/reduce conflict*/
                | CASETK Expr OFTK Case_lst ENDTK
                | FORTK Ident ASGTK Expr Dir Expr DOTK Statement
                | WHILETK Expr DOTK Statement
                | REPEATTK Statement_seq UNTILTK Expr
                | WITHTK Rec_var_lst DOTK Statement
                | ReadStmt
                | WriteStmt
                | Procedure_call
                | Label COLONTK Statement
                | Compound_stmt
                | GOTOTK Label
                ;
            Dir: TOTK
                | DOWNTOTK
                ;

            Rec_var_lst: Record_var
                | Rec_var_lst COMMATK Record_var
                ;
```

Statement productions.   The listing above contains statement productions as well as those productions related to the labeling of statements, Pascal input/output statements, and the specification of the Pascal compound statement.

Assignment statements, while relatively simple to specify, require extensive semantic checking.

```
Assignment production (parser.gram)

            Assignment: Variable ASGTK Expr
                /* must test for fn_ident */
                ;
```

Of special interest is the case when `Variable` is a function name. Naturally that should only be allowed inside a function declaration.

Almost all official Pascal grammars handle a `write` or `writeln` statement as a procedure call. Such procedures allow for any number of parameters, and place very few restrictions on their type. The grammatical pain experienced in specifying syntax for these special formatting conventions more than justifies the construction of separate productions for special input/output statements in a working grammar.

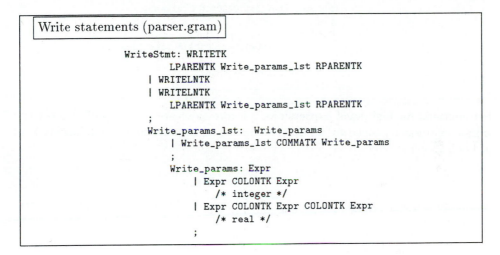

Write statements (parser.gram)

```
            WriteStmt: WRITETK
                    LPARENTK Write_params_lst RPARENTK
                | WRITELNTK
                | WRITELNTK
                    LPARENTK Write_params_lst RPARENTK
                ;
            Write_params_lst:  Write_params
                | Write_params_lst COMMATK Write_params
                ;
            Write_params: Expr
                | Expr COLONTK Expr
                    /* integer */
                | Expr COLONTK Expr COLONTK Expr
                    /* real */
                ;
```

A Pascal procedure call consists either of the procedure name or the name followed by a possibly empty list of actual parameters enclosed in parentheses. A list of actual parameters consists of any number of comma-separated expressions.

Procedure call (parser.gram)

```
        Procedure_call: Ident Actual_param_stuff
            ;
        Actual_param_stuff:  /*empty*/
            | LPARENTK RPARENTK
            | LPARENTK Actual_param_lst RPARENTK
            ;
        Actual_param_lst: Actual_param
            | Actual_param_lst COMMATK Actual_param
            ;
        Actual_param: Expr
            /* a Variable or a proc/fn id */
```

The similarity of the **case** statement to the declaration of the variant part of a record is not an accident, of course.

```
┌─────────────────────────────────────────────────────────────────┐
│  Case productions (parser.gram)                                   │
│                                                                   │
│              Case_lst: Case_lst_elem                              │
│                  | Case_lst SCTK Case_lst_elem                    │
│                  ;                                                │
│              Case_lst_elem: /*empty*/                             │
│                    | Case_label_lst COLONTK Statement             │
│                    ;                                              │
│                  Case_label_lst: Case_label                       │
│                      | Case_label_lst COMMATK Case_label          │
│                      ;                                            │
│                      Case_label: Constant                         │
│                          ;                                        │
│                                                                   │
└─────────────────────────────────────────────────────────────────┘
```

Productions for high-level expressions.   Expressions are made up of at most two simple expressions joined by a relational operator. In particular, the following kind of boolean expression

```
    4 < i < 6
```

is therefore specifically prohibited by Pascal syntax. Moreover the beginning programmer's next try

```
    4 < i and i < 6
```

is also rejected because and is a *Mulop* (page 110) and so will be associated with the surrounding expressions before either of the relational operators is applied.

```
┌─────────────────────────────────────────────────────────────────┐
│  High-level expressions (parser.gram)                             │
│                                                                   │
│ Expr_lst: Expr                                                    │
│     | Expr_lst COMMATK Expr                                       │
│     /*                                                            │
│      */                                                           │
│     ;                                                             │
│     Expr: Simple_expr                                             │
│         | Simple_expr Relational_op Simple_expr                   │
│         ;                                                         │
│         Relational_op: EQTK                                       │
│             | LTTK                                                │
│             | GTTK                                                │
│             | LETK                                                │
│             | GETK                                                │
│             | NETK                                                │
│              | INTK                                               │
│             ;                                                     │
└─────────────────────────────────────────────────────────────────┘
```

Productions for simple expressions.   Expressions constructed by using either the unary plus or minus operators or the binary operators

```
    +,  -,  or
```

are called Simple Expressions.

```
┌─────────────────────────────────┐
│ Simple expressions (parser.gram)│
└─────────────────────────────────┘

        Simple_expr: Term
              | PLUSTK Term
              | MINUSTK Term
              | Simple_expr Add_op Term
              ;
        Add_op: PLUSTK
              | MINUSTK
              | ORTK
              ;
```

Note that $4+i$ is a simple expression. You might verify that the following expression

```
    4 + i - 6
```

is also a valid simple expression.

Productions for terms. Pascal terms are built from factors by use of the various *MulOps.*

```
┌─────────────────────────────────┐
│ Term productions (parser.gram)  │
└─────────────────────────────────┘

         Term: Factor
              | Term Mul_op Factor
              ;
         Mul_op: ASTERTK
               | SLASHTK
               | DIVTK
               | MODTK
               | ANDTK
               ;
```

The fact that multiplication occurs at this lower level in the grammar ensures that it has a higher precedence than any of the AddOps.

Productions for factors. Factors are the expression work horses: Every expression must ultimately be recognized as a factor or made up of factors in some way.

```
┌─────────────────────────────────────────────────────────────────┐
│ ┌─────────────────────────────────┐                             │
│ │ Factor productions (parser.gram) │                             │
│ └─────────────────────────────────┘                             │
│                                                                   │
│               Factor: Unsigned_lit                               │
│                  | Variable                                       │
│                  | Set                                           │
│                  | NOTTK Factor                                  │
│                  | LPARENTK Expr RPARENTK                        │
│                  ;                                               │
│               Unsigned_lit: Unsigned_number                     │
│                   | STRINGTK      /* type is char if len=1 */    │
│                   | BADSTRINGTK                                  │
│                   | NILTK                                        │
│                   ;                                              │
│              Set: LBRACKTK Member_stuff RBRACKTK                 │
│                  ;                                               │
│                  Member_stuff: /*empty*/                         │
│                      | Member_lst                               │
│                      ;                                           │
│                   Member_lst: Member                            │
│                       | Member_lst COMMATK Member               │
│                       ;                                          │
│                    Member: Expr                                 │
│                        | Expr DDTK Expr                         │
│                        ;                                         │
└─────────────────────────────────────────────────────────────────┘
```

These productions specify that factors can be any of several kinds of literals, an identifier, a set, a negated boolean expression, or any expression enclosed in parentheses.

Identifier productions.   Identifiers are used extensively in expressions.

```
┌─────────────────────────────────────────────────────────────────┐
│ ┌─────────────────────────────────────┐                         │
│ │ Identifier productions (parser.gram) │                         │
│ └─────────────────────────────────────┘                         │
│                                                                   │
│ Variable: Ident Actual_param_stuff                               │
│        /* could be a const, variable or  fn_call*/               │
│     | Variable LBRACKTK Expr_1st RBRACKTK                        │
│     | Variable DOTTK Ident                                       │
│     | Variable UPARROWTK                                         │
│     ;                                                            │
│ Ident_lst: Ident                                                │
│     | Ident_lst COMMATK Ident                                   │
│     ;                                                            │
│     Ident: IDENTIFIERTK                                         │
│         ;                                                        │
│ Record_var: Variable                                            │
│     ;                                                            │
└─────────────────────────────────────────────────────────────────┘
```

Notice that the first `Variable` production can be used to recognize an identifier representing a variable in an expression as well as a function call. The second specifies an element of a (possibly higher dimensional) array. The third specifies a field of a record. The fourth is the Pascal syntax for dereferencing a pointer variable.

Supporting Programs Section

This is the third major part of the parser specification file, as illustrated in Figure 6.4. This optional section may contain a number of supporting C (or C++) functions or compiler directives to include a file containing such functions.

- The function, *yyerror()*, that allows the user to specify action taken by the parser when the finite-state machine detects an error.

- The parser also requires that a scanner *yylex()* be provided. If you decide to write your own, the code for this could be placed in this section.

User-supplied yyerror() (parser.fcts)

```
 7 void yyerror(char* s) {
 8     if (!s) {
 9         hard.err("yyerror() LOGIC ERROR!");
10     } else {
11 //      soft.err(s);
12     }
13 }
```

See page 118, below, and Appendix C for additional information on error classes.

6.2.2   Generating the Parser

In this section we describe specific information for using *yacc* to produce the parser. The details for other generators may be somewhat different, but can probably be obtained from your system documentation.

The command

```
yacc parser.spec
```

causes *yacc* to convert the parser specification file *parser.spec* into the file *y.tab.c* containing code for the parsing function *yyparse()*. Actually, *yacc* can do much more.

1. *Yacc* produces the token file, *y.tab.h*. The list of tokens in the declaration section of *parser.spec* can be automatically converted to corresponding integer constants that are stored in the file *y.tab.h*. These constants are in C (and therefore C++) *#include* format. The file can be generated by modifying the command to contain the *-d* option, as follows.

```
yacc -d parser.spec
```

2. *Yacc* produces the parser description file, *y.output*. Grammars are things we build. There is a learning curve associated with building something for the first (or even the tenth) time—you have to try your best ideas and then

somehow get feedback on how closely those ideas match the expected or required protocols. One good way to get feedback while building a grammar is to keep an eye on the following information found in the description file *y.output*.

- The list of productions not reduced or used by any other productions in the grammar
- The list of shift/reduce conflicts and information about the parser's state affected by the conflict
- The list and location specification of any reduce/reduce conflicts

The command

```
yacc -v parser.spec
```

produces the *y.output* file.

6.2.3   Testing the Parser

Clearly the best quality-control strategy is to simply not allow any errors to enter the parser or compiler during the development stages. But constructing a grammar is a slow process, one that readily lends itself to the introduction of errors. And so we need additional methods to find system errors that elude our most careful anti-error efforts during the grammar production phases.

There are two essentially different techniques to help ferret out errors that have slipped into the system: automated system testing and compiler extension. The first is most often designed to test (most) all of the paths through the grammar. The second examines the format of the output for insight into parser action.

The Test Suite

Based on a number of comments that Knuth made about his construction of TEX (Appendix D), there are two tasks on which to focus.

- Construct the data designed to *trip* the system.
- Modify the system so that it responds in an appropriate manner to the tripping data.

Constructing the test suite.   A collection of test source programs can be produced by the following activities, working from the highest level to the lowest level of the grammar.

- Write a collection of small, valid programs testing the given production.
- Produce test programs of invalid data.

1. For each token on the right side of the production, write a program segment that will do one of the following.
   - Delete the token
   - Misspell the token
   - Place the token in another location

2. Write a program that will produce invalid entries for each nonterminal on the right side of the production.

As an example, consider the following production.

```
Program:
    PROGRAMTK Ident External_files SCTK Block DOTTK
    ;
```

Our first task is to produce valid programs testing the various paths through the following production. This requires knowing at least the high-level syntax for each of the nonterminals in the production.

- `Ident`. The production for `Ident` is just the token

  ```
  Ident: IDENTIFIERTK ;
  ```

  representing any valid Pascal identifier.

- `External_files`. The following two productions prescribe valid syntax for `External_files`.

  ```
  External_files : /*empty*/
           | LPARENTK  Ident_1st RPARENTK
           ;
  ```

  The empty string would therefore be recognized as valid.

- `Block`. The following production specifies the syntax for `Block`.

  ```
  Block:
      Label_dec_part
      Const_def_part
      Type_def_part
      Var_dec_part
      Proc_fun_dec_part
      Statement_part
      ;
  ```

Each of the nonterminals except for `Statement_part` on the right side of `Block` recognize the empty string as valid. Thus a minimal set of tokens for `Block` would be the following.

```
begin
end
```

A minimal test program for the first production can now be specified.

```
program TestHeader;
begin
end.
```

This program can now be modified to produce errors in important locations of the production.

- Missing leading token.

- Misplaced semicolons or other single-character tokens.

A misspelling of the first token will actually simulate a missing

```
progrum TestHeader;
begin
end.
```

first token in this case since the scanner will then send `IDENTIFIERTK`. Another modification for testing this first production might be the program

```
program TestHeader
begin
end.
```

that does not contain the header's semicolon or

```
program TestHeader
begin
end
```

that does not contain the program's "end dot."

Additional changes such as missing program identifier and misspelled or even missing begin/end keywords actually test the validity of the parser's action on *other* productions. We may therefore consider these programs a complete test set for the production.

It is a simple (though time consuming) task to write a corresponding set of test programs for the `External_files` production, the `Block` production, each of its right-side nonterminals, and so on.

Modifying the parser: Error recovery.   Now let's see how the compiler responds to the various test files we have just created. When we submit the correct program

```
program TestHeader;
begin
end.
```

we get the following expected output.

```
[    1]    program TestHeader;
[    2]    begin
[    3]    end.
```

The syntactically incorrect program

```
program TestHeader;
begin
end.
```

produces the following compiler behavior.

```
[    1]    progrum
syntax error
```

And the missing semicolon code

```
program TestHeader
begin
end.
```

causes the compiler to output the following statements.

```
[    1]    program TestHeader
[    2]    begin
syntax error
```

Two observations are quite clear. The compiler outputs a very generic error message, and parsing terminated as soon as the error was encountered. Compiler modifications are clearly in order, since neither of these behaviors is acceptable.

Knowledge of what the parser is actually doing is obviously an important prerequisite to making the modifications. And gaining such insight about a *yacc*-generated parser is surprisingly hard to obtain, since it is a finite-state machine based upon a computer-generated next-state table. Schreiner and Friedman, in their excellent text [18, Chapter 4], actually show how to add debugging code to the parser. Information about the parser's behavior in the presence of syntax errors can then be obtained by experimentation. Their examples clearly show that the parser will do the following things when it encounters an unacceptable token.

- Changes the next (lookahead) token temporarily to a special `error` token

- Produces the required error message by a single call to *yyerror()*

- Begins popping the state stack looking for any state that will accept the `error` token

Once such a state has been located, the lookahead token is reset to the original token that generated the error and normal parser shift/reduce actions are resumed.

Since the parser is looking for states accepting the `error` token, modifications could therefore take the form of adding additional productions that contain the `error` token strategically placed immediately after those tokens that are likely places of programmer syntax error.

In the "progrum" example, the code has no valid tokens before the error; catching the error would only be possible by a kind of last-ditch production, such as the following.

```
Program:
    error
    ;
```

In this case, we would also like to output some sort of apology to the user, explaining that we simply could not get the parsing process going. This can be done by placing semantic actions in these productions.

```
Program:
    error
        {soft.err("Syntax error -- cannot recover, sorry");}
    ;
```

Appendix C contains the definition and implementation details of three objects used for reporting compiler errors. *Soft* is an object whose *err* member reports the specified error message to the user and then notifies the compiler's back end to not interpret or emit code.

The missing semicolon code could be caught with a production and error message like the following.

```
Program:
    PROGRAMTK Ident error Block DOTTK
        {soft.err("Program Header Error -- expecting semi colon");}
    ;
```

And a source program missing the program identifier or having some other header error could be intercepted by this production.

```
Program:
    PROGRAMTK error Block DOTTK
        {soft.err("Program Header Error");}
    ;
```

These new productions and others could then be added to the grammar in a form such as that listed below.

```
Program:
            {PProgramCls pgm = new ProgramCls($2,$5);}
      | PROGRAMTK Ident error Block DOTTK
            {soft.err("Program Header Error -- expecting semi colon");}
      | error
            {soft.err("Syntax error -- cannot recover, sorry");}
      | PROGRAMTK error
            {soft.err("Program Header Error");}
      | PROGRAMTK Ident External_files SCTK Block DOTTK
            {soft.err("Missing end dot");}
      ;
```

You have probably had the interesting experience of making a simple syntax error in a Pascal type or variable declaration, only to have the error semantically ripple into numerous correct statements in the following code. To stop these cascades of error messages a *yacc*-produced parser is required to recognize and shift three additional tokens after an error before normal error detection procedures are restored. Sometimes you may want to resume the detection and reporting process sooner than that, particularly if you have been able to recognize an important placement token like SCTK. Such tokens can be recognized by adding a simple production like

```
      Sc: SCTK
            {yyerrok;}
          ;
```

where the *yyerrok* action indicates that the parser should immediately resume its error-reporting activities.

Other grammar constructs, particularly lists and sequences using left recursion are more difficult to handle. Schreiner and Friedman suggest that a structure like the following one for sequences of statements

```
      Statement_seq: Statement
          | Statement_seq SCTK Statement
          ;
```

should be modified as indicated below.

```
      Statement_seq: Statement
            {$$ = new StatementSeqCls($1);}
      | Statement_seq SCTK Statement
            {yyerrok;
             $$ = PStatementSeqCls($1) -> append($3);}
      | error
            {soft.err("Statement error");
             $$ = new ErrStmtCls();}
      | Statement_seq SCTK error
            {soft.err("Statement error");
             $$ = $1;}
          ;
```

Lists, like the list of identifiers used for parameters, record fields, type specification and file specification are error protected by the following similar structure.

```
Ident_lst: Ident
        {$$ = new IdentLstCls($1);}
    | Ident_lst COMMATK Ident
        {yyerrok;
         $$ = PIdentLstCls($1) -> append($3);}
    | Ident_lst error
        {soft.err("Expecting comma in Ident list");
         $$ = $1;}
    | Ident_lst COMMATK error
        {soft.err("Error after comma in Ident list");
         $$ = $1;}
    ;
```

Adding error productions often causes shift/reduce or reduce/reduce conflicts. Since the parser's normal mode is to accept as long a string as possible, the parser's checking of correct syntax will not have been destroyed by these conflicts. Simply try the parser out on the particular error. If it behaves correctly, then resign yourself to seeing *yacc's* announcement of *nn* shift/reduce conflicts, and writing numerous disclaimers and assurances to people using your work. The Schreiner/Friedman recommendations tend to not work well in nested recursive productions like those defining the Pascal record structure. In these situations, you can at least start with the recommendations at the highest levels and then carefully insert and test lower level error productions until an acceptable truce is reached.

Additional information about specific error handling can be found in the Pascal grammar listed in Appendix E.

Testing by Extension: Pretty Printers

A second effort at verifying the correctness of a grammar is the construction of a pretty printer that is based upon the grammar. Pretty printers, or formatters, produce as output a copy of the input source code that has source indentation determined by the code's syntax. It is a very simple matter to visually compare the output from such a utility against the input code. Problems with the scanner or parser are often located by noticing different levels of indentation in the two versions of source code.

Most formatters are systems separate from the associated compiler. However, since this formatter's major purpose is checking the scanner and parser, we will make it a part of the compiler, invoked through the use of a - f formatting option.

Some formatters are quite sophisticated systems, conditioning all of a source code's white spaces, inserting carriage returns in formal parameter lists, and so on. Again, since the goal of this formatter is to serve as a scanner/parser testing device, the only function of the formatter is to modify the left margin of the source code.

Let's agree that the formatter will deal with *begin/end* pairs much like C++ programmers write the {/} pairs: *begin* and *end* do not affect the indentation of the code they bracket; instead, the statements using the *begin/end* are responsible for adjusting the indentation. The following sample output will therefore serve as a definition for the formatter.

```
Program GoodIndent;
const
    pi = 3.14158;
    jobs = 10;
    try = 3;
type
    color = (red,blue,yellow);
var
    i: integer;
begin
    for i := 1 to 10 do
        writeln;
    for i := 1 to 10 do begin
        if (i < 3) then
            writeln(1);
        writeln(i)
    end;
    if (i < 10) then begin
        writeln('less than')
    end else begin
        writeln('not less than')
    end
end.
```

Clearly the same set of indentation rules that hold for the **for** and **if** statement would also hold for the **while, repeat**, and so on. Also it is very helpful to insist that **record** cause at least one level of indentation change. Subprogram indentation should be indented one level for each declared unit. This is especially important in languages allowing nesting of subprograms.

The following are general suggestions for building a formatter.

- Notice that a formatter is really an extension of a listing option for a compiler.

- The scanner should be modified so that carriage returns indicate a left margin position.

- The scanner will need to handle white spaces differently when encountering them at the left margin.

- The scanner's *ck_reserved_wd()* could be enhanced to change indentation levels as certain reserved words are encountered.

- Indentation caused by a reserved word like **if** will need to be turned back off. One way would be to have the corresponding parse tree node representing the **if** statement change the margin to the left. This works well since the construction of the node occurs *after* the entire **if** statement has been correctly recognized by the parser.

Additional suggestions for adding this feature can be found in Exercise 6.11.

6.3   Encapsulating Scanner and Parser

Parsers generated by *yacc* communicate with their *lex*-generated scanners by means
of the following global structures.

- **yylineno**. Integer number of current source line.

- **yylex**. Array of characters containing the lexeme just recognized.

- **yyleng**. Integer number of characters in the lexeme. It does count the
  delimiting character.

Encapsulating the scanner and parser eliminates these globals and also allows
for the possibility of using several different parsers in the same compiler.

We use a *ScanParseCls* object to do the encapsulating. Figure 6.5 illustrates
the module design. The definition portion of the module contains class information
about the encapsulating *ScanParseCls* as well as *LexTokCls*, that is used by the
scanner and parser for communication.

```
Scanparse definitions (scanparse.h)

 5 typedef class LexTokCls *PLexTokCls;
 6 class LexTokCls {
 7   public:
 8         LexTokCls(int LineNo, int Token, char *Lexeme);
 9         char*   get_lexeme() {return lexeme;}
10         friend ostream& operator<<(ostream&, LexTokCls&);
11   private:
12         int       line_no;
13         char    *lexeme;
14         int       token;
15 };
16
17 class ControllerCls;
18 class PTreeCls;
19
20 typedef class ScanParseCls *PScanParseCls;
21 class ScanParseCls {
22   public:
23         ScanParseCls();
24         void        print();
25         friend class ControllerCls;
26   private:
27         PTreeCls      *parse_tree;
28         int           valid_parse;
29 };
```

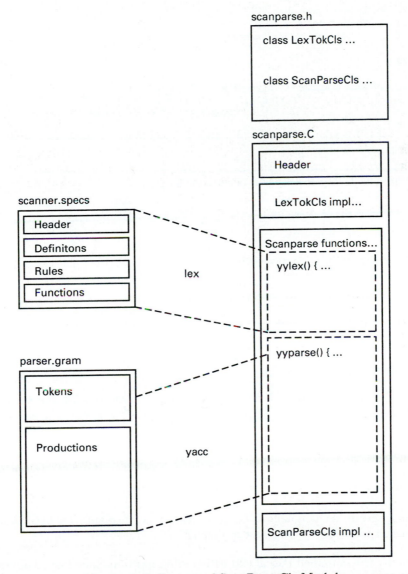

Figure 6.5. Layout of ScanParseCls Module

LexTokCls implementation (scanparse.C)

```
17 #include <string.h>
18 LexTokCls :: LexTokCls(int LineNo, int Token, char *Lexeme) {
20     line_no = LineNo;
21     token   = Token;
22     lexeme = new char[80];
23     if (Lexeme) {
24         strcpy(lexeme,Lexeme);
25     }
26 }
27
28 ostream& operator<<(ostream& s, LexTokCls& x) {
29     return s << "LexTokCls: [" << x.line_no << "] "
30                         << x.token << " " << (x.lexeme)   ;
31 }
```

ScanparseCls implementation (scanparse.C)

```
34 PPTreeNodeCls prgm_node = new PTreeNodeCls; //global, ...
35         //set by root of tree, ProgramCls
36 #include "scanparse.fct"
37
38 ScanParseCls :: ScanParseCls() {
40     //Since yyparse() is 1 on error condition ...
41     valid_parse = !yyparse();
42     parse_tree = new PTreeCls(prgm_node);
43 }
```

6.4   Exercises

1. Let G be the simplified Pascal expression grammar on page 78. For each of the following, trace through the productions of G used to reduce the expression.

   (a) $1 + 2 + 3$

   (b) $(1 + 2)$

   (c) $(1 + 2) * 3$

   Then specify the language $L(G)$ generated by G. Explain why $L(G)$ does not contain valid Pascal boolean expressions.

2. Modify the simplified Pascal expression grammar to include logical operators.

3. In this exercise we want to determine some strings that are recognized by the following grammar.

```
            %start     Pal
            %%
            Pal:  /* empty */
               |  'a'
               |  'b'
               |  'a' Pal 'a'
               |  'b' Pal 'b'
               ;
```

Illustrate how the following strings are reduced to the start symbol.

(a) 'a'

(b) 'aa'

(c) 'abba.'

(d) 'aaaa.'

4. Place the following grammar in a grammar specification file.

```
       %start          Program
       %%
       Program: Program_heading SCTK Block DOTTK
          ;

       Program_heading: PROGRAMTK Identifier Parameter_piece
          ;

       Identifier: IDENTTK
          ;

       Parameter_piece: /empty/
          | LPARENTK RPARENTK
          ;

       Block: Statement_part
          | Statement_part
          ;

       Statement_part: BEGINTK ENDTK
          ;
```

(a) Use *yacc* to produce a listing of the push-down automaton that recognizes the language generated by this grammar. (The −*v* option on *yacc* places this information in the file *y.output*.)

(b) Construct a transition matrix for this recognizer.

(c) Trace the behavior of this recognizer on the following input.

```
       program Simple;
       begin
       end.
```

5. Produce a table similar to those on page 89 for each of the following input strings.

   (a) $1 * 2 + 3$

   (b) $((1))$

   (c) $((1)$

6. This exercise explores ambiguous grammars. Consider the following excerpt from a C grammar.

```
%token IDENTTK
%token PLUSTK
%%
Expression: IDENTTK
     | Expression PLUSTK Expression
     ;
```

   (a) Do a top-down leftmost derivation on the expression $2 + 3 + 4$.

   (b) Now do a top-down rightmost derivation on the same expression.

   (c) Compare the two derivations.

   (d) Submit this grammar to *yacc*. Work up a corresponding parsing table for the *yacc*-generated parser. Trace the parser's action on the above expression. How does the corresponding parse tree compare with those above?

   (e) Add the disambiguating specification

```
%left PLUSTK
```

   to the grammar and note any changes to the parsing table.

   Do the same with the

```
%right PLUSTK
```

   specification.

7. This exercise explores the three major categories of grammars.

   (a) A grammar is called **right-linear** if all the productions are of the form $A \Rightarrow w\,B$ or $A \Rightarrow w$, where A and B are nonterminals and w is a (possibly empty) string of tokens. Similarly, a grammar is called **left-linear** if all productions are of the form $A \Rightarrow B\,w$ or $A \Rightarrow w$. Any right-linear or left-linear grammar is called a **regular grammar**. Verify that the following grammar is regular.

```
        %start   S
        %%
        S: "b" S
         | "a" A
        A: "b"
         | "b" A
         ;
```

See if you can describe the language defined by this grammar.

Incidentally, any language defined by a regular grammar can also be defined by regular expressions and so is recognized by a simple finite-state machine. (Cohen [4] and Hopcroft and Ullman [9] contain the details on this.)

(b) The definition of a grammar in Section 6.1.2 is the usual definition of a context-free grammar.

    i. Verify that the following grammar

```
        %start    Int
        %%
        Int: SignedInt
         |  UnsignedInt
         ;
        SignedInt: "+" UnsignedInt
         | "-" UnsignedInt
         ;
        UnSignedInt:  Digit
         | Digit UnsignedInt
         ;
        Digit:  "0" | "1" | "2" | "3" | "4" |
                | "5" | "6" | "7" | "8" | "9"
         ;
```

is context-free, but not regular.

    ii. Show that the language generated by the grammar above is also generated by the following *regular* grammar.

```
%start    Int
%%
Int: SignedInt
   |  UnsignedInt
   ;
SignedInt: "+" UnsignedInt
   | "-" UnsignedInt
   ;
UnSignedInt: Digit
   | Digit
   | "0" UnsignedInt
   | "1" UnsignedInt
   | "2" UnsignedInt
   | "3" UnsignedInt
   | "4" UnsignedInt
   | "5" UnsignedInt
   | "6" UnsignedInt
   | "7" UnsignedInt
   | "8" UnsignedInt
   | "9" UnsignedInt
   ;
Digit:   "0" | "1" | "2" | "3" | "4" |
       | "5" | "6" | "7" | "8" | "9"
   ;
```

(c) A grammar is called **context-sensitive** if productions have the form $\alpha \ A \ \beta \Rightarrow \alpha\gamma\beta$ where γ is required to be a nonempty string of tokens or nonterminals. Verify that the following famous grammar

```
%start    S
%%
S: "a" A B
 |  "a" B
 ;
A: "a" A C
 | "a" C
 ;
B:  D "c"
 ;
D:  "b"
 ;
CD:   CE
 ;
CE:   DE
 ;
DE:   DC
 ;
C "c":  D "c" "c"
 ;
```

is context-sensitive. In particular, show that the strings *abc* and *aabbcc* are in the language generated by the grammar.

Context-sensitive grammars are a subset of the more general **recursively enumerable** grammars. These are the grammars that can be recognized by a special machine called a Turing machine. (Hopcroft and Ullman [9, page 148] contains a discussion of these machines and the languages recognized by them.)

8. Use the PDA definition on page 95 to trace the recognizer's behavior on the following strings.

    (a) IFTK BEXPRTK THENTK

    (b) IFTK BEXPRTK THENTK IFTK BEXPRTK THENTK ELSETK

    (c) IFTK BEXPRTK IFTK BEXPRTK

    (d) IFTK BEXPRTK ELSETK

9. Submit the following grammar to *yacc*.

```
%token   NUMTK
%token   ADDOPTK
%token   MULOPTK
%token   LPARENTK
%token   RPARENTK
%start Expr

%%
Expr: Term
    | Factor
    ;
Term: NUMTK
    | Term  MULOPTK  Factor
    ;
Factor: NUMTK
      | LPARENTK  Expr  RPARENTK
      ;
```

    (a) What are the PDA's states?

    (b) What causes the reduce/reduce conflicts?

    (c) Modify the grammar to remove the conflicts.
        Hint: Try moving the common token up in the grammar.

10. This exercise is a continuation of Exercise 5.9. Modify the grammar of your (enhanced) embryonic compiler so that it now contains productions for the following.

    (a) Variable declarations

    (b) For statement

(c) If-then-else statement

Test the scanner/parser system via test programs submitted to the new embryonic compiler.

11. This exercise describes one way of implementing the formatter designed for testing the scanner and parser. The following suggestions are intended to assist you in modifying the enhanced embryonic compiler containing the scanner in Exercise 5.9 and parser in Exercise 6.10, above.

   (a) Modify *OptionCls* to allow the $-f$ option.
   - Add the definition of *set_format()* and *format()* to *OptionCls* in *ctrl.h*
   - Implement the two functions in *ctrl.C*.

   (b) Add the $-f$ option to ControllerCls::set_options().

   (c) Upgrade the scanner.
   - Modify the scanner's behavior on white spaces. You could use an action something like the following.
     ```
     {if (! at_margin || !OptionCls::format()) {ckout();}}
     ```
   - Modify the reserved word checker. On most reserved words you want to modify the left margin *after* the *ckout()* has output the lexeme. I use several global variables to try to manage the position of the left margin.
     - *at_margin*. This variable is turned true each time *ckout()* outputs a return from the source program.
     - *indent_level*. This variable is either incremented directly by the function *ck_reserved_wd()*, or in the case of lexemes like "if", "for", etc., by *ckout()* because *indent_after* has been turned on.
     - *indent_after* indicates that *indent_level* is to be incremented as soon as the current lexeme has been printed.

   Ck_reserved_wd() can modify the various globals using code like the following.

     ```
                         switch (Token) {
     case PROGRAMTK:
         indent_after++;
         break;
     case BEGINTK:
         indent_level--;
         indent_after++;
         break;
     case CASETK:
         indent_after++;
         break;
     case CONSTTK:
         indent_level--;
         indent_after++;
     ```

```
            break;
        case ELSETK:
            indent_level--;
            indent_after++;
            break;


        .
        .
        .
```

You might think about the differences between *BEGINTK* and *CASETK* margin control.

- Modify the output routine *ckout()*.

12. There are a number of public domain C grammars available. One of these was written by Jeff Lee and is available by *ftp* from *primost.cs.wisc.edu*. If you are able to obtain such a grammar, put it in a form acceptable for *yacc*. If you do not have access to such a grammar, modify a grammar from a standard text like Kernighan and Ritchie [10].

    Use *yacc* to generate a parser. Combine this parser with the scanner from Exercise 5.10 to form the beginnings of a C-compiler front end.

13. (**CLIP** Project)

    Design and implement a parser for the **CLIP** system.

Chapter 7

Symbol Tables

```
Topics:
  • Symbol table use
  • Symbol table class definition and implementation
```

As the parser (Figure 2.1) begins to work its way through a source program, it encounters various kinds of identifiers. These identifiers represent diverse program entities: program name, user-defined types, variable names, procedure or function names, standard identifiers, and so on. There are times when the compiler needs to obtain all known information on a given identifier. Has this proposed variable name already been declared? Does this identifier represent a type or a variable? At other points in the compilation process information will need to be stored in the table. Have we just completed a declaration of variables? Do we need to store a value during program interpreting? All this activity suggests that a symbol table will need to be able, at the very least, to store a wide diversity of information and it will need to provide mechanisms for its efficient use.

In this chapter we describe the design and implementation of symbol tables that are appropriate for use in compiling modern programming languages. Our symbol tables are going to be *objects*, of course. The analysis, design and construction will therefore be based on Chapter 2 ideas.

- Locate key abstractions.

- Design the classes.

- Build the classes.

We will determine the key abstractions by first creating a list-of-things and then selecting from that list candidates for objects. Once the objects have tentatively been determined, we begin placing them into classes, noting possible hierarchical relationships that suggest class derivation structures. Then based upon the increasingly complete design information, we begin to produce the C++ definition and implementation details for the classes.

Producing a list-of-things. The first task is to try to locate the key players in this symbol table game. There are essentially two ways to find these. We can often discover the higher level objects by working through well-chosen scenarios and noting the nouns occurring in our description of the process. To save space, our approach in Section 7.1.1, below is to trace the compiler's actions with one typical source program, rather than the more realistic use of a number of prototypes.

Specifying potential objects. The list-of-things contains the various items used by or in symbol tables. Some of these are central; others are more like innocent bystanders needing to go on about their own business. One excellent way to select the central items is to look for *objects*, those items that are important either because of what they contain or what they do. We often say that an item is an **object** if it exhibits at least one of the following characteristics.

- **Has state.** An item **has state** if it encapsulates data that might change or be significant during the execution of the system.

- **Exhibits behavior.** An item **exhibits behavior** if it can change its state or the state of other items.

- **Possesses important identity.** An item **possesses important identity** if there is a property or behavior that distinguishes it from all other items.

Classifying objects. Our next task is to begin to separate objects into sets or classes. A **class** is a set of objects that share common structures or have common behavior. We therefore begin to look for common encapsulated data or similar behavior in our collection of objects. Special attention is placed on noting important *subsets* of objects within a given class. These often become classes *derived* from a base class.

Specifying class membership and class relationships. Object-oriented analysis techniques do give us information about how classes are related to each other, especially if we have been able to discover some of the required behaviors as we were developing the list-of-things. But these same techniques rarely give significant assistance with the task designing the inside of classes. We have found that much of this information can be obtained by a technique from domain analysis called **interviewing experts.** In this case our domain experts will be several existing compiler texts as well as compiler implementation code.

Defining classes. This is the point at which object-oriented programming actually begins. A **class definition** is a C++ statement that describes information about the data or functions that will be available for each **instance** or object of the class. Definitions also contain information about relationships between the various classes.

Implementing classes. A *class implementation* contains the specific implementation details for the various member functions of that class. In particular, code must be provided for special **constructor** functions that are executed when each object is created.

```pascal
 1 program StackShowsTables;
 2
 3 type
 4     StackPtrType = ^StackType;
 5     StackType = record
 6                     data: integer;
 7                     next: StackPtrType
 8                 end; {StackType}
 9 var i: integer;
10     StackHead: StackPtrType;
11
12     function Empty(Stack: StackPtrType): boolean;
13     begin
14         Empty := (Stack^.next = nil)
15     end; {Empty}
16
17     procedure Init(var NewStack: StackPtrType);
18     begin
19         new(NewStack);
20         with NewStack^ do begin
21             data := 0;
22             next := nil
23         end
24     end;{Init}
25
26     procedure Push(data: integer; var Top: StackPtrType);
27     var
28         p: StackPtrType;
29     begin
30         p := Top;
31         new(Top);
32         Top^. data := data;
33         Top^. next := p
34     end;{Push}
35
36     procedure Pop(var data:integer; var Top:StackPtrType);
37     begin
38         data := Top^.data;
39         Top := Top ^.next;
40     end; {Pop}
41
42 begin {main}
43     Init(StackHead);
44     readln(i);
45     while i <> 0 do begin
46         Push(i,StackHead);
47         readln(i)
48     end;
49     while not Empty(StackHead) do begin
50         Pop(i,StackHead);
51         writeln(i);
52     end
53 end.
```

7.1   Locating Key Abstractions

As noted, above we begin by tracing through the compilation of a prototypical source program. The following items are of special note. The program contains the following items.

- Type declaration activity, including an exception to Pascal's define before use rule

- Declarations of functions and procedures

- Nontrivial formal parameter examples

- Declaration and use of local variables

- Calls to standard functions

7.1.1   List-of-Things

Initial Table Activities

$$\boxed{\text{Scenario: Part 0}}$$

Even before the first line of a source program is recognized by the scanner, the compiler must construct a symbol table, called the **standard identifier table**, containing the names and attributes of the language's default types, functions, and procedures.

Pascal has five required types: `integer`, `real`, `char`, `boolean`, and `text`.

- **Integer.** Valid `integer` values lie only in the closed interval

$$-maxint + 1 .. \ maxint$$

  where $maxint$, the largest valid integer value, is determined by the number of bits per word for the host computer. The actual object representing the type `integer` is defined and implemented in Chapter 8, since it is used directly in parse tree construction.

  Incidentally, the identifier $maxint$ is a Pascal required identifier and so will also need to be entered into this symbol table.

- **Others.** Each of the identifiers *real, char, boolean,* and *text* must also be linked with their corresponding type objects and then entered into this standard identifier table.

The identifiers representing the following required functions

Category	Function Name			
Arithmetic	$abs(x)$	$sqr(x)$	$sqrt(x)$	$sin(x)$
Type Conversion	$round(x)$	$trunc(x)$		
Ordinal	$ord(x)$	$chr(x)$	$succ(x)$	$pred(x)$
Boolean	$odd(x)$	$eoln(f)$	$eof(f)$	

must also be entered into this symbol table. Below is the list of required Pascal procedures.

Category	Procedure Name			
I/O	*read(x)*	*readln(x)*	*write(x)*	*writeln(x)*
File Handling	*rewrite(f)*	*reset(f)*	*put(f)*	*get(f)*
Device Handling	*page(f)*			
Dynamic Allocation	*new(p)*	*dispose(p)*		
Data Transfer	*pack(x,i,y)*	*unpack(x,y,i)*		

Identifiers representing each of these procedures also need to be associated with the relevant information or behaviors and then entered into this first symbol table.

List of things, 0

- **Symbol tables** are made up of **entries** that associate information or **attributes** with identifiers.

- Identifier attributes are stored for at least the following kinds of things.

  1. **Types**, such as the standard types.

  2. **Constants** , such as maxint. Constants have the following attributes.

     - The underlying type.
     - The constant value.
     - The corresponding ordinal value, if appropriate.

  3. **Functions and procedures**, such as the required functions or procedures.

Creating Symbol Tables

Scenario: Part 1
1 program StackShowsTables;

During the computation of a source program, a number of different kinds of tables need to be created and accessed by various objects in the compiler. As the parser processes the first line of a source program, the identifier for the program name must be entered into some table so that any possible future reference to the identifier will result in an error. A reasonable way to accomplish this is to create a global symbol table for user-defined identifiers at the highest, or outermost, level of the program. This second table is then made to point to the standard identifier table so that subsequent identifier existence queries will also prevent redefinition of the Pascal required identifiers.

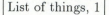

> - There are a number of **different symbol tables** present during compilation. One table contains the standard identifiers, another the global variables declared in the source program.
>
> - Symbol tables need to be placed into a **linked-list**.
>
> - Tables need to provide for table-specific **lookup** as well as for *scanning* through all appropriate tables.

Storing User-Defined Types

```
                    Scenario: Part 2
3    type
4         StackPtrType = ∧StackType;
5         StackType = record
6                          data: integer;
7                          next: StackPtrType
8         end; {StackType}
```

The production most responsible for recognizing Pascal type specifications such as lines 3 through 8 of the scenario essentially is concerned with associating the string-valued identifier recognized by *Ident* with a previously declared type represented by the nonterminal *Type*.

Type_def: Ident EQTK Type
;

A symbol table entry storing this information will therefore need to associate the identifier to the information about the particular type.

The type specifications in the scenario also bring two additional ideas to the surface.

1. Line 4 is the major exception to the 'define-it-before-you-use-it' rule. Semantic analysis of this particular construct will need to wait until the end of the type declaration.

2. Most modern languages support a structured data type that contains an arbitrary number of data items of possibly different types. In Pascal the structure is called a **record** and the data items are called **fields**. Since the various fields of a record can be accessed only by identifiers, it makes sense

to utilize a symbol table, containing these field identifiers, for each record declared in the source program.

The present collection of symbol table entries must therefore be augmented to include these fields.

List of things, 2

- Another **different symbol table** will be present during compilation. This one will need to store information associated with the various **fields** of a record.

- Symbol tables must also store information associated with a type name.

Storing User-Defined Variables

Scenario: Part 3		
9	var	i: integer;
10		StackHead: StackPtrType

The production

```
Var_dec: Ident_lst COLONTK Type
         ;
```

is the primary means for declaring Pascal variables. Clearly, a symbol table entry for such a variable declaration will need to contain information representing the type of that variable. Variables and constants also represent a particular *state* of the underlying type. This means that symbol table entries representing constants or variables must also have some way to specify and to allow for the modification of the particular value being represented by the identifier.

List of things, 3

- Symbol tables will need to store **variable attributes**.

  - The type of the variable.
  - The value of the variable.

Storing Subprogram Information

```
                        Scenario: Part 4
12    function Empty(Stack: StackPtrType): boolean;
13    begin
14        Empty := (Stack∧.next = nil)
15    end; {Empty}
16
17    procedure Init(var NewStack: StackPtrType);
18    begin
19        new(NewStack);
20        with NewStack∧ do begin
21            data := 0;
22            next := nil
23        end
24    end; {Init}
25
26    procedure Push(data: integer; var Top: StackPtrType);
27    var
28        p: StackPtrType;
29    begin
30        p := Top;
31        new(Top);
32        Top∧.data := data;
33        Top∧.next := p
34    end; {Push}
35
36    procedure Pop(var data:integer; var Top:StackPtrType);
37    begin
38        data := Top∧.data;
39        Top := Top∧.next;
40    end; {Pop}
```

Scope of a variable. One of the significant features of Algol that has been retained in nearly all procedurally oriented languages is the ability to nest procedures or functions. Each such subprogram can contain its own local variables and parameters. Moreover, standard visibility rules often specify that references to identifiers not declared in a particular subprogram can be resolved by declarations in the nearest enclosing subprogram. Needless to say, resolving such references can be a complex task, even for a language as simple as Pascal.

The region of a program in which references to a particular identifier are valid is called the **scope** of that identifier. Scope is often handled by constructing a linked-list of symbol tables and then looking through the tables, starting with the table containing variables closest to the particular section of code. If the variable is

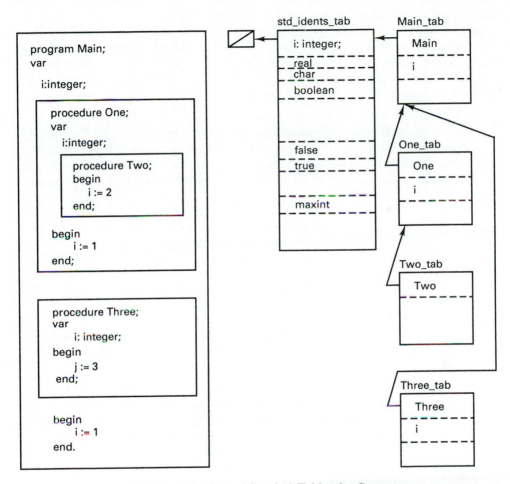

Figure 7.1. Use of Symbol Tables for Scope

not found in the closest table, then the next table in the list is searched and so on. Figure 7.1 illustrates this with a simple Pascal program containing three procedures. *One*'s table is linked to *Main*'s table, and *Main*'s is linked to the standard identifier table. Not finding "i" in *Two*'s table, the compiler then searches back up the list and so locates the variable in the enclosing procedure. The reference to "j" in *Three* is clearly an error, since the compiler cannot locate that variable in any table along its visibility path or **vista**.

Procedure/function information. The parser will construct a parse tree representing the sequence of subprogram statements. Each symbol table entry for a *subprogram identifier* must therefore provide a link to the corresponding statement tree information. In the case of functions, the symbol table entries must also contain information about the return type and value of the function.

A procedure or function symbol table entry must also maintain information about its own locally defined identifiers. This is usually accomplished by creating a local symbol table. Every Pascal subprogram has (possibly empty) sets of formal parameters and local variables. These are best stored in the local symbol table. Formal parameters are the data windows of subprograms. Pascal has three kinds.

1. **Value-parameters.** These are like subprogram local variables except that they are initialized by the values of corresponding actual-parameters at the beginning of a procedure or function call. Modification of their values by the subprogram does not affect the value of the corresponding actual-parameters.

2. **Variable-parameters.** A variable-parameter is just a local alias for a variable declared outside the subprogram. Assignment to variable-parameters is exactly the same as assignment to the corresponding actual-parameters. Actual parameters associated with formal variable-parameters must therefore be identifiers, rather than literals or more complex expressions.

3. **Procedure/function-parameters.** These are just local aliases for a procedure or function identifier declared outside the current subprogram.

In addition to the formal parameters, local symbol tables must be able to store the declaration of all locally defined items such as constants, variables, and other subprograms. On the other hand, the type identifier *StackPtrType* in the scenario lives in the distant global table. Local tables must therefore be linked to the tables of enclosing procedures or functions.

Most modern programming languages also provide for overloading standard procedure or function identifiers; some even allow for such overloading of *user-defined* subprogram identifiers. In this case, source program calls to one of a set of subprograms can be resolved by the identifier representing the class of subprograms and the *type* of the actual parameter(s) used in the call. Clearly this association of a number of subprogram attributes with a single identifier is going to place significant stress on traditional table lookup mechanisms. There are a number of schemes currently used to provide this language feature. One of these methods is to provide symbol table entries of such overloaded identifiers with the ability to form linked-lists. A first entry is entered into the table, in the same manner as any subprogram identifier would. Subsequent entries specifying the other versions of this subprogram are then simply linked to the inserted entry.

> **List of things, 4**
>
> - We need to provide some way keep track of the **set of valid variables** during the compilation process.
>
> - Symbol tables need to store attributes associated with **functions** and **procedures**. This includes the following kinds of information.
>
>   - Entries containing information about **formal parameters**.
>
>   - Entries containing information about **local variables**.
>
>   - Entries representing **overloaded standard functions** or **procedures**.

Parsing Statements

```
                     Scenario: Part 5
42   begin main
43       Init(StackHead);
44       readln(i);
45       while i <> 0 do begin
46           Push(i,StackHead);
47           readln(i)
48       end;
49       while not Empty(StackHead) do begin
50           Pop(i,StackHead);
51           writeln(i);
52       end
53   end.
```

The procedure-call object created by the parser

```
Init(StackHead);
```

must look up both *Init* and *StackHead* in the global symbol table. It must be possible to verify that *Init* is indeed a procedure expecting a single parameter and that the actual parameter, *StackHead*, is a variable of the required type. This kind of checking will be possible using the kinds of member functions we have already specified for the various symbol table entry classes.

The procedure-call in line 44 of the scenario is a different matter. In this case, *lookup()* must be able to continue its search up the current vista of tables, since the (valid) standard identifier *readln* does not exist in the global table. This actually argues for the existence of two lookup functions, one restricted to a particular table and one for searching an entire vista if necessary. It is also clear that we need to keep track of the current table as source parsing and even program execution take place.

List of things, 5a

- Symbol tables need to store attributes associated with **functions** and **procedures**. This includes the following kinds of information.

    - Entries containing information about **formal parameters**.
    - Entries containing information about **local variables**.
    - Entries representing **overloaded standard functions** or **procedures**.

- Symbol tables should have two different kinds of *lookup()* functions: one restricted to the table and the other able to access all linked tables.

Handling Labels

The grammar production

```
Label: UNSIGNEDINTTK
     ;
```

for recognizing Pascal labels, as well as the additional requirement that the number be only four digits, gives the impression that a label is an integer. Actually, labels are special identifiers built from strings of digits, and their only purpose is to point to a particular statement.

List of things, 5b

- A symbol table entry representing a program **label** needs to maintain information about the program statement being referenced.

7.1.2   List of Objects

Our next analysis task is to select system objects from the above list-of-things. As noted in the introduction of this chapter, we need to examine each "thing" to see if it posses one or more of the object criteria: state, behavior, and identity. The following nouns from the list-of-things seem to satisfy at least one of the object criteria.

- **The entire symbol table.** Tables clearly change state every time information is added. They also possess behaviors like *insert()* or *lookup()*.

- **The various symbol table entries.** The actual pieces of information stored by the table entries are also possible objects.

  - **Type attributes.** The underlying type of a particular variable, particularly if it is built up of a number of simpler types, can be very nicely described by a collection of objects.

  - **Internal constant values.** Similarly, the *value* of a constant or constant expression could be represented by a *Value* object, capable of representing a value of any type.

  - **Internal strings.** Strings of characters are used in scanning, parsing, semantic analysis, and even in program interpreting and emitting. This extensive use, as well as the number of specialized required string functions, argues strongly for the definition of string objects.

  - **Variable attributes.** Variables and constants both encapsulate the idea of type and value.

  - **Procedure and function attributes.** Subprograms have a large number of different kinds of information associated with their declaration.

  - **Label attributes.** Labels need to reference a particular instruction, at the very least.

Let's summarize these ideas by creating the following list of the objects.

Object	Description
Symtab	Table having adjustable size
TypeAtt	Points to actual parse tree type objects
ConstAtt	Contains type, value and ord information
VarAtt	Contains type, value and ord information
ProcAtt	Contains own symbol table and parse tree
FuncAtt	Also returns a value
Type	Represents various standard and user types
Value	Contains a string representation of value
String	Points to sequence of chars

We will defer further *Type* design and implementation efforts until Chapter 8, since type objects are normally constructed during the construction of the parse tree. *Value* and *String* objects are really utility objects, since they are used throughout the compiler. Their design and implementation are therefore described in Appendix C.

However, we can certainly focus on *TypeAtt* design and implementation in this chapter, as well as that of *VarAtt*, *ProcAtt*, ... And one major task is placing these objects into some hierarchical structure. Figure 7.2 contains an initial version of an **object diagram**. The main purpose of such a diagram is to assist in recognizing *groupings* of objects that have common behavior or share common data members, rather than the careful specification of that behavior or those members.

7.2   Designing Classes

7.2.1   Classifying Objects

Of the various objects described above, the *Symtab* object is fundamentally different. It *uses* the other objects in storing the various information. This suggests the need for a separate *SymtabCls* specification.

The remaining symbol table entry objects in Figure 7.2 have at least one thing in common: Each one is associated with some identifier. This suggests that we define a *SymtabEntryCls* base class that contains a *name* data member. The classes for the particular symbol table entries will then be *derived* from this base class.

Class	Description
SymtabCls	Must allow for inserting and deleting of information. Also must allow for creation of different sized tables.
TypeAttCls	Associates identifier with type object
ConstAttCls	Same as TypeAttCls, but also stores value and ordinal value.
VarAttCls	Same as ConstAttCls
ProcAttCls	Stores own symbol table and parse tree for procedure instructions.
FuncAttCls	Same as ProcAttCls but also allows for returning function value.

The above table contains a list of symbol table classes that have been identified so far. These classes now need to be arranged into at least a tentative class diagram, such as the one in Figure 7.3. This class diagram may be incomplete, since it is based on objects encountered only during the one scenario. As we continue with later design efforts in Section 7.2, we may encounter additional objects and corresponding classes that will need to be added to our list and diagrams.

7.2.2   Class Membership

Our next design activity is to try to specify the data members for the various classes. As we work on this, we also may be able to anticipate and specify class behaviors. A summary for each class is listed below.

Symbol Table Entries

```
                              TypeAttCls

Class data member
      Pointer to data type
Class behavior
      Constructor (public)
            Parameters: Ident, Type
      Function for accessing type pointer
Class relationships
      Inherits ident storage from symbol table base class
      Uses type classes in its definition
```

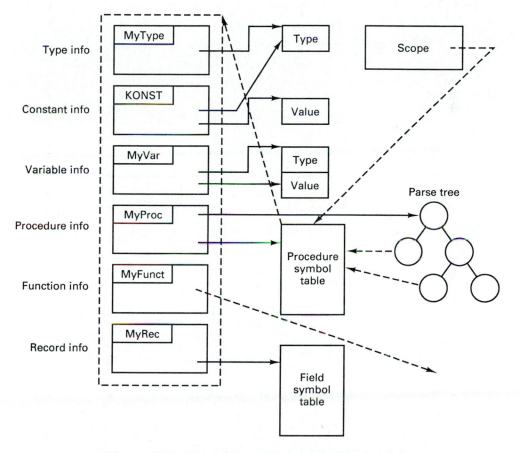

Figure 7.2. Initial Object Diagram for Symbol Table

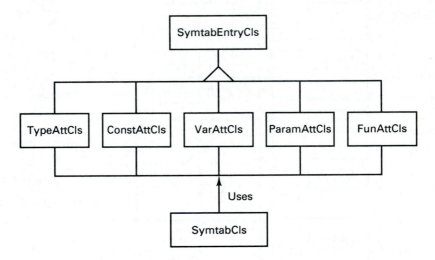

Figure 7.3. Preliminary Symbol Table Class Diagram

```
┌─────────────────────────────────────────────────────────────────────┐
│                          VarAttCls/ConstAttCls                        │
│                                                                       │
│  Class data member                                                    │
│       Pointer to data type                                            │
│       Pointer to value                                                │
│       Storage for corresponding ordinal value                         │
│  Class behavior                                                       │
│       Constructor (public)                                            │
│             Parameters: Ident, Value, Type                            │
│       Functions for accessing type, value and ordinal information     │
│  Class relationships                                                  │
│       Inherits ident storage from symbol table base class             │
│       Uses type and value classes in its definition                   │
└─────────────────────────────────────────────────────────────────────┘
```

```
┌─────────────────────────────────────────────────────────────────────┐
│                          ProcAttCls/FuncAttCls                        │
│                                                                       │
│  Class data members                                                   │
│       Pointer to symbol table                                         │
│       Pointer to parameter list                                       │
│       Pointer to parse (sub)tree                                      │
│       Pointer to return type, if a function                           │
│       Pointer to return value, if a function                          │
│  Class behavior                                                       │
│       Provide for interpreting or executing of the subprogram         │
│       Provide (public) member functions for returning type            │
│             or value information                                      │
│  Class relationships                                                  │
│       Inherits ident storage from symbol table base class             │
│       Uses type and value classes in its definition                   │
└─────────────────────────────────────────────────────────────────────┘
```

Based on the discussion in the list-of-things, *FormalParamAttCls* will be a base class having the following three subclasses.

```
┌─────────────────────────────────────────────────────────────────────┐
│                           ValParamAttCls                              │
│                                                                       │
│  Class data members                                                   │
│       Pointer to parameter type                                       │
│       Pointer to parameter (local) value                              │
│  Class behavior                                                       │
│       Requests for value return the local value                       │
│  Class relationships                                                  │
│       Subclass of FormalParamAttCls                                   │
│       Initialized by ExprCls objects during                           │
│             program interpreting or execution                         │
└─────────────────────────────────────────────────────────────────────┘
```

VarParamAttCls

Class data member
      Pointer to the symbol table entry of
          aliased variable
Class behavior
      Requests for value return the value of the
          aliased variable
Class relationships
      Subclass of FormalParamAttCls
      Not initialized by *ExprCls* objects during
          program interpreting or execution

ProcFunParamAttCls

Class data members
      Pointer to ProcAttCls if procedure
      Pointer to FunctAttCls if function
Class behavior
      Member functions for returning data members
Class relationships
      Subclass of FormalParamAttCls

Pascal records have two kinds of fields: **fixed** and **variant**. For example, in

```
StackType = record
            next: StackPtrType;
            case tag: integer of
                 1: (idata:integer);
                 2: (rdata: real)
          end; {StackType}
```

next is a fixed field of *StackType*, while idata and rdata are variants. The identifier *tag* is called a **tag field** and its type integer is the associated **tag type**. The "1" is the **tag value** for the variant *idata*.

Pascal's rather stringent semantic requirements for fields specify that all field identifiers for a given record must be unique. This requirement is very easily imposed by simply associating a separate symbol table with the record structure and then inserting the necessarily uniquely specified fields into the table as they are declared.

We therefore need to specify another symbol table entry class that will provide the data storage and behavioral requirements for such fields. The field identifier will be stored by the parent *SymtabEntryCls*. But *FieldAttCls* will also need to provide for the storage of the field type, field value (if it is a scalar type), and an optional associated tag variable and list of corresponding tag values.

```
┌─────────────────────────────────────────────────────────────────┐
│                          FieldAttCls                              │
│                                                                   │
│  Class data member                                                │
│      Pointer to field type                                        │
│      Pointer to field value                                       │
│      Pointer to tag field                                         │
│      Pointer to corresponding list of tag values                  │
│  Class behavior                                                    │
│      Provide (public) member function for returning various data members │
│  Class relationships                                              │
│      Inherits ident storage from symbol table base class          │
└─────────────────────────────────────────────────────────────────┘
```

Labels are stored in symbol tables so that references to the location by *goto* statements have a target. The only attribute associated with a label is therefore some particular statement object in the parse tree.

```
┌─────────────────────────────────────────────────────────────────┐
│                          LabelAttCls                              │
│                                                                   │
│  Class data member                                                │
│      Pointer to statement object                                  │
│  Class behavior                                                    │
│      Provide (public) member function for returning statement     │
│  Class relationships                                              │
│      Inherits ident storage from symbol table base class          │
└─────────────────────────────────────────────────────────────────┘
```

```
┌─────────────────────────────────────────────────────────────────┐
│     ConstAttCls, VarAttCls, FuncAttCls, ParamAttCls (addition)    │
│                                                                   │
│  Class behavior                                                    │
│      Ability to return present value                              │
│                                                                   │
│                                                                   │
│          VarAttCls, FuncAttCls, ParamAttCls (addition)            │
│                                                                   │
│  Class behavior                                                    │
│      Ability to modify present value                              │
└─────────────────────────────────────────────────────────────────┘
```

Interpreting source programs and emitting assembler code representing source programs also require symbol table activity.

Interpreting.   The object representing a statement like

$$\texttt{while i <> 0 do begin ...}$$

must be able to efficiently look up the value of a constant or the loop variable. Assignment statements and procedure-calls also need to be able to *set* the value associated with variables, parameters, and function identifiers.

Since Pascal procedures and functions can recursively call themselves, traditional symbol tables for these must be able to allocate their parameters and local variables to **stack frames**. Each recursive call during execution will result in a new frame or copy of the subprogram variables being created and pushed onto a stack. Upon completion of the subprogram's execution, the current frame is popped, revealing the frame corresponding to the previous version, which was interrupted by the recursive call. An object-oriented implementation of the stack frame idea is somewhat different: Each symbol table entry *object* has the ability to push present values onto its own value stack during program interpretation. So a single procedure stack frame is replaced by individual linked-lists of value objects.

Code emitting.   Each constant or variable in a symbol table must be made to correspond to some memory location in the executable module. One way to do this is to provide symbol tables and their entries with the ability to output code that allocates corresponding memory on the target machine to be used during program execution. The object-oriented approach is particularly suited to this approach. The symbol table can emit code that initializes the general data area and then request that each of its entries emit code (if it is appropriate to do so) specifying the region of memory in which that entry would be stored during execution.

SymtabCls, ConstAttCls, VarAttCls, FuncAttCls, ParamAttCls (addition)

Class behavior
   Ability to allocate data space on target machine

SymtabEntryCls. This is the base class for the various kinds of symbol table entries.

   TypeAttCls. This subclass contains information about appropriate data values and operations associated with standard and user-defined types.

   ConstAttCls. This subclass contains information about the type of the constant and its fixed value.

   VarAttCls. This subclass contains information about the type of the variable and allows for the modification of corresponding values during program interpreting.

   ProcAttCls. This subclass contains all information associated with procedures including a local symbol table for formal parameters and local variables as well as a reference to the parse tree form of the instructions that make up the procedure.

   FuncAttCls. This subclass contains all the information noted for *ProcAttCls*, above, as well as type and value information normally associated with *VarAttCls* objects.

   FormalParamAttCls. This subclass contains the type, value, and *direction* (in Pascal, **var** or simply value) of the formal parameter it represents.

   FieldAttCls. This subclass contains the type and value information for each field specified in a particular Pascal **record** structure.

   LabelAttCls. This class associates a four-digit integer string with a particular statement in the given program block.

ScopeCls. This class contains information and behaviors that facilitate determining the scope of a particular identifier.

SymtabCls. This class provides for the storage and the retrieval of information associated with the various identifiers occurring in a Pascal source program.

This information can be further summarized by the construction of a complete class diagram as illustrated in Figure 7.4.

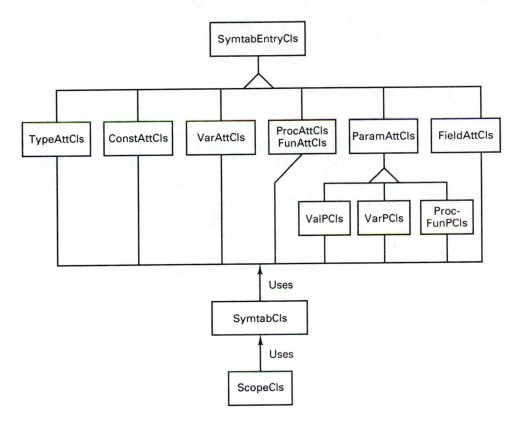

Figure 7.4. Symtab Class Diagram

Symbol Tables

An important source of information about symbol tables, particularly the interior components, are the words and the work of compiler experts. Much of our discussion below has been gleaned from Aho et al. [1], Holub [8], and Schreiner and Friedman [18]. Another excellent "text" has been the actual compiler code from early versions of Stroustrup's C++ compiler, as well as Gnu's *gcc*. Indeed, time spent reading experts' programs often provides the most accurate picture of that vital intersection of theory and practice.

There are three symbol table design issues that the experts regularly address.

- **Efficiency.** Symbol tables are utilized extensively during the compilation of a single source program. The information must be stored in a data structure allowing highly efficient access.

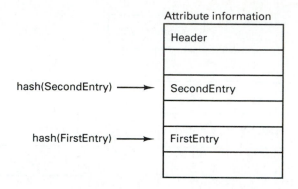

Figure 7.5. First Design of Hash Structure

- **Faithfulness.** Often the order in which an identifier is encountered will give additional information about the meaning of the identifier. Symbol tables should store information so that program structural information is faithfully represented in the table's structure.

- **Flexibility.** Arbitrarily setting limits on lengths or quantities of identifiers is clearly not a good idea. Symbol tables should be implemented so that space is dynamically allocated for the individual identifiers. Tables should also have the ability to **grow** or increase in size if the particular structure of a source program requires such action.

Efficient data structure.   We clearly are seeking a data structure that is suited to the storage and retrieval of a wide variety of information. Many structures are suggested in the compiler literature, but the predominant structure used in most compilers is that of a **hash table**. Hash tables are most often based on two essential components: an array for storing the information, and a **hash function**, that converts a search key into an array index number where the information for that key is to located (Figure 7.5).

Of course, most hash functions are not **perfect**: There will be occasions when two different keys will hash to the same index. In this case we say that a **collision** has occurred. Again, the literature is full of collision-resolution strategies, but the most popular seems to be a simple **linear resolution** strategy amounting to a linear search through the table looking for the first open location in the table where the information for the second key may be stored. Not unexpectedly, the number of such lookups, also called **probes**, depends primarily on the **load factor** λ that is the fraction of the table containing entries at any particular time. The famous text by Knuth [11] contains the derivation of the following formulas for the expected

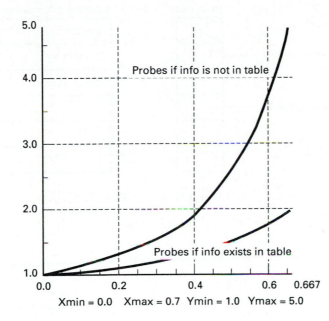

Figure 7.6. Number of Probes Due to Collisions

number of probes as functions of λ.

$$Probes_{not\_there} = \frac{1}{2}\left(1 + \frac{1}{(1-\lambda)^2}\right)$$

$$Probes_{found\_it} = \frac{1}{2}\left(1 + \frac{1}{(1-\lambda)}\right)$$

Figure 7.6 contains the graphs of these of the probe functions that indicate the following interesting information: The number of collision-induced probes remains less than 5 if the table is not more than two-thirds full. In fact, if the information exists in the table, the expected number of probes is just slightly less that 2.

Faithful representation. There are times when the order in which identifiers occur in a source program must be referenced during later stages of compilation. Certainly this is the case in the declaration of formal parameters for a subprogram; it is also true for the corresponding specification of actual parameters in the call to that

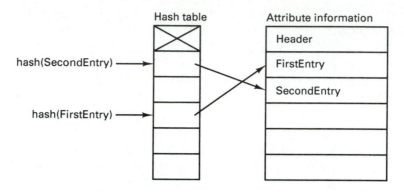

Figure 7.7. Second Design of Hash Structure

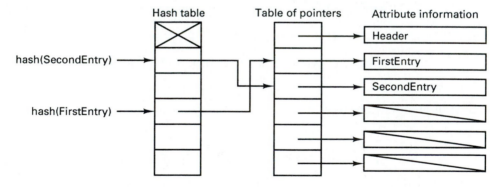

Figure 7.8. Third Design of Hash Structure

subprogram. One of the important features of hashing is that the index produced by the hash function is uniformly distributed over the range of all possible indices. Naturally such a function will therefore not place objects in the table the order in which they are encountered. A rather standard hash table modification for retaining this kind of information is illustrated in Figure 7.7, where the information array is replaced by a *pointer array* and the actual information is then free to be stored in encounter order.

Flexible implementation. The symbol table design should not impose superficial limitations on its use. In particular, the memory requirements for information stored in each symbol table entry cannot be precisely specified prior to compiler execution.

So the class data members of the various symbol table entries should almost always be *pointers* and the actual information stored on the free store as needed. Indeed, the symbol table itself should consist of such pointers and the various entries placed on the store. Similarly we cannot accurately predict optimum or even adequate sizes for the various tables. Tables must therefore be provided with an ability to *grow* when they reach the selected critical load factor of two-thirds. Figure 7.8 contains a structure we use in this text to implement these three design requirements.

We complete this section with the following table summarizing the current state of design decisions for *SymtabCls*.

```
                              SymtabCls

Class data member
      Table size
      Pointer to actual table
Class behavior
      Constructor
      Ability to insert symbol table entry
      Ability to look up an identifier
      Ability to grow if table is getting too small
      Pointer to a higher level table for additional searching
Class relationships
      Uses classes derived from SymtabEntryCls
```

```
                              ScopeCls

Class member
      Pointer to current symbol table
Class behavior
      Ability to point to new table
      Ability to return current table pointer
```

7.2.3   Class Protocols

Having just specified the complete set of symbol table classes, our next task is to design those classes so that their corresponding objects provide the services and are able to access other objects during the compilation of a Pascal source program.

Booch [3, page 40] describes this task as the specification of object **protocol**.

> A **client** is any object that uses the resources of another object. We characterize the behavior of an object by considering the operations that its clients may perform upon it, as well as the operations that it may perform upon other objects. This view forces us to concentrate upon the outside view of an object. We call the entire set of operations that a client may perform upon an object its **protocol**. A protocol denotes the ways in which an object may act and react, and thus constitutes the entire static and dynamic outside view of the abstraction.

To specify protocol, we will address the following questions.

1. Who will call the function?

2. What information needs to be passed to the function?

3. Precisely what will the function do?

These questions must be answered at least for the class constructor(s) and nontrivial member functions. The "reporter" functions that simply return the current value of a data member probably only need to be cited.

SymtabEntryCls. Base class.

- **Constructors.** Since *SymtabEntryCls* is a base class, only the constructors of the derived classes will call the base constructor.

  All symbol table entries associate various kinds of information with a particular identifier. This common identifier must therefore be specified as a member of the class. It should be passed to the constructor by the constructor of each derived class.

  The use of virtual functions for derived classes requires the existence of a default constructor, as well as one having a specified argument.

  The nondefault constructor transfers the argument value of its member value.

- **Reporter function.** Since *SymtabEntryCls* is a base class there will be no SymtabEntry objects created, nor will any other object be able to request this information. So there will be no "reporter" function corresponding to the identifier member data.

- **Virtual functions.** We heavily use the late binding capability provided by virtual functions of derived classes. (See Appendix A, Section A.1.5.) Clearly, the various derived classes do not have an identical collection of member functions. So we provide the base class with the collection of all the required functions, require that each base function return a false (0) value, and then have the various derived functions return nonzero values. This gives us the ability to ask a derived class to do something if it is able to do so without querying the object for its identity. The following functions are used by the various derived classes.

  1. *get_type()*
  2. *get_value()*
  3. *set_value()*

TypeAttCls. Derived class.

- **Constructors.** As noted earlier, a default constructor is required. The main constructor will be called by a *TypeDefCls* parse tree node representing a source program type specification. Public constructors should not pose any security problem.

  The grammar production

```
Type_def: Ident EQTK Type
```

for type specification actually creates a *TypeDefCls* object, which then sends the two nonterminals on the right of the production to the main *TypeAttCls* constructor.
The constructor simply assigns the arguments to the data members.

- **Reporter functions.** The "reporter" function *get_type()* should provide a redefinition of the *SymtabEntryCls* virtual function. It will be called extensively by various parse tree objects that are responsible for semantic checking and expression evaluation. This argues for making the function a public member.
- **Virtual functions.** Since no classes are derived from *TypeAttCls*, there are no virtual member functions.

ConstAttCls. Derived class.

- **Constructors.** The usual default and main constructors are required. The main constructor is called only by a ConstDefCls object.
  The grammar production

  ```
  Const_def: Ident EQTK Constant
  ```

  indicates that at least two arguments should be sent to the constructor. Actually, the *ConstDefCls* object can determine the value and the type from `Constant`, so it is best to pass in the following three arguments
  1. Identifier
  2. Type of constant
  3. Value of constant
- **Reporter functions.**
  1. *get_type()*
  2. *get_value()*
- **Virtual functions.** No virtual functions.

VarAttCls. Derived class.

- **Constructors.** Same as *ConstAttCls* constructors, above.
- **Reporter functions.** Same as *ConstAttCls* "reporter" functions.
- **Other functions.** Source program variables play all the roles that constants do when used in expressions. However, since they also show up on left-hand sides of assignments, in various procedure-calls and in various looping structures they must possess behaviors that allow various statement nodes of the parse tree to make appropriate modifications to their values. So the additional

  *set_value(ValueCls *)*

  function is required.

FParamAttCls. Derived or even a base type.

- **Constructors.** The following productions are a representative sample of those dealing with the specification of formal parameters for functions and procedures.

  ```
  Formal_param_stuff: LPARENTK Formal_p_sect_1st RPARENTK;
      Formal_p_sect_1st: Formal_p_sect
  ```

```
            | Formal_p_sect_lst SCTK Formal_p_sect;
   Formal_p_sect: Param_group
            | VARTK Param_group;
        Param_group: Ident_lst COLONTK Paramtype;
```

It is evident from these productions that a *FParamAttCls* symbol table entry must have a number of data members.

1. A pointer to the underlying parameter type.

2. Some indication of whether the parameter is a variable or value parameter. If it is a value parameter, then the symbol table entry needs a pointer to a *ValueCls* object. If it is a variable parameter, then the value pointer must actually reference the *ValueCls* object for the aliased variable in a higher level symbol table.

The *FParamAttCls* constructor will need the following three arguments.

1. The parameter name

2. The underlying type of the parameter

3. The (var/val) kind of the parameter

- **Reporter functions.**

  1. *get_kind()*

  2. *get_type()*

  3. *get_value()*

- **Virtual functions.**

  - *set_value(ValueCls *)*

ProcAttCls. Derived class.

- **Constructors.** The grammar productions

  ```
        Proc_or_fun_dec: Proc_heading SCTK Block SCTK;
  ```

  and

  ```
        Proc_heading: PROCEDURETK Ident Formal_param_stuff;
  ```

  indicate that constructors for *ProcAttCls* will be called by a *ProcDecCls* object and probably should have the following arguments.

  1. A pointer to the procedure's own symbol table. The first entries in this table will be the procedure's formal parameters. Local variables will also be stored here.

  2. A pointer to the parse tree objects representing the formal parameter list. Though technically not necessary, this information makes comparisons between formal and actual parameters much easier.

  3. A pointer to the parse tree objects representing the procedure's block of statements.

- **Reporter functions.** Since procedures are programs in their own right, there probably will be no need to have external classes accessing the data members of this class.

- **Virtual functions.** Procedures are called during program interpretation using the following production.

  ```
        Procedure_call: Ident Actual_param_stuff;
  ```

Corresponding to this production is a *ProcCallCls* object, which needs to be able to send an *execute()* message to the *ProcAttCls* symbol table entry associated with the procedure name stored in *Ident*.

For code production, this *ProcCallCls* object needs to request that the *ProcAttCls* actually *emit()* the code necessary for execution of the program on the host machine.

FuncAttCls. Derived class. Exercise 7.4 is concerned with the design of this class.

FieldAttCls. Derived class.

The Pascal **record** structure can be arbitrarily complex. Each field of a record associates a field name with a previously declared type. There may even be collections of fields that are individually present, based upon the value of a special tag field.

- **Constructors.** The following productions specify the recognition of the fields in a record structure.

```
Field_lst: Fixed_part Variant_part;
    Fixed_part: Field;
        Field:Ident_lst COLONTK Type;
    Variant_part:
        CASETK Ident COLONTK Ident OFTK Variant_seq;
        Variant_seq: Variant
            | Variant_seq SCTK Variant;
                Variant:Case_label_lst COLONTK
                    LPARENTK Field_lst RPARENTK;
```

These are quite complicated, to be sure, but they recognize field declarations like the following.

```
record
    name: StringType
    case person of kind
        student: (grades: GradeType);
        staff,faculty: (evaluation: EvalType)
end
```

Symbol table entries representing such information must therefore have data members such as:

1. Underlying type of the field.

2. Associated tag variable. This can be zero if the field is not part of a variant structure.

3. A pointer to a list of values for which a variant field would be selected.

The main constructor for *FieldAttCls* will be called by *RecordTypeCls* object as it attempts to build its symbol table.

If may be more obvious from the above declaration example than the corresponding productions that the constructor's arguments can be limited to the following two.

1. FieldName

2. FieldType

- **Reporter functions.**

  – *get_type()*

- **Virtual functions.**
    1. *evaluate()*
    2. *emit()*

LabelAttCls Exercise 7.5 is concerned with the design this class.

ScopeCls. We mentioned earlier in this chapter that many programming languages provide for nesting of procedures. We noted there that the scope of identifiers can be implemented by actually making a kind of reverse tree of tables, where the table of an inside procedure points to the table of the enclosing table, and so on. Starting from a given table, the set of all the tables along the path back to the root or standard identifier table therefore contains all the variables that can be viewed from that particular location. This linked-list of tables is called a **vista**. *ScopeCls* provides the entry into the "tree" of tables that specifies the vista currently in force during the parsing of the program as well as the interpreting or executing of the generated code.

Since scope or vista information is referenced by such a broad segment of the compiler's objects, I have decided to make a single copy of the class and to make it readily available. That is quite easily done in C++ by making the data and function members **static**. Static members are actually associated with the *class* rather than a specific object of that class. What this means is that a *ScopeCls* object will never be created. Instead, the static data member will be set using a public function *set_vista()*, and vista information will be obtained by the public "reporter" function *get_vista()*. Since no object will be created, no constructor will ever be called. We might as well not worry about specifying or implementing something that will not be used.

SymtabCls. Base class.

Actually *SymtabCls* is a *derived* class! It just feels like a base class. As we noted above, symbol tables need to be linked together into a kind of reverse tree to implement variable scope requirements. This behavior can be very easily added to symbol tables by *deriving* symbol tables from a special *LstSeqBldrCls* utility. This derivation then makes available the following members to tables.

1. *append()*

2. *get_next()*

- **Constructors.** There are at least five different reasons for creating symbol tables. Each of these special uses probably should be supported by one of the *SymtabCls* constructors.
    1. Standard identifier table. Probably the controller class should be responsible for creating a highest level table containing information on all the Pascal required types, constants, procedures, and functions.
    2. Global symbol table. This could also be created by the controller object. This table could start at a smaller size than the standard identifier table
    3. Enumerated types. The type declaration nodes of the parse tree need to be able to create tables that contain the enumerated type information. Actually, a separate symbol table is rarely used to record enumerated type or enumerated value information. Most often, *ConstAttCls* objects

are associated with each enumerated value and then stored in the current table immediately before the declaration of the enumerated type.

4. Record structures. Parse tree nodes related to the declaration of record structures also must be able to create tables that faithfully represent the record structure. Such structures, especially those used in connection with pointers, are often recursive, since they may contain fields that are pointers to their own record type.

5. Subprogram tables. Parse tree nodes representing procedures and functions need to be able to create tables containing their (formal) parameters and local variables.

All of these requirements can be serviced by the following two constructors.

1. *SymtabCls.* This default constructor can be used by the controller object to create the standard identifier table.

2. *SymtabCls(PSymtabCls OuterTable).* This creates a small table and makes it point to the next table in the vista.

- **Reporter functions.** None! It turns out that there are some five or six different private data or function members for this class that are used primarily for implementation details. Good design demands that this information not be made available to any client objects.

- **Virtual functions.** A large number of objects need to reference these tables. The primary requests are for inserting or looking up information related to a given identifier.

  1. *lookup()*
  2. *vista_lookup()*
  3. *emit()*

7.3 Designing the Module

Our final design decision is to organize the symbol table module contents. The symbol table subsystem is sufficiently small that it can consist of a single file containing all the definitions and a single file of class function implementation details.

- Definition module: (*symtab.h*)

  - *SymtabEntryCls*

    * *TypeAttCls*
    * *ConstAttCls*
    * *VarAttCls*
    * *FParamAttCls*
    * *ProcAttCls*
    * *FuncAttCls*

* * *FieldAttCls*

* * *LabelAttCls*

- * *ScopeCls*

- * *SymtabCls*

- Implementation module: (*symtab.C*)

The order of implementation follows the definition order.

7.4   Constructing the Classes

7.4.1   Definitions

The listing below is our first C++ example of nontrivial inheritance. There are six different subclasses of symbol table entries, each designed to store and provide attribute information for the various identifiers that are encountered in a source program. This means that the base class, *SymtabEntryCls*, must provide for the following kinds of design decisions that were prescribed in Section 7.2.3.

- General data members, used by all symbol table entries

- Visibility of data and function members

- Late binding of function members

The only piece of data common to all symbol table entries is the character string containing the entry's identifier.

Visibility issues are a little more complex. Protected members are available only to classes derived from the base class. The actual implementation of the data member **name** is also **protected**. So a special member function **get_name()** is **publicly** provided for use by other members.

Virtual function members of the base class are usually not intended to be executed. Their declaration in the base class just creates the C++ mechanisms so that when a general symbol table variable points to a specific symbol table object, the general function call will result in a call to the corresponding function of the specific object. For more information on this, see Appendix A, Section A.1.5.

Symbol table entry definition (symtab.h)

```
 9 typedef class SymtabEntryCls *PSymtabEntryCls;
10 class SymtabEntryCls   {
11   public:
12       virtual char    *get_name()
13                  {return name;};
14       virtual TypeCls *get_type()
15                  {return 0;}
16       virtual ValueCls *get_value()
17                  {return 0;}
18       virtual void    set_value(PTreeNodeCls*,ValueCls *);
19
20       virtual void    push_value() {;}
21             //For recursion: "stack frame"
22
23       virtual void    pop_value() {;}
24
25       virtual int     is_TypeAtt()
26                  {return 0;}
27       virtual int     is_ConstAtt()
28                  {return 0;}
29       virtual int     is_VarAtt()
30                  {return 0;}
31       virtual int     is_ProcAtt()
32                  {return 0;}
33       virtual int     is_FuncAtt()
34                  {return 0;}
35       virtual int     is_FParamAtt()
36                  {return 0;}
37       virtual int     is_FieldAtt()
38                  {return 0;}
39       virtual int     is_LabelAtt()
40                  {return 0;}
41       virtual ValueCls *evaluate();
42
43       virtual int     execute(PTreeNodeCls*)
44                  {return 0;}
45       virtual int     emit();
46
47       virtual void    print();
48
49       friend class    SymtabCls;
50   protected:
51       SymtabEntryCls() {;}
52       SymtabEntryCls(char *Name);
53
54       char            *name;
55 };
```

Type attribute entries (symtab.h)

```
58 typedef class TypeAttCls *PTypeAttCls;
59 class TypeAttCls : public SymtabEntryCls {
60    public:
61         TypeAttCls(char* Name, TypeCls *Type);
62         TypeCls         *get_type()
63                     {return type;}
64       int             is_TypeAtt()
65                     {return 1;}
66    private:
67         TypeCls         *type;
68 };
```

Note the syntax for deriving *TypeAttCls* from the base class. The keyword `public` in the declaration just means that `public` members of the base class remain so (when they are inherited) for the derived class.

Constant attribute entries (symtab.h)

```
73 typedef class ConstAttCls *PConstAttCls;
74 class ConstAttCls : public SymtabEntryCls,
75                      public LstSeqBldrCls {
76    public:
77       ConstAttCls()   {;}
78       ConstAttCls(char* Name,
79                     TypeCls *Type,
80                       ValueCls *Val);
81       TypeCls         *get_type()
82                     {return type;}
83       ValueCls        *get_value()
84                     {return value;}
85       void          push_value();
86
87       void          pop_value();
88
89       int             is_ConstAtt()
90                     {return 1;}
91       ValueCls        *evaluate()
92                     {return value;}
93       int             emit();
94    private:
95         TypeCls         *type;
96         ValueCls        *value;
97 };
```

Identifiers representing constants are stored in symbol tables, and so are derived from *SymtabEntryCls*. But later implementation details will indicate that identifiers representing constants will also need to be able to construct linked-lists of various kinds of objects. This functionality is provided by also deriving constants from a linked-list utility class, *LstSeqBldrCls*.

The first trivial constructor is called a **default** constructor. Its requirement is somewhat difficult to understand or even predict when programming in C++. Most programmers simply defer to the C++ compiler and place these constructors in the definition whenever demanded. The *get_type()* and *get_value()* functions are the usual "reporter" functions. *Push_value()* and *pop_value()* are used during recursive subprogram calls to simulate stack frame activities during program interpreting. The *evaluate()* and *emit()* functions are used during program interpreting and code generating, respectively. Evaluating constants is performed by just returning the constant value stored in the data member.

```
     Variable attribute entries (symtab.h)

101 typedef class VarAttCls *PVarAttCls;
102 class VarAttCls : public SymtabEntryCls {
103    public:
104         VarAttCls()      {;}
105         VarAttCls(char* Name, TypeCls *Type, ValueCls *Value);
106
107         TypeCls        *get_type()
108                    {return type;}
109         ValueCls       *get_value()
110                    {return value;}
111         void              set_value(PTreeNodeCls*,ValueCls *Value);
112
113         void              push_value();
114
115         void              pop_value();
116
117         int               is_constant()
118                    {return const_expr;}
119         void              set_is_constant()
120                    {const_expr = 1;}
121         int               get_ord()
122                    {return ord;}
123         int               is_VarAtt()
124                    {return 1;}
125         ValueCls       *evaluate()
126                    {return value;}
127         int               emit();
128
129         void              print();
130
131    private:
132         int               const_expr;  //boolean
133          TypeCls         *type;
134         ValueCls        *value;
135         int               ord;
136 };
```

Symbol table entries representing variables would certainly contain the data members found in entries for constants. The additional member *const_expr* is a flag indicating that the variable represents a value that can be determined at compile time. This greatly simplifies both the *evaluate()* and *emit()* member functions. The other data member *ord* contains ordinal information for identifiers representing enumerated constants. In addition to the usual collection of "reporter" and the push/pop functions that support recursive subprogram calls, there is a public member function *set_value()* used by statement nodes in the parse tree. The *set_is_constant()* is called primarily by parse tree objects during the construction of the parse tree.

```
    Procedure attribute entries (symtab.h)

    183 typedef class ProcAttCls *PProcAttCls;
    184 class ProcAttCls : public SymtabEntryCls {
    185    public:
    186        ProcAttCls()      {;}
    187
    188        ProcAttCls(char* Name,
    189                PTreeNodeCls *FormalParamStuff,
    190                    SymtabCls *ProcTab);
    191        int         is_ProcAtt()
    192                    {return 1;}
    193        FParamAttCls    *get_param_lst()
    194                    {return param_lst;}
    195        int             execute(PTreeNodeCls *);
    196
    197        int             emit();
    198        friend class    ProcDecCls;
    199                    // for setting block
    200    private:
    201        SymtabCls       *proc_tab;
    202        FParamAttCls    *param_lst;
    203        BlockCls        *block;
    204 };
```

The data members for objects representing procedures are made up of a symbol table containing all parameters local variables, a pointer to a linked-list of parameters and a pointer to the actual block of instructions contained in the procedure.

In the case that this object is representing a forward reference to a procedure, the block information object is left uninitialized. Parse tree objects of class *ProcDecCls* are friends. As such, they can initialize the *block* member when that information becomes available.

Functions are more complex than procedures.

- They have a return value and so also a return type.

- They are part of expressions rather than statement calls, and so it is convenient to update a linked-list of actual parameters during program interpreting.

- *FuncCallCls* must have friendly access to the actual parameter list prior to function evaluation.

```
   Function attribute entries (symtab.h)

209 typedef class FuncAttCls *PFuncAttCls;
210 class FuncAttCls : public SymtabEntryCls {
211    public:
212         FuncAttCls()      {;}
213         FuncAttCls(char* Name,
214                    PTreeNodeCls *FormalParamStuff,
215                       SymtabCls *FuncTab,
216                         PTreeNodeCls *Type);
217         int           is_FuncAtt()
218                    {return 1;}
219         int           is_forward_refd()
220                    {return !block;}
221         SymtabCls     *get_tab()
222                    {return func_tab;}
223         TypeCls       *get_type()
224                    {return type;}
225         ValueCls      *get_value()
226                       //Compile time.
227                    {return value;}
228         void          set_value(PTreeNodeCls*,ValueCls *Value);
229
230         void          push_value();
231
232         void          pop_value();
233
234         ValueCls      *evaluate();
235
236         int           emit();
237
238         friend class  FuncDecCls;
239                       //setting block
240         friend class  FuncCallCls;
241                       //setting a_param_lst
242    private:
243         SymtabCls     *func_tab;
244         FParamAttCls  *param_lst;
245         ActualParamLstCls  *a_param_lst;
246         BlockCls      *block;
247         TypeCls       *type;
248         ValueCls      *value;
249 };
```

```
Field attribute entries (symtab.h)

254 typedef class FieldAttCls *PFieldAttCls;
255 class FieldAttCls : public SymtabEntryCls {
256    public:
257         FieldAttCls()    {;}
258         FieldAttCls(char* FieldName,
259                        TypeCls *FieldType);
260         TypeCls        *get_type()
261                    {return type;}
262         int            is_FieldAtt()
263                    {return 1;}
264         int            emit();
265    private:
266         TypeCls        *type;
267         PSymtabEntryCls tag_var;
268              //Field is variant if non-zero.
269         FSigmaCls      *selector_list;
270 };
```

Fields have the following information associated with them.

- The first data member listed is the field type.

- In the event that the field is part of a variant structure, the data member *tag_var* points to the symbol table entry containing the tag variable or tag type information.

- *FSigmaCls* handles the messy task of keeping the various selector values in a nice order so that checking values at runtime is more efficient. Details can be found in Appendix C.

```
ScopeCls definition (symtab.h)

331 typedef class ScopeCls *PScopeCls;
332 class ScopeCls {
333    public:
334         static void set_vista(PSymtabCls NewSymtab);
335
336         static SymtabCls       *get_vista()
337                        {return vista;}
338    private:
339         static SymtabCls       *vista;
340 };
```

As noted in our earlier description of *ScopeCls* and also in Appendix A, Section A.2, static members such as *vista* and *get_vista()* are not associated with any particular *ScopeCls* object, and so are readily available by just calling the class functions.

Symbol table definition (symtab.h)

```
298 typedef class SymtabCls *PSymtabCls;
299 class SymtabCls : public LstSeqBldrCls {
300    public:
301         SymtabCls();
302         SymtabCls(PSymtabCls OuterTab);
303
304         int             insert(PSymtabEntryCls);
305
306         PSymtabEntryCls lookup(char*);
307
308         PSymtabEntryCls vista_lookup(char*);
309
310         void            push_values();
311
312         void            pop_values();
313
314         int             emit();
315
316         void            print();
317    private:
318         int             tab_size_index;
319         int             tablesize;
320                //set by ctr and grow
321         int             next_location;
322         int             *hashtable;
323         PSymtabEntryCls *symtab;
324                //N.B.:  pointers!
325         int             hash(char *);
326         void            grow();
327 };
```

We recall that symbol tables consist of a hash table and an array of pointers to the actual attribute entries, as displayed in Figure 7.8.

Symbol table data members consist of the following items.

- An index into the table containing the value of the last table activity.

- A specification of the current size of the two arrays. This number is also called the size of the symbol table.

- An index pointing to the next unused position in the array of pointers of pointers.

- The array of hash entries.

- The array of pointers to attributes.

The function members are as follows.

- The usual public constructors.

- The public access functions *insert()* and *lookup()*.

- Two private members, *hash()* and *grow()*. The hash function is called by the *insert()* to determine the entry into the table; the grow function is also called by *insert()* if the table has reached the magic two-thirds full level where hash collisions begin to frequently occur.

7.4.2   Implementation

```
SymtabEntryCls (symtab.C)

20 SymtabEntryCls :: SymtabEntryCls(char *Name) {
21     //cout << "SymtabEntryCls()" << endl;
22     name = Name;
23 }
24
25 void SymtabEntryCls :: set_value(PPTreeNodeCls Variable,
26                                     PValueCls Value) {
27     cout << "SymtabEntryCls::set_value() BASE CLASS!! " <<
28                                 Variable << Value << endl;
29 }
30
31 PValueCls SymtabEntryCls :: evaluate() {
32     hard.err("SymtabEntryCls::evaluate() BASECLASS!!");
33     return 0;
34 }
35
36 int SymtabEntryCls :: emit() {
37     cout << "SymtabEntryCls::emit() BASE CLASS!!!!" << endl;
38     return 0;
39 }
```

The *SymtabEntryCls* constructor will be called only during the construction of derived objects. Its major purpose is therefore to initialize the *name* data member to the identifier being stored in the table.

The virtual functions *set_value()* and *emit()* are examples of implementation of base class functions, which are not intended to be executed. Indeed, if they are executed it is because of a design problem in a derived class and the "BASE CLASS!!!!" error message will then indicate the existence of the problem.

```
TypeAttCls (symtab.C)

46 TypeAttCls :: TypeAttCls(char *Name, PTypeCls Type) :
47                                 SymtabEntryCls(Name){
48     //cout << "TypeAttCls" << endl;
49     type = Type;
50 }
```

TypeCls is derived from *SymtabEntryCls*. The peculiar-looking syntax in the second line of the listing above is the C++ mechanism for invoking the parent class constructor and passing it any information. In this case, name information is being sent to the parent.

```
ConstAttCls (symtab.C)

53 ConstAttCls :: ConstAttCls(char* Name,
54                                     TypeCls *Type,
55                                     ValueCls *Value)  :
56                                     SymtabEntryCls(Name){
57     //cout << "ConstAttCls(Name,Type,Vale)" << endl;
58     type  = Type;
59     if (!Value) {
60         value = new ValueCls(0);
61     } else {
62         value = Value;
63     }
64 }
65
66 void ConstAttCls :: push_value() {
67     //cout << "ConstAttCls::push_value()" << endl;
68     value = PValueCls(value -> prepend(new ValueCls(0)));
69 }
70
71 void ConstAttCls :: pop_value() {
72     //cout << "ConstAttCls::pop_value()" << endl;
73     value = PValueCls(value -> get_next());
74 }
```

- The *ConstAttCls* constructor creates a new *ValueCls* object if necessary. Since this usually occurs because a Pascal programmer has accessed a variable without previously initializing it, the *ValueCls* constructor can be given responsibility for sending a warning message and for selecting an appropriate initial value.

The following implementation details of *push()* and *pop()* behaviors for *ConstAttCls* are typical of what is done for all the symbol table entry classes. The definition of *ConstAttCls* above indicates that it is derived not only from the general *SymtabEntryCls* but also from the utility class *LstSeqBldrCls* providing linked-list behaviors. And since we are essentially implementing a stack in terms of a linked-list, a *push()* will amount to placing the value at the beginning of the list.

```
VarAttCls (symtab.C)

 77 VarAttCls :: VarAttCls(char *Name,
 78                        PTypeCls Type,
 79                             PValueCls Value) :
 80                                  SymtabEntryCls(Name){
 81     //cout << "VarAttCls(Name,Value) " << endl;
 82     type  = Type;
 83     if (!Value) {
 84         value = new ValueCls(0);
 85     } else {
 86         value = Value;
 87     }
 88 }
 89
 90
 91 void VarAttCls :: push_value() {
 92     //cout << "VarAttCls::push_value()" << endl;
 93     value = PValueCls(value -> prepend(new ValueCls(0)));
 94 }
 95
 96 void VarAttCls :: pop_value() {
 97     //cout << "VarAttCls::pop_value()" << endl;
 98     value = PValueCls(value -> get_next());
 99 }
100
101 void VarAttCls :: print() {
102     //cout << "VarAttCls::print()" << endl;
103     SymtabEntryCls::print();
104     cout << "   this "<< this << endl;
105     cout << "   const_expr" << const_expr << endl;
106     cout << "   type      " << type << endl;
107     cout << "   value     " << value ;
108     cout << "   " ; value -> print(); cout << endl;
109     cout << "   ord       " << ord << endl;
110 }
111
```

- The above *VarAttCls* constructor just initializes the data members.

- Coding details for push and pop values for *VarAttCls* are exactly the same as those used in *ConstAttCls*.

The next listing contains implementation details for *ProcAttCls*. Identifiers representing procedure names must be associated with a substantial amount of information, all of which must be gleaned by the parser during the procedure declaration process. Details of this can be found in Sections 6.2.1 and 9.5.

The first piece of information stored is a pointer to the subprogram's symbol table *ProcTab*, that is created during parsing by the declaration objects. It contains the identifiers of any formal parameters, inserted in the order specified by the Pascal subprogram header.

ProcAttCls (symtab.C)

```
155 ProcAttCls :: ProcAttCls(char* Name,
156                             PPTreeNodeCls FormalParamStuff,
157                               PSymtabCls ProcTab):
158                                 SymtabEntryCls(Name){
159     //cout << "ProcAttCls(Actual Declaration)" << endl;
160     proc_tab = ProcTab;
161     if (!proc_tab) {
162         hard.err("ProcAttCls() LOGIC ERROR 0");
163     }
164     if (!FormalParamStuff) {
165         param_lst = 0;
166     } else {
167         PIdentCls param_ident =
168                     PFParamStuffCls(FormalParamStuff)
169                         -> get_fpsl()
170                             -> get_seq_head()
171                                 -> get_param_grp()
172                                     -> get_ident_lst()
173                                         ->get_seq_head();
174
175         PSymtabEntryCls found_it =
176             proc_tab -> lookup(param_ident -> get_name());
177         if (!(found_it && found_it -> is_FParamAtt())) {
178             hard.err("ProcAttCls() LOGIC ERROR 1");
179         }
180         param_lst = PFParamAttCls(found_it);
181     }
182     //block = PBlockCls(Block); Set by ProcDecCls
183 }
```

- The commented assignment in the last line indicates that sufficient information about the actual parse tree representing the instructions for the subprogram has not yet been processed when this constructor is called.

- The data member for this information will be updated by the declaring *ProcDecCls* object as soon as all instruction and expression objects have been created.

- The long chain of function calls can probably best be understood by looking at the following grammar segment and then looking ahead to the corresponding definitions of the corresponding parse tree objects in Chapter 8. In particular, formal parameter stuff consists of parameter sections, header sections contain parameter groups, groups contain lists of identifiers representing the formal parameters, and the lists have leading identifiers.

Formal parameters (parser.gram)

```
                         Formal_param_stuff: /*empty*/
                           | LPARENTK Formal_p_sect_lst RPARENTK
                           ;
                         Formal_p_sect_lst: Formal_p_sect
                           | Formal_p_sect_lst SCTK Formal_p_sect
                           ;
                         Formal_p_sect: Param_group
                           | VARTK Param_group
                           | Proc_heading
                           | Func_heading
                           ;
                         Param_group: Ident_lst COLONTK Paramtype
                           ;


                         Paramtype: Ident
                           | ARRAYTK
                               LBRACKTK Index_spec_seq RBRACKTK
                                                     OFTK Paramtype
                           | PACKEDTK
                               ARRAYTK LBRACKTK Index_spec RBRACKTK
                                                     OFTK Ident
                           ;
                         Index_spec_seq: Index_spec
                           | Index_spec_seq SCTK Index_spec
                           ;
                         Index_spec:
                               Ident DDTK Ident COLONTK Ident
                                      ;
```

Once the first parameter identifier has been determined, the above code for the *ProcAttCls* constructor stores this information in the data member *param_lst*, unless the leading parameter is not in the procedure's symbol table. *Hard.err()* is used, since this could happen only if a design (rather and a programmer) error has occurred.

The listing of the *FieldAttCls* constructor, below, is included primarily for completeness. Note the following.

- The specific constructor arguments are prescribed by the corresponding production in the grammar.

- The specific values of these arguments are obtained from the parser's value stack and are therefore stored in corresponding value members for later use by the parse tree.

FieldAttCls (symtab.C)

```
246 FieldAttCls :: FieldAttCls(char* FieldName,
247                            TypeCls *FieldType):
248                            SymtabEntryCls(FieldName){
249     cout << "FieldAttCls(Name)" << endl;
250     type = FieldType;
251 }
```

We stated in Section 7.1 that object-oriented tables can take on an appropriate initial size and then expand if the particular compilation application requires more space. Most hashing algorithms will produce quality hashing values, based upon some implementation-dependent parameters. The particular algorithm used in this text assumes that the table contains a prime number of cells. So the listing below contains a number of possible prime integer values for use by the *SymtabCls* constructors when building various tables during program compilation.

SymtabCls sizes (symtab.C)

```
266 int tablesizes[] = { //primes so that hash works well
267     17,
268     37,
269     67,
270     131,
271     257,
272     521,
273     1031,
274     2053,
275     4099,
276     8209,
277     16411
278 };
```

The specific values in this table are based upon expected table sizes for typical programs written by beginning programmers. Modification of this table could and should be done if profiling information indicates an unsatisfactorily large number of changes of table size.

The following listing contains code used to create part of the standard identifier table. Its ultimate size can be determined initially, since no user identifiers are stored in it. The various arrays and symbol table entries are then constructed and initialized. Standard types and values are then constructed from parse tree objects in a way that closely parallels the construction of programmer defined types or values. These standard identifiers are then *insert()*ed into the table.

```
┌─────────────────────────────────────────────────────────────┐
│  SymtabCls constructor – standard identifiers (symtab.C)      │
└─────────────────────────────────────────────────────────────┘

281 SymtabCls :: SymtabCls() { //Standard Identifier table
282     //cout << "SymtabCls::() "<< this << endl;
283     tab_size_index = 2;  //Start it out big
284     tablesize = tablesizes[tab_size_index];
285     hashtable = new int[tablesize];
286     next_location = 1;
287         // sacrifice 0th spot - hashtable empty:NIL
288     symtab = new PSymtabEntryCls[tablesize]; // Note "P" !!!!
289     PSymtabEntryCls tmp = new SymtabEntryCls("      ");
290     for (int i=0; i<tablesize; i++) {
291         hashtable[i] = 0;
292         symtab[i] = tmp;
293     }
294
295     // create standard types integer, real and char
296     PTypeAttCls s_type;
297     s_type = new TypeAttCls("integer",std_type.integer());
298     this -> insert(s_type);
299     s_type = new TypeAttCls("real",std_type.real());
300     this -> insert(s_type);
301     s_type = new TypeAttCls("char",std_type.CHAR());
302     this -> insert(s_type);
303
304     // boolean values
305     PValueCls f_val  = new ValueCls(0);
306         PVarAttCls f_att =
307             new VarAttCls("false",std_type.boolean_type,f_val);
308         this -> insert(f_att);
309
310     PValueCls t_val  = new ValueCls(1);
311         PVarAttCls t_att =
312             new VarAttCls("true",std_type.boolean_type,t_val);
313         this -> insert(t_att);
314
315     PTypeAttCls b_type =
316             new TypeAttCls("boolean",std_type.boolean());
317         this -> insert(b_type);
318
319     // maxint
320     PValueCls m_val = new ValueCls(MAXINT);
321         PVarAttCls s_var =
322             new VarAttCls("maxint",std_type.integer(),m_val);
323         this -> insert(s_var);
324
325 }
```

Tables used throughout the rest of the compilation process all start at the first table size listed above. Since variable visibility/scope is implemented by requiring each table to point to the table associated with the enclosing scope of the present table, we therefore distinguish the constructor for these tables from those of the standard identifier table by using the enclosing table in the argument list.

SymtabCls constructor – general (symtab.C)

```
328 SymtabCls :: SymtabCls(PSymtabCls OuterTab) {
329     //cout << "SymtabCls::(OuterTab) "<< this << endl;
330     this -> LstSeqBldrCls::append(OuterTab);
331     tab_size_index = 0; //.. to begin with
332     tablesize = tablesizes[tab_size_index];
333     hashtable = new int[tablesize];
334     next_location = 1;
335     symtab = new PSymtabEntryCls[tablesize];
336     PSymtabEntryCls tmp = new SymtabEntryCls("    ");
337     for (int i=0; i<tablesize; i++) {
338         hashtable[i] = 0;
339         symtab[i] = tmp;
340     }
341 }
```

The dragon book [1, page 436] attributes the following hash function to P. J. Weinberger's C-compiler. The algorithm was tested using collections of identifiers, including the following.

- The most frequently occurring names and keywords in C programs.

- The set of nearly 1000 external names in the UNIX operating system kernel.

- A collection of extended C identifiers produced by C++.

- Nearly 1000 randomly generated character strings.

- A collection of words occurring in scientific English prose.

- A collection of names with the identical 4-character string as a suffix and a prefix.

It was a consistently a good performer (fast and few collisions) so long as the symbol table had a prime number of entries.

SymtabCls hash function (symtab.C)

```
411 int SymtabCls :: hash(char *s) {
412     //cout << "SymtabCls :: hashing for " << s ;
413     char* ss = s;
414     unsigned int h = 0, g;
415     for (; *ss != '\0'; ss++) {
416         h = (h << 4) + *ss;
417         if (g = h & 0xf0000000) {
418             h ^= g >> 24;
419             // fold top 4 bits onto ------X-
420             h ^= g;
421             // clear top 4 bits
422         }
423     }
424     return h % tablesize;
425 }
```

The following insert function is a good example of adaptive object behavior. Recall that this is a *Symtab* class function and that such functions are accessed through an object of that class, in this case, a symbol table. If a particular table has reached a load factor of two-thirds (see page 155), then we probably need to increase the size of the table by calling the *grow()* function (page 182).

SymtabCls insert function (symtab.C)

```
344 int SymtabCls :: insert(PSymtabEntryCls info) {
345     //cout << "SymtabCls::insert()" << endl;
346     //Return 0 if insert successful; else location in symtab.
347
348      //First, check tablesize and grow() if necessary....
349      if (next_location >= (tablesize * 2) / 3) {
350          //cout << "SymtabCls :: insert -- growing ....\n";
351          grow(); // automatically updates tablesize, so ...
352      }
353
354      //Look for open slot in the hashtable....
355      int try, hash_try;
356      char *Name = info -> name;
357      try = hash(Name);
358
359      while (hash_try = hashtable[try]) { //something's there
360          //Check to see if it's what we want to insert...
361          if (!strcmp((symtab[hash_try] -> name), Name)) {
362              return hash_try; //it's already there!
363          } else if (++try >= tablesize) {
364              //resolve collision by looking for open spot ...
365              try = 0; //wrap around
366          }
367          //Tables can be at most 2/3 full,
368      }
369      // So an open spot MUST be found
370      hashtable[try] = next_location;
371      symtab[next_location++] = info; //They're both pointers
372      return 0; // success!
373 }
```

We enter the table at the hash location and proceed to check all contiguous entries for a match. If no match occurs we insert the name at the first available location and indicate a successful insertion by returning the C++ true value of 0. An unsuccessful insertion can occur only if the identifier is already in the table, and this can be efficiently indicated by returning the (nonzero) location value of the existing entry.

```
     SymtabCls lookup function (symtab.C)

376 PSymtabEntryCls SymtabCls :: lookup(char *Name) {
377     //cout << "SymtabCls :: lookup for " << Name ;
378     int try, orig_try, hash_try;
379
380     orig_try = try = hash(Name);
381     hash_try = hashtable[try];
382     while (hash_try) {
383         if (!strcmp((symtab[hash_try] -> name), Name)) {
384             return symtab[hash_try]; //found it!
385         }
386         if (++try >= tablesize) try = 0; // wrap around
387         if (try == orig_try) {
388             return symtab[0];
389         } else {
390             hash_try = hashtable[try];
391         }
392     }
393         return 0; //Failure!
394 }
395
396 PSymtabEntryCls SymtabCls :: vista_lookup(char *Name) {
397     //cout << "vista_lookup for " << *Name << "\n";
398     PSymtabCls table = this;
399     //cout << "present_table " << table << endl;
400     PSymtabEntryCls look_info = table -> lookup(Name);
401     while ((table != 0) && (!look_info)) {
402 //cout <<"looking back up the list of tables \n";
403 //cout << " table  " << table;
404         table = PSymtabCls(table -> get_next());
405         look_info = table -> lookup(Name);
406     }
407     return look_info;
408 }
```

The two kinds of lookup behaviors needed for symbol tables are described in the code above. The ideas for this function come primarily from Stroustrup's implementation of tables in the C++ translator. The function *lookup()* first looks directly at the table entry specified by the hash algorithm. If the entry does not match the required identifier, then it is assumed that a collision may have occurred during insertion and the nonzero entries immediately following in the table are then also compared. Note that searching in a table is not terminated by the physical end of the table, since the index will wrap back to the beginning if necessary. The *vista_lookup()* function first performs a standard lookup for the identifier in the present table. If that fails, it then calls the *lookup()* function for each enclosing table.

SymtabCls grow function (symtab.C)

```
430 void SymtabCls :: grow() {
431     //cout << "SymtabCls::grow()" << endl;
432     PSymtabEntryCls* tmp_s_tab;
433         // (temporary) larger symtab array.
434     if (!(tab_size_index < LEN(tablesizes) -1)) {
435         hard.err("Compiler tables too small");
436     } else {
437         tablesize = tablesizes[++tab_size_index];
438         delete hashtable;
439         hashtable = new int[tablesize];  //next size
440         tmp_s_tab = new PSymtabEntryCls[tablesize];
441             // array! not constructor!
442         for (int i = 0; i<tablesize; i++) {
443             hashtable[i] = 0;
444             tmp_s_tab[i] = ((i < next_location) ?
445                 symtab[i] : symtab[0]);
446         }
447         for (i = 1; i < next_location; i++) {
448             for (int try = hash(symtab[i] -> name);
449                     hashtable[try];
450                         try = (try + 1) % tablesize);
451             hashtable[try] = i;
452         }
453         delete symtab;
454         symtab = tmp_s_tab;
455     }
456 }
```

Naturally, we do not want to impose arbitrary size limitations on source programs. *SymtabCls* must therefore have some mechanism for creating tables of appropriate sizes and then allowing the tables to increase in size as source program complexity might require. If a table needs to grow, it first creates the necessary hash table and pointer tables and then rehashes each symbol table entry in the present table into the new table structure. It then deletes the old tables and again initializes its data members to the new arrays.

7.5   Exercises

1. Check your favorite Pascal text for answers to the following questions.

   (a) What are the maximum and minimum values possible for char?

   (b) In what order are the char values arranged on your computing system?

   (c) What are the ordinal values of true and false?

   (d) What integer value has an ordinal value of 0?

2. For each of the following functions, specify the allowable input and corresponding output types.

   (a) *abs()*

   (b) *sqr()*

   (c) *sqrt()*

   (d) *float()*

3. Sections 7.1.1 – 7.1.1 contain segments of a program used to assist in the design of the symbol table classes. Assume that the following list of tables is created during the compilation of this program.

   - Standard identifier table

   - Globals table

   - Table of fields

   - Subprogram symbol tables

   (a) Draw an object diagram illustrating how each of these tables would look at the end of the parsing stage.

   (b) Indicate the sequence of creation of the various tables by the use of a timing diagram. Make the horizontal (time) axis a function of source program statement numbers rather than seconds.

4. Complete the design of *FuncAttCls* by doing each of the following items.

   (a) Using *ProcDecCls* as a pattern, specify and implement *FuncDecCls* constructor that is responsible for constructing the FuncAttCls symbol table entry.

   (b) Specify the main *FuncAttCls* constructor.

   (c) Specify any *FuncAttCls* public member functions. Recall that Pascal functions are not called by statements but used in expressions. This means that *FuncAttCls* would not have an *execute()* member function. What would it have instead?

5. Complete the design of *LabelAttCls* by doing each of the following items.

   (a) Specify the main *LabelAttCls* constructor.

   (b) Specify any *LabelAttCls* public member functions.

   (c) Summarize your design work using a C++ class definition format.

6. (a) Specify the definition for the *FParamAttCls* class.

   (b) Write C++ code for the constructors for *FParamAttCls*.

7. (a) Specify the definition for the *LabelAttCls* class.

   (b) Write C++ code for the constructors for *LabelAttCls*

8. This exercise deals with the task of testing the symbol table module.

   (a) Test the performance of the hash function by entering the following kinds
       of identifiers and noting when collisions occur.

       i. Identifiers that are five characters long and that differ only on the
          last character.

       ii. Identifiers that differ only in the first character.

       iii. Identifiers chosen at random from a dictionary. There are a num-
            ber of on-line dictionaries available for most systems. It would be
            instructive to do this exercise with a large number of identifiers if
            such resources are available. In this case also keep track of timing
            information.

   (b) Test the lookup function. Enter an identifier and perform a lookup on
       the same identifier and one differing in only a single location.

   (c) Test the vista-lookup function.

       i. Create two tables, linked by the *LstSeqBldrCls* mechanisms.

       ii. Insert an identifier into the outermost table and search for it, starting
           in the inner table.

       iii. Search for an identifier that is in the inner table.

       iv. Search for an identifier that is in neither table.

   (d) Test the *grow()* feature of *SymtabCls*

       i. Design a sequence of events that will verify that a *SymtabCls* object
          will actually increase its size. Be sure to address the issue of preser-
          vation of data: Is the stuff in the bigger table *exactly* the same as it
          was in the smaller? When dealing with pointers, an exact copy of
          something is *not* the same thing!

       ii. Run your test.

   (e) Comment on the appropriateness of the set of prime numbers chosen
       for the various table sizes. Gather sample source programs from your
       environment and estimate the number of times tables must *grow()*.

9. (**CLIP** Project)

   (a) Design and implement the symbol table entry classes necessary for **CLIP**.

   (b) Implement and test a symbol table class for **CLIP**.

Parse Tree Nodes

```
┌─────────────────────────────────────────────────────┐
│  Topics:                                            │
│                                                     │
│      •  Discovering objects used in parse trees     │
│                                                     │
│      •  Organizing parse tree objects into classes  │
│                                                     │
│      •  Specifying the various parse tree classes    │
│                                                     │
└─────────────────────────────────────────────────────┘
```

We noted in Chapter 1 that in traditional compiler construction the compiler front end most often communicates with the code generator by means of a data structure called an **intermediate representation**, or **IR**. Even for non object-oriented compiler implementations this IR is often a tree structure, called a *parse tree*, in which each node represents an important aspect of the original Pascal source program. Many of these nodes need data, called **semantic attributes**, that have been determined by one or more children. Various mechanisms are used to allow this information to move up, or be **synthesized**, through the tree and stored as fields or members of the appropriate syntax tree nodes. There are also a few situations where Pascal program information needs to move down from parent node to a child. Semantic information that is **inherited** from a parent node is traditionally passed down the tree during one of a number of traversals made of the parse tree.

In this text, the IR is taken to be a parse tree of a very special sort. Each node of the tree is an *object* that contains not only member data for storing the traditional semantic information but also member *functions* that are capable of imposing the Pascal language specifications, both at compile time and at execution time. We sometimes use the term **semantic objects** to emphasize the new activities of these nodes.

The object-oriented approach makes a considerable difference in the way that we construct an interpreter. Since the IR consists of *objects*, and since each object has member functions that can prescribe the object's activity during the execution of the corresponding Pascal program segment, the tree can *itself* be executed! Not only that, but Pascal dynamic semantics normally imposed at run time can now be included as member functions of the very objects doing the execution. Chapter 10 contains the details of the member functions that support such interpreter behavior for the various parse tree objects.

The object-oriented approach allows another innovation. In this compiler the code generator does not even exist, at least not in the way traditional compilers define and use code generators. Since each *object* in the IR has been given the ability to emit its own code, *the* code generator is actually an *aggregate* of all the objects' emitter member functions, that are invoked for each object by the corresponding parent node's emitter function! Chapter 11 contains a description of SPARC ® code associated with each of the various parse tree nodes.

8.1   Discovering Parse Tree Objects

Roughly speaking, the task of analysis is to discover the appropriate classes for the problem domain, while the design phase is responsible for the specification of class communication and membership. The analysis method we use almost exclusively in this text is called **definition by abstraction**, a general procedure of first discovering the *objects* and then arranging them into clusters that ultimately become *classes*.

Of course, the successful use of this method depends on being able to accurately and completely answer the following questions.

1. What are the required objects?

2. What are the criteria used to arrange or cluster the objects?

The following are clearly requirements of whatever method we might use to answer these questions.

- The method must be **complete**. It need not generate every required object, but at least one object of each important class should be produced at the current level of analysis.

- The method must produce objects in an **orderly manner**. Since the overall goal is to use clusters of objects to aid in the definition of classes, related objects should bubble up at approximately the same point in the process.

- The method should be **informative**. Insight into class *behavior* is often obtained by looking at object behaviors common to a cluster. The process of generating objects should therefore also provide information about how the various objects behave.

One obvious technique for discovering parse tree objects would be to simply start at the top of the grammar and make a list of all the nonterminals. Unfortunately, this produces a kind of maximal set of objects, blindly suggesting their presence at parse tree locations that may not even be needed. It also gives very little understanding of required object behavior or data members. So it provides a complete set of objects but does not give any real insight into ultimate class membership or behavior.

Another object-generating technique, that we used in Chapter 7, is the tracing of scenarios. Objects are certainly encountered using this method, and the order in which objects are encountered during a simulated execution of the system really does give insight into what the classes should be, how those classes are related to each other, and what behaviors are appropriate. But if the system is complex, completeness can often be obtained only by tracing a large number of scenarios. Such multiple scenario activity obviously makes the organization of the various objects a much more difficult task, since the objects have now been encountered in parallel strings. Scenarios seem to give information about the third property, above, and provide only a partial answer to the questions of how to generate a complete set of objects and how to organize them into classes.

A third approach to the generation of objects is to try to specify categories of objects, based upon the structure of the language. In Pascal, the various kinds of objects that might occur in a parse tree would fall into one of the categories listed below.

- Program productions

- Declaration productions

- Type productions

- Statement productions

- Expression productions

- Name and literal productions

Each of these categories will in fact become a subclass of the general class of parse tree nodes. So we need to examine the various parse tree nodes and place in the parent node those data members and member functions that are common to all nodes. Specific data members or member functions for each category can then be defined for each of the subcategories.

Somewhat surprisingly, the language *grammar* provides yet another way to solve the completeness problem. Actually, it is the *parser* generated by the grammar that we need to watch most closely. Since our parser recognizes programs and therefore builds parse trees from the bottom up, the first grammar productions to be completely recognized are those specifying or containing references to the language tokens. These tokens most often correspond to parser tree nodes, which are the leaves of the tree. The next productions to be completely recognized are those that call these token-productions. Parse tree nodes for these productions will be produced when these lowestlevel leaf productions are recognized. And this process continues until the highestlevel program production has been accepted.

One way to encounter a complete set of parse tree node objects would therefore be to mimic the parser recognition of process: Consider the lowest level productions first and then work carefully up the grammar, making certain that all lower level nodes have been identified below the present node.

- Start with a widely used lowest level production.

- Add the corresponding leaf to the list of objects.

- Then move "up and down" the grammar.

  - Find a production up one level that calls one of the present production.

  - Trace down the grammar. Find all leaves referenced by this production and add the objects for parse tree nodes and leaves using the order in which they would be recognized by the parser.

The discussion above is intended to be descriptive rather than the specification of an actual algorithm. Essentially, the method tries to discover important parse tree leaves and their ancestors first. Once all or most of the leaves have been specified, higherlevel objects connecting the various leaves or leaf ancestors are discovered. Essentially, moving up in the grammar corresponds to moving up in the parse tree. Moving down in the grammar, while not really mimicking corresponding tree structure, will terminate at nodes that either have already been discovered or will be candidates for new objects. Then moving back up the grammar from these produces a list of objects, gives insight into their behaviors and clues as to appropriate classification. Even rather complex language constructs rarely require more than a half-dozen major up-steps.

A good place to start this process would be at a leaf node that is used throughout the tree. One leaf meeting this requirement is that of an identifier. Let's therefore begin the up/down discovery process by looking for a higherlevel production that calls the grammar production

```
Ident: IDENTIFIERTK
    ;
```

for *Ident.*

Since one of the productions

```
Variable: Ident Actual_param_stuff
    | Variable LBRACKTK Expr_seq RBRACKTK
    | Variable DOTTK Ident
    | Variable UPARROWTK
    ;
```

for *Variable* contains the nonterminal *Ident* on its right side, this should be an appropriate production on which to work our way toward additional leaves.

First, let's introduce some terminology that assists in organizing our work. We say that a nonterminal α **precedes** the nonterminal β if α occurs on the right side of a production for β, and we indicate this by the following notation.

$$\alpha \prec \beta$$

So, for example, the previous production for *Variable* indicates that

$$Ident \prec Variable \tag{8.1}$$

since *Ident* will be recognized by the parser before *Variable*.

A word of caution is in order. Precedence is not even a partial order in the mathematical sense. Language grammars containing recursive productions often produce a circular precedence string. A certain amount of subjective judgment must then be exercised to try to break the circle into one or more linear precedence strings. Of course, when arranging these linear precedence substrings for the C++ compiler, we must appease the compiler by inserting forward references to objects or classes that occur later on the precedence circle. Indeed, the smaller number of forward references demanded by C++, the better the circle cutting has been performed.

Now let's move down the productions. The *Variable* productions, above, also give the following precedence.

$$Actual\_param\_stuff \prec Variable \tag{8.2}$$

And the following grammar segment

```
Actual_param_stuff:  /*empty*/
    | LPARENTK Actual_param_lst RPARENTK
    ;
Actual_param_lst: Actual_param
    | Actual_param_lst COMMATK Actual_param
    ;
Actual_param: Expr
```

provides information about additional nonterminals that precede *Actual_param_stuff* (and therefore *Variable*).

$$Expr \prec Actual\_param \prec Actual\_p\_lst \prec Actual\_p\_stuff \tag{8.3}$$

Now let's look at grammar productions dealing with *Expr*. Section 6.2.1 contains a number of productions that boil down to the following.

```
Expr: Simple_expr
    | Simple_expr RelationalOp Simple_expr
    ;
    RelationalOp : EQTK
        | ...
        ;
Simple_expr: Term
        | PLUSTK Term
        | MINUSTK Term
        | Simple_expr Add_op Term
        ;
        Add_op: PLUSTK
            | ...
```

```
            ;
    Term: Factor
        | Term Mul_op Factor
        ;
        Mul_op: ASTERTK
            | ...
            ;
        Factor: Unsigned_lit
            | Variable
            | ...
            ;
            Unsigned_lit: Unsigned_number
                | STRINGTK
                | NILTK
                ;
            Unsigned_number: UNSIGNEDINTTK
                | UNSIGNEDREALTK
                ;
```

This grammar segment provides the following precedence string

$$Unsigned\_lit \prec Factor \prec Term \prec Simple\_expr \prec Expr \qquad (8.4)$$

that suggests parse tree leaves for the various Pascal literals. Notice also the additional precedence strings

$$Relational\_op \quad \prec \quad Expr \qquad (8.5)$$

$$Add\_op \quad \prec \quad Simple\_expr \qquad (8.6)$$

$$Mul\_op \quad \prec \quad Term \qquad (8.7)$$

that, though they do not result in the production of parse tree leaves, certainly do behave similarly to leaf-producing productions in that they call no further grammar productions.

The productions

```
        Factor: Unsigned_lit
            | Variable
            | Set
            | NOTTK Factor
            | LPARENTK Expr RPARENTK
            ;
```

for *Factor* sends us either back to *Variable* or to *Expr* or call the productions related to *Set*. The following productions are related to *Set*.

```
        Set: LBRACKTK Member_stuff RBRACKTK
            ;
            Member_stuff: /*empty*/
                | Member_lst
                ;
            Member_lst: Member
```

```
                    | Member_1st COMMATK Member
                    ;
                Member: Expr
                    | Expr DDTK Expr
                    ;
```

The above grammar segments allow us to complete the precedence strings for *Expr*

$$Member \prec Member\_1st \prec Member\_stuff \prec Set \prec Factor \qquad (8.8)$$

since *Member* takes us back to the highest level *Expr* production.

A quick look up the grammar for additional productions using *Ident* yields the two important productions listed below.

```
        Type_def: Ident EQTK Type
        ;
        Var_dec: Ident_1st COLONTK Type
        ;
```

The nonterminal *Type* on the right side of each of these productions suggest that we next need to work down the grammar for *Type* objects.

Section 6.2.1 also contains the listings of the various productions related to the declaration of user-defined types. These can be summarized as follows.

```
    Type: Simple_type
        | PACKEDTK Structured_type
        | Structured_type
        | UPARROWTK IDENTIFIERTK
        ;
        Simple_type: LPARENTK Ident_1st RPARENTK
            | Constant DDTK Constant
            | Ident
            ;
        Ident_1st: Ident
            | Ident_1st COMMATK Ident
            ;
        Constant: Unsigned_number
            | PLUSTK Unsigned_number
            | MINUSTK Unsigned_number
            | Ident
            | PLUSTK Ident
            | MINUSTK Ident
            | STRINGTK
            ;
        Structured_type: ARRAYTK LBRACKTK Index_t_1st RBRACK OFTK Type
            | RECORDTK Field_1st ENDTK
            | SETTK OFTK Type
            ;
        Index_t_1st: Simple_type
            | Index_t_1st COMMATK Simple_type
            ;
```

These productions suggest that several levels of precedence strings are required. The highest level precedence relations are clearly as follows.

$$Simple\_type \quad \prec \quad Type \tag{8.9}$$

$$Structured\_type \quad \prec \quad Type \tag{8.10}$$

The next-level relations specify nonterminals that precede *Simple_type* and *Structured_type*.

$$Ident \prec Ident\_lst \prec Simple\_type \tag{8.11}$$

$$Constant \prec Simple\_type \tag{8.12}$$

$$Simple\_type \prec Index\_type \prec Index\_t\_lst \prec Structured\_type \tag{8.13}$$

$$Field\_lst \prec Structured\_type \tag{8.14}$$

Parse tree structures representing record structures are quite complex, especially when they must include provision for user-defined variants. Section 6.2.1 described the following productions for such structures.

```
Field_lst: Fixed_part Variant_part
    ;
    Fixed_part: Field
        | Fixed_part SCTK Field
        ;
        Field: /*empty*/
            | Ident_lst COLONTK Type
            ;
    Variant_part: /* empty */
        | CASETK Ident OFTK Variant_seq
        | CASETK Ident COLONTK Ident OFTK Variant_seq
        ;
        Variant_seq: Variant
            | Variant_seq SCTK Variant
            ;
            Variant: /*empty*/
                |Case_label_lst COLONTK
                        LPARENTK Field_lst RPARENTK
            ;
```

The corresponding highest level precedence strings are as follows.

$$Fixed\_part \quad \prec \quad Field\_lst \tag{8.15}$$

$$Variant\_part \quad \prec \quad Field\_lst \tag{8.16}$$

And the lower level precedence strings

$$Ident\_lst \prec Field \prec Fixed\_part \tag{8.17}$$

$$Ident \prec Variant\_part \tag{8.18}$$

$$Case\_label\_lst \prec Variant \prec Variant\_seq \prec Variant\_part \qquad (8.19)$$

follow directly.

Since all the nonterminals below *Type* have been encountered, it is time to look up the grammar for another production higher than *Ident* or *Variable* or *Expr*. The next such production seems to be the following.

```
Assignment: Variable ASGTK Expr
```

And the major production directly above this one is the specification of all statements.

```
Compound_stmt: BEGINTK Statement_seq ENDTK
    ;
Statement_seq: Statement
    | Statement_seq SCTK Statement
    ;
Statement: /*empty*/
    | Assignment
    | IFTK Expr THENTK Statement
    | IFTK Expr THENTK Statement
      ELSETK Statement
    | CASETK Expr OFTK Case_lst ENDTK
    | FORTK Ident ASGTK Expr Dir Expr DOTK Statement
    | WHILETK Expr DOTK Statement
    | REPEATTK Statement_seq UNTILTK Expr
    | WITHTK Rec_var_lst DOTK Statement
    | WriteStmt
    | Procedure_call
    | Label COLONTK Statement
    | Compound_stmt
    | GOTOTK Label
    ;
Assignment: Variable ASGTK Expr
    ;
Case_lst: Case_lst_elem
    | Case_lst SCTK Case_lst_elem
    ;
Case_lst_elem: Case_label_lst COLONTK Statement
    ;
Case_label_lst: Case_label
    | Case_label_lst COMMATK Case_label
    ;
Case_label: Constant
    ;
Dir: TOTK
    | DOWNTOTK
    ;
Rec_var_lst: Record_var
    | Rec_var_lst COMMATK Record_var
    ;
Record_var: Variable
    ;
```

```
Procedure_call: Ident Actual_param_stuff
    ;
    Actual_param_stuff:  /*empty*/
        | LPARENTK Actual_param_lst RPARENTK
        Actual_param_lst: Actual_param
            | Actual_param_lst COMMATK Actual_param
            ;
            Actual_param: Expr


WriteStmt: WRITETK LPARENTK Write_params_lst RPARENTK
    | WRITELNTK LPARENTK Write_params_lst RPARENTK
    ;
    Write_params_lst:  Write_params
        | Write_params_lst COMMATK Write_params
        ;
        Write_params: Expr
            | Expr COLONTK Expr  /* integer */
            | Expr COLONTK Expr COLONTK Expr  /* real */
            ;
```

The highest precedence strings are determined in the same way as they were for *Expr* and *Type*.

$$Statement \prec Statement\_seq \prec Compound\_stmt \tag{8.20}$$

$$Assignment \quad \prec \quad Statement \tag{8.21}$$

$$Case\_lst \quad \prec \quad Statement \tag{8.22}$$

$$Dir \quad \prec \quad Statement \tag{8.23}$$

$$Write\_stmt \quad \prec \quad Statement \tag{8.24}$$

$$Procedure\_call \quad \prec \quad Statement \tag{8.25}$$

$$Label \quad \prec \quad Statement \tag{8.26}$$

Of all the nonterminals above, only *Case_list* has a precedence string containing new information. The grammar segment

```
Case_lst: Case_lst_elem
    | Case_lst SCTK Case_lst_elem
    ;
    Case_lst_elem: /*empty*/
        | Case_label_lst COLONTK Statement
        ;
        Case_label_lst: Case_label
            | Case_label_lst COMMATK Case_label
            Case_label: Constant
                ;
```

suggests the following precedence string.

$$Const \prec CaseLabelLst \prec CaseElt \prec CaseLst \tag{8.27}$$

We are now ready to look up for additional grammar productions, not yet considered. The two immediately above the *Statement_seq* production are in fact the highest level productions.

```
Program: PROGRAMTK Ident External_files SCTK Block DOTTK
    ;
    Block:
        Label_dec_part
        Const_def_part
        Type_def_part
        Var_dec_part
        Proc_fun_dec_part
        Compound_stmt
    ;
```

Label declarations simply amount to storing *numeric* identifiers in a particular symbol table. There are no new parse tree objects needed for this activity. Constant definitions also require no new parse tree objects, since productions for constants are essentially a subset of expression productions, and *VarAttCls* objects representing constants differ from variables only by setting the *const_expr* field. Type definition does require a *TypeDef* object, but it is purely a service object and does not *itself* get placed into the parse tree. The specification and implementation of this kind of object is therefore placed in a *defdec* module rather than *p_tree*. The same thing is true for Variable declarations and, to some extent, for the declaration of functions and procedures. However, the declaration of such subprogram segments does require a surprisingly complex set of parse tree objects that represent formal parameter specification in all its generality.

So the highest level precedence strings are as follows.

$$Ident \quad \prec \quad Program \qquad (8.28)$$

$$External\_files \quad \prec \qquad (8.29)$$

$$Block \quad \prec \qquad (8.30)$$

And *Block* can be described by the strings below.

$$Label\_dec \quad \prec \quad Block \qquad (8.31)$$

$$Const\_def \quad \prec \quad Block \qquad (8.32)$$

$$Type\_def \quad \prec \quad Block \qquad (8.33)$$

$$Var\_dec \quad \prec \quad Block \qquad (8.34)$$

$$Proc\_fun\_dec \quad \prec \quad Block \qquad (8.35)$$

$$Statement\_part \quad \prec \quad Block \qquad (8.36)$$

Of these nonterminals, only *Proc_fun_dec* will introduce any significant new parse tree nodes. The grammar segment describing the declaration of procedures or functions is somewhat complex.

The highest level productions

```
Proc_or_fun_dec:  Proc_heading SCTK Body SCTK
   |  Func_heading SCTK Body SCTK
   ;
Proc_heading: PROCEDURETK Ident Formal_param_stuff
   ;
Body: Block
   |  FORWARDTK
   ;
Func_heading: FUNCTIONTK Ident Function_form
   ;
      Function_form: /* empty */
         |  Formal_param_stuff COLONTK Ident
         ;
```

give rise to the following two precedence strings.

$$F\_param\_stuff \prec Proc\_heading \prec Proc\_or\_fun\_dec \qquad (8.37)$$

$$F\_param\_stuff \prec Func\_form \prec Func\_heading \prec Proc\_or\_fun\_dec \qquad (8.38)$$

The next level of productions, dealing directly with formal parameters,

```
Formal_param_stuff: /*empty*/
   |  LPARENTK Formal_p_sect_lst RPARENTK
   ;
Formal_p_sect_lst: Formal_p_sect
   |  Formal_p_sect_lst SCTK Formal_p_sect
   ;
Formal_p_sect: Param_group
   |  VARTK Param_group
   |  Proc_heading
   |  Func_heading
   ;
Param_group: Ident_lst COLONTK Paramtype
   ;
Paramtype: Ident
   |  ARRAYTK LBRACKTK Index_spec_seq RBRACKTK
                              OFTK Paramtype
   |  PACKEDTK
         ARRAYTK LBRACKTK Index_spec_seq RBRACKTK
                              OFTK Paramtype
   ;
Index_spec_seq: Index_spec
   |  Index_spec_seq SCTK Index_spec
   ;
Index_spec:
      Ident DDTK Ident COLONTK Ident
      ;
```

then give us our last collection of precedence strings.

$$Param\_gp \prec Formal\_p\_sec \prec Formal\_p\_lst \prec F\_param\_stuff \qquad (8.39)$$

$$Index\_spec \prec Index\_spec\_sec \prec Param\_type \prec Param\_gp \qquad (8.40)$$

8.1.1   Leaf Objects

The precedence relations in the previous section certainly indicate that there are two primary lowest level productions in our Pascal grammar: *Ident* and *Unsigned_lit*. Our first task is therefore to specify as much as possible about the objects that correspond to these leaves.

Identifiers

The grammar production

        Ident: IDENTIFIERTK

for *Ident* corresponds to the following parse tree leaf object.

Ident. This object should take the current value of the lexeme and store it as a member for future access. The naive scheme of immediately storing the lexeme value in "the" symbol table is not appropriate in a larger compiler having multiple symbol tables. Indeed, the selection of the appropriate symbol table is often not even possible at the early, bottom-up recognition of many identifiers.

There does not seem to be any other kind of object playing the same role. This suggests that we should define a class *IdentCls* consisting of a single constructor *IdentCls()*, that directly accesses the lexeme value corresponding to the recognized identifier.

Literals

The grammar contains the following productions for literals.

- UNSIGNEDINTTK

- UNSIGNEDREALTK

- STRINGTK

- NILTK

IntLiteral. The actual lexeme value corresponding to *UNSIGNEDINTTK* is really a string of characters representing an integer.

RealLiteral. The actual lexeme value corresponding to *UNSIGNEDREALTK* is one of a number of possible strings of characters representing a real number.

StringLiteral. The lexeme passed by the scanner actually contains the enclosing apostrophe " ' " character. These will need to be removed from the actual string.

NilLiteral. The lexeme value for this literal need not be stored.

Actually, the productions also suggest that we should define a class, *LiteralCls*, that will encapsulate the lexemes and corresponding types for *Integer, Real*, string and NIL literals. A new *LitFactor* object would then be used to convert the *Unsigned_number*, STRINGTK and NILTK to expressions, as suggested by precedence 8.4 and illustrated in Figure 8.1.

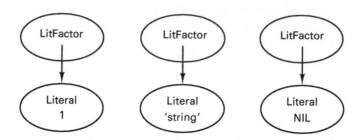

Figure 8.1. Objects for Literals

8.1.2   Expression Objects

It seems fairly clear from the precedence strings 8.4 through 8.7, that there are a large number of different kinds of expression objects available for the construction of any given parse tree. All these objects would be instances of subclasses of an *ExprCls*, as suggested by our version of King's taxonomy. Indeed, multiple or lengthy precedence strings often indicate the possibility of inheritance situations based on the existence of similar data or function members. Almost all authors of program(ming) language(s) texts agree that there are two things common to all expressions.

1. Every expression must have a type. Though this may not be true in some languages, it certainly holds in all strongly typed languages.

2. Every expression must have a mechanism for evaluating that expression.

So all expression objects would have a member specifying the *type* of the expression and a function allowing for expression evaluation during compilation, and source code emitting time. It therefore makes sense to specify that *ExprCls* is a parent class consisting of at least these two members and then require that all expression objects be instances of other classes that are derived from this one class.

Literal Expressions

We have already described the need for an object to convert the various kinds of literals to card-carrying expressions.

LitFactor. We can convert each of the four kinds of Pascal literals to an expression by simply providing it with a type and the ability to be evaluated. This can be easily accomplished by deriving *LitFactorCls* directly from *ExprCls* as described directly above.

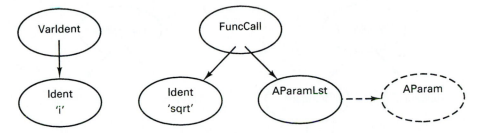

Figure 8.2. Expression Objects for Identifiers

Primitive Expressions

The precedence string 8.1 indicates that the *Ident* object needs to have a *Variable* parent object sitting above it on the parse tree. Actually it is a bit more difficult than that, as evidenced by the following scenario.

Expressions on the right side of an assignment statement like

$$j := i$$

or

$$j := rand()$$

are built up from an identifier and recognized by the following production.

```
Variable: Ident Actual_param_stuff
```

Of course the "i" and "rand" will first be recognized by the parser as an *Ident* and so will be represented by an *IdentCls* object. What is needed here is another object to convert the rather sterile identifier into an expression. In exactly the same way as we converted literals to expressions, we just define tree objects *VarIdent* and *FuncCall* and insert them into the tree, as illustrated in Figure 8.2. Most function calls such as

$$CFac = gcd(a, b)$$

utilize actual parameters. Actual parameters are represented by *ActualParam* objects that are linked and referenced by an *ActualParamLst* object. This is also illustrated in Figure 8.1.

If a variable like *Scores* is an array, then assignment statements such as

$$j := Scores[i]$$

are possible. The expression on the right side of the assignment statement needs to be represented in the parse tree in such a way that later expression behaviors

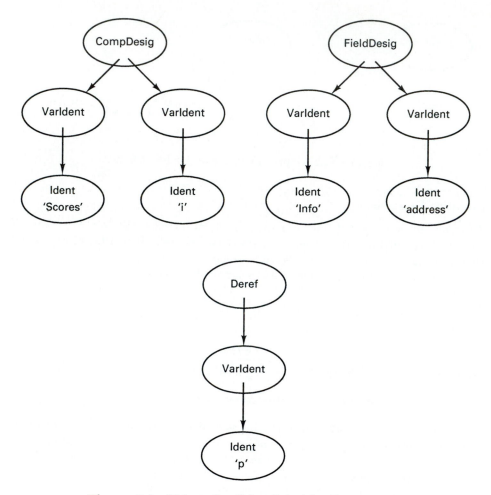

Figure 8.3. Objects for Other Primitive Expressions

know an array component is being specified. Notice that the second production of the *Variable* production is responsible for recognizing this kind of expression. What is needed here is a *ComponentDesig* object that will point to the *VarIdent* object representing *Scores* and the *VarIdent* object representing *i*, as illustrated in Figure 8.3

Similarly a field designator object and a pointer dereferencing object are needed for expressions like *Info.address* or *p^* that specify a particular field of a record or the value of an anonymous variable.

The following objects therefore need to be added to our list.

VarIdent. This object should have data members to store the underlying identifier, and the symbol table entry specified by the Pascal scope rules.

FuncCall. This object has the same members as *VarIdent*, except for an additional pointer to the subtree of actual parameters used in the function call.

ActualParamLst. This object represents the head of a list of actual parameters. It should be able to automatically append additional actual parameters to its list as they are encountered in the recursive production for *Actual_param_lst*.

ActualParam. This is essentially any possible expression.

ComponentDesig. These objects point on the left to identifier representing the entire array and on the right to an expression whose value represents a particular component of the array. Actually for multidimensional arrays, these objects are placed one above the other. For example, an expression like a[i,j] would consist of a *ComponentDesig* pointing at *a* on the left and *i* on the right. This set of nodes is pointed to on the left by another *ComponentDesig* object directly above. This second object then points to the *j* on the right.

FieldDesig. All that is required here are pointers on the left to the record identifier and on the right to the field identifier.

Dereference. This object has only one pointer to the identifier being dereferenced.

Expressions Constructed from Multiplicative Operators

Expressions such as

```
i * 2
i div divisor
bool1 and bool2
```

are built from simpler expressions by using any one of the five multiplicative operators, below.

$$*, /, div, mod, and$$

The following productions

```
Term:   Term Mul_op Factor
    ;
    Mul_op:  ASTERTK
        |   SLASHTK
        |   ...
```

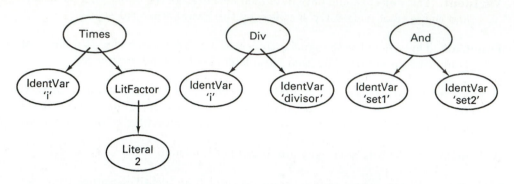

Figure 8.4. Multiplicative Objects for Expressions

form the principal grammar segment that recognizes these expressions. Clearly we will need five corresponding objects that represent the various multiplication operators: *Times, Divide, Div, Mod* and *And*. Then, to represent an expression like *i ∗ 2*, a *Times* object would point on the left to the *VarIdent* object representing *i* and point on the right to the *LitFactor* object representing *2*, as shown in Figure 8.4.

All multiplicative operators have two data members pointing to the left and right subexpressions. In the same way as *ExprCls* containing the common data members for all expressions, we will need to define a *MulOpCls* having the required *left* and *right* pointers and then have the other five objects be instances of classes derived from this (intermediate) base class.

Times. A *Times* object should have its own versions of three functions, *evaluate()*, *make_tree()*, and a function to test the types of the left and right expressions called *is_defined_for()*. These functions are the usual redefinitions of virtual ones defined for the base class *MulOpCls*.

Divide. Note that this operation *is_defined_for()* only *real*.

Div. This operation *is_defined_for()* only *integer*.

Mod. For *integer* only.

And. For *boolean* and set types.

Expressions Constructed from Addition Operators

We will need to define an *AddOpCls* base class for these operators in exactly the same way as we did for *MulOpCls* in the previous section. It will have the same *left*

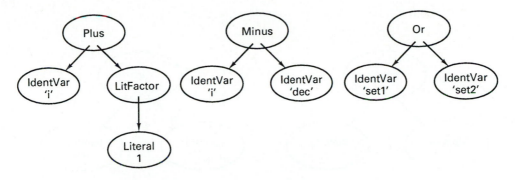

Figure 8.5. Additive Objects for Expressions

and *right* data members as well as the virtual versions of *evaluate()*, *make_tree()*, and is_defined_for() behaviors.

An analogous collection of expressions built from additive operators is given below.

```
i := i + 1;
j := i - dec;
test := bool1 or bool2;
```

Parse tree representations for such expressions are traditionally constructed by using tree nodes representing any of the three addition operations, below.

$$+, -, or$$

Figure 8.5 illustrates the tree construction.

Plus, Minus. A *Plus* object *is_defined_for()* nearly every standard type and also for sets. Its class will redefine the three virtual *AddOpCls* functions.

Or. This operation *is_defined_for() boolean* and set types only.

Expressions Constructed from Relational Operators

The six relational operators,

$$=, <, >, <=, >=, <>, in$$

are represented by corresponding objects, listed below. Each of these are derived from a base class, *RelOpCls* having the usual *left* and *right* data members. Each also redefines virtual functions *is_defined_for()*, *make_tree()*, and *evaluate()*.

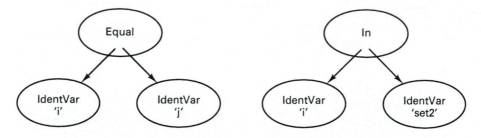

Figure 8.6. Relational Objects for Expressions

- **EQ**
- **LT**
- **GT**
- **LE**
- **GE**
- **NE**
- **IN**

Set Expressions

The productions for expressions involving sets

```
Set: LBRACKTK Member_stuff RBRACKTK
     ;
   Member_stuff: /*empty*/
        | Member_lst
        ;
      Member_lst: Member
           | Member_lst COMMATK Member
           ;
         Member: Expr
              | Expr DDTK Expr
              ;
```

clearly indicate that set membership could be represented by a list of expressions. Thus we need to be sure that the base class *ExprCls* inherits the ability to form lists from *LstSeqBldrCls* and to provide a header class *ExprLstCls*.

Set. An object representing a set expression just needs to reference the underlying list of expressions representing elements.

Range. One possible specification for set membership is a range like 1..4. A range object should be able to convert such a range into a list of objects representing $1, 2, 3, 4$.

8.1.3 Type Objects

A data type is really two things: (i) A specification of valid literal values and (ii) A list of operations and functions that may be applied to the literal values. Parse tree entries representing a type must therefore contain the following two items.

- A member describing a valid value of the type

- A list of associated operations and functions

Standard Types

Each of the following types admits the usual six relational operations.

$$=, \ldots, \diamondsuit$$

Integer. The parse tree node for the Pascal integer type must specify the range of valid Pascal integers and a list of operations like +, -, ..., mod, ... and procedures or functions like ord and odd.

Real. The node for real type must specify the valid operations, most notably /, and procedures such as *trunc()* and *round()*.

Char. There are no operations on char, other than the relational operators described above. The set of standard procedures and functions available to any discrete type are valid for char, e.g., *ord()*, *pred()*, and succ().

String. Though technically not a specified type in Pascal, string literals are handled as though they are a distinct type. All the relational operators are defined for such literals.

Boolean. Boolean type is essentially an enumerated type based upon the two values of false and true. Again, this type admits the usual relational operators, procedures and functions associated with any discrete type.

Simple Types

The next major category of type declaration productions are those associated with the simple types that are defined by the following grammar segment.

```
Simple_type: LPARENTK Ident_1st RPARENTK
           | Constant DDTK Constant
           | Ident
```

The first production is clearly recognizing the user specified list of identifiers that specifies an **enumerated type**. The second production is clearly defining a **subrange type**. And the third is referencing or **specifying** a type that has been previously declared in the source program.

EnumeratedType. Enumerated types use programmer identifiers for literal values and associate a type name to the entire collection of identifiers. The usual method for implementing enumerated types is to store the literal values in the symbol table that is closest to the type declaration statement. So *EnumeratedType* objects need to have data members referencing not only the list of identifiers, but also the corresponding list[1] of symbol table entries containing those identifiers. It is also helpful for these objects to have a data member containing the number of identifiers, or equivalently the maximum ordinal value of the type's values.

SubrangeType. There are essentially three things that *Subrange* objects must reference.

1. The type, called the **underlying type**, from which the subrange has been chosen
2. The start value for the subrange
3. The stop value for the subrange

SpecifiedType. More complex type structures are constructed from earlier types by specifying the name or identifier associated with the simpler type. A *SpecifiedType* object must therefore have a data member pointing to the actual type structure associated with the identifier.

ArrayType

The remaining type specification productions are for structured types.

```
Structured_type: ARRAYTK LBRACKTK Index_t_lst RBRACK OFTK Type
    | RECORDTK Field_lst ENDTK
    | SETTK OFTK Type
    ;
Index_t_lst: Simple_type
    | Index_t_lst COMMATK Simple_type
    ;
```

The first production recognizing array types contains two nonterminals *Index_t_lst* and *Type* on the righthand side. An *ArrayType* object must therefore have data members referencing the following two things.

1. A list of index types (these are often subranges)
2. The type object(s) specifying the array's components

---

[1] This is the reason that *ConstAttCls* is also derived from *LstSeqBldrCls* in Chapter 7.

RecordType

Most modern languages support a structured data type that contains an arbitrary number of data items of possibly different types. In Pascal the structure is called a record and the data items are called **fields**. Since the various fields of a record can be accessed only by identifiers, it makes sense to utilize a symbol table, containing these field identifiers, for each record declared in the source program.

An object representing such a type will only need a data member referencing the symbol table of field identifiers.

PointerType

Variables declared to be of pointer type contain the addresses of data of a specified type. So *PointerType* objects need to reference that specified type. In the event that the pointer type is referencing a record with fields that are themselves pointers back to the entire record, the original pointer declaration will necessarily be allowed to reference the undeclared record structure.

SetType

An object representing a Pascal set type must contain the underlying type of the elements making up the universal set.

8.1.4   Statement Objects

Statements represent the last major category of parse tree nodes. The following grammar productions

```
Program: PROGRAMTK Ident External_files SCTK Block DOTTK
    ;
Block:
    Label_dec_part
    Const_def_part
    Type_def_part
    Var_dec_part
    Proc_fun_dec_part
    Compound_stmt
    ;
    Compound_stmt: BEGINTK Statement_seq ENDTK
        ;
        Statement_seq: Statement
            | Statement_seq SCTK Statement
            ;
```

certainly indicate that programs consist of blocks and that blocks consist of sequences of statements. In much the same way as we have handled previous lists or sequences, we will represent such statement sequences in the parse tree by a *StatementSeq* object that then points to the corresponding linked-list of *Statement* objects. This argues that *StatementCls* should be derived from *LstSeqBldrCls*.

The grammar production for statements

```
Statement: /*empty*/
    | Assignment
    | IFTK Expr THENTK Statement
    | IFTK Expr THENTK Statement ELSETK Statement
    | CASETK Expr OFTK Case_lst ENDTK
    | FORTK Ident ASGTK Expr Dir Expr DOTK Statement
    | WHILETK Expr DOTK Statement
    | REPEATTK Statement_seq UNTILTK Expr
    | WITHTK Rec_var_lst DOTK Statement
    | WriteStmt
    | Procedure_call
    | Label COLONTK Statement
    | Compound_stmt
    | GOTOTK Label
    ;
```

shows very clearly that Pascal has a rather complete collection of statements. The objects representing these will be instances of subclasses of the base class *StatementCls*. Naturally, this base class will have virtual functions *execute()*[2] and *emit()* that will then be redefined for each of its subclasses.

EmptyStmt. Pascal's original use of the semicolon has probably caused more trouble for students than any other language symbol. Somehow, it is easier to think of this symbol as terminating a statement rather than separating two statements. Since empty statements are now valid Pascal statements, any semicolon after the "last" statement can be recognized as separating that statement from a following empty one.

Assignment. The grammar production recognizing the assignment has the following two nonterminals on the production's right side.

- Variable. We are interested in the location of this variable.

- Expr. The value of this expression is the important issue.

Assignment objects therefore need two data members to reference the corresponding objects.

IfStmt. One *IfStmt* object can be used to represent the two different `If_stmt` productions, above. This object will need the following data members.

- *b_expr*. To point to the boolean expression used for the statement's selection.

---

[2]In some languages, most notably C, statements also return values. But Pascal statement execution is significantly different from expression evaluation. Expression objects therefore have *evaluate()* function members, while statement objects have *execute()* function members.

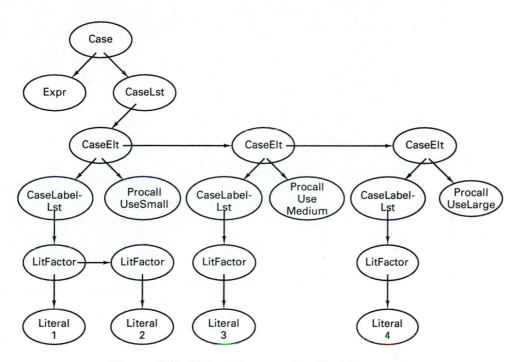

Figure 8.7. Objects Representing Case Statement

- *stmt.* The (possibly compound) statement to be executed if *b_expr* is true.

- *else_stmt.* The (possibly compound) statement to be executed if *b_expr* if false. This member is set to nil if the first If_stmt production is used.

CaseStmt. Perhaps the best way to understand how a parse tree represents a case statement is to look at an example. Let's consider the following Pascal code.

```
case count of
    1,2: GetSmallBag;
    3: GetNormalBag;
    4: GetLargeBag
end
```

As illustrated in Figure 8.7, the 1,2,3 are represented by a list of *CaseLabel* objects. A *CaseLstElem* object can be created and made to point at the list of labels and the corresponding statement. These are in turn made into a linked-list referenced by a *CaseLst* object. A *CaseStmt* object needs to point

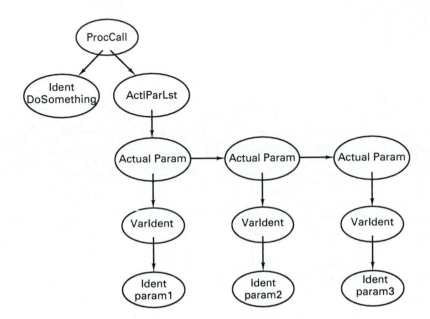

Figure 8.8. Objects Representing Procedure Call

to the case expression used for the selection and then the list of case elements. Objects for these case elements are as follows.

ForStmt. See Section 8.2.5.

WhileStmt. See Section 8.2.5.

RepeatStmt. See Section 8.2.5.

ProcCall. Again, it is probably helpful to consider an example. The following Pascal code

```
DoSomething(param1, param2, param3);
```

is somewhat representative of a normal procedure call. As illustrated in Figure 8.8, `param1` ... `param3` are represented by an expression list to which the *ProcCall* object must point. It is also somewhat helpful to be able to reference the procedure's name.

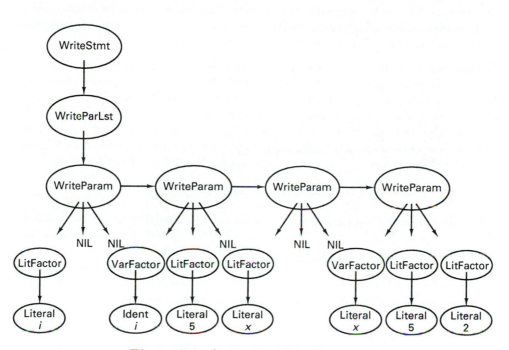

Figure 8.9. Objects for Write Statements

WithStmt. *WithStmt* objects must point to a list of record variables. Record variables are just variable expressions specifying the name of a particular record type structure.

WriteStmt. Wirth's definition of Pascal does not include these statements, since they can be recognized by procedure call productions. But most compiler writers like to handle them separately, since their parameters often contain formatting information. Figure 8.9 contains a tree representation for the following write statement.

```
writeln('i',i:5,'x',x:5:2);
```

8.1.5   Higher Level Objects

The last set of productions to be considered specify the declaration section of a Pascal program. Most of these productions, while creating and utilizing objects of various kinds, do not require the construction of parse tree objects. A label declaration creates a *symbol table* entry object associated with the numeric identifier and the corresponding statement. Similarly, productions for constants and variables do not actually create new parse tree objects, since their task is to insert symbol table entries representing the constants or variables. There is one notable exception to this pattern: procedure or function declaration.

Declaration objects. Subprogram declaration is almost identical to the process of the main program declaration. Subprograms have their own symbol tables and their own block of statements. In addition to this, they have communication devices called parameters, that may come in at least two fundamental flavors.

It is helpful to look at an example as we begin to specify the objects necessary for subprogram declaration. Actually, the real focus is just the subprogram's header. Figure 8.10 illustrates the parse tree structure for the following header.

```
procedure DoSomething(a,b: integer; var c: real);
```

The identifiers *a* and *b* are first made into a list and referenced by an *IdentLst* object. Then a *ParamGrp* object points at this identifier list as well as the corresponding type of the group. Since this parameter group is not declared to be variable, it is referenced by a *ValParamGrp* object. In much the same way, a *VarParamGrp* object points at the parse tree nodes representing the declaration for the parameter *c*. These are two of the various kinds of parameter sections that are then formed into a linked-list and referenced by the highest level *FParamStuff* object.

But recognition of the parameters is only one of several rather tricky parts. As the identifiers for these parameters are found, they need to be placed in the symbol table for the subprogram. And since the production for the recognition of the subprogram is not yet complete, the grammar action

```
$$ = new ProcDecCls;
```

or

```
$$ = new FuncDecCls;
```

normally placed at the end of the production will not yet have been executed! This of course means that the creation of the symbol table for the subprogram by the corresponding constructors has not yet taken place either! The usual method used to solve this tail-chasing problem is to insert an action near the *beginning* of the production and then provide the corresponding object with a member function, *finish()* to grab the pointers to the remaining nonterminals. This is illustrated in the following grammar segment.

```
Proc_heading: PROCEDURETK
        {$$ = new ProcHeadCls;}
     Ident Formal_param_stuff
        {$$ = PProcHeadCls($2) -> finish($3,$4);}
   ;
Func_heading: FUNCTIONTK
```

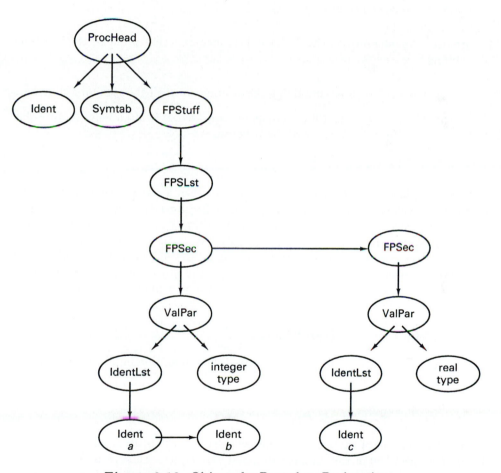

Figure 8.10. Objects for Procedure Declaration

```
                {$$ = new FuncHeadCls;}
            Ident Function_form
                {$$ = PFuncHeadCls($2) -> finish($3,$4);}
    ;
```

Top nodes.

Block. The production for Block indicates that a *Block* object should point to the
statement sequence of that block.

Program. *Program* objects should have data members that point to the following
items.

- The symbol table containing the declaration of all the standard identifiers
- The program identifier (though not required, it is often helpful to be able
  to tell what the name of the program is)
- The program's block

The tree. There is, of course, a distinction between a parse tree and the nodes
of that tree. When abstract data types are specified for tree structures, very often
a special object is placed at the head of the tree that contains data members and
operations supporting important tree activity. It turns out that parse trees in
compilers seem to not really need this additional level of abstraction. This object
has therefore been retained so that you can see the object-oriented equivalent of
ideas you may have already seen in a Data Structures course.

8.2   Defining Parse Tree Classes

This section contains the complete[3] parse tree class definition information stored in
the header file *p_tree.h*.

8.2.1   Parse Tree Base Class

With the exception of the parse tree object itself, all the objects and therefore all
the classes described in this chapter are parse tree nodes. All such nodes represent
some lexeme and this information is stored in the data member of the base class
object. This will allow the recreation of portions of the original source code for error
messages. This base class also includes the virtual *execute()* and *emit()* functions
that are redefined by all but the expression nodes.

---

[3] There are times when the specification of one class (e.g., *EQCls*) gives sufficient information
for other, omitted classes (like *LECls*, *GTCls*, ...). These listings also do not contain some of the
forward referencing information required by C++.

```
  PTreeNodeCls definition (p_tree.h)

  7 typedef class PTreeNodeCls *PPTreeNodeCls;
  8 class PTreeNodeCls {
  9   public:
 10        PTreeNodeCls();
 11        virtual int             emit();
 12        virtual int             execute();
 13        virtual int             optimize();
 14        virtual int             peephole();
 15        virtual void            print();
 16        virtual LexTokCls       *get_lex_tok()
 17                                    {return lt;}
 18        friend ostream  &operator<< (ostream&, PTreeNodeCls&);
 19   protected:
 20        LexTokCls               *lt;
 21 };
```

8.2.2 Leaf Classes

IdentCls

```
  IdentCls definition (p_tree.h)

 24 typedef class IdentCls  *PIdentCls;
 25 class IdentCls : public PTreeNodeCls , public LstSeqBldrCls {
 26    public:
 27        IdentCls();
 28        IdentCls(char *Name);
 29        char                *get_name()
 30                               {return name;}
 31    private:
 32        char                *name;
 33 };
```

Note that this section also includes *IdentLstCls* that is used to represent lists of identifiers.

```
  IdentCls definition (p_tree.h)

 36 typedef class IdentLstCls *PIdentLstCls;
 37 class IdentLstCls : public PTreeNodeCls {
 38    public:
 39        IdentLstCls()    {;}
 40        IdentLstCls(PPTreeNodeCls Ident);
 41        PPTreeNodeCls    append(PPTreeNodeCls);
 42        PIdentCls        get_seq_head()
 43                              {return seq_head;}
 44    private:
 45        PIdentCls        seq_head;
 46        PIdentCls        seq_tail;
 47 };
```

LiteralCls

The following literal class definitions follow directly from the discussion of the corresponding objects in Sections 8.1.1 and 8.1.2.

```
LiteralCls definition (p_tree.h)

55 typedef class LiteralCls  *PLiteralCls;
56 class LiteralCls : public PTreeNodeCls {
57    public:
58          LiteralCls(PTypeCls Type);
59          ValueCls             *evaluate()
60                                   {return value;}
61          PTypeCls             get_type()
62                                   {return type;}
63    private:
64          ValueCls             *value;
65          PTypeCls             type;
66 };
```

8.2.3   Expression Classes

```
ExprCls definition (p_tree.h)

71 typedef class ExprCls  *PExprCls;
72 class ExprCls : public PTreeNodeCls, public LstSeqBldrCls {
73    public:
74          ExprCls();
75          ExprCls(PTypeCls Type);
76
77          virtual int          is_var()
78                                   {return 0;}
79          virtual int          is_fun()
80                                   {return 0;}
81          //virtual ValueCls   *get_value();
82
83          //virtual void        set_value(ValueCls*)
84
85          PTypeCls             get_type()
86                                   {return type;}
87          virtual void         set_type(PTypeCls Type)
88                                   {type = Type;}
89          virtual SymtabEntryCls *get_att()
90                                   //redefined by VarIdentCls
91                                   {return 0;}
92          virtual ValueCls    *evaluate();
93
94          virtual int          emit();
95    protected:
96          PTypeCls             type;
97          ValueCls             *value;
98 };
```

```
ExprLstCls definition (p_tree.h)

101 typedef class ExprLstCls *PExprLstCls;
102 class ExprLstCls : public PTreeNodeCls {
103    public:
104        ExprLstCls()      {;}
105        ExprLstCls(PPTreeNodeCls Expr);
106
107        PExprCls        get_seq_head()
108                            {return seq_head;}
109        PExprCls        get_seq_tail()
110                            {return seq_tail;}
111        PPTreeNodeCls   append(PPTreeNodeCls);
112
113        friend class    VarDecCls;
114    private:
115        PExprCls        seq_head;
116        PExprCls        seq_tail;
117 };
```

Relational Operators

```
EQCls definition (p_tree.h)

120 typedef class RelOpCls *PRelOpCls;
121 class RelOpCls: public ExprCls {
122    public:
123        RelOpCls()      {;}
124        virtual int     is_defined_for(PTypeCls Left,
125                                       PTypeCls Right);
126        virtual PPTreeNodeCls
127                        make_tree(PPTreeNodeCls Left,
128                                  PPTreeNodeCls Right);
129        ValueCls        *evaluate();
130    protected:
131        PExprCls        left;
132        PExprCls        right;
133 };
135
136 typedef class EqCls *PEqCls;
137 class EqCls : public RelOpCls {
138    public:
139        EqCls()         {;}
140        int             is_defined_for(PTypeCls Left,
141                                       PTypeCls Right);
142        PPTreeNodeCls   make_tree(PPTreeNodeCls Left,
143                                  PPTreeNodeCls Right);
144        ValueCls        *evaluate();
145 };
```

The other six derived classes are essentially identical to *EQCls* and are therefore omitted.

Unary and Additive Operators

```
220 typedef class UMinusCls *PUMinusCls;
221 class UMinusCls: public ExprCls {
222    public:
223         UMinusCls()      {;}
224         UMinusCls(PPTreeNodeCls Term);
225         int           is_defined_for(PTypeCls TermType);
226         ValueCls      *evaluate();
227         PTypeCls      get_type();
228    private:
229         PExprCls      term;
230 };
232
233 typedef class UNotCls *PUNotCls;
234 class UNotCls : public ExprCls {
235    public:
236         UNotCls()        {;}
237         UNotCls(PPTreeNodeCls Factor);
238         int           is_defined_for(PTypeCls FactorType);
239         ValueCls      *evaluate();
240    private:
241         PExprCls      factor;
242 };


245 typedef class AddOpCls *PAddOpCls;
246 class AddOpCls: public ExprCls {
247    public:
248         AddOpCls()       {;}
249         virtual int   is_defined_for(PTypeCls Left,
250                                      PTypeCls Right);
251         virtual PPTreeNodeCls
252                       make_tree(PPTreeNodeCls Left,
253                                      PPTreeNodeCls Right);
254         ValueCls      *evaluate();
255    protected:
256         PExprCls      left;
257         PExprCls      right;
258 };
260
261 typedef class PlusCls *PPlusCls;
262 class PlusCls : public AddOpCls {
263   public:
264         PlusCls()        {;}
265          int           is_defined_for(PTypeCls Left,
266                                       PTypeCls Right);
267         PPTreeNodeCls  make_tree(PPTreeNodeCls Left,
268                                       PPTreeNodeCls Right);
269         ValueCls      *evaluate();
270 };
```

Multiplicative Operators

```
┌─────────────────────────────────────────────────────────────────────┐
│ Multiplication operation class definitions (p_tree.h)               │
│                                                                       │
│ 297 typedef class MulOpCls *PMulOpCls;                                │
│ 298 class MulOpCls: public ExprCls {                                  │
│ 299    public:                                                        │
│ 300         MulOpCls()      {;}                                       │
│ 301         virtual int     is_defined_for(PTypeCls Left,             │
│ 302                                         PTypeCls Right);           │
│ 303         virtual PPTreeNodeCls                                      │
│ 304                         make_tree(PPTreeNodeCls Left,             │
│ 305                                       PPTreeNodeCls Right);        │
│ 306         ValueCls        *evaluate();                              │
│ 307    protected:                                                     │
│ 308         PExprCls        left;                                     │
│ 309         PExprCls        right;                                    │
│ 310 };                                                                │
│ 312                                                                   │
│ 313 typedef class TimesCls *PTimesCls;                                │
│ 314 class TimesCls : public MulOpCls {                                │
│ 315   public:                                                         │
│ 316         TimesCls()      {;}                                       │
│ 317         int             is_defined_for(PTypeCls Left,             │
│ 318                                         PTypeCls Right);           │
│ 319         PPTreeNodeCls   make_tree(PPTreeNodeCls Left,             │
│ 320                                       PPTreeNodeCls Right);        │
│ 321         ValueCls        *evaluate();                              │
│ 322 };                                                                │
└─────────────────────────────────────────────────────────────────────┘
```

Primitive Expressions

```
┌─────────────────────────────────────────────────────────────────────┐
│ Factor class definitions (p_tree.h)                                  │
│                                                                       │
│ 373 typedef class FactorCls *PFactorCls;                              │
│ 374 class FactorCls : public ExprCls {                                │
│ 375   public:                                                         │
│ 376         FactorCls();                                              │
│ 377         FactorCls(PTypeCls Type);                                 │
│ 378 };                                                                │
│ 380                                                                   │
│ 381 typedef class LitFactorCls *PLitFactorCls;                        │
│ 382 class LitFactorCls : public FactorCls {                           │
│ 383   public:                                                         │
│ 384         LitFactorCls()  {;}                                       │
│ 385         LitFactorCls(PPTreeNodeCls Lit);                          │
│ 386                                                                   │
│ 387         ValueCls        *evaluate();                              │
│ 388                                                                   │
│ 389         int             emit();                                   │
│ 390 };                                                                │
└─────────────────────────────────────────────────────────────────────┘
```

Variable classes. As noted in Section 8.1.2, Pascal factors are either literal factors or essentially one of the following forms of a 'variable.'

First we have the *VariableCls* base class.

```
VariableCls definition (p_tree.h)

440 typedef class VariableCls *PVariableCls;
441 class VariableCls : public FactorCls {
442   public:
443         virtual TypeCls  *get_var_type();
444         virtual ValueCls *locate_val(ValueCls*);
445         virtual int      is_arr_desig()
446                              {return 0;}
447   protected:
448         VariableCls() {;}
449
450         VariableCls(PTypeCls Type, ValueCls *Value);
451
452 };
```

Next, we have the corresponding derived class representing an actual variable, rather than a function call.

```
VarIdentCls definition (p_tree.h)

455 typedef class VarIdentCls *PVarIdentCls;
456 class VarIdentCls : public VariableCls {
457   public:
458         VarIdentCls() {;}
459         VarIdentCls(PIdentCls VarIdent,
460                         SymtabEntryCls *Att,
461                           PTypeCls Type,
462                             ValueCls *Value);
463         int          is_var()
464                          {return 1;}
465         SymtabEntryCls *get_att();  //The associated
466                                     //symbol table entry
467         TypeCls       *get_var_type();
468
469         ValueCls      *evaluate();
470
471         ValueCls      *locate_val(ValueCls *);
472
473         int           emit();
474   private:
475         PIdentCls     ident;
476         SymtabEntryCls *att;
477 };
```

Is_var() redefines the base class virtual function (see page 216) which normally returns false, while *get_value()* and *set_value()* are inherited from the base class.

We then have the classes used for function call expressions. First we define those which specify the actual parameters occurring in a function call.

FuncCallCls definition (p_tree.h)

```
480 typedef class ActualParamCls *PActualParamCls;
481 class ActualParamCls : public ExprCls {
482    public:
483          ActualParamCls() {;}
484          ActualParamCls(PPTreeNodeCls Expr);
485
486       PExprCls      get_expr()
487                       {return expr;}
488       PTypeCls      get_type()
489                       {return expr -> get_type();}
490       int           is_var()
491                       {return expr -> is_var();}
492       int           is_fun()
493                       {return expr -> is_fun();}
494       ValueCls      *evaluate()
495                       {return expr -> evaluate();}
496       int           emit();
497    private:
498          PExprCls      expr;
499 };
500
501 typedef class ActualParamLstCls *PActualParamLstCls;
502 class ActualParamLstCls : public PTreeNodeCls {
503    public:
504          ActualParamLstCls() {;}
505          ActualParamLstCls(PPTreeNodeCls ActualParam);
506
507       PActualParamCls get_seq_head()
508                        {return seq_head;}
509       PPTreeNodeCls   append(PPTreeNodeCls);
510
511       int             emit();
512    private:
513          PActualParamCls seq_head;
514          PActualParamCls seq_tail;
515 };
```

- Actual parameters used in function calls can be any valid expression, of course. The data member *expr* points to this expression.

- Actual parameters corresponding to variable formal parameters must represent a location where values can be stored. Tests *is_var()* and *is_fun()* are therefore needed to support such semantic analysis.

- Function calls allow for arbitrary lists of actual parameters.

Then we define the class which represents the actual function call.

FuncCallCls definition (p_tree.h)

```
520 typedef class FuncCallCls *PFuncCallCls;
521 class FuncCallCls : public VariableCls {
522   public:
523         FuncCallCls() {;}
524         FuncCallCls(PIdentCls FuncIdent,
525                     SymtabEntryCls *Att,
526                        PTypeCls Type,
527                          ValueCls *Value,
528                            PActualParamLstCls ActualParamLst);
529         int             is_fun()
530                            {return 1;}
531     SymtabEntryCls  *get_att()
532                            {return att;}
533                     //The associated symbol table entry
534     TypeCls         *get_type();
535
536     ValueCls        *evaluate();
537
538         int             emit();
539   private:
540         PIdentCls ident;
541         PActualParamLstCls  actual_param_lst;
542         SymtabEntryCls *att;
543 };
```

And finally, we specify the class whose constructor determines whether an identifier or function has indeed been specified in the expression.

VarFuncDesignatorCls definition (p_tree.h)

```
546 typedef class VarFuncDesignatorCls *PVarFuncDesignatorCls;
547 class VarFuncDesignatorCls {
548   public:
549         VarFuncDesignatorCls(PPTreeNodeCls Ident,
550                             PPTreeNodeCls ActualParamLst);
551     PPTreeNodeCls  get_factor(); //Either var or fct.
552   private:
553     PExprCls        factor;
554 };
```

Variables can also be built up by using various designator expressions. The classes representing these are listed below.

```
┌─────────────────────────────────────────────────────┐
│ ┌──────────────────────────────────────────────┐    │
│ │ Designator expression definitions (p_tree.h) │    │
│ └──────────────────────────────────────────────┘    │
│                                                      │
│  557 typedef class ArrayDesigCls *PArrayDesigCls;    │
│  558 class ArrayDesigCls: public VariableCls {       │
│  559    public:                                      │
│  560         ArrayDesigCls() {;}                     │
│  561                                                 │
│  562         ArrayDesigCls(PPTreeNodeCls Variable,   │
│  563                          PPTreeNodeCls IndexLst);│
│  564         int            is_arr_desig()           │
│  565                           {return 1;}           │
│  566                                                 │
│  567         PExprLstCls    get_index_lst()          │
│  568                           {return index_lst;}   │
│  569         SymtabEntryCls *get_att();              │
│  570                                                 │
│  571         TypeCls        *get_var_type(); //Of designator│
│  572                                                 │
│  573         ValueCls       *locate_val(ValueCls*);  │
│  574                                                 │
│  575         ValueCls       *evaluate();             │
│  576    private:                                     │
│  577         PVariableCls   variable;                │
│  578         PExprLstCls    index_lst;               │
│  579 };                                              │
│  580                                                 │
│  581 typedef class FieldDesigCls *PFieldDesigCls;    │
│  582 class FieldDesigCls: public VariableCls {       │
│  583    public:                                      │
│  584         FieldDesigCls() {;}                     │
│  585         FieldDesigCls(PPTreeNodeCls Variable,   │
│  586                          PPTreeNodeCls Ident);  │
│  587    private:                                     │
│  588         PVariableCls   variable;                │
│  589         PIdentCls      ident;                   │
│  590 };                                              │
│  592                                                 │
│  593 typedef class DereferenceCls *PDereferenceCls;  │
│  594 class DereferenceCls: public VariableCls {      │
│  595    public:                                      │
│  596         DereferenceCls() {;}                    │
│  597         DereferenceCls(PPTreeNodeCls Variable); │
│  598    private:                                     │
│  599         PVariableCls   variable;                │
│  600 };                                              │
└─────────────────────────────────────────────────────┘
```

Write parameter classes.   Actual parameters used in the calls for Pascal output statements have a slightly more general form than normal expressions. Classes representing these expressions must therefore provide additional data members to allow access to this formatting information.

Write parameter definitions (p_tree.h)

```
634 typedef class WriteParamCls *PWriteParamCls;
635 class WriteParamCls: public ExprCls {
636    public:
637         WriteParamCls() {;}
638
639         WriteParamCls(PPTreeNodeCls Expr,
640                                  PPTreeNodeCls Field1,
641                                          PPTreeNodeCls Field2);
642         PExprCls        get_expr()
643                               {return expr;}
644         ValueCls        *evaluate();
645         int             emit();
646         void            print();
647         friend class    WriteStmtCls;
648         friend class    WritelnStmtCls;
649    private:
650         PExprCls        expr;
651         PPTreeNodeCls   field1;
652         PPTreeNodeCls   field2;
653 };
654
655 typedef class WriteParamLstCls *PWriteParamLstCls;
656 class WriteParamLstCls : public PTreeNodeCls {
657    public:
658         WriteParamLstCls() {;}
659         WriteParamLstCls(PPTreeNodeCls WriteParam);
660         int             emit();
661          PPTreeNodeCls   append(PPTreeNodeCls);
662         friend class    WriteStmtCls;
663         friend class    WritelnStmtCls;
664    private:
665         WriteParamCls   *seq_head;
666         WriteParamCls   *seq_tail;
667 };
```

- Write parameters are a special expression list, where the delimiters are colons. Since there are at most three expressions in this list, it is much easier to pass these directly to the *WriteParamCls* constructor, rather than have the parser build a special linked list representing this structure.

  - The first expression in a write parameter can be any valid Pascal expression.

  - Field width parameters can be any positive valued expression. Semantic tests for such expressions are sufficiently different that we have chosen to store them simply as base class nodes which will be tested during execution.

- Pascal output statements also allow for any number of such write parameters. We do require that the parser construct a normal linked list of these.

8.2.4   Type Classes

Base Class

```
TypeCls definition (p_tree.h)

671 class TypeCls : public PTreeNodeCls, public LstSeqBldrCls {
672     public:
673         TypeCls();
```

The specification for this class is quite complicated. Virtual functions about the nature of the individual type are initialized to return 0 and redefined to return 1 by the corresponding derived type or types. Finally, special type comparison operators are defined. These allow elegant checking of various semantic type compatibility requirements.

```
TypeCls IsA definitions (p_tree.h)

675        virtual int     is_enum()
676                            {return 0;}
677        virtual int     is_subrange()
678                            {return 0;}
679        virtual int     get_min_ord()
680                            {return 0;}
681        virtual int     get_max_ord()
682                            {return 0;}
683        virtual PTypeCls get_underlying_type()
684                            {return 0;}
685                        //Re-defined by SubrangeTypeCls
686        virtual int     is_ordinal()
687                            {return 0;}
688        virtual int     is_scalar()
689                            {return 0;}
690        virtual int     is_array()
691                            {return 0;}
692        virtual int     is_record()
693                            {return 0;}
694        virtual int     is_pointer()
695                            {return 0;}
696        virtual int     is_set()
697                            {return 0;}
698        virtual int     is_string()
699                            {return 0;}
700        virtual ValueCls *make_value()
701                            {return 0;}
702        virtual int     is_valid_val(ValueCls*)
703                            {return 1;}
```

Each possible type operation is specified for the base class and then will be redefined if it exists for a derived type.

```
┌─────────────────────────────────────────────────────────────────┐
│  ┌──────────────────────────────┐                                 │
│  │ TypeCls operations (p_tree.h) │                                │
│  └──────────────────────────────┘                                 │
│   705        virtual ValueCls  *not(PPTreeNodeCls Val);           │
│   706        virtual ValueCls  *uplus(PPTreeNodeCls Val);         │
│   707        virtual ValueCls  *uminus(PPTreeNodeCls Val);        │
│   708                                                             │
│   709        virtual ValueCls                                     │
│   710                *eq(PPTreeNodeCls LVal, PPTreeNodeCls RVal); │
│   711        virtual ValueCls                                     │
│   712                *lt(PPTreeNodeCls LVal, PPTreeNodeCls RVal); │
│   713        virtual ValueCls                                     │
│   714                *gt(PPTreeNodeCls LVal, PPTreeNodeCls RVal); │
│   715        virtual ValueCls                                     │
│   716                *le(PPTreeNodeCls LVal, PPTreeNodeCls RVal); │
│   717        virtual ValueCls                                     │
│   718                *ge(PPTreeNodeCls LVal, PPTreeNodeCls RVal); │
│   719        virtual ValueCls                                     │
│   720                *ne(PPTreeNodeCls LVal, PPTreeNodeCls RVal); │
│   721        virtual ValueCls                                     │
│   722                *in(PPTreeNodeCls LVal, PPTreeNodeCls RVal); │
│   723                                                             │
│   724        virtual ValueCls                                     │
│   725               *add(PPTreeNodeCls LVal, PPTreeNodeCls RVal); │
│   726        virtual ValueCls                                     │
│   727                *sub(PPTreeNodeCls LVal, PPTreeNodeCls RVal);│
│   728        virtual ValueCls                                     │
│   729                *or(PPTreeNodeCls LVal, PPTreeNodeCls RVal); │
│   730                                                             │
│   731        virtual ValueCls                                     │
│   732              *times(PPTreeNodeCls LVal, PPTreeNodeCls RVal);│
│   733                                                             │
│   734        virtual ValueCls                                     │
│   735           *divide(PPTreeNodeCls LVal, PPTreeNodeCls RVal);  │
│   736                                                             │
│   737        virtual ValueCls                                     │
│   738               *div(PPTreeNodeCls LVal, PPTreeNodeCls RVal); │
│   739        virtual ValueCls                                     │
│   740               *mod(PPTreeNodeCls LVal, PPTreeNodeCls RVal); │
│   741        virtual ValueCls                                     │
│   742               *and(PPTreeNodeCls LVal, PPTreeNodeCls RVal); │
│   743                                                             │
│   744        virtual ValueCls                                     │
│   745                *inc(ValueCls *Val);                         │
│   746        virtual ValueCls                                     │
│   747                *dec(ValueCls *Val);                         │
└─────────────────────────────────────────────────────────────────┘
```

A lot of the compiler use of *TypeCls* objects involves checking the operands of various expression objects to see if their types are valid for a given operation expression. Some operations require operands of identical types. Others allow one type to be a subrange of the other. Still others just require that the type of one could be legally stored in a variable of the other type. The following definitions specify operations for such testing of types. They are our first nontrivial example of the use of C++ operator overloading, since we are changing the meaning of normal

C++ operators for the use of *TypeCls*.

```
┌─────────────────────────────────────────────────────────────────────────┐
│ ┌─────────────────────────────────┐                                      │
│ │ TypeCls recognition (p_tree.h)  │                                      │
│ └─────────────────────────────────┘                                      │
│                                                                          │
│   749     //Can't overload operators for pointers (Bjarne,p178), so ...  │
│   750        friend int operator==(TypeCls&, TypeCls&);                  │
│   751                            //Identical/equivalent to               │
│   752        friend int operator!=(TypeCls&, TypeCls&);                  │
│   753                            //Not Identical to                      │
│   754        friend int operator<<(TypeCls&, TypeCls&);                  │
│   755                            //Strict subrange of ..                 │
│   756        friend int operator<=(TypeCls&, TypeCls&);                  │
│   757                            //Subrange of ..                        │
│   758        friend int operator|=(TypeCls&, TypeCls&);                  │
│   759                            //Assignment compat with..              │
│   760    };                                                              │
└─────────────────────────────────────────────────────────────────────────┘
```

The index types for multidimensional arrays are essentially lists of type speci-fications. Objects representing such index types must therefore be a linked-list of type objects, having a header object of the following class.

```
┌─────────────────────────────────────────────────────────────────────────┐
│ ┌──────────────────────┐                                                 │
│ │ TypeLstCls (p_tree.h)│                                                 │
│ └──────────────────────┘                                                 │
│                                                                          │
│   764 class TypeLstCls : public TypeCls { //Primarily for array indices  │
│   765    public:                                                         │
│   766        TypeLstCls() {;}                                            │
│   767        TypeLstCls(PPTreeNodeCls Type);                             │
│   768                                                                    │
│   769        PPTreeNodeCls   append(PPTreeNodeCls);                      │
│   770                                                                    │
│   771        PTypeCls        get_seq_head()                              │
│   772                {return seq_head;}                                  │
│   773    private:                                                        │
│   774        PTypeCls        seq_head;                                   │
│   775        PTypeCls        seq_tail;                                   │
│   776 };                                                                 │
└─────────────────────────────────────────────────────────────────────────┘
```

Standard Types

```
IntegerTypeCls (p_tree.h)

779 typedef class IntegerTypeCls *PIntegerTypeCls;
780 class IntegerTypeCls : public TypeCls {
781    public:
782        IntegerTypeCls();
783
784        int            is_ordinal()
785                          {return 1;}
786        int            is_scalar()
787                          {return 1;}
788        ValueCls       *make_value();
789
790        ValueCls       *uplus(PPTreeNodeCls Val);
791        ValueCls       *uminus(PPTreeNodeCls Val);
792
793        ValueCls       *eq(PPTreeNodeCls LVal,
794                              PPTreeNodeCls RVal);
795        ValueCls       *lt(PPTreeNodeCls LVal,
796                              PPTreeNodeCls RVal);
797        ValueCls       *gt(PPTreeNodeCls LVal,
798                              PPTreeNodeCls RVal);
799        ValueCls       *le(PPTreeNodeCls LVal,
800                              PPTreeNodeCls RVal);
801        ValueCls       *ge(PPTreeNodeCls LVal,
802                              PPTreeNodeCls RVal);
803        ValueCls       *ne(PPTreeNodeCls LVal,
804                              PPTreeNodeCls RVal);
805
806        ValueCls       *add(PPTreeNodeCls LVal,
807                              PPTreeNodeCls RVal);
808        ValueCls       *sub(PPTreeNodeCls LVal,
809                              PPTreeNodeCls RVal);
810
811        ValueCls       *times(PPTreeNodeCls LVal,
812                              PPTreeNodeCls RVal);
813        ValueCls       *div(PPTreeNodeCls LVal,
814                              PPTreeNodeCls RVal);
815        ValueCls       *mod(PPTreeNodeCls LVal,
816                              PPTreeNodeCls RVal);
817
818        ValueCls       *inc(ValueCls *Val);
819        ValueCls       *dec(ValueCls *Val);
820 };
```

RealTypeCls (p_tree.h)

```
823 typedef class RealTypeCls *PRealTypeCls;
824 class RealTypeCls : public TypeCls {
825    public:
826         RealTypeCls();
827
828         int              is_scalar()
829                             {return 1;}
830      ValueCls        *make_value();
831
832      ValueCls        *uplus(PPTreeNodeCls Val);
833      ValueCls        *uminus(PPTreeNodeCls Val);
834
835      ValueCls        *eq(PPTreeNodeCls LVal,
836                                 PPTreeNodeCls RVal);
837      ValueCls        *lt(PPTreeNodeCls LVal,
838                                 PPTreeNodeCls RVal);
839      ValueCls        *gt(PPTreeNodeCls LVal,
840                                 PPTreeNodeCls RVal);
841      ValueCls        *le(PPTreeNodeCls LVal,
842                                 PPTreeNodeCls RVal);
843      ValueCls        *ge(PPTreeNodeCls LVal,
844                                 PPTreeNodeCls RVal);
845      ValueCls        *ne(PPTreeNodeCls LVal,
846                                 PPTreeNodeCls RVal);
847
848      ValueCls        *add(PPTreeNodeCls LVal,
849                                 PPTreeNodeCls RVal);
850      ValueCls        *sub(PPTreeNodeCls LVal,
851                                 PPTreeNodeCls RVal);
852
853      ValueCls        *times(PPTreeNodeCls LVal,
854                                 PPTreeNodeCls RVal);
855      ValueCls        *divide(PPTreeNodeCls LVal,
856                                 PPTreeNodeCls RVal);
857 };
```

CharTypeCls (p_tree.h)

```
860 typedef class CharTypeCls *PCharTypeCls;
861 class CharTypeCls : public TypeCls {
862    public:
863         CharTypeCls();
864
865         int              is_ordinal()
866                             {return 1;}
867         int              is_scalar()
868                             {return 1;}
869         ValueCls            *make_value();
870
871         ValueCls         *eq(PPTreeNodeCls LVal,
872                                  PPTreeNodeCls RVal);
873         ValueCls         *lt(PPTreeNodeCls LVal,
874                                  PPTreeNodeCls RVal);
875         ValueCls         *gt(PPTreeNodeCls LVal,
876                                  PPTreeNodeCls RVal);
877         ValueCls         *le(PPTreeNodeCls LVal,
878                                  PPTreeNodeCls RVal);
879         ValueCls         *ge(PPTreeNodeCls LVal,
880                                  PPTreeNodeCls RVal);
881         ValueCls         *ne(PPTreeNodeCls LVal,
882                                  PPTreeNodeCls RVal);
883
884         ValueCls         *inc(ValueCls *Val);
885         ValueCls         *dec(ValueCls *Val);
886 };
```

StringLitTypeCls (p_tree.h)

```
889 typedef class StringLitTypeCls *PStringLitTypeCls;
890 class StringLitTypeCls : public TypeCls {
891    public:
892         StringLitTypeCls();
893
894         ValueCls            *make_value();
895
896         ValueCls         *eq(PPTreeNodeCls LVal,
897                                  PPTreeNodeCls RVal);
898         ValueCls         *lt(PPTreeNodeCls LVal,
899                                  PPTreeNodeCls RVal);
900         ValueCls         *gt(PPTreeNodeCls LVal,
901                                  PPTreeNodeCls RVal);
902         ValueCls         *le(PPTreeNodeCls LVal,
903                                  PPTreeNodeCls RVal);
904         ValueCls         *ge(PPTreeNodeCls LVal,
905                                  PPTreeNodeCls RVal);
906         ValueCls         *ne(PPTreeNodeCls LVal,
907                                  PPTreeNodeCls RVal);
908
909 };
```

```
BooleanTypeCls and StandardTypeCls (p_tree.h)

912 typedef class BooleanTypeCls *PBooleanTypeCls;
913 class BooleanTypeCls : public TypeCls {
914    public:
915        BooleanTypeCls();
916
917        int             is_ordinal()
918                            {return 1;}
919        int             is_scalar()
920                            {return 1;}
921        ValueCls        *make_value();
922
923        ValueCls        *eq(PPTreeNodeCls LVal,
924                            PPTreeNodeCls RVal);
925        ValueCls        *ne(PPTreeNodeCls LVal,
926                            PPTreeNodeCls RVal);
927
928        ValueCls        *or(PPTreeNodeCls LVal,
929                            PPTreeNodeCls RVal);
930        ValueCls        *and(PPTreeNodeCls LVal,
931                            PPTreeNodeCls RVal);
932        ValueCls        *unot(PPTreeNodeCls BVal);
933
934        ValueCls        *inc(ValueCls *Val);
935        ValueCls        *dec(ValueCls *Val);
936 };

939 class StandardTypeCls {
940    public:
941        PTypeCls                undeclared()
942                                    {return undeclared_type;}
943        PTypeCls                integer()
944                                    {return integer_type;}
945        PTypeCls                real()
946                                    {return real_type;}
947        PTypeCls                CHAR()
948                                    {return char_type;}
949        PTypeCls                string_lit()
950                                    {return strlit_type;}
951        PTypeCls                boolean()
952                                    {return boolean_type;}
953    friend class            ControllerCls;
954    friend class            SymtabCls;
955    private:
956        void init();
957        static PTypeCls         undeclared_type;
958        static PTypeCls         integer_type;
959        static PTypeCls         real_type;
960        static PTypeCls         char_type;
961        static PTypeCls         strlit_type;
962        static PTypeCls         boolean_type;
963 };
964 extern StandardTypeCls std_type; //Defined in p_tree/type.C
```

Simple Types

As we noted in previous sections of this chapter, Pascal simple types consist of enumerated, subrange and previously specified types.

```
      EnumTypeCls (p_tree.h)

967 typedef class EnumTypeCls *PEnumTypeCls;
968 class EnumTypeCls : public TypeCls {
969    public:
970         EnumTypeCls()    {;}
971         EnumTypeCls(PPTreeNodeCls Ident);
972
973         int             is_enum()
974                             {return 1;}
975         int             is_ordinal()
976                             {return 1;}
977         int             is_scalar()
978                             {return 1;}
979         int             get_min_ord()
980                             {return 0;}
981         int             get_max_ord()
982                             {return max_ord;}
983         ValueCls        *make_value();
984
985         ValueCls        *eq(PPTreeNodeCls LVal,
986                                 PPTreeNodeCls RVal);
987         ValueCls        *lt(PPTreeNodeCls LVal,
988                                 PPTreeNodeCls RVal);
989         ValueCls        *gt(PPTreeNodeCls LVal,
990                                 PPTreeNodeCls RVal);
991         ValueCls         *le(PPTreeNodeCls LVal,
992                                 PPTreeNodeCls RVal);
993         ValueCls        *ge(PPTreeNodeCls LVal,
994                                 PPTreeNodeCls RVal);
995         ValueCls        *ne(PPTreeNodeCls LVal,
996                                 PPTreeNodeCls RVal);
997
998         ValueCls        *inc(ValueCls *Val);
999         ValueCls        *dec(ValueCls *Val);
1000   private:
1001        PIdentLstCls     ident_lst;
1002        SymtabEntryCls  *enum_const_lst;
1003        int              max_ord;
1004 };
```

```
SubrangeTypeCls (p_tree.h)

1007 typedef class SubrangeTypeCls *PSubrangeTypeCls;
1008 class SubrangeTypeCls : public TypeCls {
1009    public:
1010        SubrangeTypeCls()        {;}
1011        SubrangeTypeCls(PPTreeNodeCls LowConst,
1012                               PPTreeNodeCls HighConst);
1013
1014        int             is_subrange()
1015                           {return 1;}
1016        int             is_ordinal()
1017                           {return 1;}
1018        int             is_scalar()
1019                           {return 1;}
1020        int             get_min_ord();
1021
1022        int             get_max_ord();
1023
1024        PTypeCls        get_underlying_type()
1025                           {return underlying_type;}
1026        ValueCls        *make_value();
1027
1028        int             is_valid_val(ValueCls *Val);
1029
1030        ValueCls        *eq(PPTreeNodeCls LVal,
1031                               PPTreeNodeCls RVal);
1032        ValueCls        *lt(PPTreeNodeCls LVal,
1033                               PPTreeNodeCls RVal);
1034        ValueCls        *gt(PPTreeNodeCls LVal,
1035                               PPTreeNodeCls RVal);
1036        ValueCls        *le(PPTreeNodeCls LVal,
1037                               PPTreeNodeCls RVal);
1038        ValueCls        *ge(PPTreeNodeCls LVal,
1039                               PPTreeNodeCls RVal);
1040        ValueCls        *ne(PPTreeNodeCls LVal,
1041                               PPTreeNodeCls RVal);
1042
1043        ValueCls        *inc(ValueCls *Val);
1044        ValueCls        *dec(ValueCls *Val);
1045    private:
1046        PTypeCls        underlying_type;
1047        ValueCls        *low_const;
1048        ValueCls        *high_const;
1049 };
```

Specified types. Any reference to a previously defined type in the source program is done by the use of an identifier that is first recognized by the parser and then stored in an appropriate symbol table. A *SpecifiedTypeCls* object essentially points to the underlying type being referenced by the identifier.

```
┌─────────────────────────────────────────────────────────────┐
│ SpecifiedTypeCls (p_tree.h)                                   │
│                                                               │
│  1052 typedef class SpecifiedTypeCls *PSpecifiedTypeCls;      │
│  1053 class SpecifiedTypeCls : public TypeCls {               │
│  1054    public:                                              │
│  1055        SpecifiedTypeCls()      {;}                       │
│  1056        SpecifiedTypeCls(PPTreeNodeCls Ident);            │
│  1057         PTypeCls        get_type()                       │
│  1058                              {return type;}              │
│  1059    private:                                             │
│  1060        PTypeCls        type;                             │
│  1061 };                                                      │
└─────────────────────────────────────────────────────────────┘
```

Structured Types

One of the real strengths of modern languages is the provision for user-defined data structures of arbitrary complexity. The way this is usually done is to allow programmers to build complex types from those previously declared. Such structured types require rather complex parse tree structures for their representation.

```
┌─────────────────────────────────────────────────────────────┐
│ ArrayTypeCls (p_tree.h)                                       │
│                                                               │
│  1064 typedef class ArrayTypeCls *PArrayTypeCls;              │
│  1065 class ArrayTypeCls : public TypeCls {                   │
│  1066    public:                                              │
│  1067        ArrayTypeCls()  {;}                               │
│  1068        ArrayTypeCls(PPTreeNodeCls IndexTypeLst,          │
│  1069                     PPTreeNodeCls ComponentType);        │
│  1070        PTypeCls        get_index_type()                  │
│  1071                            {return index_type;}          │
│  1072        PTypeCls        get_component_type()              │
│  1073                            {return component_type;}      │
│  1074        int             is_array()                        │
│  1075                            {return 1;}                   │
│  1076        ValueCls        *make_value();                    │
│  1077    private:                                             │
│  1078        PTypeCls        index_type;                       │
│  1079                            //TypeList is converted        │
│  1080        PTypeCls        component_type;                   │
│  1081 };                                                      │
└─────────────────────────────────────────────────────────────┘
```

```
RecordTypeCls (p_tree.h)

1084 typedef class RecordTypeCls *PRecordTypeCls;
1085 class RecordTypeCls : public TypeCls{
1086    public:
1087          RecordTypeCls() {;}
1088          int            is_record()
1089                            {return 1;}
1090          ValueCls       *make_value();
1091    private:
1092          SymtabCls       *fields;
1093 };
```

```
PointerTypeCls (p_tree.h)

1096 typedef class PointerTypeCls *PPointerTypeCls;
1097 class PointerTypeCls : public TypeCls{
1098    public:
1099          PointerTypeCls() {;}
1100          int            is_pointer()
1101                            {return 1;}
1102          ValueCls       *make_value();
1103    private:
1104          PTypeCls        deref_type;
1105 };
```

```
SetTypeCls (p_tree.h)

1108 typedef class SetTypeCls *PSetTypeCls;
1109 class SetTypeCls : public TypeCls{
1110    public:
1111          SetTypeCls() {;}
1112          SetTypeCls(PPTreeNodeCls SimpleType);
1113          int            is_set()
1114                            {return 1;}
1115          ValueCls       *make_value();
1116    private:
1117          PTypeCls        elt_type;
1118 };
```

8.2.5   Statement Classes

As noted earlier, program blocks consist of sequences of statements. The base class *StatementCls* is therefore derived from *LstSeqBldrCls*, and a special header class *StatementSeqCls* is provided in exactly the same manner as for lists of identifiers and lists of expressions.

```
(p_tree.h)

1121 typedef class StatementCls *PStatementCls;
1122 class StatementCls : public PTreeNodeCls, public LstSeqBldrCls {
1123    public:
1124         StatementCls()  {;}
1125         int             emit();
1126 };
1128
1129 typedef class StatementSeqCls *PStatementSeqCls;
1130 class StatementSeqCls : public PTreeNodeCls {
1131    public:
1132         StatementSeqCls() {;}
1133         StatementSeqCls(PPTreeNodeCls Stmt);
1134         int             execute();
1135         int             emit();
1136         PPTreeNodeCls   append(PPTreeNodeCls);
1137    private:
1138         PStatementCls   seq_head;
1139         PStatementCls   seq_tail;
1140 };
```

Empty Statement

```
(p_tree.h)

1150 typedef class EmptyStmtCls *PEmptyStmtCls;
1151 class EmptyStmtCls : public StatementCls {
1152    public:
1153         EmptyStmtCls()  {;}
1154         int             execute();
1155         int             emit();
1156 };
```

Assignment Statement

```
(p_tree.h)

1159 typedef class AssignmentStmtCls *PAssignmentStmtCls;
1160 class AssignmentStmtCls : public StatementCls {
1161    public:
1162         AssignmentStmtCls() {;}
1163         AssignmentStmtCls(PPTreeNodeCls Variable,
1164                            PPTreeNodeCls Expr);
1165         int             execute();
1166         int             emit();
1167    private:
1168         PVariableCls    variable;       //lhs
1169         PExprCls        expr;           //rhs
1170 };
```

Selection Statements

```
If statement (p_tree.h)

1173 typedef class IfStmtCls *PIfStmtCls;
1174 class IfStmtCls : public StatementCls {
1175    public:
1176          IfStmtCls() {;}
1177          IfStmtCls(PPTreeNodeCls Expr,
1178                      PPTreeNodeCls Statement,
1179                        PPTreeNodeCls ElseStatement);
1180          int              execute();
1181          int              emit();
1182    private:
1183          PExprCls         expr;          //boolean
1184          PStatementCls stmt;             //then part
1185          PStatementCls else_stmt;        //else part
1186 };
1188
1189 typedef class ElseStmtCls *PElseStmtCls;
1190 class ElseStmtCls : public StatementCls {
1191    public:
1192          ElseStmtCls() {;} //Really an error statement!
1193          ElseStmtCls(PPTreeNodeCls ElseStatement);
1194    private:
1195          PPTreeNodeCls else_stmt;        //else part
1196 };
```

```
Case label classes (p_tree.h)

1199 typedef class CaseLabelCls *PCaseLabelCls;
1200 class CaseLabelCls : public ExprCls {
1201    public:
1202          CaseLabelCls() {;}
1203          CaseLabelCls(PPTreeNodeCls Constant);
1204          int              emit();
1205          friend class CaseStmtCls;
1206    private:
1207          PExprCls         constant;
1208 };
1209
1210 typedef class CaseLabelLstCls *PCaseLabelLstCls;
1211 class CaseLabelLstCls : public PTreeNodeCls {
1212    public:
1213          CaseLabelLstCls() {;}
1214          CaseLabelLstCls(PPTreeNodeCls CaseLabelElt);
1215          int              emit();
1216          PPTreeNodeCls    append(PPTreeNodeCls);
1217          friend class CaseStmtCls;
1218    private:
1219          PCaseLabelCls    seq_head;
1220          PCaseLabelCls    seq_tail;
1221 };
```

Case label classes (p_tree.h)

```
1224 typedef class CaseEltCls *PCaseEltCls;
1225 class CaseEltCls : public StatementCls {
1226    public:
1227         CaseEltCls() {;}
1228         CaseEltCls(PPTreeNodeCls CaseLabelLst,
1229                               PPTreeNodeCls Stmt);
1230         int             emit();
1231         friend class CaseStmtCls;
1232    private:
1233         PCaseLabelLstCls case_label_lst;
1234         PStatementCls    stmt;
1235 };
1237
1238 typedef class CaseLstCls *PCaseLstCls;
1239 class CaseLstCls : public PTreeNodeCls {
1240    public:
1241         CaseLstCls() {;}
1242         CaseLstCls(PPTreeNodeCls CaseElt);
1243         int             emit();
1244         PPTreeNodeCls   append(PPTreeNodeCls);
1245         friend class CaseStmtCls;
1246    private:
1247         PCaseEltCls     seq_head;
1248         PCaseEltCls     seq_tail;
1249 };
```

Case label classes (p_tree.h)

```
1253 class CaseStmtCls : public StatementCls {
1254    public:
1255          CaseStmtCls() {;}
1256         CaseStmtCls(PPTreeNodeCls Expr,
1257                            PPTreeNodeCls CaseList);
1258         int            execute();
1259         int            emit();
1260    private:
1261         PExprCls        expr;
1262         PCaseLstCls     case_lst;
1263 };
```

Iteration Statements

ForStmtCls definition(p_tree.h)

```
1266 typedef class DirectionCls *PDirectionCls;
1267 class DirectionCls : public PTreeNodeCls {
1268    public:
1269         DirectionCls() {;}
1270         DirectionCls(int Dir);
1271    friend class ForStmtCls;
1272    private:
1273         int            dir;
1274 };
1275
1276 typedef class ForStmtCls *PForStmtCls;
1277 class ForStmtCls : public StatementCls {
1278    public:
1279         ForStmtCls() {;}
1280         ForStmtCls(PPTreeNodeCls Ident,
1281                     PPTreeNodeCls StartExpr,
1282                         PPTreeNodeCls Direct,
1283                             PPTreeNodeCls StopExpr,
1284                                 PPTreeNodeCls Statement);
1285         int            execute();
1286         int            emit();
1287    private:
1288         PIdentCls      ident;
1289         PExprCls       start_expr;
1290         PDirectionCls  dir;
1291         PExprCls       stop_expr;
1292         PStatementCls  stmt;
1293 };
```

WhileStmtCls definition(p_tree.h)

```
1296 typedef class WhileStmtCls *PWhileStmtCls;
1297 class WhileStmtCls : public StatementCls {
1298    public:
1299         WhileStmtCls() {;}
1300         WhileStmtCls(PPTreeNodeCls Expr,
1301                     PPTreeNodeCls Statement);
1302         int            execute();
1303         int            emit();
1304    private:
1305         PExprCls       expr;          //boolean
1306         PStatementCls  stmt;
1307 };
```

RepeatStmtCls definition(p_tree.h)

```
1310 typedef class RepeatStmtCls *PRepeatStmtCls;
1311 class RepeatStmtCls : public StatementCls {
1312    public:
1313          RepeatStmtCls() {;}
1314          RepeatStmtCls(PPTreeNodeCls StatementSeq,
1315                        PPTreeNodeCls Expr);
1316          int         execute();
1317          int         emit();
1318    private:
1319          StatementSeqCls *stmt_seq;
1320          PExprCls         expr;          //boolean
1321 };
```

Procedure call statement

```
1325 typedef class ProcCallCls *PProcCallCls;
1326 class ProcCallCls : public StatementCls {
1327    public:
1328          ProcCallCls() {;}
1329          ProcCallCls(PPTreeNodeCls Ident,
1330                      PPTreeNodeCls ActualParamLst);
1331          int         execute();
1332          int         emit();
1333    private:
1334          PIdentCls ident;
1335          PActualParamLstCls actual_param_lst;
1336 };
```

With Statement

```
1361 typedef class WithStmtCls *PWithStmtCls;
1362 class WithStmtCls : public StatementCls {
1363    public:
1364          WithStmtCls() {;}
1365          WithStmtCls(PPTreeNodeCls RecVarLst,
1366                      PPTreeNodeCls Statement);
1367          int         execute();
1368          int         emit();
1369    private:
1370          PRecVarLstCls rec_var_lst;
1371          PStatementCls stmt;
1372 };
```

Write Statements

```
1399 typedef class WriteStmtCls *PWriteStmtCls;
1400 class WriteStmtCls : public StatementCls {
1401    public:
1402         WriteStmtCls()   {;}
1403         WriteStmtCls(PPTreeNodeCls WriteParamLst);
1404         int              execute();
1405         int              emit();
1406    private:
1407         PWriteParamLstCls write_param_lst;
1408 };
1410
1411 typedef class WritelnStmtCls *PWritelnStmtCls;
1412 class WritelnStmtCls : public StatementCls {
1413    public:
1414         WritelnStmtCls()         {;}
1415         WritelnStmtCls(PPTreeNodeCls WriteParamLst);
1416         int              execute();
1417         int              emit();
1418    private:
1419         PWriteParamLstCls write_param_lst;
1420 };
```

8.2.6   Declaration of Procedures and Functions

Parameter Group

```
1423 typedef class ParamGrpCls *PParamGrpCls;
1424 class ParamGrpCls : public PTreeNodeCls {
1425    public:
1426         ParamGrpCls() {;}
1427         ParamGrpCls(PPTreeNodeCls IdentLst, PPTreeNodeCls Type);
1428         PIdentLstCls    get_ident_lst()
1429                              {return ident_lst;}
1430         friend VarParamGrpCls;
1431    private:
1432         PIdentLstCls    ident_lst;
1433         PTypeCls        param_type;
1434 };
```

Value and variable parameters (p_tree.h)

```
1437 typedef class FParamSecCls *PFParamSecCls;  //Base class
1438 class FParamSecCls : public PTreeNodeCls, public LstSeqBldrCls {
1439    public:
1440         FParamSecCls() {;}
1441         virtual PParamGrpCls get_param_grp()
1442                             {return 0;}
1443 };
1444
1445 typedef class ValParamGrpCls *PValParamGrpCls;
1446 class ValParamGrpCls : public FParamSecCls {
1447    public:
1448         ValParamGrpCls() {;}
1449         ValParamGrpCls(PPTreeNodeCls ParamGrp);
1450         PParamGrpCls    get_param_grp()
1451                             {return param_grp;}
1452    private:
1453          PParamGrpCls    param_grp;
1454 };
1455
1456 typedef class VarParamGrpCls *PVarParamGrpCls;
1457 class VarParamGrpCls : public FParamSecCls {
1458    public:
1459         VarParamGrpCls() {;}
1460         VarParamGrpCls(PPTreeNodeCls ParamGrp);
1461         PParamGrpCls    get_param_grp()
1462                             {return param_grp;}
1463    private:
1464         PParamGrpCls    param_grp;
1465 };
```

Procedure and function parameters (p_tree.h)

```
1470 typedef class ProcParamCls *PProcParamCls;
1471 class ProcParamCls : public FParamSecCls {
1472    public:
1473         ProcParamCls() {;}
1474         ProcParamCls(PPTreeNodeCls ProcHead);
1475    private:
1476         ProcHeadCls    *proc_head;
1477 };
1478
1479 class FuncHeadCls;
1480
1481 typedef class FuncParamCls *PFuncParamCls;
1482 class FuncParamCls : public FParamSecCls {
1483    public:
1484         FuncParamCls() {;}
1485         FuncParamCls(PPTreeNodeCls FuncHead);
1486    private:
1487         FuncHeadCls    *func_head;
1488 };
```

Formal parameter list classes (p_tree.h)

```
1491 typedef class FParamSecLstCls *PFParamSecLstCls;
1492 class FParamSecLstCls : public PTreeNodeCls {
1493    public:
1494         FParamSecLstCls(); //Called by gram for param error
1495         FParamSecLstCls(PPTreeNodeCls FParamSec);
1496         PPTreeNodeCls   append(PPTreeNodeCls);
1497         PFParamSecCls   get_seq_head()
1498                            {return seq_head;}
1499    private:
1500         PFParamSecCls   seq_head;
1501         PFParamSecCls   seq_tail;
1502 };
1504
1505 typedef class FParamStuffCls *PFParamStuffCls;
1506 class FParamStuffCls : public PTreeNodeCls {
1507    public:
1508         FParamStuffCls() {;}
1509         FParamStuffCls(PPTreeNodeCls FParamSecLst);
1510         PFParamSecLstCls get_fpsl()
1511                            {return fpsl;}
1512    private:
1513         PFParamSecLstCls fpsl; //temporarily typed this way
1514 };
```

Subprograms

```
1519 typedef class ProcHeadCls *PProcHeadCls;
1520 class ProcHeadCls : public PTreeNodeCls {
1521    public:
1522         ProcHeadCls();
1523         PPTreeNodeCls   finish(PPTreeNodeCls Ident,
1524                                         PPTreeNodeCls FormalParam);
1525         friend class    ProcDecCls;
1526    private:
1527         PIdentCls        ident;
1528         SymtabCls        *proc_tab;
1529         PFParamStuffCls formal_param_stuff;
1530 };
1532
1533 typedef class FuncFormCls *PFuncFormCls;
1534 class FuncFormCls : public PTreeNodeCls {
1535    public:
1536         FuncFormCls() {;}
1537         FuncFormCls(PPTreeNodeCls FPStuff, PPTreeNodeCls Type);
1538         friend class    FuncHeadCls;
1539    private:
1540         PFParamStuffCls fp_stuff;
1541         PTypeCls         type;
1542 };
1543
1544 typedef class FuncHeadCls *PFuncHeadCls;
1545 class FuncHeadCls : public PTreeNodeCls {
1546    public:
1547         FuncHeadCls();
1548         PPTreeNodeCls   finish(PPTreeNodeCls Ident,
1549                                         PPTreeNodeCls FuncForm);
1550         friend class    FuncDecCls;
1551    private:
1552         PIdentCls        ident;
1553         PTypeCls         func_type;
1554         SymtabCls        *func_tab;
1555         PFParamStuffCls formal_param_stuff;
1556 };
```

8.2.7 Root Classes

Block

```
1559 typedef class BlockCls *PBlockCls;
1560 class BlockCls : public PTreeNodeCls {
1561    public:
1562         BlockCls()       {;}
1563         BlockCls(PPTreeNodeCls StmtSeq);
1564         int              execute();
1565         int              emit();
1566    private:
1567         PStatementSeqCls stmt_seq;
1568 };
```

Program

```
1571 typedef class ProgramCls *PProgramCls;
1572 class ProgramCls : public PTreeNodeCls {
1573   public:
1574          ProgramCls()    {;}
1575          ProgramCls(PPTreeNodeCls Ident, PPTreeNodeCls Block);
1576          int             execute();
1577          int             emit();
1578          void            print();
1579   private:
1580          SymtabCls       *std_table;
1581          PIdentCls       ident;
1582          PBlockCls       block;
1583 };
```

8.2.8   Parse Tree Class

```
1586 typedef class PTreeCls *PPTreeCls;
1587 class PTreeCls {
1588   public:
1589          PTreeCls(PPTreeNodeCls Root);
1590          int             execute();
1591          int             emit();
1592          int             optimize();
1593          int             peephole();
1594          int             decorate();
1595          void            print();
1596          friend ostream& operator<< (ostream&, PTreeCls&);
1597   private:
1598          PPTreeNodeCls   root;
1599 };
```

8.3   Parse Tree Module

This chapter has described the single definition file for the parse tree module *p_tree*. The implementation of the various class functions are contained in a number of different files, as illustrated in Figure 8.11. Since all static semantic checking can be done by the constructors of the various parse tree objects during the parsing phase, the implementation of the various constructors is discussed in Chapter 9 on semantics. Semantics that must be checked at run time can be most easily implemented in an interpreter, and then these checks can be used as a benchmark for the output of the code generator. Details for *interp.C* and *emit.C* can be found in Chapters 10 and 11, respectively.

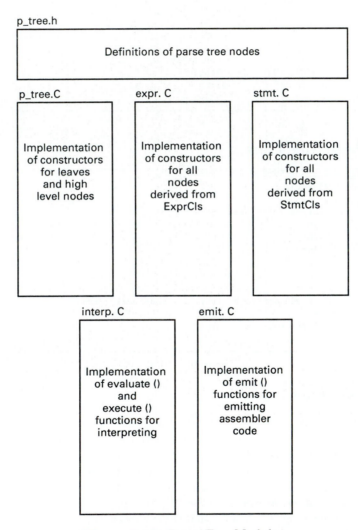

Figure 8.11. Parse Tree Module

8.4   Exercises

1. Construct a precedence string for each of the following.

   (a) *Constant.*

   (b) *Assignment.*

   (c) *Procedure_call.*
       Hint: There are two strings. One is rather extensive and includes actual parameter nonterminals.

   (d) *Write_stmt.*

2. For each of the precedence strings in Exercise 1,

   (a) List parse tree objects that would be appropriate for representing the corresponding source program structure.

   (b) Specify any class structures suggested by the discovered objects.

   (c) Construct C++ grammar action(s) needed to produce the corresponding parse tree nodes.

3. Specify the data membership of an *IfStmt* object by answering the following question.

   (a) What are the nonterminals on the right side of the *If_stmt* production?

   (b) Do any of these nonterminals not yet have objects associated with them? If so, spend some time describing these objects.

   (c) Make a list of *IfStmt* object data members. Note that these are almost always *pointers*.

4. Using a Pascal grammar (Appendix E) and the set of case-class definitions in Section 8.2.5, trace through the construction of the various objects for the following Pascal code segment.

```
case i of
      1: doOneThing;
    2,4: doTwoFourThing;
  3,5,6: doOtherThing
end
```

5. Trace through the construction of the various objects for the following Pascal declaration.

```
        procedure example(invar1,invar2: integer;
                           var outvar1, outvar2: real);
        begin

        end
```

6. Trace through the construction of the various objects for the following Pascal instruction.

   `for i := 10 downto 1 do`

7. (**CLIP** Project)

   Define the parse tree classes for **CLIP**.

Chapter 9

Static Semantics

> Topics:
> - Terms
> - Strategy
> - Implementing semantic checks

9.1 Examples

Expressions. In Pascal, as in most languages, complex expressions are constructed from simpler ones by means of unary and binary operations such as $+$, $*$, *in*, ... Expressions like

$$2 + 3$$

and $2 + 3.0$ are valid, of course, while one like

$$2 + \text{`a'}$$

is not. The integer expression in $2 + 3.0$ is **lifted** to a real.

Assignment statement. The left-hand side of a Pascal assignment must be a variable of the same type as the expression on the right-hand side.

If *ivar* is a variable of integer type, then the assignment

```
ivar := 0
```

is valid, while the assignment, below, is not.

```
ivar := 0.0
```

Of course Pascal assignment statements have the same lifting rule for integers to reals as do expressions: the assignment, below, is therefore valid for a variable *rvar* of real type.

```
rvar := 0
```

249

Procedure call.   Given that the procedure header

```
procedure GetUserResponse(Prompt: string; var Resp: string);
```

has been recognized by the parser, the two statements

```
GetUserResponse('Please enter last name',Response);
```

and

```
GetUserResponse(Pmpt,Response);
```

are clearly valid calls, since they abide by the well-known Pascal rule about parameters: The number and type of formal and actual parameters must agree.

The procedure calls

```
GetUserResponse(i,j)
```

and

```
GetUserResponse(Prompt,Response,Success)
```

are not valid, since the first has actual parameters whose types do not match those of the formal parameters and the second call has more actual than formal parameters.

A more subtle kind of error is illustrated in the following command.

```
GetUserResponse(Prompt,'response')
```

Actual parameters corresponding to variable formal parameters must not be literals.

Declarations.   In the following valid Pascal declarations,

```
type
    ArrayType = array [1 .. MAX] of integer;
var
    IntArray: ArrayType;
```

the (standard) identifier `integer` already has been defined. By the time *ArrayType* is encountered in the variable declaration it also has been declared. These are just examples of usual "declare-it-before-using-it" rule.

Pascal relaxes this rule for recursively defined record declarations like the following.

```
type
    NodePtrType = ^NodeType;
    NodeType = record
                    data: integer;
                    next: NodePtrType;
                end;
```

9.2 Terms

The compiler components we have developed so far would have significant difficulty enforcing the rules illustrated in any of these examples. A scanner can certainly recognize a particular literal and so produce information about its corresponding type. But determining the type associated with a user-defined variable is not even possible for a parser. Counting parameters could be done with a finite-state machine having a stack. But again the matching of types and the checking of variable actual parameter requirements cannot even be done by the most powerful LR(1) machines. And selective application of matching-type or define-before-use rules is far beyond the capabilities of any machine based solely upon the specification of syntax.

Recall (Chapters 1 and 5) that scanners are primarily responsible for breaking the Pascal source program into meaningful chunks and to screen out individual characters that are not meaningful (i.e., illegal characters) or are not relevant information for the compiler. Lexical rules are language restrictions related to the individual characters and the recognition of valid chunks or lexemes. Recall also (Chapters 1 and 6) that the parser is responsible for checking the *order* of the Pascal program's tokens against the order prescribed by the Pascal grammar. Syntax rules are language restrictions that can be imposed by a (context-free) grammar testing token order. All language restrictions that are not lexical nor syntax are called **semantic rules**. Semantic checks that are best performed during the compilation process are called **contextual constraints** or **static semantics**. Language requirements that are best detected at runtime are called **dynamic semantics**.

9.3 Strategy for Checking Static Semantics

The object-oriented design work of the earlier chapters really pays handsomely at this juncture of compiler construction. Since each node in the parse tree is now an *object*, the semantic data that is relevant for that particular part of the program can be encapsulated in the *attributes* of the corresponding object. Any static semantic checks can then be built into the *behavior* of the object, that represents that grammatical structure during compilation, most often when the object is created.

9.3.1 Examples Revisited

Expression. The process of checking the types of two operands of the expression $2 + 3$ is illustrated in Figure 9.1. The first task is to spot the 2 and 3 as unsigned integer literals, that is of course performed by the scanner. Then the bottom-up parser, when receiving the *UNSIGNEDINTTK* token, uses the production

```
Unsigned_number: UNSIGNEDINTTK
             ;
```

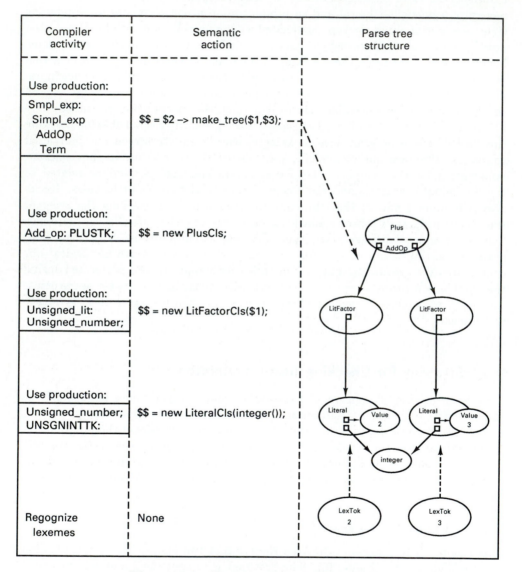

Figure 9.1. Checking Types in Expressions

to recognize each literal. It is possible to insert commands to create the parse tree objects directly into the grammar. For example, the command

$$\$\$ = \text{new LiteralCls(std\_type.integer())};$$

creating a *LiteralCls* object can be added to the following production.

```
Unsigned_number: UNSIGNEDINTTK
        {$$ = new LiteralCls(std_type.integer();}
      ;
```

The parser, once it has recognized the right-hand side of the production, will then execute the C++ code, where $$ refers to a special parser's value stack onto which is pushed the pointer to the *LiteralCls* object just created.

The next production used in the recognition process is

```
Unsigned_lit: Unsigned_number
      ;
```

where a literal is converted to an expression by constructing a *LitFactorCls* expression object as its parent node in the tree. We therefore add the action

$$\$\$ = \text{new LitFactorCls(\$1)};$$

to the production as follows.

```
Unsigned_lit: Unsigned_number
        {$$ = new LitFactorCls($1);}
      ;
```

Next, the + is recognized as an *Add_op* and the corresponding object is created by the following production.

```
Add_op: PLUSTK
        {$$ = new PlusCls;}
      ;
```

What remains is to make the *PlusCls* object point to the literal expressions for 2 and 3. This is accomplished by the parser action

$$\$\$ = \$2 \rightarrow \text{make\_tree(\$1,\$2)};$$

that is placed in the following *Simple_expr* production.

```
Simple_expr: Simple_expr AddOp Term
        {$$ = $2 -> make_tree($1,$2);}
      ;
```

It is here that the semantic requirement of identical types is checked. First the *PlusCls* member function *make_tree()* calls its base class *AddOpCls* function *make_tree()*, that establishes the links to the left and right expressions.

```
PPTreeNodeCls PlusCls :: make_tree(PPTreeNodeCls Left,
                                   PPTreeNodeCls Right) {
    PPTreeNodeCls check = AddOpCls::make_tree(Left,Right);

    //now, test for valid types
    PTypeCls l_type = left -> get_type();
    PTypeCls r_type = right -> get_type();
    if (this -> is_defined_for(l_type,r_type)) {
        this -> ExprCls::type = l_type;
    } else {
        soft.err("+ not valid for this type");
    }
}
```

Then the *PlusCls* function *make_tree()* requests the left and right expressions to send their types. And finally the types are checked by the *PlusCls* function *is_defined_for()* illustrated in the following code.

```
int PlusCls :: is_defined_for(PTypeCls Left, PTypeCls Right) {
    if (*Left != *Right) {
        soft.err("'+' requires identical types");
        return 0;
    } else if (*Left == *std_type.integer()) {
        return 1;
    } else if (*Left == *std_type.real()) {
        return 1;
    } else {
        return 0;
    }
}
```

Assignment.   Figure 9.2 contains a portion of a parse tree representing the assignment statement `ivar := 0`. The production that recognizes such a statement of course is the following.

`Assignment: Variable ASGTK Expr;`

And this is then augmented with the indicated action,

`{$$ = new AssignmentStmtCls($1,$3);}`

designed to perform the semantic check that is included in the object's constructor.

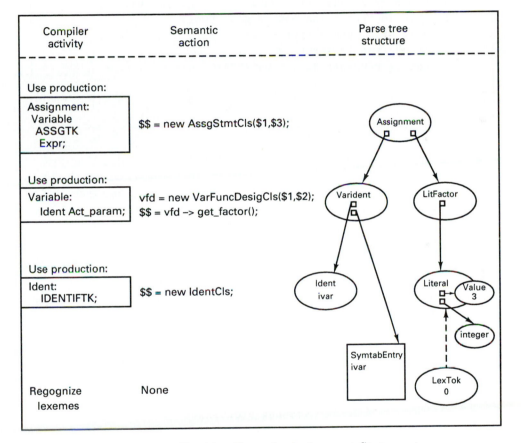

Figure 9.2. Checking Types in Assignment Statements

Code for the *AssignmentStmtCls* constructor is listed below.

```
AssignmentStmtCls :: AssignmentStmtCls(
                          PPTreeNodeCls Variable,
                            PPTreeNodeCls Expr) {
    variable = PVariableCls(Variable);
    expr = PExprCls(Expr);
    PSymtabEntryCls lhs_att = variable -> get_att();
    PTypeCls id_type = lhs_att -> get_type();
    PTypeCls expr_type = expr -> get_type();
    if (!(*id_type |= *expr_type)) {
        soft.err("Types do not match");
    }
}
```

- Since the left-hand side of an assignment is a *Variable*, rather than just an *Ident*, and since the variable object references an appropriate symbol table, a pointer *lhs_att* to that symbol table entry can be updated and then used to determine the type of the memory location(s) being referenced.

- The right-hand side is an expression object that contains a member containing its type information. In Pascal, these types need only be **assignment compatible**. This is symbolized by the |= *TypeCls* operator, that essentially requires that either the types are identical or that an integer is being assigned to a real.

Procedure call. A procedure call is recognized by the following production.

```
Procedure_call: Ident Actual_param_stuff
                {$$=new ProcCallCls($1,$2);}
```

As the tree illustrated in Figure 9.3 is constructed the *ProcCallCls* object's constructor performs the various checks on the parameters. The constructor first finds the identifier's symbol table entry, determines that it indeed does represent a procedure (code for this has been omitted), and then begins working down the two lists of parameters, formal and actual, matching type and checking "variable-ness". At the end of either list, information about the total numbers of each list of parameters is used to send a relevant error message to the user.

```
ProcCallCls :: ProcCallCls(PPTreeNodeCls Ident,
                           PPTreeNodeCls ActualParamLst) {
    char *name = Ident -> get_name();
    PSymtabEntryCls found_it = ScopeCls::get_vista() ->
                                      vista_lookup(name);
    actual_param_lst = PActualParamLstCls(ActualParamLst);

    // Params must match in number, type and order.
    PFParamAttCls f_param = PProcAttCls(found_it) ->
                                        get_param_lst();
    if (f_param) {
        PActualParamCls a_param = actual_param_lst ->
                                        get_seq_head();
        while (f_param && a_param) {
            PTypeCls f_type = f_param -> get_type();
            PTypeCls a_type = a_param -> get_type();
            // Match in type ....
            if (!(*f_type == *a_type)) {
                soft.err("Types don't match");
            }
            //var formal must have
            //          variable access actual param.
            if (f_param -> get_is_var() &&
                            !(a_param -> is_var())) {
                soft.err("Must have variable actual param");
            }
            // Get the next pair of parameters
            f_param = PFParamAttCls(f_param -> get_next());
            a_param = PActualParamCls(a_param -> get_next());
        }
        // Match in number ....
        if (f_param) {
            soft.err("Not enough actual parameters");
        } else if (a_param) {
            soft.err("Too many actual parameters");
        }
    }
}
```

Declaration.   Objects produced during the recognition of most declarations are not parse tree nodes and so don't officially belong to the list of classes described in this chapter. But these declaration (and other definition) objects are created by the parser in essentially the same way as are parse tree objects, and the constructors for these objects similarly enforce the associated semantic requirements.

When type or variable declarations like

```
type
    ArrayType = array [1 .. MAX] of integer;
var
    IntArray: ArrayType;
```

are recognized by the parser, a declaration or definition object is created; it is not

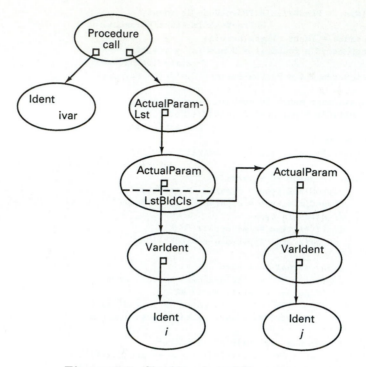

Figure 9.3. Checking Actual Parameters

placed on the parser's stack, since no other object needs to refer to its attributes and it is not directly used during either the interpreter or code generation phases. So the grammar production for type definition looks like

```
Type_def: Ident EQTK Type
          {new TypeDefCls($1,$3);}
        ;
```

and the production for variable declaration is as follows.

```
Var_dec: Ident_lst COLONTK Type
         {new VarDecCls($1,$3);}
       ;
```

Note that each action simply creates the corresponding object. The constructors

```
TypeDefCls :: TypeDefCls(PPTreeNodeCls Ident,
                         PPTreeNodeCls Type) {
    char* name = Ident -> get_name();
    char *name = p -> get_name();
    PSymtabEntryCls found_it = scp -> lookup(name);
    if (found_it) {
        soft.err("Variable already declared");
    }
    PTypeAttCls t_att = new TypeAttCls(name, Type);
    ScopeCls::get_vista() -> insert(t_att);
}
```

and

```
VarDecCls :: VarDecCls(PPTreeNodeCls IdentList,
                       PPTreeNodeCls Type) {
    PIdentCls p = PIdentLstCls(Ident_lst) ->
                                    get_seq_head();
    PSymtabCls scp = ScopeCls::get_vista();
    while (p) {
        char *name = p -> get_name();
        PSymtabEntryCls found_it = scp -> lookup(name);
        if (found_it) {
            soft.err("Variable already declared");
        } else {
            PValueCls default_val = type ->
                                    make_value();

            PVarAttCls va =
                new VarAttCls(name,type,default_val);
            scp -> insert(va);
        }
        p = PIdentCls(p -> get_next());
    }
}
```

do the required semantic checking and insert the relevant information into appropriate symbol tables.

9.3.2 Role of the Parser

The idea of using the parser to assist in semantic checking is a well-known technique, often called **syntax-directed translation**. The main idea is that each item on the left-hand side of a production has associated with it an potentially diverse set of data items, called **attributes**. The values of these attributes are determined and also set by **semantic actions** or functions that are invoked by parser actions placed on the right-side of the corresponding productions. Naturally if you are using a bottom-up parser, you will be able to update attributes of parent tree nodes based upon values of the children. All such **synthesized** attributes are determined during the parsing phase. Those attributes not properly updated at the conclusion of the parsing phase most probably require information from a parent. These **inherited** attributes are then usually determined by one or more traversals of the parse tree.

There are two aspects of such syntax-directed translation that have required major effort in the past.

- Finding convenient means for implementing and then accessing the various attribute data structures, often complex record structures

- Providing robust procedures for the traversal of parse trees of unpredictably varied shapes

Object-oriented implementation languages provide mechanisms that make each of these problems more manageable. The first problem is conveniently solved by simply declaring a parse tree node's attributes to be data members of the object representing the particular language structure. In fact, these data members are usually pointers to other parse tree objects, making for very simple structures at each node in the tree.

Object-oriented ideas also greatly simplify the second problem. Instead of one or more routines designed to traverse the entire parse tree, all the while locating and then decorating the remaining inherited attributes, *each object of the tree* is given specific behavior, suitable for passing information to the children *of that specific object*. Rather than one complex tree-traversal procedure, we now have many objects doing what each one knows best: exhibiting its *own* behavior.

In summary, implementing static semantic requirements can be achieved as follows.

General Procedure

1. Determine a set of parse tree objects.

2. For each object, determine the collection of possible semantic attributes. This involves looking at the items on the right side of the production that is associated with the object. It also requires knowing what semantic requirements should be checked at that point in the recognition of the source program.

3. Encapsulate each semantic attribute as a class attribute or member.

4. Implement the relevant semantic requirement(s) into the object's constructor.

5. Modify the corresponding grammar production to include an action creating the object and (in most cases) placing that object on the parser's value stack.

Steps 1, 2, and 3 in the general procedure have been completed in Chapter 8. Section 9.4 focuses on step 4. The last step is discussed in Section 9.5.

9.4   Implementing Static Semantic Checks

Actually this section contains listing for all parse tree class constructors. While most of these do contain static semantic checks, some are simply bookkeeping constructors whose main task is to be sure that attributes arriving from children nodes are placed in the appropriate data members of the parent.

9.4.1   PTreeNode Base Class

Since all parse tree nodes are created by the parser upon recognition of the entire right-hand side of a production, we have decided to store (a pointer to) the current *LexTokCls* object at the time of recognition. In particular, for leaf nodes this will provide lexical information about the particular lexeme just recognized.

```
(p_tree.C)

19 PTreeNodeCls :: PTreeNodeCls() {
20     //cout << "PTreeNodeCls" << endl;
21     extern LexTokCls *lex_tok;
22     lt = lex_tok;
23 }
24
25 int PTreeNodeCls :: emit() {
26     cout << "PPTreeNodeCls::emit() BASECLASS " << endl;
27     return 0;
28 }
29
30 int PTreeNodeCls :: execute() {
31     cout << "PPTreeNodeCls::execute() BASECLASS " << endl;
32     return 0;
33 }
34
35 int PTreeNodeCls :: optimize() {
36     cout << "PPTreeNodeCls::optimize() BASECLASS " << endl;
37     return 0;
38 }
39
40 int PTreeNodeCls :: peephole() {
41     cout << "PPTreeNodeCls::peephole() BASECLASS " << endl;
42     return 0;
43 }
44
45 void PTreeNodeCls :: print() {
46     cout << "PTreeNodeCls::print() " << " lex_tok " << *lt ;
47 }
48
49 ostream& operator<<(ostream& s, PTreeNodeCls& x) {
50     return s << "PTreeNodeCls: "  << x.lt ;
51 }
```

As described in Appendix A, defining functions for the base class that are intended to be redefined by derived classes is performed by using the `virtual` keyword.

The parent functions contain an output statement to warn the implementor that a derived class function has probably not been correctly defined.

9.4.2   Literal and Identifier Classes

This might be a good time to review the important *ValueCls* ideas found in Appendix C, Section C.4. Essentially all internal compiler variable values are handled by objects of this class.

LiteralCls

LiteralCls objects are created normally when a production recognizing a numeric, character or string literal has been completed. The normal convention is that a nil argument to the constructor signifies that a character or string literal has been encountered.

```
Constant:  STRINGTK      /*type is char if len=1*/
            {PLiteralCls lit = new LiteralCls(0)}
```

```
(p_tree.C)

54 LiteralCls :: LiteralCls(PTypeCls Type) {
55     //cout << "LiteralCls " << Type << endl;
56     //cout << " this " << this << endl;
57     if (Type) {
58         //numeric
59         value = new ValueCls(this ->
60                         PTreeNodeCls::lt -> get_lexeme());
61         type = Type;
62     } else {
63         char *lit_ch = this ->
64                         PTreeNodeCls::lt -> get_lexeme();
65         if (! *lit_ch == '\'') {
66             hard.err("LiteralCls() Logic error!");
67          }
68         //need to strip off the outer string delimiters: '
69         int str_len = strlen(lit_ch);
70         Pchar short_str = new char[str_len];
71         strncpy(short_str,++lit_ch,str_len -2);
72
73         //now set value and type
74         value = new ValueCls(short_str);
75         if (strlen(short_str) == 1) {
76             type = std_type.CHAR();
77         } else {
78             type = std_type.string_lit();
79         }
80     }
81 }
```

In this case, the string delimiters are removed and the value is stored as a scalar in a *ValueCls* object. If the string is one character long, it is associated with a Pascal char type; otherwise it is typed as an internal string.

A numeric literal will have either an integer or real type associated with it, and this can be sent to the constructor by the following semantic actions in the grammar.

```
Unsigned_number: UNSIGNEDINTTK
            {$$ = new LiteralCls(std_type.integer());}
          | UNSIGNEDREALTK
                {$$ = new LiteralCls(std_type.real());}
          ;
```

In either case, the actual literal value of the integer or real number is a string that is stored as a scalar in a *ValueCls* object.

IdentCls

There are no required Pascal static semantics to test with these constructor. The first constructor is the one most often used. It is called by the grammar production

```
        Ident: IDENTIFIERTK
                {$$ = new IdentCls();}
              ;
```

that recognizes any leaf identifier. This constructor therefore requests the corresponding *LexTokCls* data member of the *PTreeNodeCls* parent to return its lexeme value, and this is stored in the *IdentCls* data member *name*.

The second constructor is called internally in the compiler. The *ControllerCls* object creates standard identifier *IdentCls* objects prior to storing them in the main symbol table. This constructor gets its member data through the argument list, rather than a *LexTokCls* object, since the scanner/parser is not involved in the process.

Lists of identifiers are used many places in Pascal. These lists are recognized by the following productions.

```
        Ident_lst: Ident
                {$$ = new IdentLstCls($1);}
              | Ident_lst COMMATK Ident
                {$$ = PIdentLstCls($1) -> append($3);}
              ;
```

The first identifier causes the *IdentLstCls* object to be created, and then subsequent identifiers are appended to the list by calling the previous object's *append()* function. Note the use of the $1 and the $3 to refer to the corresponding parse tree objects previously stored on the value stack. Note also that an *IdentLstCls* object has such an *append()* function, since it is derived from a *LstSeqBldrCls*. More information about *LstSeqBldrCls* can be obtained from Section C.1.

```
(p_tree.C)

 84 IdentCls :: IdentCls() {
 85     //cout << "IdentCls" << endl;
 86     name = this -> PTreeNodeCls::lt -> get_lexeme();
 87     //cout << " name " << name << endl;
 88 }
 89
 90 IdentCls :: IdentCls(char *Name) {
 91     //cout << "IdentCls(Name)" << endl;
 92     name = Name;
 93 }
 94
 95 IdentLstCls :: IdentLstCls(PPTreeNodeCls Ident) {
 96     //cout << "IdentLstCls" << endl;
 97     seq_head = seq_tail = PIdentCls(Ident);
 98 }
 99
100 PPTreeNodeCls IdentLstCls :: append(PPTreeNodeCls Ident) {
101     //cout << "IdentLstCls::append()" << endl;
102     if (!seq_tail) {
103         cerr << "IdentLstCls::append() -- Logic Error" << endl;
104     } else {
105         seq_tail = PIdentCls(seq_tail ->
106                     LstSeqBldrCls::append(PIdentCls(Ident)));
107     }
108     return this;
109 }
```

9.4.3   Expression Classes

Expression Base Class

```
(p_tree.C)

112 ExprCls :: ExprCls() {
113     //cout << "ExprCls" << endl;
114 }
115
116 ExprCls :: ExprCls(PTypeCls Type) {
117     //cout << "ExprCls" << endl;
118     type = Type;
119 }
```

As noted in Section 8.1.2, expressions are essentially characterized by their type and their value. Neither of the *ExprCls* constructors are called by semantic actions placed in the grammar. The first is just a default constructor necessarily called by the constructors of any objects derived from this base class. The second could possibly be called directly by derived objects' constructors, though the present version of the compiler does not use it in any way.

Relational Operator

If you look back to Section 8.2.3, you will note that *RelOpCls* is a base class from which are derived the various relational operator classes like *EqCls*, *LtCls*, and so on. As such the *RelOpCls* constructors are not designed to be called from grammatical semantic actions. The same is true for the first function (virtual!) implemented below.

```
(expr.C)

34  int RelOpCls :: is_defined_for(PTypeCls Left, PTypeCls Right) {
35      cout << "RelOpCls::is_defined_for()--BASE CLASS!!" << endl;
36      if (!Left || !Right) {
37          hard.err("RelOpCls::is_defined_for() logic error");
38      }
39      hard.err("Execution of base class");
40      return 0;
41  }
42
43  PPTreeNodeCls RelOpCls :: make_tree(PPTreeNodeCls Left,
44                                      PPTreeNodeCls Right) {
45      //cout << "RelOpCls::make_tree()" << endl;
46      if (!Left || !Right) {
47          hard.err("RelOpCls::make_tree logic error");
48      }
49      left =  PExprCls(Left);
50      right = PExprCls(Right);
51      return this;
52
53  }
```

The second function is also redefined by each derived class, though in this case the redefined function actually calls this one. An example would probably be helpful at this point. Suppose that the parser is trying to recognize a boolean expression like $i = 3$. After the identifier i and the literal 3 have been recognized and the corresponding parse tree nodes created, the following productions handle the relational expression.

```
Expr: Simple_expr
    | Simple_expr Relational_op Simple_expr
      {$$ = PRelOpCls($2) -> make_tree($1,$3);}
    ;
      Relational_op: EQTK
              {$$ = new EqCls;}
      ;
```

```
(expr.C)

56  int EqCls :: is_defined_for(PTypeCls Left, PTypeCls Right) {
57      //cout << "EqCls::is_defined_for()" << endl;
58      if (!Left || !Right) {
59          hard.err("RelOpCls::is_def_for() logic error");
60      } else if (!(*Left |= *Right)) {
61          soft.err("= requires identical types");
62          return 0;
63      } else if (*Left == *std_type.integer()) {
64          return 1;
65      } else if (*Left == *std_type.real()) {
66          return 1;
67      } else if (*Left == *std_type.CHAR()) {
68          return 1;
69      } else if (Left -> is_enum()) {
70          return 1;
71      } else if (Left -> is_subrange()) {
72          return 1;
73      } else {
74          return 0;
75      }
76  }
77
78  PPTreeNodeCls EqCls ::  make_tree(PPTreeNodeCls Left,
79                                    PPTreeNodeCls Right) {
80      PPTreeNodeCls check = RelOpCls::make_tree(Left,Right);
81      //checks for null left and right
82      PTypeCls l_type = left -> get_type();
83      PTypeCls r_type = right -> get_type();
84      if (this -> is_defined_for(l_type,r_type)) {
85          this -> ExprCls::type = std_type.boolean();
86      } else {
87          soft.err(" '=' not valid for this type");
88      }
89      return this;
90
91  }
```

When the = is recognized, an *EqCls* object is created. Because *EqCls* is derived from *RelOpCls*, the default *RelOpCls* constructor (that has really nothing to do) will be executed. Then when the entire expression is recognized, $2 now represents the *EqCls* object just created. That object's *make_tree()* is then called. Its first task is to call the *RelOpCls* function to store the types of the left and right expressions, and then to perform the following semantic checks.

1. Are the left and right types identical? (Actually, we should allow for lifting an integer to a real here.)

2. Does the type admit a relational operator of equal?

If the answer is yes, then the type of the *EqCls* object is set to Pascal boolean. If not, an error message is sent to the programmer.

Unary Operators

A unary expression like $-i$ is recognized by the following production.

```
Simple_expr:
        MINUSTK Term
        {$$ = new UMinusCls($2);}
    ;
```

When the *UMinusCls* object is created the first two of the following functions are called.

```
(expr.C)

303 UMinusCls :: UMinusCls(PPTreeNodeCls Term) {
304     //cout << "UMinusCls() " << endl;
305     term = PExprCls(Term);
306     ExprCls::type = term -> get_type();
307     if (! this -> is_defined_for(ExprCls::type)) {
308         soft.err("Unary minus is not valid for this type");
309     }
310 }
311
312 int UMinusCls :: is_defined_for(PTypeCls Type) {
313     //cout << "UMinusCls::is_defined_for()" << endl;
314     if (*Type |= *std_type.integer()) {
315         return 1;
316     } else if (*Type == *std_type.real()) {
317         return 1;
318     } else {
319         return 0;
320     }
321 }
322
323 PTypeCls UMinusCls :: get_type() {
324     //cout << "UMinusCls::get_type()" << endl;
325     return term -> get_type();
326 }
```

Additive Operators

The creation of a parse tree for an expression like $1 + 2$ is also essentially the same as for expressions involving relational operators. In this case the productions are like the following.

```
Simple_expr:  Term
        | Simple_expr Add_op Term
          {$$ = PAddOpCls($2) -> make_tree($1,$3);}
        ;
Add_op: PLUSTK
            {$$ = new PlusCls;}
        ;
```

The implementation details of the *AddOpCls* versions of *is_defined_for()* and *make_tree()* are exactly the same as those for *RelOpCls* and are therefore omitted. The same is true for the *is_defined_for()* of the derived *PlusCls*.

```
(expr.C)

388  PPTreeNodeCls PlusCls :: make_tree(PPTreeNodeCls Left,
389                                      PPTreeNodeCls Right) {
390    //cout << "PlusCls::make_tree()" << endl;
391    PPTreeNodeCls check = AddOpCls::make_tree(Left,Right);
392    //checks for null left and right
393    PTypeCls l_type = left -> get_type();
394    PTypeCls r_type = right -> get_type();
395
396    //check to see if need to lift to real
397    if ((*l_type == *std_type.real()) &&
398            (*r_type == *std_type.integer())) {
399      r_type = std_type.real();
400      right -> set_type(r_type);
401    }
402
403    if ((*l_type == *std_type.integer()) &&
404            (*r_type == *std_type.real())) {
405      l_type = std_type.real();
406      left -> set_type(l_type);
407    }
408
409    //now, check for valid types
410    if (this -> is_defined_for(l_type,r_type)) {
411        this -> ExprCls::type = l_type;
412    } else {
413        soft.err("+ not valid for this type");
414    }
415    return this;
416
417 }
```

There is one addition to the *make_tree()* implementation for some of the objects derived from *AddOpCls* not found in our discussion on relational operators. This has to do with Pascal's specification that integers are to be lifted to reals in certain mixed expressions. If the type of one of the children is integer and the other is real, then the integer one is modified to real. Most compiler implementations would have inserted a special lifting parse tree node between the integer child and the parent "+", but since we are using objects, and since *ValueCls* objects deal with their data members based on the type, a simple change of type to real produces the required lifting. Not all Pascal *AddOpCls* operations perform the lifting: In fact *MinusCls* is the only other one.

Multiplicative Operators

Since the implementation details for the *MulOpCls* base class and sample derived *TimesCls* are essentially the same as those for *AddOpCls* and *PlusCls*, the listings are omitted. Note that in this case only *TimesCls*, and *DivideCls* preform the required lifting of integer to real in mixed expressions.

Literals and Variables

Literals, once recognized by the parser, are converted to expressions by the following productions.

```
Factor: Unsigned_lit
        ;
        Unsigned_lit: Unsigned_number
                      {$$ = new LitFactorCls($1);}
```

Variables are a bit more complex.

```
Factor: Variable
        ;
        Variable: Ident Actual_param_stuff
                  {PVarFuncDesignatorCls vfd = new
                        VarFuncDesignatorCls($1,$2);
                   $$ = vfd -> get_factor();}
                | Variable LBRACKTK Expr_seq RBRACKTK
                  {PComponentSeqCls p = new
                                ComponentSeqCls($1,$3);
                   $$ = p -> get_idx_tree();}
                | Variable DOTTK Ident
                  {$$ = new FieldDesigCls($1,$3);}
                | Variable UPARROWTK
                  {$$ = new DereferenceCls($1);}
                ;
```

Essentially, the first production says that a *Variable* could be the following.

- An identifier (no *Actual_param_stuff*) representing an entire data structure

- A function call (with or without the parentheses or the actual parameters)

The second production describes a Variable as a reference to a particular component of an array. Variables can also be specifications of fields or a pointer dereferencing. Figure 9.4 summarizes these ideas. Recall also that the same structure was described in Chapter 8, where the following parse tree classes were declared.

```
class FactorCls : public ExprCls { ...
   class LitFactorCls : public FactorCls { ...
   class SetFactorCls : public FactorCls { ...
   class VariableCls : public FactorCls { ...
```

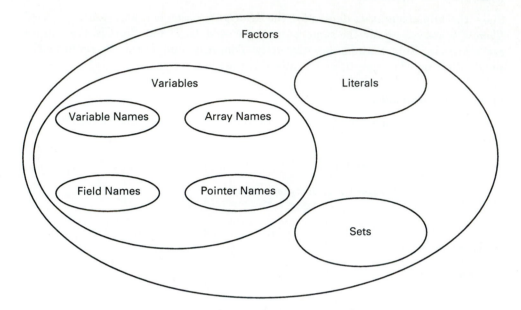

Figure 9.4. Classification of Factors

```
class VarIdentCls : public VariableCls { ...
class FuncCallCls : public VariableCls { ...
class VarFuncDesignatorCls { ...
class ArrayDesigCls: public VariableCls { ...
class FieldDesigCls: public VariableCls { ...
class DereferenceCls: public VariableCls { ...
```

The constructor for the first of these is contained in the next C++ code segment.

```
LitFactorCls constructor (expr.C)

705 LitFactorCls :: LitFactorCls(PPTreeNodeCls Lit) {
706     //cout << "LitFactorCls() " << endl;
707     if (!Lit) {
708         cerr << "LitFactorCls - Logic Error" << endl;
709     }
710     this -> ExprCls::value = PLiteralCls(Lit) -> evaluate();
711     ExprCls::type  = PLiteralCls(Lit) -> get_type();
712 }
```

The *LiteralCls* object is converted to an expression by storing the appropriate type and value in the parent *ExprCls* data members.

Constructing *SetFactorCls* literals is done by specifying the various members of the set. Pascal set elements are specified by lists of expressions that must be of the same type and of constant value.

```
SetMemberCls constructor (expr.C)

715 SetMemberCls :: SetMemberCls(PPTreeNodeCls StartElt,
716                              PPTreeNodeCls StopElt) {
717     cout << "SetMemberCls" << endl;
718     start_elt = PExprCls(StartElt);
719
720     if (!StopElt) {
721         stop_elt = start_elt;
722     } else {
723         stop_elt = PExprCls(StopElt);
724     }
725
726     if (*(start_elt -> get_type()) != *(stop_elt -> get_type())) {
727         soft.err("Set members not of same type");
728         stop_elt = start_elt; //for recovery
729     }
730
731     if (!(start_elt -> get_type() -> is_ordinal())) {
732         soft.err("Sets require ordinal types");
733     } else if ((start_elt -> is_var()) ||
734                (stop_elt -> is_var())) {
735         soft.err("Sets require constant member values");
736     }
737 }
```

Then a set literal is implemented by declaring it to be of set type having the given set of members and by setting its value to be a *ValueCls* object also determined by the members. (See Appendix C for more detail on *SetValueCls*.)

```
SetFactorCls constructor (expr.C)

760 SetFactorCls :: SetFactorCls(PPTreeNodeCls MemberLst) {
761     cout << "SetFactorCls() " << endl;
762     if (!MemberLst) {
763         hard.err("SetFactorCls - Logic Error");
764     }
765     this -> member_lst = PSetMemberLstCls(MemberLst);
766     this -> ExprCls::type =
767             new SetTypeCls(member_lst -> get_type());
768     PSetValCls sval = new SetValCls(member_lst);
769     this -> ExprCls::value = new ValueCls(sval);
770 }
```

The next segment describes the constructors for the variable subclass of factors illustrated in Figure 9.4. *VariableCls* is just a base class. This constructor for the base class is called by the constructors for the derived children by the colon operator as illustrated in the header of the *VarIdentCls*:

```
VarIdentCls :: VarIdentCls(...): Variable(Type,Val) { ...
```

```
Variable and VarIdent (expr.C)

773 VariableCls :: VariableCls(PTypeCls Type, PValueCls Value) {
774     //cout << "VariableCls()" << endl;
775     ExprCls::type = Type;
776     value = Value;
777 }
778
779 PTypeCls VariableCls :: get_var_type() {
780     hard.err("VariableCls::get_var_type() BASE CLASS!!");
781     return 0;
782 }
783
784 VarIdentCls :: VarIdentCls(PIdentCls VarIdent,
785                           PSymtabEntryCls Att,
786                             PTypeCls Type,
787                               PValueCls Val):
788                                 VariableCls(Type,Val) {
789     //cout << "VarIdentCls() " << endl;
790     if (!VarIdent) {
791         cerr << "VarIdentCls() - Logic Error" << endl;
792     }
793     ident = VarIdent;
794     att = Att;
795 }
```

The next variable listed is that of a function call. These look just like a variable identifier, except for the actual parameter list.

```
ActualParamCls (expr.C)

808 ActualParamCls :: ActualParamCls(PPTreeNodeCls Expr) {
809     //cout << "ActualParamsCls " << endl;
810     expr = PExprCls(Expr);
811 }
812
813 ActualParamLstCls ::
814               ActualParamLstCls (PPTreeNodeCls ActualParam) {
815     //cout << "ActualParamSeqCls() " << endl;
816     seq_head = seq_tail = PActualParamCls(ActualParam);
817 }
818
819 PPTreeNodeCls ActualParamLstCls ::
820                        append(PPTreeNodeCls ActualParam) {
821     //cout << "ActualParamLstCls::append()" << endl;
822     if (!seq_tail) {
823         cerr <<
824           "ActualParamLstCls::append()--Logic Error" << endl;
825     } else {
826         seq_tail = PActualParamCls(seq_tail ->
827             LstSeqBldrCls::append(PActualParamCls(ActualParam)));
828     }
829     return this;
830 }
```

```
  FuncCallCls (expr.C)

833 FuncCallCls :: FuncCallCls(PIdentCls FuncIdent,
834                 PSymtabEntryCls Att,
835                   PTypeCls Type,
836                     PValueCls Value,
837                       PActualParamLstCls ActualParamLst):
838                                   VariableCls(Type,Value) {
839     cout << "FuncCallCls(FuncIdent, ActualParamLst)" << endl;
840
841     ident = FuncIdent;
842     att = Att;
843     actual_param_lst = ActualParamLst;
844
845 }
846
847 PTypeCls FuncCallCls :: get_type() {
848     //cout << "FuncCallCls::get_type()" << endl;
849     return att -> get_type();
850 }
851
```

```
  VarFuncDesignator, Part 1 (expr.C)

854 VarFuncDesignatorCls :: VarFuncDesignatorCls(
855                         PPTreeNodeCls Ident,
856                         PPTreeNodeCls ActualParamLst) {
857     //cout << "VarFuncDesigCls(Ident,ActualparamLst)" ;
858
859     PSymtabCls vista = ScopeCls::get_vista();
860
861     PIdentCls ident = PIdentCls(Ident);
862     char *name = ident -> get_name();
863     PSymtabEntryCls found_it = vista  -> vista_lookup(name);
864     if (!found_it) {
865         soft.err("Variable not yet declared");
866
867         PValueCls val = new ValueCls(0);
868         PVarAttCls va =
869                 new VarAttCls(name,std_type.undeclared(),val);
870         vista -> insert(va);
871
872         factor =
873             new VarIdentCls(ident,va,std_type.undeclared(),val);
874
```

```
VarFuncDesignator, Part 2 (expr.C)

876        } else if (!(found_it -> is_ConstAtt() ||
877                       found_it -> is_VarAtt() ||
878                          found_it -> is_FParamAtt() ||
879                             found_it -> is_FuncAtt())) {
880          soft.err("Identifier is not a  variable or function");
881          strcpy(name,"_error");
882          PValueCls val = new ValueCls(0);
883          PVarAttCls va =
884                   new VarAttCls(name,std_type.undeclared(),val);
885          vista -> insert(va);
886
887          factor =
888             new VarIdentCls(ident,va,std_type.undeclared(),val);
```

```
VarFuncDesignator, Part 3 (expr.C)

890        } else {
891          PValueCls value =
892                   PSymtabEntryCls(found_it) -> get_value();
893          PTypeCls type  = PSymtabEntryCls(found_it) -> get_type();
894          if (found_it -> is_ConstAtt() ||
895               found_it -> is_VarAtt() ||
896                  found_it -> is_FParamAtt()) {
897            factor = new VarIdentCls(ident,found_it,type,value);
898          } else { // is_FuncAtt()
899            PActualParamLstCls apl =
900                        PActualParamLstCls(ActualParamLst);
901            factor =
902                new FuncCallCls(ident,found_it,type,value,apl);
903          }
904        }
905 }
```

The previous, somewhat involved code segment is the constructor of an object that is not a node of the parse tree. Since identifiers and function calls are recognized by the same production in the parser, this one object first does various static semantic analyses and then creates either a *VarIdentCls* or *FuncCallCls* object, that is then placed on the tree by its *get_factor()* member function.

The following listing contains the implementation of the constructor for one of the last categories of variables, the *ArrayDesigCls*. After determining that the underlying variable being referenced is indeed an array, the linked-list of index values is updated and the final type of the variable is updated.

```
ArrayDesigCls (expr.C)

913 ArrayDesigCls :: ArrayDesigCls(PPTreeNodeCls Variable,
914                                 PPTreeNodeCls IndexLst) {
915     //cout << "ArrayDesigCls" << Variable << IndexLst << endl;
916
917     PVariableCls tmp_variable = PVariableCls(Variable);
918     PExprLstCls tmp_index_lst = PExprLstCls(IndexLst);
919
920     PTypeCls var_type  = tmp_variable -> get_var_type();
921     if (! var_type -> is_array()) {
922         soft.err("Identifier is not an array");
923         this -> ExprCls::type = tmp_variable -> get_type();
924     } else {
925         if (PVariableCls(tmp_variable) -> is_arr_desig()) {
926             PArrayDesigCls a_desg = PArrayDesigCls(tmp_variable);
927             this -> variable =
928                 a_desg -> variable;
929             this -> index_lst =
930                 PExprLstCls(a_desg ->
931                     index_lst ->
932                         append(tmp_index_lst ->
933                             get_seq_head()));
934         } else {
935             this -> variable = tmp_variable;
936             this -> index_lst = tmp_index_lst;
937         }
938         PExprCls p = this -> index_lst -> get_seq_head();
939         while (p) {
940             var_type = PArrayTypeCls(var_type) ->
941                                     get_component_type();
942             p = PExprCls(p -> get_next());
943         }
944         this -> ExprCls::type = var_type;
945     }
946 }
```

9.4.4   Type Classes

Base Class

```
(p_tree.C)

122 TypeCls :: TypeCls() {
123     //cout << "TypeCls" << endl;
124 }
```

Standard Types

While there are some differences between the various standard types, the great number of similarities would render complete listings for all standard types highly uninstructive. The constructors and member functions of these types are represented well by those of the standard type `integer`.

```
IntegerTypeCls constructor(type.C)

17 IntegerTypeCls :: IntegerTypeCls() {
18     //cout << "IntegerTypeCls()" << endl;
19 }
20
21 PValueCls IntegerTypeCls :: make_value() {
22     //cout << "IntegerTypeCls::make_value()" << endl;
23     return new ValueCls(rand());
24 }
```

```
IntegerTypeCls unary operations (type.C)

35 PValueCls IntegerTypeCls :: uminus(PPTreeNodeCls Val) {
36     //cout << "IntegerTypeCls::uminus() " << endl;
37     if (!Val) {
38         hard.err("IntegerTypeCls::uminus -- LOGIC ERROR");
39     }
40     return
41         new ValueCls(- atoi(PExprCls(Val) ->
42                               evaluate() ->to_char()));
43 }
```

Types are both a specification of valid values and a specification of the operations on those values. In this object-oriented setting, each type class therefore contains the implementation of the actual operations of the type. These functions are then called by the corresponding binary operators during evaluation (Chapter 10).

```
(IntegerTypeCls relational operators type.C)

46 PValueCls IntegerTypeCls :: eq(PPTreeNodeCls LVal,
47                                PPTreeNodeCls RVal){
48     //cout << "IntegerTypeCls::eq()" << endl;
49     if (!LVal || !RVal) {
50         hard.err("IntegerTypeCls::eq() LOGIC ERROR");
51     }
52     int i_val = atoi(PExprCls(LVal) ->
53                           evaluate() -> to_char()) ==
54                 atoi(PExprCls(RVal) ->
55                           evaluate() -> to_char()) ;
56     return new ValueCls(i_val);
57 }
```

IntegerTypeCls additive operators (type.C)

```
110 PValueCls IntegerTypeCls :: add(PPTreeNodeCls LVal,
111                                       PPTreeNodeCls RVal){
112     //cout << "IntegerTypeCls::add()" << endl;
113     if (!LVal || !RVal) {
114         hard.err("IntegerTypeCls::add() LOGIC ERROR");
115     }
116     int i_val = atoi(PExprCls(LVal) ->
117                               evaluate() -> to_char()) +
118               atoi(PExprCls(RVal) ->
119                               evaluate() -> to_char()) ;
120     return new ValueCls(i_val);
121 }
```

IntegerTypeCls multiplicative operators (type.C)

```
134 PValueCls IntegerTypeCls :: times(PPTreeNodeCls LVal,
135                                       PPTreeNodeCls RVal){
136     //cout << "IntegerTypeCls::times()" << endl;
137     if (!LVal || !RVal) {
138         hard.err("IntegerTypeCls::times() LOGIC ERROR");
139     }
140     int i_val = atoi(PExprCls(LVal) ->
141                               evaluate() -> to_char()) *
142               atoi(PExprCls(RVal) ->
143                               evaluate() -> to_char()) ;
144     return new ValueCls(i_val);
145 }
```

IntegerTypeCls standard operators (type.C)

```
174 PValueCls IntegerTypeCls :: inc(PValueCls Val){
175     //cout << "IntegerTypeCls::inc()" << endl;
176     if (!Val) {
177         hard.err("IntegerTypeCls::inc() LOGIC ERROR");
178     }
179     int i_val = atoi(Val -> to_char()) + 1;
180
181     return new ValueCls(i_val);
182 }
183
184 PValueCls IntegerTypeCls :: dec(PValueCls Val){
185     //cout << "IntegerTypeCls::dec()" << endl;
186     if (!Val) {
187         hard.err("IntegerTypeCls::dec() LOGIC ERROR");
188     }
189     int i_val = atoi(Val -> to_char()) - 1;
190
191     return new ValueCls(i_val);
192 }
```

User-Defined Types

Enumerated constants are identifiers that cannot be visible at the time of their declaration. If the identifier has already been used in the current vista, store _error as the new name of the present constant so that compilation can continue. Then determine the associated ordinal value of the constant, insert it into the appropriate symbol table, and add the identifier to the linked-list of constant names.

```
EnumTypeCls constructor (type.C)

566 EnumTypeCls :: EnumTypeCls(PPTreeNodeCls IdentLst) {
567     //cout << "EnumTypeCls()" << endl;
568     ident_lst = PIdentLstCls(IdentLst);
569     PIdentCls p = ident_lst -> get_seq_head();
570     PConstAttCls enum_lst_head = 0;
571     PConstAttCls enum_lst_tail = 0;
572     int ord = 0;
573     while (p) {
574         char* name = p -> get_name();
575         PValueCls e_val = new ValueCls(ord++);
576         PConstAttCls e_cnst  = 0;
577
578         PSymtabCls cur_vista = ScopeCls::get_vista();
579         PSymtabEntryCls found_it =
580                         cur_vista -> vista_lookup(name);
581         if (found_it) {
582             soft.err("Enum constant already declared");
583             e_cnst = new ConstAttCls("_error", this, e_val);
584         } else {
585             e_cnst = new ConstAttCls(name, this, e_val);
586         }
587         cur_vista -> insert(e_cnst);
588         if (!enum_lst_tail) {
589             enum_lst_head = enum_lst_tail = e_cnst;
590         } else {
591             enum_lst_tail =
592                 PConstAttCls(enum_lst_tail -> append(e_cnst));
593         }
594
595         p = PIdentCls(p -> get_next());
596     }
597     enum_const_lst = enum_lst_head;
598     max_ord = --ord;
599 }
600
601 PValueCls EnumTypeCls :: make_value() {
602     //cout << "EnumTypeCls::make_value()" << endl;
603     return new ValueCls(0);
604 }
```

The *make_value()* function is only used to assign an initial value to a variable of this type during declaration.

Enumerated types enjoy all the standard relational operators. The following listing for *EnumTypeCls::eq* is representative of the others.

```
     ┌─────────────────────────────────────────────┐
     │ EnumTypeCls relational operator (type.C)     │
     └─────────────────────────────────────────────┘
607 PValueCls EnumTypeCls :: eq(PPTreeNodeCls LVal,
608                                        PPTreeNodeCls RVal) {
609     //cout << "EnumTypeCls::eq()" << endl;
610     if (!LVal || !RVal) {
611         hard.err("EnumTypeCls::eq() LOGIC ERROR");
612     }
613     int i_val = *PExprCls(LVal) -> evaluate() -> to_char() ==
614                     *PExprCls(RVal) -> evaluate() -> to_char();
615     return new ValueCls(i_val);
616 }
```

There are no valid binary operations for Pascal enumerated types.

```
     ┌─────────────────────────────────────────────┐
     │ EnumTypeCls standard functions (type.C)      │
     └─────────────────────────────────────────────┘
679 PValueCls EnumTypeCls :: inc(PValueCls Val){
680     //cout << "EnumTypeCls::inc()" << endl;
681     if (!Val) {
682         hard.err("EnumTypeCls::inc() LOGIC ERROR");
683     }
684     int i_val = atoi(Val -> to_char());
685     if (i_val < max_ord) {
686         i_val++;
687     }
688     return new ValueCls(i_val);
689 }
690
691 PValueCls EnumTypeCls :: dec(PValueCls Val){
692     //cout << "EnumTypeCls::dec()" << endl;
693     if (!Val) {
694         hard.err("EnumTypeCls::dec() LOGIC ERROR");
695     }
696     int i_val = atoi(Val -> to_char());
697     if (i_val) {
698         i_val--;
699     }
700     return new ValueCls(i_val);
701 }
```

The above listing contains the implementation for the valid standard functions of *inc* and *dec*.

```
   ┌─────────────────────────────────────────────────┐
   │ SubrangeTypeCls constructor (type.C)            │
   └─────────────────────────────────────────────────┘

   704 SubrangeTypeCls :: SubrangeTypeCls(PPTreeNodeCls LowConst,
   705                                     PPTreeNodeCls HighConst) {
   706     //cout << "SubrangeTypeCls()" << endl;
   707     if (!LowConst || !HighConst) {
   708         hard.err("SubrangeTypeCls() LOGIC ERROR");
   709     }
   710     PTypeCls  low_type = PExprCls(LowConst) -> get_type();
   711     PTypeCls  high_type = PExprCls(HighConst) -> get_type();
   712     if (!(*low_type == *high_type)) {
   713         soft.err("Subrange bounds not of the same type");
   714     } else if (!((*low_type == *std_type.integer()) ||
   715                  (*low_type == *std_type.CHAR()) ||
   716                  (*low_type == *std_type.boolean()) ||
   717                  (low_type -> is_enum())))) {
   718         soft.err("Subrange valid only for ordinal types");
   719     } else {
   720         underlying_type = low_type;
   721     }
   722
   723     low_const = PExprCls(LowConst) -> evaluate();
   724     high_const = PExprCls(HighConst) -> evaluate();
   725     //low_const -> print();
   726     //high_const -> print();
   727 }
   728
   729 PValueCls SubrangeTypeCls :: make_value() {
   730     //cout << "SubrangeTypeCls::make_value()" << endl;
   731     return underlying_type -> make_value();
   732 }
```

```
   ┌─────────────────────────────────────────────────┐
   │ SubrangeTypeCls relational operator (type.C)    │
   └─────────────────────────────────────────────────┘

   781 PValueCls SubrangeTypeCls :: eq(PPTreeNodeCls LVal,
   782                                 PPTreeNodeCls RVal) {
   783     //cout << "SubrangeTypeCls::eq()" << endl;
   784     if (!LVal || !RVal) {
   785         hard.err("SubrangeTypeCls::eq() LOGIC ERROR");
   786     }
   787     return underlying_type -> eq(LVal,RVal);
   788 }
```

A low and high value are used to specify a subrange type. Both values must be of the same ordinal type.

All binary operations and standard functions for a subrange are implemented in terms of the corresponding actions for the underlying type. The listings below should include some dynamic semantic check for range of values. Methods for implementing such checks can be found in Chapter 10. When such changes take place, the implementation code for the operations and functions would more naturally be located in the *interp.C* portion of the p_tree module.

```
SubrangeTypeCls standard functions(type.C)

832 PValueCls SubrangeTypeCls :: inc(PValueCls Val){
833     //cout << "SubrangeTypeCls::inc()" << endl;
834     if (!Val) {
835         hard.err("SubrangeTypeCls::inc() LOGIC ERROR");
836     }
837     return underlying_type -> inc(Val);
838 }
839
840 PValueCls SubrangeTypeCls :: dec(PValueCls Val){
841     //cout << "SubrangeTypeCls::dec()" << endl;
842     if (!Val) {
843         hard.err("SubrangeTypeCls::dec() LOGIC ERROR");
844     }
845     return underlying_type -> dec(Val);
846 }
```

When a declaration statement uses a previously declared type, the specification is just an identifier. Such an identifier must have already been declared and then as a type specifier.

```
SpecifiedTypeCls (type.C)

849 SpecifiedTypeCls :: SpecifiedTypeCls(PPTreeNodeCls Ident) {
850     //cout << "SpecifiedTypeCls" << endl;
851     char *t_name = PIdentCls(Ident) -> get_name();
852     PSymtabCls scp = ScopeCls::get_vista();
853     PSymtabEntryCls found_it = scp -> vista_lookup(t_name);
854     if (found_it) {
855         this -> type = found_it -> get_type();
856         if (!(this -> type)) {
857             soft.err("Identifier is not a type");
858         }
859     } else {
860         soft.err("Type not yet declared");
861         PTypeAttCls vt =
862             new TypeAttCls(t_name,std_type.undeclared());
863         scp -> insert(vt);
864         this -> type = std_type.undeclared();
865     }
866 }
```

The last major category of user-defined types are the structured types, array, record, and pointer. Each of these has its own set of required static semantic checks. In the case of *ArrayTypeCls*, the components can be themselves arrays. In the non-nested situation, the 'final' component type must be ordinal.

```
ArrayTypeCls (type.C)

869 ArrayTypeCls :: ArrayTypeCls(PPTreeNodeCls IndexTypeLst,
870                              PPTreeNodeCls ComponentType){
871     //cout << "ArrayTypeCls()" << IndexTypeLst <<
872     //                       ComponentType << endl;
873     PTypeLstCls index_type_lst = PTypeLstCls(IndexTypeLst);
874     PTypeCls c_type = PTypeCls(ComponentType);
875
876     PTypeCls p = index_type_lst -> get_seq_head();
877     this -> index_type = p;
878
879     if (p -> get_next()) { //Nested array type
880         p = PTypeCls(p -> get_next());
881         PTypeLstCls q = new TypeLstCls(p);
882         component_type = new ArrayTypeCls(q,c_type);
883     } else { // Non nested array type
884         if (! p -> is_ordinal()) {
885             soft.err("Array indices must be of ordinal type");
886         }
887         component_type = c_type;
888     }
889 }
890
891 PValueCls ArrayTypeCls :: make_value() {
892     //cout << "ArrayTypeCls::make_value()" << endl;
893     PTypeCls p = index_type;
894     PTypeCls c_type = component_type;
895     PArrayValCls aval = new ArrayValCls(p,c_type);
896     return new ValueCls(aval);
897 }
```

Type Operators

The following listings show the implementation of the various type operators. In the first one, two types are recognized as identical if they are (pointers to) the same object.

```
TypeCls type operator: identical types (p_tree.C)

295 int operator==(TypeCls &Type1, TypeCls &Type2)  {
296     //cout << "== " << "Type1 " << &Type1
297     //                   << " Type2 " << &Type2 << endl;
298     if (&Type1 == &Type2)
299         return 1;
300     else
301         return 0;
302 }
```

Note that this is an excellent example of the use of C++ **operator overloading**.

TypeCls type operator: distinct types (p_tree.C)

```
306 int operator!=(TypeCls &Type1, TypeCls &Type2) {
307     //cout << "!= " << "Type1 " << &Type1 <<
308     //                 " Type2 " << &Type2 << endl;
309     if (&Type1 == &Type2)
310         return 0;
311     else
312         return 1;
313 }
```

TypeCls type operator: strict subrange (p_tree.C)

```
317 int operator<<(TypeCls &Type1, TypeCls &Type2) {
318     //cout << "<< " << "Type1 " << &Type1 <<
319     //                 " Type2 " << &Type2 << endl;
320     if (!(&Type1 && &Type2)) {
321         return 0;
322     } else if ((Type1.is_subrange()) &&
323             (*Type1.get_underlying_type() == Type2)) {
324         return 1;
325     } else {
326         return 0;
327     }
328 }
```

TypeCls type operator: subrange (p_tree.C)

```
332 int operator<=(TypeCls &Type1, TypeCls &Type2) {
333     // A (general-purpose) subrange check
334     //cout << "<= " << "Type1 " << &Type1 <<
335     //                 " Type2 " << &Type2 << endl;
336     if (&Type1 == &Type2)  {//Identical
337         return 1;
338     } else if (Type1 << Type2) { // Strict Subrange
339         return 1;
340     } else {
341         return 0;
342     }
343 }
```

```
    TypeCls type operator: assignment compatible(p_tree.C)

347 int operator|=(TypeCls &Type1, TypeCls &Type2) {
348     //Is assignment compatible with ...
349     //cout << "|= " << "Type1 " << &Type1 <<
350     //                        " Type2 " << &Type2 << endl;
351     if (Type1 == Type2) {    //if Compatible then no sweat ...
352         return 1;
353     } else if ((Type1 == *std_type.real()) &&
354                         (Type2 == *std_type.integer()))) {
355         return 1;
356     } else if ((Type1 << Type2) || (Type2 << Type1)) {
357         return 1;
358     } else if ((Type1.is_set()) && (Type2.is_set())) {
359         return 1;
360     } else {
361         return 0;
362     }
363 }
```

9.4.5 Statement Classes

The definition of *StatementCls* indicates that since it is merely an organizing base
class, it will have only a trivial constructor containing no semantic checks.

The first derived statement class is *AssignmentStmtCls*. Semantic requirements
for Assignment statement objects include checking that the type of the right-hand
member is assignment compatible with the type of the left-hand side. *Indent_level*
is used by a pretty printer option.

```
    AssignmentStmtCls (stmt.C)

19 AssignmentStmtCls :: AssignmentStmtCls(
20                         PPTreeNodeCls Variable,
21                         PPTreeNodeCls Expr) {
22     //cout << "AssignmentStmtCls() " << endl;
23     if (!Variable || !Expr) {
24         hard.err("AssignmentStmtCls() - Logic Error ");
25     }
26     variable = PVariableCls(Variable);
27     expr = PExprCls(Expr);
28
29     PTypeCls id_type = variable -> get_type();
30     PTypeCls expr_type = expr -> get_type();
31     if (!(*id_type |= *expr_type)) {
32         soft.err("Types not assignment compatible");
33     }
34 }
```

The major semantic requirement of an *if* statement is that the expression be of
boolean type.

```
IfCls (stmt.C)

37 IfStmtCls :: IfStmtCls(PPTreeNodeCls Expr,
38                             PPTreeNodeCls Statement,
39                                 PPTreeNodeCls ElseStatement) {
40     //cout << "IfStmtCls()" << endl;
41     if (!Expr || !Statement) {
42         hard.err("IfStmtCls() - Logic Error ");
43     }
44     expr = PExprCls(Expr);
45     if (*expr -> get_type() != *std_type.boolean()) {
46         soft.err("Condition expression is not boolean");
47     }
48     stmt = PStatementCls(Statement);
49     else_stmt = PStatementCls(ElseStatement);
50     indent_level--;
51 }
52
53 ElseStmtCls :: ElseStmtCls(PPTreeNodeCls ElseStatement) {
54     //cout << "ElseStmtCls()" << endl;
55     //just placed in tree to allow continued compilation
56     else_stmt = ElseStatement;
57 }
```

```
Case labels (stmt.C)

60 CaseLabelCls :: CaseLabelCls(PPTreeNodeCls Constant) {
61     //cout << "CaseLabelCls() " << endl;
62     constant = PExprCls(Constant);
63 }
64
65 CaseLabelLstCls :: CaseLabelLstCls
66                         (PPTreeNodeCls CaseLabel) {
67     //cout << "CaseLabelLstCls() " << endl;
68     seq_tail = seq_head = PCaseLabelCls(CaseLabel);
69 }
70
71 PPTreeNodeCls CaseLabelLstCls :: append(PPTreeNodeCls Stmt) {
72     //cout << "CaseLabelLstCls::append()" << endl;
73     if (!seq_tail) {
74       hard.err("CaseLabelLstCls::append()--Logic Error");
75     } else {
76       seq_tail = PCaseLabelCls(seq_tail ->
77                 LstSeqBldrCls::append(PStatementCls(Stmt)));
78     }
79     return this;
80 }
```

```
   Case elements (stmt.C)

   60 CaseLabelCls :: CaseLabelCls(PPTreeNodeCls Constant) {
   61     //cout << "CaseLabelCls() " << endl;
   62     constant = PExprCls(Constant);
   63 }
   64
   65 CaseLabelLstCls :: CaseLabelLstCls
   66                              (PPTreeNodeCls CaseLabel) {
   67     //cout << "CaseLabelLstCls() " << endl;
   68     seq_tail = seq_head = PCaseLabelCls(CaseLabel);
   69 }
   70
   71 PPTreeNodeCls CaseLabelLstCls :: append(PPTreeNodeCls Stmt) {
   72     //cout << "CaseLabelLstCls::append()" << endl;
   73     if (!seq_tail) {
   74       hard.err("CaseLabelLstCls::append()--Logic Error");
   75     } else {
   76       seq_tail = PCaseLabelCls(seq_tail ->
   77                    LstSeqBldrCls::append(PStatementCls(Stmt)));
   78     }
   79     return this;
   80 }
```

```
   CaseStmtCls (stmt.C)

   107 CaseStmtCls :: CaseStmtCls(PPTreeNodeCls Expr,
   108                             PPTreeNodeCls CaseList) {
   109     //cout << "CaseStmtCls()" << endl;
   110     if (!Expr || !CaseList) {
   111         hard.err("CaseStmtCls() - Logic Error ");
   112     }
   113     expr = PExprCls(Expr);
   114     case_lst = PCaseLstCls(CaseList);
   115     indent_level--;
   116 }
```

Since Pascal does not allow a possibly negative incremental value for the *for* statement loop variable, we have designed the following *DirectionCls* object to encapsulate at least the positive or negative incremental value.

```
   DirectionCls (stmt.C)

   119 DirectionCls :: DirectionCls(int Dir) {
   120     //cout << "DirectionCls() " << Dir << endl;
   121     dir = Dir;
   122 }
```

For statements require by their syntax an identifier for the loop variable. This identifier must previously have been declared, of course.

```
ForStmtCls (stmt.C)

125 ForStmtCls :: ForStmtCls(PPTreeNodeCls Ident,
126                           PPTreeNodeCls StartExpr,
127                            PPTreeNodeCls Dir,
128                             PPTreeNodeCls StopExpr,
129                              PPTreeNodeCls Statement) {
130     //cout << "ForStmtCls()" << endl;
131     if (!Ident ||
132            !StartExpr ||
133               !Dir ||
134                 !StopExpr ||
135                    !Statement) {
136        hard.err("ForStmtCls() - Logic Error ");
137     }
138     ident     = PIdentCls(Ident);
139     start_expr = PExprCls(StartExpr);
140     dir       = PDirectionCls(Dir);
141     stop_expr  = PExprCls(StopExpr);
142     stmt      = PStatementCls(Statement);
143     indent_level--;
144
145     char* name = ident -> get_name();
146     PSymtabEntryCls found_it =
147        ScopeCls::get_vista() -> vista_lookup(name);
148     if (!found_it) {
149        soft.err("Loop variable not yet declared");
150        PValueCls val = new ValueCls(0);
151        found_it =
152           new VarAttCls(name,std_type.undeclared(),val);
153        ScopeCls::get_vista() -> insert(found_it);
154     }
155     PTypeCls start_type = start_expr -> get_type();
156     PTypeCls stop_type = stop_expr -> get_type();
157     if (!(*start_type == *stop_type)) {
158        soft.err("Start and stop expression types don't match");
159     }
160
161 }
```

```
WhileStmtCls(stmt.C)

164 WhileStmtCls :: WhileStmtCls(PPTreeNodeCls Expr,
165                              PPTreeNodeCls Statement) {
166     //cout << "WhileStmtCls()" << endl;
167     if (!Expr || !Statement) {
168        hard.err("WhileStmtCls() - Logic Error ");
169     }
170     expr = PExprCls(Expr);
171     stmt = PStatementCls(Statement);
172     indent_level--;
173 }
```

RepeatStmtCls (stmt.C)

```
176 RepeatStmtCls :: RepeatStmtCls(PPTreeNodeCls StatementSeq,
177                                         PPTreeNodeCls Expr) {
178     //cout << "RepeatStmtCls()" << endl;
179     if (!StatementSeq || !Expr) {
180         hard.err("RepeatStmtCls() - Logic Error ");
181     }
182     stmt_seq = PStatementSeqCls(StatementSeq);
183     expr = PExprCls(Expr);
184     indent_level--;
185 }
```

WithStmtCls (stmt.C)

```
188 RecVarCls :: RecVarCls(PPTreeNodeCls Variable) {
189     cout << "RecVarCls() " << endl;
190     rec_var = PIdentCls(Variable);
191 }
192
193 RecVarLstCls :: RecVarLstCls (PPTreeNodeCls RecVar) {
194     cout << "RecVarLstCls() " << endl;
195     seq_tail = seq_head = PRecVarCls(RecVar);
196 }
197
198 PPTreeNodeCls RecVarLstCls :: append(PPTreeNodeCls Stmt) {
199     //cout << "RecVarLstCls::append()" << endl;
200     if (!seq_tail) {
201       hard.err("RecVarLstCls::append() -- Logic Error");
202     } else {
203         seq_tail = PRecVarCls(seq_tail ->
204                 LstSeqBldrCls::append(PStatementCls(Stmt)));
205     }
206     return this;
207 }
208
209 WithStmtCls :: WithStmtCls(PPTreeNodeCls RecVarLst,
210                                 PPTreeNodeCls Statement) {
211     //cout << "WithStmtCls()" << endl;
212     if (!RecVarLst || !Statement) {
213         hard.err("WithStmtCls() - Logic Error ");
214     }
215     rec_var_lst = PRecVarLstCls(RecVarLst);
216     stmt = PStatementCls(Statement);
217     indent_level--;
218 }
```

```
  ProcCallCls (part 1) (stmt.C)

221  ProcCallCls :: ProcCallCls(PPTreeNodeCls Ident,
222                             PPTreeNodeCls ActualParamLst) {
223     //cout << "ProcCallCls()" << endl;
224     if (!Ident ) {
225         hard.err("ProcCallCls() - Logic Error0 ");
226     }
227     ident = PIdentCls(Ident);
228     actual_param_lst = PActualParamLstCls(ActualParamLst);
229
230     //1. Be certain it really is a procedure
231     char *name = ident -> get_name();
232     PSymtabEntryCls found_it =
233                 ScopeCls::get_vista() -> vista_lookup(name);
234     if (!found_it) {
235         soft.err("Procedure identifier not yet declared");
236     } else if (!(found_it -> is_ProcAtt())) {
237         soft.err("Identifier is not a procedure");
238     } else {
```

Procedure calls have almost identical semantic requirements as do function calls, though the latter are expressions rather than statements. In the code directly above, the identifier is first checked to see if it is a visible procedure name.

In the code that follows, the usual matching of actual and formal parameters is checked.

- Formal and actual parameters must match in type.

    - *F_type* and *a_type* respectively point to the types of the formal and actual parameters.

    - The C++ equals operator has been extended[1] to test for identical type objects (see page 282).

- Variable formal parameters must be associated with *VarIdentCls* actual parameters.

    - *Get_is_var()* and *is_var()* return boolean (integer) values describing the nature of each of the parameters.

    - Note the use of C++'s provision for termination of boolean expressions: If the left expression is false, the right expression is not evaluated.

- Formal and actual parameters must match in number. A non-zero pointer value indicates that there are yet more items to examine in the particular list.

---

[1] Actually, the official C++ jargon would say that == has been **overloaded**.

```
ProcCallCls (part 2) (stmt.C)

240          // 2. Params must match in number, type and order.
241          PFParamAttCls f_param =
242                      PProcAttCls(found_it) -> get_param_lst();
243          if ((!actual_param_lst)&&(f_param)) {
244              soft.err(
245                "Procedure declaration requires actual parameters");
246          } else if (actual_param_lst && (!f_param)) {
247              soft.err("Procedure declaration has no parameters");
248          } else if (f_param) {
249              PActualParamCls a_param =
250                          actual_param_lst -> get_seq_head();
251              if (!a_param) {
252                  hard.err("ProcCallCls() LOGIC ERROR1");
253              }
254              while (f_param && a_param) {
255                  PTypeCls f_type = f_param -> get_type();
256                  PTypeCls a_type = a_param -> get_type();
257                  if (!(*f_type == *a_type)) {
258                    soft.err(
259                    "Formal and actual param types don't match");
260                  }
261
262                  //Check: var formal has variable access actual?
263                  if (f_param -> get_is_var() &&
264                    !(a_param -> is_var())) {
265                    soft.err(
266                    "Var param requires variable for actual param");
267                  }
268
269                  f_param = PFParamAttCls(f_param -> get_next());
270                  a_param = PActualParamCls(a_param -> get_next());
271              }
272              if (f_param) {
273                  soft.err("Not enough actual parameters");
274              } else if (a_param) {
275                  soft.err("Too many actual parameters");
276              }
277          }
278      }
279 }
```

Each of the following constructors just use a cast conversion operator to lift the class definitions of the arguments to their proper level.

WriteStmtCls (stmt.C)

```
299 WriteStmtCls :: WriteStmtCls(PPTreeNodeCls WriteParamLst) {
300     //cout << "WriteStmtCls() " << endl;
301     if (!WriteParamLst) {
302         hard.err("WriteStmtCls() - Logic Error ");
303     }
304     write_param_lst = PWriteParamLstCls(WriteParamLst);
305 }
306
307 WritelnStmtCls :: WritelnStmtCls(PPTreeNodeCls WriteParamLst) {
308     //cout << "WritelnStmtCls() " << endl;
309     if (!WriteParamLst) {
310         hard.err("WritelnStmtCls() - Logic Error ");
311     }
312     write_param_lst = PWriteParamLstCls(WriteParamLst);
313 }
```

9.4.6 Declaration Classes

Pascal named constants require an identifier that has not been declared in the current vista. Relevant type and value information are then placed in a special attribute object and stored in the appropriate symbol table.

ConstDefCls (defdec.C)

```
19 ConstDefCls :: ConstDefCls(PPTreeNodeCls Ident,
20                            PPTreeNodeCls Constant) {
21     //cout << "ConstDefCls" << endl;
22     ident = PIdentCls(Ident);
23     constant = PExprCls(Constant);
24
25     PSymtabCls vista = ScopeCls::get_vista();
26     char *name = ident -> get_name();
27     PSymtabEntryCls found_it = vista -> lookup(name);
28     if (found_it) {
29         soft.err("Constant already declared");
30     } else {
31         PTypeCls type = constant -> get_type();
32         PValueCls val = constant -> evaluate();
33         PConstAttCls va = new ConstAttCls(name,type,val);
34         vista -> insert(va);
35     }
36 }
```

```
TypeDefCls (defdec.C)

39 TypeDefCls :: TypeDefCls(PPTreeNodeCls Ident,
40                              PPTreeNodeCls Type) {
41     //cout << "TypeDefCls" << endl;
42     if (!(Ident && Type)) {
43         hard.err("TypeDefCls() HARD ERROR");
44     }
45
46     ident = PIdentCls(Ident);
47     PSymtabCls vista = ScopeCls::get_vista();
48     char *name = ident -> get_name();
49     PSymtabEntryCls found_it = vista -> lookup(name);
50     if (found_it) {
51         soft.err("Identifier already declared");
52     } else {
53         char* name = ident -> get_name();
54         type = PTypeCls(Type);
55         PTypeAttCls t_att = new TypeAttCls(name, type);
56         ScopeCls::get_vista() -> insert(t_att);
57     }
58 }
```

```
VarDecCls (defdec.C)

61 VarDecCls :: VarDecCls(PPTreeNodeCls IdentList,
62                             PPTreeNodeCls Type) {
63     //cout << "VarDecCls" << endl;
64     ident_lst = PIdentLstCls(IdentList);
65     type = PTypeCls(Type);
66     PIdentCls p = PIdentLstCls(ident_lst) -> get_seq_head();
67
68     PSymtabCls scp = ScopeCls::get_vista();
69     while (p) {
70         char *name = p -> get_name();
71         PSymtabEntryCls found_it = scp -> lookup(name);
72         if (found_it) {
73             soft.err("Variable already declared");
74         } else {
75             //to encourage user initialization ...
76             PValueCls default_val = type -> make_value();
77             PVarAttCls va = new VarAttCls(name,type,default_val);
78             scp -> insert(va);
79         }
80         p = PIdentCls(p -> get_next());
81     }
82 }
```

Formal parameter groups (p_tree.C)

```
383 ValParamGrpCls :: ValParamGrpCls(PPTreeNodeCls ParamGrp) {
384     //cout << "ValParamGrpCls(ParamGrp)" << endl;
385     param_grp = PParamGrpCls(ParamGrp);
386 }
387
388 VarParamGrpCls :: VarParamGrpCls(PPTreeNodeCls ParamGrp) {
389     //cout << "VarParamGrpCls(ParamGrp)" << endl;
390     param_grp = PParamGrpCls(ParamGrp);
391     if (!param_grp) {
392         hard.err("VarParamGrpCls() LOGIC ERROR!");
393     }
394     PIdentLstCls id_lst = param_grp -> ident_lst;
395     PIdentCls p = id_lst -> get_seq_head();
396     while (p) {
397         PSymtabEntryCls found_it =
398                 ScopeCls::get_vista() -> lookup(p -> get_name());
399         if (!found_it) {
400             hard.err("VarParamGrpCls() LOGIC ERROR!");
401         }
402         PFParamAttCls(found_it) -> is_var = 1;
403         p = PIdentCls(p -> get_next());
404     }
405 }
```

Procedure headings (p_tree.C)

```
492 ProcHeadCls :: ProcHeadCls() {
493     //cout << "ProcHeadCls()" << endl;
494     proc_tab = new SymtabCls(ScopeCls::get_vista());
495     ScopeCls::set_vista(proc_tab);
496 }
497
498 PPTreeNodeCls ProcHeadCls :: finish(PPTreeNodeCls Ident,
499                                     PPTreeNodeCls FormalParam) {
500     //cout << "ProcHeadCls::finish(Ident,Block)";
501     ident = PIdentCls(Ident);
502     if (!ident) {
503         hard.err("ProcHeadCls::finish LOGIC ERROR!");
504     }
505     char *name = ident -> get_name();
506     PSymtabEntryCls found_it =
507                 ScopeCls::get_vista() -> vista_lookup(name);
508     if (found_it) {
509         soft.err("Procedure name already declared");
510     }
511     formal_param_stuff = PFParamStuffCls(FormalParam);
512     return this;
513 }
```

The constructor for *ProcHeadCls* on the previous page is called early in the production so that the symbol table will be available for parameters, etc.

```
Proc_head: PROCEDURE {$$ = new ProcHeadCls;} Ident F_p_stuff
          {$$ = PProcHeadCls($2) -> finish($3,$4);}
     ;
```

The *finish()* member function then makes the majority of formal parameter assignments and semantic checks.

```
┌─────────────────────────────────────────────────────────────────┐
│ ┌──────────────────────────────┐                                │
│ │ Function headings (p_tree.C) │                                │
│ └──────────────────────────────┘                                │
│ 516 FuncHeadCls :: FuncHeadCls() {                              │
│ 517     //cout << "FuncHeadCls()" << endl;                      │
│ 518     func_tab = new SymtabCls(ScopeCls::get_vista());        │
│ 519     ScopeCls::set_vista(func_tab);                          │
│ 520 }                                                           │
│ 521                                                             │
│ 522 PPTreeNodeCls FuncHeadCls :: finish(PPTreeNodeCls Ident,    │
│ 523                                     PPTreeNodeCls FuncForm) {│
│ 524     //cout << "FuncHeadCls::finish(Ident,FuncForm)";        │
│ 525     ident = PIdentCls(Ident);                              │
│ 526     if (!ident) {                                          │
│ 527         hard.err("FuncHeadCls::finish LOGIC ERROR!");      │
│ 528     }                                                       │
│ 529     char *name = ident -> get_name();                      │
│ 530     PSymtabEntryCls found_it =                             │
│ 531             ScopeCls::get_vista() -> vista_lookup(name);    │
│ 532     if (found_it && FuncForm ) { //then not forward referenced│
│ 533         soft.err("Function name already declared");        │
│ 534     } else if (found_it && !FuncForm) {                    │
│ 535         if ((found_it -> is_FuncAtt()) &&                  │
│ 536             (!(PFuncAttCls(found_it) -> is_forward_refd())))│ {
│ 537             soft.err(                                       │
│ 538             "Function declaration requires more specification");│
│ 539         } else {                                            │
│ 540             func_tab = PFuncAttCls(found_it) -> get_tab();  │
│ 541             ScopeCls::set_vista(func_tab);                 │
│ 542         }                                                   │
│ 543     } else {                                                │
│ 544         PFuncFormCls f_form = PFuncFormCls(FuncForm);       │
│ 545         if (! f_form) {                                     │
│ 546             soft.err(                                       │
│ 547             "Function declaration requires more specification");│
│ 548         } else {                                            │
│ 549             formal_param_stuff = f_form -> fp_stuff;        │
│ 550             func_type = f_form -> type;                    │
│ 551         }                                                   │
│ 552     }                                                       │
│ 553                                                             │
│ 554     return this;                                            │
│ 555 }                                                           │
└─────────────────────────────────────────────────────────────────┘
```

In the same way, the constructor for the *ProcDec* class is divided into a first part, that is created immediately after recognizing the procedure header, and a second part, that is called at the end of the following production.

```
Proc_dec:
      Proc_heading SCTK
            {$$ = new ProcDecCls($1);}
      Body SCTK
            {$$ = PProcDecCls($3) -> finish($4);}
      ;
```

Notice the use of $1 to refer to the first item on the right side of the production; $3 and $4 are used similarly.

```
ProcDecCls (defdec.C)

85 ProcDecCls :: ProcDecCls(PPTreeNodeCls ProcHead){
86      //cout << "ProcDecCls::" << endl;
87      proc_head = PProcHeadCls(ProcHead);
88
89      char *name = proc_head -> ident -> get_name();
90      proc_tab = proc_head -> proc_tab;
91      this -> proc_att = new ProcAttCls(name,
92                                proc_head -> formal_param_stuff,
93                                     proc_tab);
94      // Do it early for recursion...
95      PSymtabCls(proc_tab -> get_next()) -> insert(proc_att);
96 }
97
98 PPTreeNodeCls ProcDecCls :: finish(PPTreeNodeCls Block) {
99      //cout << "ProcDecCls::finish()" << Block << endl;
100     PProcAttCls(proc_att) -> block = PBlockCls(Block);
101
102     ScopeCls::set_vista(PSymtabCls(proc_tab -> get_next()));
103
104     return this;
105 }
```

- The cast conversion of *ProcHead* allows easy access to the procedure name and symbol table, created by "lower-level" productions.

- A symbol table entry is created for this new procedure and inserted in the *enclosing* symbol table.

```
FuncDecCls (defdec.C)

108 FuncDecCls :: FuncDecCls(PPTreeNodeCls FuncHead){
109     //cout << "FuncDecCls::" << endl;
110     func_head = PFuncHeadCls(FuncHead);
111
112     char *name = func_head -> ident -> get_name();
113     PSymtabEntryCls found_it =
114             ScopeCls::get_vista() -> vista_lookup(name);
115     if (found_it) {
116         if (! found_it -> is_FuncAtt()) {
117             soft.err(
118             "Function identifier has already been declared");
119         } else if (!PFuncAttCls(found_it) -> is_forward_refd()) {
120             soft.err("Function has already been declared");
121         } else {
122             this -> func_att = found_it;
123             this -> func_tab = PFuncAttCls(found_it) -> func_tab;
124         }
125     } else {
126         func_tab = func_head -> func_tab;
127         PTypeCls func_type = func_head -> func_type;
128         this -> func_att = new FuncAttCls(name,
129                             func_head -> formal_param_stuff,
130                                 func_tab,
131                                     func_type);
132         PSymtabCls(func_tab -> get_next()) -> insert(func_att);
133     }
134 }
135
136 PPTreeNodeCls FuncDecCls :: finish(PPTreeNodeCls Block) {
137     //cout << "FuncDecCls::finish()" << Block << endl;
138     PFuncAttCls(func_att) -> block = PBlockCls(Block);
139
140     ScopeCls::set_vista(PSymtabCls(func_tab -> get_next()));
141
142     return this;
143 }
```

9.4.7   Top Level Classes

```
BlockCls (p_tree.C)

565 BlockCls :: BlockCls(PPTreeNodeCls StmtSeq) {
566     //cout << "BlockCls" << endl;
567     stmt_seq = PStatementSeqCls(StmtSeq);
568 }
```

```
┌─────────────────────────────────┐
│ Program (p_tree.C) │
└─────────────────────────────────┘

572 ProgramCls :: ProgramCls(PPTreeNodeCls Ident,
573                           PPTreeNodeCls Block) {
574     //cout << "ProgramCls() " << endl;
575     ident = PIdentCls(Ident);
576     block = PBlockCls(Block);
577     std_table = ScopeCls::get_vista();
578     prgm_node = this;
579 }
```

9.5 Grammar Actions

In this section we briefly sketch the modifications to the grammar that will cause the various constructors to be executed. Essentially, **grammar actions** are inserted into the productions, usually at the end of a production. These actions are C++ code which is executed as soon as all the preceding nonterminals have been recognized.

In our compiler example, grammar action almost always have the form

$$\{\$\$ = newParseTreeClass(\$<n>, \$<n>, \ldots);\}$$

Where the C++ code for creating a pointer to the new parse tree object is indicated on the right side of the action, and the value of the pointer is stored on the parser's value stack on the left side so that it can be made available to other productions calling this particular grammar item.

We will illustrate this by returning to the four prototypical examples and describing the corresponding grammar modifications in each case.

- Expressions

- Assignment statements

- Procedure calls

- Declarations

General grammar modifications for the remaining productions are similar and may be found in Appendix E.

9.5.1 Expressions

As you recall from Chapter 6, the set of productions describing Pascal expressions is somewhat lengthy. We will focus on the collection of productions that are related to *simple expressions*, i.e., those that are formed by additive operations.

```
(parser.gram)

  568          Simple_expr: Term
  569             | PLUSTK Term
  570                {$$ = $2;}
  571             | MINUSTK Term
  572                {$$ = new UMinusCls($2);}
  573             | Simple_expr Add_op Term
  574                {$$ = PAddOpCls($2) -> make_tree($1,$3);}
  575             | Simple_expr Add_op error
  576                {soft.err("Simple Expression error");}
  577             ;
  578          Add_op: PLUSTK
  579                {$$ = new PlusCls;}
  580             | MINUSTK
  581                {$$ = new MinusCls;}
  582             | ORTK
  583                {$$ = new OrCls;}
  584             ;
```

Notice that one kind of simple expression is a term. These are recognized by lower productions having similar kinds of grammar actions. Since they have already created parse tree objects, the pointer to these objects is automatically placed directly on the parser's value stack. In the case of a term preceded by a unary plus, the original term, now represented by $2, is placed on the value stack. For a simple expression preceded by a unary minus, a new *UMinusCls* object is created and its pointer placed on the stack.

Parse tree objects for binary operations are created in a two-stage process. First, the particular binary operation object is created by the lower production, and then it is passed to the higher production as $2, where its *make_tree()* member function is called. Since we have chosen to type the value stack as *PTreeNodeCls* and since we didn't want this base class to have literally hundreds of virtual functions, the *AddOpCls* identity of the derived object is required by the C++ compiler.

9.5.2   Assignment Statements

The next grammar segment just creates an assignment object and passes its (pointer) value to the stack. Again notice that this will cause the corresponding constructor to be executed and to perform any static semantic checking that is included therein.

```
(parser.gram)

  433          Assignment: Variable ASGTK Expr
  434                {$$ = new AssignmentStmtCls($1,$3);}
  435             | Variable EQTK error
  436                {soft.err("Use ':=' for assignment");}
  437             /* must test for fn_ident */
  438             ;
```

9.5.3   Procedure Calls

After converting an expression to an actual parameter in the last production and pasting the parameters into a linked-list using the *append()* member of *LstSeqBldrCls*, the *ProcCallCls* constructor creates the parse tree node representing the actual procedure call.

```
(parser.gram)

441            Procedure_call: Ident Actual_param_stuff
442                {$$ = new ProcCallCls($1,$2);}
443                ;
444            Actual_param_stuff: /*empty*/
445                    {$$ = 0;}
446                | LPARENTK RPARENTK
447                    {$$ = 0;}
448                | LPARENTK Actual_param_lst RPARENTK
449                    {$$ = $2;}
450                | LPARENTK Actual_param_lst error
451                    {soft.err("Actual parameter error");}
452                ;
453            Actual_param_lst: Actual_param
454                    {$$ = new ActualParamLstCls($1);}
455                | Actual_param_lst COMMATK Actual_param
456                    {$$ = PActualParamLstCls($1) ->
457                                        append($3);}
458                ;
459            Actual_param: Expr
460                    {$$ = new ActualParamCls($1);}
461                /* a Variable or a proc/fn id */
```

- An empty actual parameter list can occur in two different ways.

    - Use of the function name only

    - No actual parameters listed between the parens

- If we forget to include an action like `$$ = $2;`, the parser will by default place a pointer to the first item on the left. In this case, since the first item is a token, a nil-pointer will also be placed on the stack, often causing segmentation errors when the parse tree is requested to exhibit some sort of behavior.

9.5.4   Declarations

A Pascal statement like

```
var i,j,k: integer;
```

is recognized by the following productions.

```
(parser.gram)

226 Var_dec_part: /* empty */
227     | VARTK Var_dec_lst SCTK
228     | VARTK error
229         {soft.err("Declaration error -- missing semicolon?");}
230     | VARTK Var_dec_lst error
231         {soft.err("Declaration error -- missing semicolon?");}
232     ;
233     Var_dec_lst: Var_dec
234         | Var_dec_lst SCTK Var_dec
235             {yyerrok;}
236         | error
237             {soft.err("Error in variable declaration");}
238         | Var_dec_lst error Var_dec
239             {soft.err("Expecting semicolon");}
240         | Var_dec_lst SCTK error
241             {soft.err("Error in variable declaration");}
242         ;
243     Var_dec: Ident_lst COLONTK Type
244             {new VarDecCls($1,$3);}
245         | Ident_lst COLONTK error
246             {soft.err("Variable declaration error");}
247         ;
```

A lower production recognizing *Ident:* will create the *IdentCls* object corresponding to each identifier *i*, *j*, and *k*. These objects are again formed into a list using the *append()* function. Then the list, together with the underlying type, is made available to the *Var_dec:* production that creates (but does not bother to store on the value stack) a *VarDecCls* object. This causes the *VarDecCls* constructor to be executed, applying the appropriate semantic checks.

9.6   Exercises

1.   (a) Draw a partial tree (such as those in Figures 9.1, 9.2, and 9.3) representing an *if* statement.

     (b) Indicate that constructor(s) should be responsible for being sure that the expression is of `boolean` type.

     (c) Give a grammar production for the **if** statement that would cause the `boolean` check to be made.

2.   Explain why a constructor like that of *ProcDecCls* needs to be split up. Why not just wait until the entire production has been recognized and then execute the constructor?

3.   Checking the number and type and order of actual parameters in a function call against the formal parameters in the function definition is a static semantic activity and should be done in the *FuncCallCls* constructor, rather than in the *evaluate()* member function (Chapter 10 as, perhaps incorrectly, done in

our Pascal example). Modify the *FuncCallCls* constructor so that it makes these important semantic checks.

4. Implement the *get_type()* member function for *FuncCallCls*.

   Hint: The information can be found indirectly from one of its data members.

5. Specify the implementation for the constructor for *FieldDesigCls*. You might use *ArrayDesigCls* as a prototype. Be sure to include relevant semantic analysis on the names of the fields and their types. In particular, Pascal does not allow a record to contain a field of its own type.

6. Modify the *SubrangeTypeCls* constructor to include the following important static semantic checks.

   (a) The expressions for the low and high constants must be constant expressions.

   (b) The value for the low constant should not exceed the value for the high constant.

7. What kinds of changes might you make to the *ArrayTypeCls* constructor so that it enforces the semantic requirement that its components not be of its own type?

8. Modify the constructors for the case labels, elements, and statements so that the following semantic requirements are met.

   - The case index expression must be of ordinal type.
   - The types of all the types of the various case labels (See the grammar in Appendix E) are the same as the type of the case index expression.
   - The values of the various case labels must not overlap.

   Hint: You might want to consider using *FSigmaCls* objects described in Appendix C to represent the (possible intervals of the) case label values. Issues of order, overlap, etc. have all been built into that class.

9. Why not impose semantic requirements on *for* statement start and stop expressions that would requiring the obviously implied sizes of the values.

   Hint: What is known about these expressions when the *ForStmtCls* constructor is executed?

10. Modify the *WhileStmtCls* and *RepeatStmtCls* constructors so that they impose the usual requirement that their expression have `boolean` type.

11. What static semantic requirements are specified for a Pascal record variable list in a *With* statement? Modify the *RecVarCls* to implement these checks. You may also want to modify the *WithStmtCls* constructor.

12. Specify the definition of a *LabelCls*, that is declared with the grammar productions

```
Label_dec_part:  /* empty */
   | LABELTK Label_lst SCTK
   ;
   Label_lst: Label
        | Label_lst COMMATK Label
        ;
```

recognizes a labeled statement. Include in the *LabelCls* constructor the normal Pascal semantic requirements for labels.

13. Modify the *ConstDefCls* constructor to test that its expression is indeed a constant.

14. (**CLIP** Project)

Implement the constructor for all **CLIP** parse tree classes. Be sure to include code for testing semantic checks relevant for your system.

Chapter 10

Interpreter

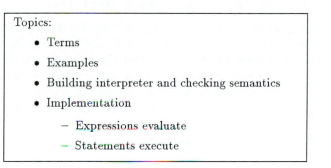

Topics:

- Terms
- Examples
- Building interpreter and checking semantics
- Implementation
    - Expressions evaluate
    - Statements execute

10.1   Terms

10.1.1   An Interpreter Is a Virtual Computer

Historically the computer science use of the term **interpreter** is a bit of a misnomer, since it has been used to describe a program or system that accepts and then *simulates* commands in some high-level language. As such, it is really a simulated or virtual computer rather than a translator from one computer language to another. Some interpreters execute the source language instructions directly. Others translate the source program into some internal representation and then perform the program simulation by processing the intermediate representation in some way. The first approach is much easier to implement; the second approach allows more efficient simulation, especially if the intermediate representation is optimized for expensive loop constructs.

Most modern interpreters are some variant of the second approach. The famous Berkeley Pascal student interpreter *pi* constructs an intermediate tree structure, and then simulates the program by performing a tree traversal. User interfaces for large systems are also often interpreters that convert the user commands into tree structures, and then issue system commands as the tree is traversed. Such an implementation allows system commands to be treated as procedure calls in a more powerful **command language**. Commands for interacting directly with individual data sets can be entered in an interactive mode, while routine or complex tasks can be performed on large quantities of data by using instructions stored in a source file or **script**.

Modern interpreters often execute at surprisingly fast speeds. With today's operating systems utilizing shared libraries even for compiled modules, interpreted code is often only a factor of two or three times slower than the corresponding machine language module, even for rather extensive and complex instructions. The major increases of machine speed and highly efficient implementation environments also have combined to greatly improve interpreter performance.

10.1.2   An Interpreter Is a Language Definition

A specific implementation of an interpreter or compiler for a given programming language certainly becomes a *local* definition of the language in the sense that users of that implementation must conform to the language checks and then can associate observed behavior in response to a given source program. However, carefully constructed interpreters can also become an *operational definition* of a programming language, providing a semantic standard against which the output of a corresponding code generator may be tested.

Lexical requirements of a language can be reasonably accurately translated from the language specification document into a scanner specification and from there to a corresponding scanner. Syntactic specifications of a language can also be accurately specified and then used to produce the related parser. But producing compiled code for implementing run-time semantic checks, especially since the semantic specifications are usually written in an informal prose, is no trivial task. It is much easier to implement and verify such semantic analysis in an interpreter, as it is usually implemented in a high-level language. Then the interpreter behavior can be compared to the behavior of the corresponding code generated by an actual compiler.

10.2   Examples

Let's begin our discussion of dynamic semantic analysis by looking at four examples.

Example: Assignment statement.   Consider the following assignment statement.

```
i := 1;
```

Interpreting this statement requires evaluating the expression on the right-hand side, locating the store bound to the identifier, i, and then placing the value of the expression in the appropriate memory location. Locating the memory store associated with an identifier can be a nontrivial task in a program containing nested procedures or functions.

Example: Definite iteration.

```
for i := 1 to n do <stmt>
```

Executing a `for` statement is a bit more complex.

1. The assignment i := 1 is first executed, as in the previous example.

2. Then the stop expression n is evaluated.

3. Compare the value of the loop variable with the value of the stop expression. If the value of the loop variable is less than or equal to the value of the stop expression, then perform the following.

    (a) Execute <stmt>.

    (b) Increment the loop variable according to the loop variable's type.

    (c) Goto to Step 3.

4. Execution of the **for** statement has been completed normally.

Example: Procedure call.   Suppose that the following procedure has been previously declared.

```
procedure DoExample(In: integer; var InOut: integer);
begin
    InOut := 2 * In
end
```

When this procedure is called

```
DoExample(i,j)
```

a number of things must take place.

1. Locate the executable statements, local store, and formal parameters bound to the identifier *DoExample*.

2. Evaluate the actual parameters, i and j.

3. Since Pascal allows for recursion, create a new version, called a **stack frame**, of the store for local variables and formal parameters. In this example there are no local variables. Push the previous frame onto a stack.

4. Store the actual parameters in the new store associated with the formal parameters.

5. Execute the procedure's instructions. In this case there is only the one assignment statement, that will modify the value of the store associated with the formal parameter j.

6. Pop the saved local values and bind them to the procedure identifier.

This example does not display all the problems associated with procedure calls, of course. We didn't experience recursion. And we didn't talk about the possibility of modifying store associated with global variables, a process called **side effects**.

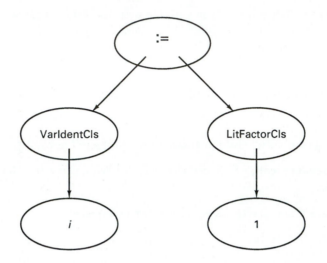

Figure 10.1. Parse Tree for Single Statement Program

Example: Input/output.   In many ways an output statement like

```
write('i,x', i:5, x:7:2)
```

is like a procedure call. There is a procedure name. There are actual parameters
that must be evaluated and passed to the procedure. But there are also significant
differences. The usual "agree in number, type, order" restriction on the actual
parameters is no longer enforced: There may be any number of parameters, and
the parameters can assume a number of different forms.

Execution of this example statement amounts to evaluating the first write-
parameter, and then outputting that to standard output. Then the next write-
parameter i is evaluated, along with the field width expression 5 and the value of
i is written in a field of width 5, if possible. Finally, x is evaluated, along with the
expressions for field width and decimal width. The first value is then formatted
according to the two width specifiers and the result also written.

10.3   Strategy

10.3.1   Interpreter: Behavior of the Parse Tree

Recall that the front-end for the interpreter produces a parse tree of objects as
the source program is processed. Since each object can display any of its class
behaviors, an object-oriented approach to the construction of an interpreter is

to place interpreter behavior appropriate for the given tree node *in* that object. Interpreting a program then amounts to requesting that the tree execute itself. The root (program) node requests that its *BlockCls* child perform its *execute()* member function. This function, in turn, requests that the block node's *StatementSeq* child *execute()*. This function requests that each *StatementCls* object *execute()*, and so on.

This process can be more precisely understood by examining several of the above examples more closely.

Assignment statement. As the parser processes the statement `i := 1` it produces a parse tree essentially like that in Figure 10.1. The *ControllerCls* object first requests the *ProgramCls* object *execute()*. This results in a call to the block object and then to the statement sequence object to execute. Finally, the *AssignmentStmtCls* object *execute()* is called. An assignment statement object has two data members representing the left and right sides of the assignment. The expression on the right side is requested to evaluate itself. This results in a *ValueCls* object that can then be placed in the symbol table entry representing the identifier on the left side of the expression.

It is important to see that a more complicated expression on the right side presents no more work for the assignment statement *execute()*. For example, the tree for

$$i := 3 * j + 5$$

would essentially be that illustrated in Figure 10.2. In this case, the same *evaluate()* request is sent to the right-hand expression. Now, the *PlusCls* object requests the left and right expressions to evaluate themselves and then returns the *ValueCls* object representing the sum of each of these two as returned by the appropriate *TypeCls::add()* function. The left side value is similarly produced: A *TimesCls* object would request its left and right children to evaluate() themselves and then produce a *ValueCls* object representing the product. If the expression had been even more complex, then the process would just continue.

The key idea is that increased complexity in a source program statement does not require any change to the *execute()* structure. Because of the powerful joining of inheritance and late binding, an assignment statement object doesn't need to know anything about the construction of the expression on the right side. It only sends the *evaluate()* message, and then the expression itself determines the manner in which that expression is evaluated.

For statement. One additional example may be helpful. Consider a statement like the following trivial *for* statement.

$$for\ i := 1\ to\ n\ do\ writeln(i)$$

Again the front-end will have produced a parse tree intermediate representation like that found in Figure 10.3. The *execute()* member function of the top *ForStmtCls* object first calls the *evaluate()* function of the start expression and then assigns that

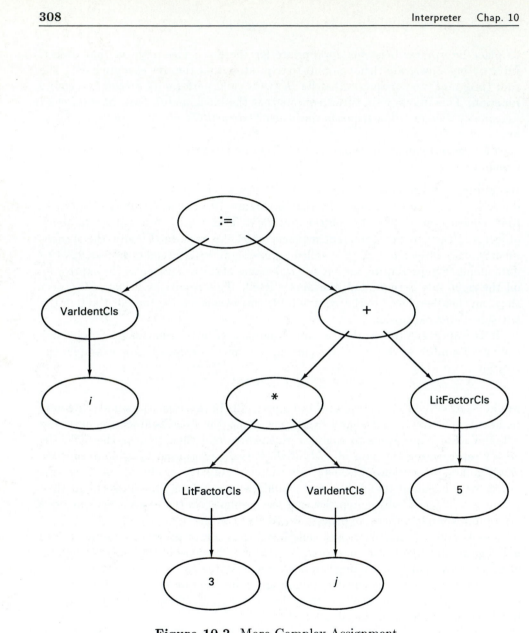

Figure 10.2. More Complex Assignment

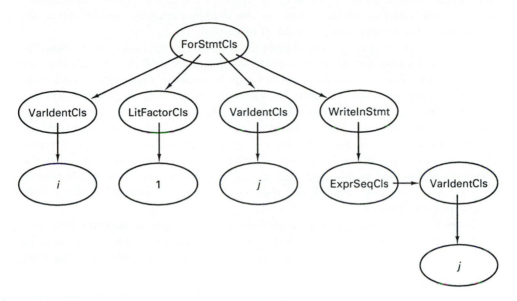

Figure 10.3. For Statement

to the control variable. This value is compared with the *ValueCls* object returned by the stop expression's *evaluate()* function. If it not greater (as determined by the common type of the expressions), then the *WriteLnStmtCls* object is executed. The control expression is incremented, again by its type. The value compared with the stop expression value. And so on....

In the event that the *writeln* statement is replaced with a compound statement, the *execute()* algorithm remains exactly the same. This time, the *StatementSeqCls* object's *execute()* will be polymorphically selected and it will send an *execute()* message to each node in the linked-list of statements making up that compound statement. Similarly additional complexity in the start or stop expressions will not require any changes to the *for* statement's *execute()* function.

10.3.2 Performing Dynamic Semantic Checks

We noted in Chapter 9 that **semantic analysis** involved those language requirements that were not already specified as either lexical or syntactical. We also divided semantic requirements into two categories, **static** and **dynamic**. The first category contains those rules that can be enforced during the program analysis phase. The second category of language semantics must be enforced during the execution of the source program.

We saw that in an object-oriented setting, the implementation of static checks could be conveniently placed in the constructors for the parse tree objects. The code for dynamic semantics can be placed in the *evaluate()* or *execute()* member functions of those same objects. Indeed, many of the dynamic semantic requirements are *definitions* of the corresponding *execute()* functions.

If the programming language is descriptively specified, the task of translating the requirements into object *execute()* or *evaluate()* behavior is often accomplished in a series of stages. First, expression objects are given *evaluate()* behaviors, using standard types, such as integer or reals. A collection of important language statements are then given *execute()* behaviors, based upon the language description. Usually, this work on statements brings clarification of expression evaluation behaviors that are then included. Expression evaluation is then extended to additional types. These extensions usually point to corrections in earlier implementation details for both expressions and statements. Then additional statements are implemented. This process continues until all specified expressions and statements have been implemented and tested.

Recently a powerful symbolic formalism called **action semantics** has been developed by P. Mosses [13] and by Watt [24], which specifies language semantics by first defining the languages symbolic entities and then specifying semantic functions on those entities.

- The symbolic entities in that specification are very closely related to the parse tree objects in an object-oriented interpreter/compiler.

- The semantic functions translate almost directly into implementation code for the corresponding *execute()* and *evaluate()* functions.

The process of developing an action semantic specification for a programming language is still in the developmental stage. Indeed, Mosses and Watt have just released a complete, soon-to-be-published specification of Pascal. However, a number of researchers are currently working on supporting tools and environments that may make this a very effective way to describe a language, both from the language developer's and the language implementor's points of view.

10.4   Implementing Interpreter

The following C++ implementation code for the Pascal interpreter described in this text can be viewed as a semantic definition of Pascal. Much of the it has been based directly on the Mosses/Watt Pascal specification.

10.4.1   Expressions Evaluate

Expression base class.   Expressions have type and value. The behavior characterizing expressions is evaluation. This translates into an *ExprCls* base class, which has *type* and *value* data members, and a virtual *evaluate()* function, which is not intended to be actually executed.

```
        ExprCls::evaluate() (eval.C)

    17 PValueCls ExprCls :: evaluate() {
    18      hard.err("ExprCls::evaluate()  BASE CLASS!!");
    19      return 0;
    20 }
```

Relational operators. Relational operators consist of a *RelOpCls* base class and seven derived operations. The code below contains the *evaluate()* details for the base class and *EqCls*, which is representative of the various derived classes.

```
      EqCls::evaluate() (eval.C)

    23 PValueCls RelOpCls :: evaluate() {
    24      hard.err("RelOpCls::evaluate() -- BASE CLASS!!");
    25      return 0;
    26 }
    27
    28 PValueCls EqCls :: evaluate() {
    29      //cout << "EqCls::evaluate()" << endl;
    30      if (!left || ! right) {
    31          hard.err("EqCls logic error");
    32      }
    33      PTypeCls ltype = left -> get_type();
    34      return ltype -> eq(left,right);
    35 }
```

After checking for a possible design error (null pointer) *EqCls::evaluate()* requests that the type of the left expression perform its eq() test. The result from that test is then returned as the value of the *EqCls::evaluate()*.

Unary operators. In Pascal, there are essentially only two unary operators. The *evaluate()* for UMinusCls just requests the expression to which it points to return its *uminus()* value.

```
      (eval.C)

    92 PValueCls UMinusCls :: evaluate() {
    93      //cout << "UMinusCls::evaluate()" << endl;
    94      PTypeCls t_type = term -> get_type();
    95      return t_type -> uminus(term);
    96 }
    97
    98 PValueCls UNotCls :: evaluate() {
    99      //cout << "UNotCls::evaluate()" << endl;
   100      PTypeCls t_type = factor -> get_type();
   101      return PBooleanTypeCls(t_type) -> unot(factor);
   102 }
```

The extra *PBooleanType* cast in the *UNotCls* is required because *unot()* was not declared as a virtual member of the base class *TypeCls*. It certainly could have been, but the length of the list of *TypeCls* virtual functions seemed to argue against additional members, unless they were widely used.

Additive operators.   The *AddOpCls* base class has three operator classes derived from it, *PlusCls* being representative.

```
(eval.C)

105 PValueCls AddOpCls :: evaluate() {
106     hard.err("AddOpCls::evaluate() -- BASE CLASS!!" );
107     return 0;
108 }
109
110 PValueCls PlusCls :: evaluate() {
111     //cout << "PlusCls::evaluate()" << endl;
112     if (!left || ! right) {
113         hard.err("PlusCls logic error");
114     }
115     PTypeCls ltype = left -> get_type();
116     return ltype -> add(left,right);
117 }
```

The base class *evaluate()* is not intended to be executed. *PlusCls::evaluate()* returns the value received from the left expressions type *plus()* function.

Multiplicative operators.   Multiplicative operators are evaluated in essentially the same way as additive ones.

```
(eval.C)

138 PValueCls MulOpCls :: evaluate() {
139     hard.err("MulOpCls::evaluate() -- BASE CLASS!!");
140     return 0;
141 }
142
143 PValueCls TimesCls :: evaluate() {
144     //cout << "TimesCls::evaluate()" << endl;
145     if (!left || ! right) {
146         hard.err("TimesCls logic error");
147     }
148     PTypeCls ltype = left -> get_type();
149     return ltype -> times(left,right);
150 }
```

Variables and functions.   Evaluating variables simply amounts to finding the present value of the variable that has been stored in the symbol table. The *VarIdentCls* data member *att* points to the symbol table entry currently attached to the variable. All that is required is to request each entry evaluate itself.

```
(eval.C)

201 PValueCls VarIdentCls :: evaluate() {
202     //cout << "VarIdentCls::evaluate()" << endl;
203     return  att -> evaluate();
204 }
205
206 PValueCls VarIdentCls :: locate_val(PValueCls Value) {
207     //cout << "VarIdentCls::locate_val()" << Value << endl;
208     //Since value associated with an identifier is itself...
209     return Value;
210 }
212
213 PValueCls FuncCallCls :: evaluate() {
214     //cout << "FuncCallCls::evaluate()" << att << endl;
215     PFuncAttCls(att) -> a_param_lst = actual_param_lst;
216     return att -> evaluate();
217 }
```

A function is evaluated by first updating the list of actual parameters, and then performing the function's instructions. The complexity surrounding a possibly recursive evaluation of a function has been placed in the *evaluate()* of the *FuncAttCls* symbol table entry, described below.

Array components.   Expressions subtrees representing a particular array component are built by the semantic action of second production in the following grammar segment.

```
Variable: Ident Actual_param_stuff
          /* could be a const, variable or  fn_call*/
        | Variable LBRACKTK Expr_lst RBRACKTK
        | Variable DOTTK Ident
        | Variable UPARROWTK
        ;
```

An expression like the array designator $A[i]$ is therefore represented by a subtree like that in Figure 10.4. Evaluating such an expression amounts to first looking up the array's identifier in the symbol table, finding the current (array) value of that identifier, calculating the present value of the index i, and then returning the ith component of the value.

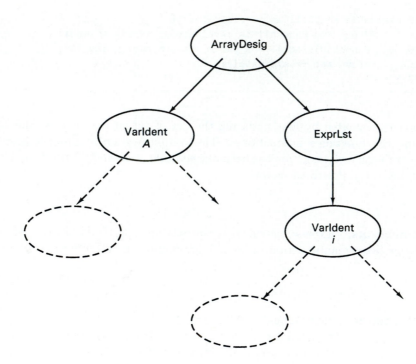

Figure 10.4. Tree Segment for A[i]

(eval.C)

```
222 PValueCls ArrayDesigCls :: evaluate() {
223     //cout << "ArrayDesigCls::evaluate()" << endl;
224
225     //First get the variable
226     PSymtabEntryCls var_att = this -> variable -> get_att();
227     PTypeCls var_type = var_att -> get_type();
228
229     //Then the value of the entire array
230     PValueCls arr_val = var_att -> evaluate();
231
232     //Next, get the requested component
233     PExprCls p = index_lst -> get_seq_head();
234     while (p) {
235         PTypeCls arr_ind_type = PArrayTypeCls(var_type) ->
236                                          get_index_type();
237         PTypeCls index_type = p -> get_type();
238         if ((*arr_ind_type == *index_type) || //identical
239             ((*arr_ind_type <= *index_type) && //subrange
240             (arr_ind_type -> is_valid_val(p->evaluate())))) {
241             int index;
242             char *ind_str = p -> evaluate() -> to_char();
243             if (is_numeric(ind_str)) {
244                 index = atoi(ind_str);
245             } else {
246                 index = int(*ind_str);
247             }
248             arr_val = arr_val -> get_component(index);
249         } else {
250             runtime.err("Array index out of bounds");
251             arr_val = new ValueCls(0);
252         }
253
254         p = PExprCls(p -> get_next());
255     }
256     return arr_val;
257 }
```

Note that the code for getting the required component involves a loop that handles array designators containing multiple index values, such as $B[i, j]$. Understanding this code may be easier if you also consider the corresponding subtree in Figure 10.5. The overall structure representing the array type of B is contained in *var_type*. *Arr_ind_type* contains the type of the (first) index. So the code in the loop first checks to see if the value p -> evaluate() of the index is valid for the array's index type. Then the component of the value for B is referenced by *arr_val*. In the first pass through the loop, this would be pointing at $B[i]$. After the second (and last) pass through the loop, it would point at

$$B[i][j] = B[i, j]$$

which is the required component.

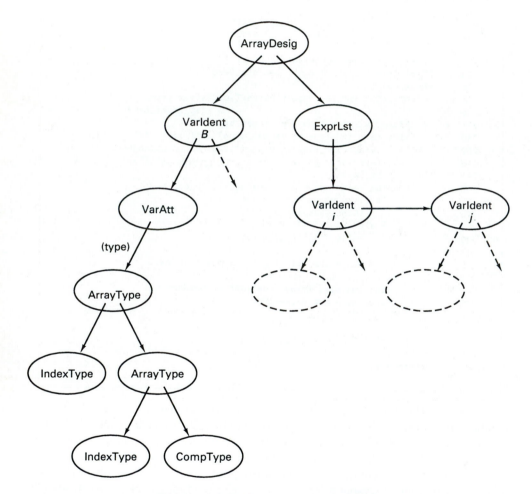

Figure 10.5. Tree Segment for B[i,j]

Write parameters. Write parameters are just objects whose data members contain an expression that is to be displayed and optional formatting field information. Evaluating such objects is accomplished by sending the *evaluate()* message to the write parameter's *expr* data member.

```
(eval.C)

288 PValueCls WriteParamCls :: evaluate() {
289     //cout << "WriteParamCls::evaluate()" << endl;
290     return PExprCls(expr) -> evaluate();
291 }
```

Symbol Table Entries

If program interpreting is desired, a symbol table entry itself can serve as the storage location for the corresponding variable or constant. This section therefore addresses the issue of providing the various symbol table entries with *evaluate()* behavior.

Entries for symbolic constants. Symbol table entries representing symbol constants contain the fixed value of the constant. The value object representing the constant is created by the parser during the analysis phase. Since the value does not change during program interpreting or execution, the *evaluate()* function can trivially return (the pointer to) this object.

```
ConstAttCls :: evaluate() (symtab.h)

PValueCls ConstAttCls :: evaluate() {
    return value
}
```

This code is actually replaced by a single line function definition in the symbol table definition module *symtab.h* to allow the C++ compiler to replace it as in-line code if possible.

Entries for variables. Symbol table entries associated with an identifier in a program can represent items of a variety of types: Integer, real, array, record. But since *ValueCls* is able to represent values for all types, the implementation for *VarAttCls::evaluate()* is exactly the same as for constants! It too can be placed in the symbol table definition module for possible system performance improvement.

Variables differ from constants in that their values can be changed during execution. The *VarAttCls* function responsible for such changes is *set_val()*.

```
(eval.C)

294 void VarAttCls :: set_value(PPTreeNodeCls Variable,
295                                       PValueCls Value) {
296     //cout << "VarAttCls::set_value" << endl;
297     //rval is (a pointer) to the value of right assignment expr.
298     PValueCls rval = Value;
299
300     if (!(this -> type -> is_valid_val(rval))) {
301         runtime.err("Assigning invalid value");
302     } else {
303         PValueCls new_val = new ValueCls(*Value); // New copy.
304         //lval is the address of the left assignement expr value.
305         //      i.e., the location in the present value.
306         PValueCls lval;
307         PVariableCls var = PVariableCls(Variable);
308         if (Variable) { //an assign from designators
309             lval =  var -> locate_val(this -> value);
310         } else { //an assign from fun/proc/other calls
311             lval = this -> value;
312         }
313         if (lval && lval -> get_next()) {
314             this -> value = lval = PVariableCls(lval ->
315                             get_next() -> prepend(new_val));
316         } else {
317             *lval = *new_val;
318         }
319     }
320 }
```

There are essentially three classes of objects calling this function.

- *AssignmentStmtCls*

- Various loop classes

- Function and procedure call classes

The first of these presents the function with the most work, since the left side of an assignment can be any valid designator. This designator, passed as the *Variable* argument must be used to locate the **lval** or address of the value that is to be changed. All classes derived from *VariableCls* have a special member function *locate_val()*, that returns this address. *VarIdentCls* objects represent the entire left-hand-side structure, so their *lval* is just the address of the *ValueCls* associated with the variable.

```
(eval.C)

206 PValueCls VarIdentCls :: locate_val(PValueCls Value) {
207     //cout << "VarIdentCls::locate_val()" << Value << endl;
208     //Since value associated with an identifier is itself...
209     return Value;
210 }
```

Locating the *lval* of an ArrayDesigCls expression should look somewhat familiar. Since *ValueCls* objects are referenced by their pointers, the (pointer to the) rval value returned by *ArrayDesigCls::evaluate()* is essentially the *lval* of that expression. The code for *ArrayDesigCls::locate_val()* has therefore been included below only for completeness.

```
(eval.C)

260  PValueCls ArrayDesigCls :: locate_val(PValueCls Value) {
261      //cout << "ArrayDesigCls::locate_val()" << endl;
262
263      PValueCls desg_value = Value;
264      PSymtabEntryCls var_att = this -> variable -> get_att();
265      PTypeCls var_type =  var_att -> get_type();
266
267      PExprCls p = index_lst -> get_seq_head();
268      while (p) {
269          PValueCls index_value = p -> evaluate();
270          PTypeCls arr_ind_type = PArrayTypeCls(var_type) ->
271                                          get_index_type();
272          if (arr_ind_type -> is_valid_val(index_value)) {
273              int i = index_value -> to_integer();
274              desg_value = desg_value -> get_component(i);
275          } else {
276              runtime.err("Array index is out of bounds");
277              //leave desg_value the same
278          }
279
280          p = PExprCls(p -> get_next());
281          var_type = PArrayTypeCls(var_type) ->
282                                  get_component_type();
283      }
284      return desg_value;
285  }
```

Entries for functions.   The fundamental difference between a Pascal procedure and function is the location of the invocation. Functions are called when their identifiers occur in expressions. Procedures are called when their identifiers are used in a statement sequence. Aside from a few minor differences (e.g., var parameters in a function should produce warning messages and a mechanism for returning a value for a function), the details for the *evaluate()* behavior of a function symbol table object and the *execute()* behavior of a procedure symbol table object are essentially the same.

Functions and procedures provide the following three items for programmers.

- An encapsulation of variables local to the subprogram.

- A mechanism for controlling the visibility of the data and identifiers in the subprogram.

- An economy of thought. A subprogram identifier is a macro-like representation of the complete set of commands found in that subprogram.

These three items form the major sections in the implementation following *evaluate()* code. After an initialization section, in which a linked list of actual parameters is created, the following instructions are given.

- The subprogram's symbol table *func_tab* is located and requested to create new locations for the values of all local variables so that recursive subprogram calls are possible.

  - Traditionally constructed interpreters accomplish this by creating a data structure called a **stack frame**, that contains all local variables and relevant parameters. These frames are pushed prior to the execution of the subprogram and popped upon subprogram completion.

  - The approach taken here is to have the symbol table take the place of the stack frame. Instead of pushing the entire symbol table onto another stack, each entry of the symbol table is requested to create a stack of values, which are pushed and popped at the appropriate times.

- The actual and formal parameters are associated.

  - Variable parameters are really aliases for the location of the associated actual parameters.

  - Value parameters have their values set to the value of the corresponding actual parameter.

- The entire sequence of subprogram statements is executed by sending the *execute()* message to the *BlockCls* object, that sits directly above the sequence in the parse tree.

```
345 PValueCls FuncAttCls :: evaluate() {
346     //cout << "FuncAttCls::evaluate()" << endl;
347     PActualParamCls a_param = 0;
348     PValueCls a_param_val_head = 0;
349     PValueCls a_param_val_tail = 0;
350
351     if (a_param_lst) {
352         a_param = a_param_lst ->get_seq_head();
353         while (a_param) {
354             //Stop aliasing of values in stack frame...
355             PValueCls a_param_val =
356                 new ValueCls(*a_param -> evaluate());
357             if (!a_param_val_tail) {
358                 a_param_val_head =
359                     a_param_val_tail = a_param_val ;
360             } else {
361                 a_param_val_tail =
362                     PValueCls(a_param_val_tail ->
363                                 append(a_param_val));
364             }
365             a_param = PActualParamCls(a_param -> get_next());
366         }
367     }
368     PSymtabCls stk_fm = func_tab;
369     stk_fm -> push_values(); //For recursion
370     if (a_param_lst) {
371         a_param = a_param_lst ->get_seq_head();
372         PFParamAttCls   f_param = this -> param_lst;
373         PTypeCls f_param_type = f_param -> get_type();
374         while (f_param) {
375             if (f_param -> get_is_var()) {
376                 f_param -> set_aliased_to(a_param ->
377                                 get_expr() -> get_att());
378             } else { // is_val!
379                 if (! f_param_type ->
380                                 is_valid_val(a_param_val_head)) {
381                     runtime.err("Actual param value invalid");
382                     return new ValueCls(0);
383                 }
384                 f_param -> set_value(0,a_param_val_head);
385             }
386             f_param = PFParamAttCls(f_param -> get_next());
387             a_param = PActualParamCls(a_param -> get_next());
388             a_param_val_head =
389                     PValueCls(a_param_val_head -> get_next());
390         }
391     }
392     ScopeCls::set_vista(stk_fm);
393     block -> execute();
394     //Pop the stack frame
395     stk_fm -> pop_values();
396     //Reset vista back to outer scope, since now done with proc.
397     ScopeCls::set_vista(PSymtabCls(stk_fm -> get_next()));
398     return this -> value;
399 }
```

After completion, the now useless values of the local variables are popped and discarded, the *ScopeCls* variable, that describes variable visibility, is restored to the symbol table of the calling routine, and in the case of a function subprogram the value of the *FuncAttCls* object representing the function is returned.

10.4.2   Statements Execute

Parse Tree Nodes

Empty statement.   Since it is a valid statement, the empty statement *execute()* returns an termination condition of zero, indicating a normal execution.

```
(execute.C)

17 int EmptyStmtCls :: execute() {
18     //cout << "EmptyStmtCls::execute()" << endl;
19     return 0;
20 }
```

Assignment statement.   An assignment statement calculates the value *rval* of the right-hand expression, locates the variable on the left-hand side *lval*, and sets the value. Any valid variable, including array designators, record fields, and pointer dereferencing, is a valid *lval*. So the *set_val* function needs to modify the current *ValueCls* object associated with the variable's identifier.

```
(execute.C)

23 int AssignmentStmtCls :: execute() {
24     //cout << "AssignmentStmtCls::execute() " << endl;
25     PValueCls rval = PExprCls(expr) -> evaluate();
26
27     PSymtabEntryCls found_it = variable -> get_att();
28     if (!found_it) {
29         hard.err("AssignmentStmtCls::execute() LOGIC ERROR");
30     } else {
31         PVarAttCls(found_it) -> set_value(variable,rval);
32     }
33     return 0;
34 }
```

The error message is left over from the design phases and could be removed at this stage.

If statement.   The Pascal *if* statement is significantly simpler than the corresponding structure in many other languages.

```
(execute.C)

37 int IfStmtCls :: execute() {
38     //cout << "IfStmtCls::execute()" << endl;
39     if (PExprCls(expr) -> evaluate() -> to_integer()){
40         stmt -> execute();
41     } else if (else_stmt) {
42         else_stmt -> execute();
43     }
44     return 0;
45 }
```

If the boolean expression is true, that is, if it evaluates to a nonzero integer, then
execute the single statement *stmt*. If the boolean expression is false and if there is
an else clause, execute the statement *else_stmt*.

Case statement. Consider the following example of a simple Pascal case statement.

```
case val of
    1,4: writeln('1 or 4');
      2: writeln('2');
      3: writeln('3')
end
```

The identifier *val* is called a **case index** The three inner statements

```
    1,4: writeln('1 or 4');
      2: writeln('2');
      3: writeln('3')
```

are called **case elements**. The values 1, 4, 2, and 3 are called **case constants**.
    In the following implementation of *CaseStmtCls::execute()*, the first task is to
evaluate the case index value.

```
        (execute.C)

     48  int CaseStmtCls :: execute() {
     49      //cout << "CaseStmtCls::execute()" << endl;
     50      char *case_index_val = expr -> evaluate() -> to_char();
     51      PCaseEltCls p = case_lst -> seq_head;
     52      while (p) {
     53          PCaseLabelLstCls q = p -> case_label_lst;
     54          PCaseLabelCls r = q -> seq_head;
     55          while (r) {
     56              char *case_lbl_cnst =
     57                  r -> constant -> evaluate() -> to_char();
     58              if (!strcmp(case_index_val,case_lbl_cnst)) {
     59                  return p -> stmt -> execute();
     60              }
     61              r = PCaseLabelCls(r -> get_next());
     62          }
     63          p = PCaseEltCls(p -> get_next());
     64      } //else, default to....
     65      return 0;
     66  }
```

Then, for each case element *p*, the case constant `r -> constant` is compared with the case index value. If the values are the same, then the corresponding statement `p -> stmt` is executed.

For statement. Implementing *ForStmtCls::execute()* amounts to initializing the start variable with the start expression and then recursively executing the loop's statement as long as the incremented or decremented loop variable has not met the stop condition.

All of that sounds very simple. The problem however is that the loop variable may be any of the following.

- It may (and probably should) be a variable local to the program section in which is being used.

- It may be an external variable visible in an enclosing program segment.

- It may even be even a *var* parameter that is aliased to such an external variable.

Incrementing the loop variable can therefore not be done internally to *ForStmtCls::execute()*. For this reason the loop variable's *TypeCls* object `id_type` must first produce the incremented value by using its `inc()` member function. The symbol table entry *id_att* for the loop variable must then set its value member to this incremented value.

(execute.C)

```
69 int ForStmtCls :: execute() {
70     //cout << "ForStmtCls::execute()" << endl;
71     PSymtabEntryCls id_att =
72                 ScopeCls::get_vista() ->
73                     vista_lookup(ident -> get_name());
74     PTypeCls id_type = id_att -> get_type();
75
76     PValueCls s_val = start_expr -> evaluate();
77     if (! id_type ->is_valid_val(s_val)) {
78         runtime.err("Invalid value for control variable");
79         return 1;
80     }
81     id_att -> set_value(0,s_val);
82
83     char *start = s_val -> to_char();
84     char *stop  = stop_expr -> evaluate() -> to_char();
85     int start_val = 0;
86     int stop_val = 0;
87     if (isalpha(*start)) {
88         start_val = int(*start);
89         stop_val  = int(*stop);
90     } else {
91         start_val = atoi(s_val -> to_char());
92         stop_val  = atoi(stop_expr -> evaluate() -> to_char());
93     }
94
95     if (dir -> dir == 1) { // up
96         for (int counter = start_val;
97                         counter <= stop_val;
98                                     counter++) {
99             stmt -> execute();
100
101             PValueCls id_val = id_att -> get_value();
102             if (! id_type ->is_valid_val(id_val)) {
103                 runtime.err("Invalid value for control variable");
104                 return 1;
105             }
106             id_att -> set_value(0,id_type -> inc(id_val));
107         }
108     } else {
109         for (int counter = start_val;
110                         counter >= stop_val;
111                                     counter--) {
112             stmt -> execute();
113
114             PValueCls id_val = id_att -> get_value();
115             if (! id_type ->is_valid_val(id_val)) {
116                 runtime.err("Invalid value for control variable");
117                 return 1;
118             }
119             id_att -> set_value(0,id_type -> dec(id_val));
120         }
121     }
122     return 0;
123 }
```

While statement.   Implementing *WhileStmtCls::execute()* is significantly easier.

```
(execute.C)

126 int WhileStmtCls :: execute() {
127     //cout << "WhileStmtCls::execute()" << endl;
128     while (atoi(expr -> evaluate() -> to_char())) {
129         stmt -> execute();
130     }
131     return 0;
132 }
```

Since *expr* is a boolean expression, and since the *while* control structure is a pretest, the boolean value of the expression is converted to a truth-value integer that is used as the C++ control variable.

Implementation details for *RepeatStmtCls::execute()* are very similar. Additional comments can be found in Exercise 10.3.

With statement.   The development of implementation code for all Pascal record type activity has been the content of a number of exercises. Hints for implementing *WithStmtCls::execute()* may be found in Exercise 10.4.

Procedure call.   *ProcCallCls::execute()* passes all the difficult work off to the symbol table entry *found_it* containing all the information for the procedure.

```
(execute.C)

151 int ProcCallCls :: execute() {
152     //cout << "ProcCallCls::execute()" << endl;
153
154     char *name = PIdentCls(ident) -> get_name();
155     PSymtabEntryCls found_it =
156                 ScopeCls::get_vista() -> vista_lookup(name);
157     if (!found_it) {
158         hard.err("ProcCallCls::execute() LOGIC ERROR");
159     }
160
161     return PProcAttCls(found_it) -> execute(actual_param_lst);
162 }
```

The use of *vista_lookup()* just searches through all the visible symbol tables for the procedure's name. *Hard.err* is an object that prints out the indicated messages and terminates the entire system. Since it is more a design tool than an implementation tool, it could be removed at this point with little loss of system integrity.

Write statement. Calls to Pascal standard procedures *write* and *writeln* are different from those made to user-defined procedures.

- Procedure calls to these standard procedures can have any number of parameters of (almost any) type.

- Similar situations exist for Pascal standard functions like *abs*, *sqrt*, ... that allow a fixed number of parameters but allow for a certain collection of valid types.

The usual way to handle this problem is to recognize such calls with separate grammar productions so that their parse tree objects can be built using whatever special techniques are necessary.

Figure 10.6 illustrates the parse tree segment that represents the following Pascal *write()* statement `write(i : 5, x : 12 : 3)`. The *WriteStmtCls* object representing this statement would *execute()* by first evaluating the expression `p -> get_expr`, evaluating a possible field width value `p -> field1` so that a default value can be set if necessary, and then requesting that the *ValueCls* object `p -> evaluate()` print itself.

```
(execute.C)

183 int WriteStmtCls :: execute() {
184     //cout << "WriteStmtCls::execute() " << expr << endl;
185     PWriteParamCls p =
186         PWriteParamLstCls(write_param_lst) -> seq_head;
187     while (p) {
188         int wide;
189         PExprCls p_xpr = p -> get_expr();
190         PExprCls fld_wdth = PExprCls(p -> field1);
191         if (*(p_xpr -> get_type()) == *std_type.CHAR()) {
192             wide = 1;
193         } else if (fld_wdth) {
194             wide = fld_wdth -> evaluate() -> to_integer();
195         } else {
196             wide = 10;
197         }
198         PWriteParamCls(p) -> evaluate() -> print(wide);
199         p = PWriteParamCls(p -> get_next());
200     }
201     return 1;
202 }
```

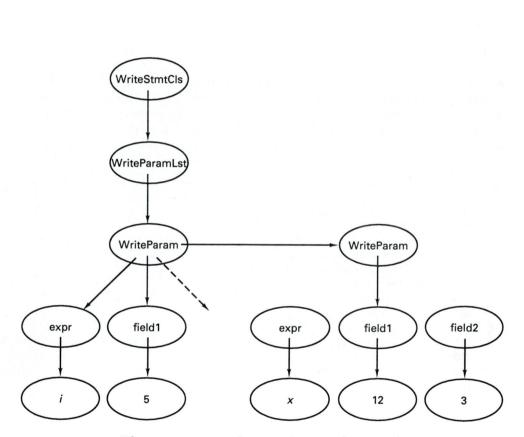

Figure 10.6. Tree Segment for write(i:5,x:12:3)

Higher level nodes. *Execute()* functions for higher level parse tree nodes are very simple.

```
(execute.C)

229 int StatementSeqCls :: execute() {
230     //cout << "StatementSeqCls::execute() " << endl;
231     PPTreeNodeCls p = this -> seq_head;
232     while (p) {
233         p -> execute();
234         p = PStatementCls(PStatementCls(p) -> get_next());
235     }
236     return 0;
237 }
238
239 int BlockCls :: execute() {
240     //cout << "BlockCls::execute() " << endl;
241     return this -> stmt_seq -> execute();
242 }
243
244 int ProgramCls :: execute() {
245     //cout << "ProgramCls::execute() " << endl;
246     return this -> block -> execute();
247 }
248
249 int PTreeCls :: execute() {
250     //cout << "PTreeCls::execute() " << endl;
251     if (root) {
252         return root -> execute();
253     } else {
254         cerr << "PTreeCls::execute - logic error" << endl;
255     }
256 }
```

The highest level *PTreeCls* requests that the parse tree *ProgramCls* node *execute()*. This, in turn, requests that its *BlockCls* child *execute()*. The block node then sends a similar message to its *StatementSeqCls* child, that just requests that each statement in its linked-list of statements execute itself.

Once again, the combination of late binding and inheritance in object-oriented programming has removed much of the complexity.

Symbol Table

The only symbol table entry class that needs to have the *execute()* behavior is the *ProcAttCls*. The implementation details are essentially the same as they were for the *FuncAttCls::evaluate()*, except that no *ValueCls* object is returned when a procedure is executed. The details are included below only for completeness and with the hope that a second presentation will clarify additional issues.

```
      ProcAttCls::execute(), Part 1(execute.C)

259 int ProcAttCls :: execute(PPTreeNodeCls ActualParamLst) {
260     //cout << "ProcAttCls::execute(ActualParamLst)" << endl;
261
262     //First evaluate the actual paramaters
263     PActualParamCls a_param = 0;
264     PValueCls a_param_val_head = 0;
265     PValueCls a_param_val_tail = 0;
266     if (ActualParamLst) {
267         a_param =
268             PActualParamLstCls(ActualParamLst)->get_seq_head();
269
270         while (a_param) {
271             //Separate copy to stop aliasing.
272             PValueCls a_param_val =
273                 new ValueCls(*a_param -> evaluate());
274             if (!a_param_val_tail) {
275                 a_param_val_head =
276                     a_param_val_tail = a_param_val ;
277             } else {
278                 a_param_val_tail =
279                     PValueCls(a_param_val_tail ->
280                         append(a_param_val));
281             }
282
283             a_param = PActualParamCls(a_param -> get_next());
284         }
285     }
```

For each actual parameter *a_param* used in the procedure call do the following.

- Create a new *ValueCls* object to be sure that any changes to these values resulting from the execution of the procedure will not result in unexpected changes to the original values in the calling program segment.

- Make these new values into a linked-list to be assigned to corresponding formal parameters in Part 2, below.

If there are actual parameters, then for each formal parameter, either alert the corresponding formal parameter that it is aliased to the actual parameter variable (if it is a var parameter) or set its value to the value of the actual parameter (if it is a value parameter).

ProcAttCls::execute(), Part 2(execute.C)

```
288        //Then simulate creating the stack frame..
289        //   ..Making a list of values for each symbol table entry.
290        PSymtabCls stk_fm = proc_tab;
291        stk_fm -> push_values(); //For recursion
292
293        //Now update the formal parameters
294        if (ActualParamLst) {
295            a_param =
296                PActualParamLstCls(ActualParamLst)->get_seq_head();
297            PFParamAttCls   f_param = this -> param_lst;
298            PTypeCls f_param_type = f_param -> get_type();
299
300            while (f_param) {
301                if (f_param -> get_is_var()) {
302                    f_param ->
303                        set_aliased_to(a_param ->
304                            get_expr() -> get_att());
305                } else { // is_val!
306                    if (!f_param_type ->
307                        is_valid_val(a_param_val_head)) {
308                        runtime.err("Invalid parameter value");
309                        return 1;
310                    }
311                    f_param -> set_value(0,a_param_val_head);
312                }
313
314                f_param = PFParamAttCls(f_param -> get_next());
315                a_param = PActualParamCls(a_param -> get_next());
316                a_param_val_head =
317                    PValueCls(a_param_val_head -> get_next());
318            }
319        }
```

Then, in Part 3, adjust the identifier visibility value so that the present vista begins with the symbol table for this procedure, request that the instructions in the procedure's block be executed, and throw away the variable values that were pushed earlier, since execution of the procedure is now complete.

ProcAttCls::execute(), Part 3(execute.C)

```
322        //Adjust vista in preparation for execution of statements
323        ScopeCls::set_vista(stk_fm);
324        block -> execute();
325
326        //Pop the stack frame
327        stk_fm -> pop_values();
328
329        //Reset vista back to outer scope, since now done with proc.
330        ScopeCls::set_vista(PSymtabCls(stk_fm -> get_next()));
331        return 0;
332 }
```

10.5   Testing the Interpreter

We noted in Section 10.1.2 that an interpreter serves as an operation definition of the programming language for both the compiler developer during the construction of the code generator and for the system user. It is therefore extremely important that the behavior of the interpreter accurately reflect the semantic specifications of the programming language.

The amount of work required for verifying this level of compliance with standards is extensive.

- Each expression operation needs to be tested on various arrangements of operand types. If the specifications indicate that type lifting is required, then it must be done for all operations that will encounter such a combination. If a run-time error is to be generated instead, then the error should be generated for all operations.

- Each statement must be tested for its compliance with semantic specifications. Preconditions on each component of the statement must be checked. Postconditions must be verified upon completion of the statement execution.

Fortunately, the test suit of programs used to test the parser can be of great assistance here. Since each program is essentially testing one of the grammar's productions, the output from the program can be slightly modified to produce information relevant to the verification process. Any semantic specifications not covered by such existing programs can be tested by adding appropriate programs to the test suite.

But it is hard work. The output from *each* program needs to be carefully verified and dated with a comment in the program. Any later changes in system behavior on the program needs to be immediately noted, and appropriate steps taken to return the system to its proper behavior.

10.6   Exercises

1. Which lines of code in the *execute()* function for the *for* statement do the following items?

   (a) Check dynamic semantics.
   (b) Perform the statement in the *for* body.

   If you have C or C++ documentation, find out what the *atoi* function is and then note its use here. Why is it valid to use it for all types of loop variables?

2. Explain how the width parameters in a Pascal write statement are implemented in the *execute()* function for *WriteStmtCls*.

   Hint: A C++ manipulator is being used with the *iostream* object.

3. Implement *RepeatStmtCls::execute()*.

   Hint: *Repeat* is a posttest loop, whose implementation is only a minor variation of that for *While*.

4. Implement *WithStmtCls::execute()*.

   Hint: Modify the vista so that the record's symbol table is seen first. Don't forget to return the scope values to their previous value upon completion.

5. Modify the details of *WriteStmtCls::execute()* to produce the implementation for *WritelnStmtCls::execute()*.

6. (a) List the semantic requirements associated with the Pascal *for* statement. You may want to consult the error appendix in Cooper's text [5] or the Pascal semantic specification by Mosses and Watt [14]. Section 2.6.1 of the revised specification will also be helpful.

   (b) Produce a set of Pascal test programs that will verify the above semantic requirements.

   (c) If you have access to a Pascal compiler, use your test suite to test its faithfulness to the language specification.

7. (**CLIP** Project) Build a **CLIP** interpreter. Commands made to specific statistical routines should now be operational.

Chapter 11

Code Generator

```
Topics:

  • Target machine information

  • Implementation strategy

  • Assembler templates
```

The code generator and optimizer described in this chapter and the next form the last major component of a compiler, as illustrated in Figure 2.1. The quality expectations placed on these components are extraordinarily severe. The code generator must faithfully reproduce the original source program with error-free, low-level code. Any optimizer, while not required to maintain order of operations and calculations, must still produce code with the same output as a program generated by the code generator. In addition to the unachievable requirement that components be bug free, the implementation of the components is often based on complex ideas, requiring mastery of the range of concepts from the voluminous details of a specific assembly language to mathematical graph-coloring algorithms applied to register allocation schemes.

The purpose of this chapter is to present a nontrivial, though very basic introduction to the ideas and methods commonly used in code production. Important terms and actual code production algorithms are presented at a level suitable for a first course. Texts by Aho [1], Wulf et al. [25] and others contain excellent discussions of the more advanced ideas and are highly recommended for a second pass through this material.

11.1 Target Machine

The target machine used for the example compiler of this text is the popular SPARCstation by SUN. The hardware and software of this system have been based upon the SPARC ® specification, much of which may be found in the SPARC ® Architecture Manual [21].

SPARC International is a consortium of both hardware and software companies. It is an open standard computing environment, focusing on the specification of a microprocessor architecture, rather than a specific, proprietary microprocessor chip. The SPARC ℗ instruction set has been derived from reduced instruction set designs engineered at the University of California at Berkeley in the early 1980s. The SPARC ℗ standard also specifies a highly efficient configuration of machine registers that has been specifically designed to increase system performance and provide features needed by a number of specific applications such as compiler constructions.

11.1.1   Special Features

The SPARC ℗ architecture has a number of special features, including the following.

1. A linear, 32-bit address space.

2. A small number of instructions.

3. Simple instruction format. Most instructions operate on two register operands and place the result in a third register.

4. Simple addressing modes.

5. A large "windowed" register configuration, specifically designed for efficient procedure calls.

6. A set of registers for handling floating-point operations.

11.1.2   Components

Though not required to do so physically, SPARC ℗ processors abstractly consist of the following three components.

- Integer unit (**IU**)

- Floating-point unit (**FPU**)

- Coprocessor (**CP**)

The **IU**, in addition to providing resources for integer valued computation, also controls the overall operation of the processor. It contains at least 40 general-purpose registers that are efficiently grouped into a circular window arrangement described in Section 11.1.5, below.

The **FPU** has 32 floating-point registers, capable of holding up two 32 single precision values. The **FPU** also provides facilities for grouping these registers into even-odd pairs and to quad-aligned groups of four registers to provide for increased floating-point precision. For this reason, compilers designed for a particular SPARC ℗ processor often implement their base floating-point types using the 64-bit pair arrangement and their double-precision floating-point types using the 128-bit quad arrangement.

The **CP** is an implementation-dependent component, containing its own set of registers and instructions for moving data between the coprocessor and main memory. Its presence, though not specifically required by the SPARC ® standard, simplifies the production of code for languages, such as Modula2, which support concurrent processing.

11.1.3 Instructions

There are essentially six kinds of SPARC ® processor instructions.

- Load/store

- Arithmetic/logical/shift

- Control transfer

- Floating-pointing operations

- Read/write control

- Coprocessor

The first four are of primary importance for the Pascal compiler example of this text, since program input/output is accomplished by calls to external functions and since coprocessing is not an issue in Pascal.

The load and store instructions are the only ones that can access memory. The integer instructions support access to byte (8-bit), halfword (16-bit), word (32-bit) and doubleword (64-bit) data, though there are the usual alignment restrictions. Specific SPARC ® load/store instruction format is really not that important for us. We will address instruction format information when we discuss assembly language requirements in Section 11.2, below.

The arithmetic/logical/shift instructions expect two source operands that are used to compute a result that is either placed in a destination register or discarded. This same general format is maintained in the set of corresponding assembly language instructions. It is interesting that SUN assembly language materials recommend performing integer multiplication by calling an external system function that is dynamically linked to the executable module. Only in cases involving extensive use of integer multiply do they recommend the use of the SPARC ® multiply instruction. Shift instructions can be used to shift the contents of a general-purpose register left or right by a given distance. Logical instructions perform the usual "and-ing" and "or-ing" of information stored in registers. There is one specialized instruction, SETHI, that can be used to create a 32-bit constant in a register. This instruction is routinely used in our model compiler to reference memory associated with program variables.

The SPARC ® instruction set contains a rather rich collection of control-transfer instructions. Branches and calls can be based on information stored in the program counter. Most control-transfer instructions are **delayed** where the instruction

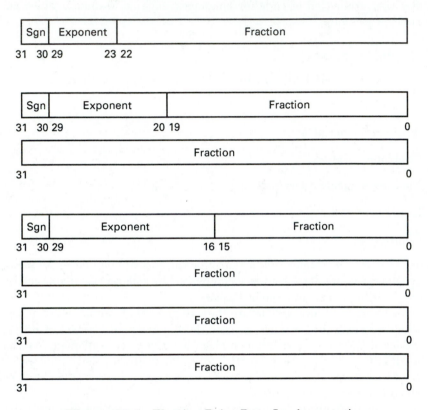

Figure 11.1. Floating-Point Data Implementation

immediately following the control instruction is executed before the transfer to the target address is completed.

The SPARC ® architecture also includes a convenient set of floating-point instructions. There are register-to-register instructions operating only on the floating-point registers. They use the same two-source registers/one-destination format of the integer instructions.

11.1.4   Data Formats

There are three fundamental data types: signed and unsigned integer and floating-point. Signed integer format uses two's-complement format. The floating-point format conforms to industry standard regulations. There are special tagged format integers that can be used to support environments like Lisp or Small-talk, that allow for dynamic typing. The single-word floating-point follows the usual conventions of the leading sign bit, followed by an 8-bit (binary) exponent and then a 23-bit (binary) fraction as illustrated in Figure 11.1.

11.1.5   Registers

Register use is the critical resource allocation in compilers, especially in those performing nontrivial optimization. The SPARC ® architecture has been specifically designed to provide efficient register utilization.

Like most processors, SPARC ® processors contain **control/status** registers and **working** registers.

Control/status registers include the integer unit's **Processor state register**, or **PSR** and the program counter pair **PC** and **nPC**. The PSR contains condition code information set by integer arithmetic and logical operations that can then be used by special *Bicc* and *Ticc* branch and trap instructions. PC contains the address of the instruction currently being executed by the integer unit. The nPC register contains the address of the next instruction to be executed, unless an error trap is generated.

Working registers or general-purpose registers are used primarily to access information or addresses of data being processed by various instructions. The working registers are partitioned into eight **global** registers plus a number of 24-register windows consisting of eight local-, eight in-, and eight out-registers. These windows are arranged in such a way that adjacent windows share registers. In fact the in-registers of one window are the out-registers of its neighbor, as illustrated in Figure 11.2. Function or procedure calls often account for extensive amounts of processor time. Minimizing this overhead was a primary motivation for the innovative register window structure described above.

11.2   Assembly Language

Most of the information in this section comes from SUN-4 ™ Assembly Language Reference Manual [23]. Additional information can also be obtained from corresponding manuals for an earlier SUN-3 ™ assembler.

SUN has designed the SPARCstation assembly language so that its instructions and data declarations match the hardware instructions specified by the SPARC ® instruction set architecture documentation.

11.2.1   Lexemes

The following set of regular expressions defines the more important lexemes in the SUN-4 ™ assembly language.

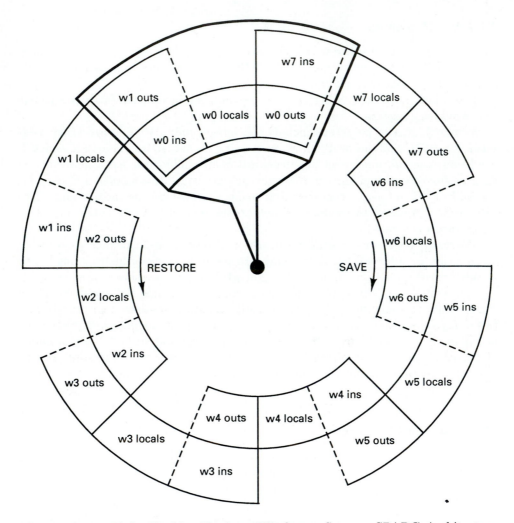

Figure 11.2. Eight Working Register Windows. Source: SPARC Architecture Manual, Copyright 1992, page 27. Used by permission of Prentice Hall, Englewood Cliffs, NJ.

```
 1  digit    [0-9]
 2  digits   {digit}+
 3  letter   [A-Za-z]
 4  u_score  "_"
 5  dollar   "$"
 6  dot      "."
 7  l_u_d_d  ({letter}|{u_score}|{dollar}|{dot})
 8  val_ch   ({l_u_d_d}|{digit})
 9  ident    {l_u_d_d}{val_ch}*
10  r_head   "0r"
11  dtdgts   {dot}{digits}
12  sign     [+\-]
13  exponent [Ee]{sign}?{digits}
14  real     {r_head}{digits}({dtdgts}|{exponent}|{dtdgts}{exponent})
15  string   ([']['^\n\']*[']|["]['^\n\"]*["])
16  other    .
```

Decimal, octal, and hex integers can be written using the same lexical rules as C. Floating-point numbers use a special notation that greatly simplifies code production, since the code emitted is just a string representation of a the usual (decimal) representation of a real number preceded by the two-character *0r* sequence. In our Pascal compiler, all real number values are stored as decimal representation strings.

The lexical rule specifying identifiers allow a much more general string consisting of any sequence of letters, numbers, underscores or dots, not starting with a digit. A standard convention is to reserve all identifiers beginning with the letter *L* for labels. Most compilers will generate label identifiers using a scheme *Lnnnnnnn* where *nnnnnnn* is a six- or seven-digit integer. The assembler is case specific, with the exception of identifiers, which are used for **special symbols**

Special symbols are identifiers preceded by the % sign so that they will not conflict with user-defined identifiers. A list of the more important special symbols is contained in the table below.

Special Symbol	Description	Comment
%0 ... %31	General-purpose registers	
%g0 ... %g7	General-purpose global registers	Same as %0 ... %7
%o0 ... %o7	General-purpose out registers	Same as %8 ... %15
%l0 ... %l7	General-purpose local registers	Same as %16 ... %23
%i0 ... %i7	General-purpose global registers	Same as %24 ... %31
%sp	Stack-pointer register	$\%sp \equiv \%o6 \equiv \%l4$
%fp	Frame-pointer register	$\%fp \equiv \%i6 \equiv \%30$
%f0 ... %f31	Floating-point registers	
%fsr	Floating-point status register	
%psr	Program status register	
%tsr	Trap base vector register	
%lo	Unary operators	Extract least sig (10) bits
%hi	Unary operators	Extract most sig (22) bits

Comments can be either the normal C type /* ... */ or the more traditional line terminated variety that begin with a *!* character.

11.2.2   Assembler Expressions

Expressions are used to specify constant values or to describe addresses of information to be moved into registers. The SUN-4 ™ assembler recognizes the following operations.

Operators			
Binary	Description	Operators	Description
+	Integer Addition	+	No effect
−	Integer Subtraction	−	2's complement
	Integer Multiplication	~	1's complement
/	Integer Division	%lo	Extracts 10 least sig bits
%	Integer Remainder	%lo	Extracts 22 most sig bits
ˆ	Exclusive OR		
≪	Left Shift		
≫	Logical Right Shift		
&	Bitwise AND		
		Bitwise OR		

The integer remainder or modulo operator is usually followed by a parenthesized expression when writing assembly language programs by hand. This is to avoid the distinct possibility that an expression like *high % lo* might be parsed to an erroneous expression *high %lo* containing a special identifier. In the Pascal compiler, we simple output a % followed by a space each time we are emitting the modulo operation.

11.2.3   Assembler Instructions

Assembler instructions are newline-terminated; that is, they may not be continued across lines. The general format for an assembly language instruction is as follows.

$$[label :] \quad [instruction]$$

As indicated, *label* and *instruction* are both optional. The *instruction* can consist of either assembly language instructions or newline terminated comments. The most frequently used assembly language instructions are listed in Tables 11.1, 11.2, and 11.3.

11.2.4   Directives

Assembler **directives**, or **pseudo ops** as they are often called, direct the activities of the assembler as it produces object code.

Some allow switching between various sections or segments of the program.

Format	Description
.seg "string"	Changes the current segment to *string* *string* can be text, data or bss
.text.	same as .seg "text"
.data.	same as .seg "data"
.bss.	same as .seg "bss"

Format		Description
sethi	%hi(_i),%o0	Set the 22 high-bits of register %o0 to those of variable i.
ld	[%o0+%lo(_i)],%o1	Load the contents at address in $\%o0$ into $\%o1$.
sethi	%hi(_j),%o2	
st	%o1,[%o2+%lo(_j)]	Store the contents of $\%o1$ in the variable j.
set	_x,%o1	Set the contents of $\%o1$ equal to the address of $\_x$.
ld2	[%o1],%f4	Load two words starting at $\%o1$ into the floating-point register.
set	_y,%o2	
st2	%f4,[%o2]	Store the contents of $\%f4$ in the variable y.
mov	0x1,%o0	Move the (hex) value 1 to $\%o1$.
sethi	%hi(_test),%o0	
ldsb	[%o0+%lo(_test)],%o0	Load signed byte at $test$ to $\%o0$.
sethi	%hi(_test),%o1	
stb	%o0,[%o1+%lo(_test)]	Store byte in variable $test$.

Table 11.1. Load/Store Instructions

Format		Description
or	%o0,%o1,%o2	Inclusive *or* contents of *%o0* with *%o1* and store in *%o2*.
and	%o0,%o1,%o2	*And* contents of *%o0* with *%o1*, store in *%o2*.
add	%o1,%o0,%o1	Integer add contents of *%o0* with *%o1*, store in *%o2*.
fadds	%f4,%f2,%f4	Floating add contents of *%o0* with *%o1*, store in *%o2*. (Floating add single).
faddd	%f4,%f2,%f4	Floating add double.
fitod	%f0,%f2	Convert integer to floating double.
sethi	%hi(_i),%o0	
ld	[%o0+%lo(_i)],%o0	
sethi	%hi(_j),%o1	
ld	[%o1+%lo(_j)],%o1	
call	.mul,2	Call the dynamically linked system
nop		routine for multiplying ints.
call	.div,2	
nop		
fmuld	%f8,%f6,%f8	Floating (double) multiply.

Table 11.2. Arithmetic/Logical Shift Instructions

Format		Description
sethi	%hi(_i),%o0	
ld	[%o0+%lo(_i)],%o0	
tst	%o0	Test contents of *%o0*, place results in the condition bits of PSR.
bne	L00000010	Branch if not zero to label.
nop		
be	L00000010	Branch if zero to label.
nop		
b	L00000009	Unconditional branch to label.
nop		

Table 11.3. Control Transfer Instructions

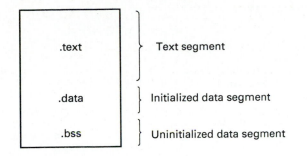

Figure 11.3. Assembly Language Program Structure

Some allocate and initialize memory for various kinds of literals.

Format	Description
.align bbb.	Aligns the location counter to boundary bbb (2,4,8)
.byte. vvvv	Generates a byte, initialized by 8-bit literal vvvv
.half. vvvv	Generates a halfword, initialized by 16-bit literal vvvv
.word. vvvv	Generates a word, initialized by any 32-bit literal
.single. vvvv	Generates a word, initialized by any real literal
.double. vvvv	Generates 2 words, initialized by any real literal

Others describe the visibility of identifiers from outside the program.

Format	Description
.global ssss	Marks the user symbol *ssss* as global. Such identifiers are then accessible by other modules.
.common ssss	Places the symbol *ssss* in a FORTRAN-style global area

The following special pseudo op has a FORTRAN-like syntax.

Format
symbol_name = constant_expression

Description
Assigns the value of *constant_expression* to *symbol_name*

11.2.5 Program Layout

A SPARC ® assembly language program (Figure 11.3) looks a lot like the final
executable file, with the various segments. Though the various program segments
do not have to occur in the illustrated order, such an arrangement is at least a
standard for the compiler's output.

A sample assembly language output file from the Pascal compiler is listed below.
The file is the output from a source program containing the single instruction
writeln(123);.

```
        .text
        .global _main

_main:
        save    %sp,-MINWINDOW,%sp
!    writeln(123)
        mov     0x7b,%o0
        call    _Writeln,1
        nop
        ret
        restore %o0, 0, %o0

        .data
#define DW(x)   (((x)+7)&(~0x07))
#define MINFRAME ((16+1+6)*4)
        MINWINDOW = 96 /* DW(MINFRAME) */
        .bss
```

The text segment begins with the declaration of an identifier _main, which is then used as the entry point to the start of the program. The first nontrivial instruction saves the present register window and moves the current window by one unit (Figure 11.2). Then the (hex) value of 123 is placed in working register %o0 and the external procedure _Writeln is called with one argument. Since a procedure call is a **delayed control-transfer instruction**, the instruction immediately following would normally be executed before the control transfer is complete. A no-op is placed in this so-called **delay slot** to prevent any optimizing surprises. The return and corresponding restore of the register window complete the tasks performed by the program.

The data segment contains an assignment of the minimum window size to the identifier MINWINDOW.

The bss segment, normally containing space allocated to user-defined variables, is not used in this simple program.

11.2.6   Memory Management

The placement of machine instructions and assigning of storage for data are often described as **storage organization**. A SPARC ®(UNIX) executable file consists of the following items.

- Header

- Program code

- Program data

  - Static data

  - Stack

  - Heap

- (Optional)

  - Text and data reallocation information
  - Table containing list of all the executable symbols
  - String table of the source level identifiers associated with the symbols

The header contains information about the size and location of the major sections. These data are stored in an extensive and quite well document record structure.

The section containing program code can be quite complex, especially if the amount of code exceeds a standard size limitation that can reside in RAM at one time. In this case separate pages must be designated and data structures supporting the swapping of one page for another also provided.

The data section consists of a static and dynamic section. The static section is located directly beneath the program instruction section. The dynamic section then is allocated space beneath that. The stack is a downward-growing stack. An upward-growing heap (for run-time allocation of dynamic variables) is placed at the very bottom of the data section.

In the case where the compiler actually generates machine code, the specific details of this executable file must be produced by the code generator. However, if the compiler produces assembly language code, then the system's loader or link editor can produce this file directly from the assembled code. This greatly simplifies the code generation process.

- The header section does not need to be created by the compiler.

- Generated instructions can be mnemonic assembly language and assembler directives, rather than actual binary instructions. Most assemblers provide for comments to be placed in assembly code. The original source program can in this way be placed in the compiler output to aid in debugging the system.

- Data can be symbolically referenced, rather than locationally referenced.

- Data segments in an assembly language program are considerably simpler to create and access. The creation and use of stacks supporting procedure calls are easily accomplished by using simple instructions.

- Separate compilation of program modules is much easier. The link editor can resolve references to symbols that are in other modules.

11.3   Code Production

The approach taken in this text has been to provide the parse tree objects with behaviors so that the tree itself performs many of the functions of normal compiler components. As noted in earlier chapters, the responsibility for system control is pushed as far down in the hierarchy structure as possible. While this strategy works quite well for implementing semantic checks and produces a very efficient interpreter, it does not seem to lend itself well to the production of quality code. Parse tree objects, that are expected to emit their own code, often do not have sufficient information to cooperate with other objects who may need to emit similar or even identical code. The generated code can therefore often have a number of sections of almost identical instructions. This object-oriented approach is still presented, however, since the method is quite easy to implement and since modern processors have sufficient speed to overcome such inefficiencies. Moreover, there are fairly easy optimization techniques that can be used to improve the quality of the generated code if performance or code size is an issue.

11.3.1   Example

Consider the following Pascal source program.

```
program sample(output);
    var
        i: integer;
begin
    i := 123;
    writeln(i)
end.
```

Our compiler needs to translate this program into an assembly language program like the following.

```
        .text
        .global _main

_main:
        save    %sp,-MINWINDOW,%sp
!   i := 123
        mov     0x7b,%o0
        sethi   %hi(_i),%o1
        st      %o0,[%o1+%lo(_i)]
!   writeln(i)
        sethi   %hi(_i),%o0
        ld      [%o0+%lo(_i)],%o0
        call    _Writeln,1
        nop
        ret
        restore %o0, 0, %o0

        .data
#define DW(x)    (((x)+7)&(~0x07))
#define MINFRAME ((16+1+6)*4)
        MINWINDOW = 96 /* DW(MINFRAME) */
        .bss
        .align  4
        .common _i,4
```

As noted above, the structure of the assembly language program corresponds to the SPARC ® specifications for the executable file.

- **Text segment.**

  1. Declare the entry point _main as a global so that it can be referenced by external modules if necessary.

  2. Output code corresponding to each statement of the source program.

     (a) The hex value of 123 is placed in register %o0, the (top 22 bits of) the address of the variable i are loaded into %o1 and then the literal value stored at that location.

     (b) The contents at i are loaded into %o0 and then an external program _Writeln is called. The no op is just a place holder in the delay slot.

  3. The program terminates and restores the stack to its original state.

- **Data segment.** The minimum amount of space for registers is assigned to *MINWINDOW*.

- **Bss segment.** After aligning the current address to the next nearest word boundary, space is assigned for the program variable i.

11.3.2   Object Emitters

The above program is produced by issuing an *emit()* request to the root node of the corresponding parse tree, as illustrated in Figure 11.4. This then results in the following actions.

- The parse tree root node is a *ProgramCls* object. Its *emit()* function will first output the initializing assembly language instructions, such as the global declaration of _main, and push the old registers on the stack.

- It then requests that its block member emit itself.

  - Each *StatementCls* object in the block is then requested to emit its own code.

    * Almost all statements involve expressions of various kinds. The statement object interrupts its output of code to request that the various expression objects emit code for their evaluation.

    * The statement object then continues outputting code that uses the results from the above expression evaluation.

- The root then outputs code for system constants such as *MINWINDOW*.

- The root node finally requests that the outer symbol table emits code for declaring the various variables in the program.

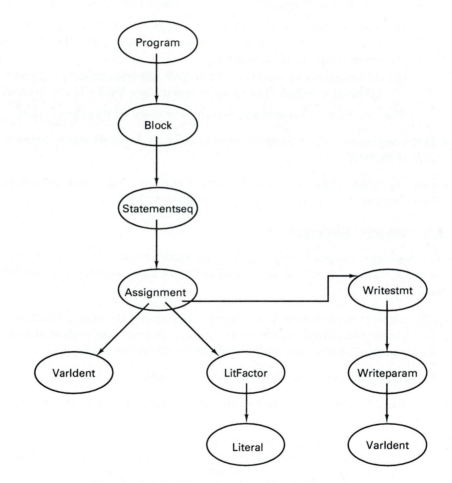

Figure 11.4. Parse Tree for Simple Program

11.3.3 Selection of Instructions

Evaluation of programming languages is usually based on the following four criteria. [19]

- **Readability.** Even assembly languages need to be read by humans at times, especially when a compiler is being constructed. One major factor in readability is simplicity of structure. The SUN SPARC ®assembly language has greatly simplified instruction addressing modes, allowing improved accuracy in specifying and in understanding instructions.

- **Orthogonality.** A major goal in the construction of modern languages has been to provide a small number of primitive language constructs that can be combined in a relatively small number of ways (or even uniquely) to produce all the possible control and data structures supported by the language. While this noble goal is not attainable in a low-level assembly language, much progress has been made in this direction. SPARC ® design has been based on extensive work done on reduced instruction set (RISC) machines. The lean SPARC ® instruction design has translated directly into a correspondingly small set of SUN assembly instructions, many of which are designed especially for use by compiler code generators.

- **Writability.** The issue of simplicity can be taken to far, of course. A programming language needs to have sufficient instructions that normal algorithms are easily specified. SPARC ®'s design meets this objective by retaining instructions, based upon usage patterns in programs over an extended development period.

- **Reliability** Languages enhance the reliability of programs in a number of ways, though primarily by type checking. The SPARC ® model of separate registers and operations for integer and floating-point values is one way an assembly language can facilitate some type consciousness. A second major way languages can contribute to program reliability is to provide mechanisms for handling program exceptions, such as the extensive trap recourses available on SPARC ®systems.

11.3.4 Allocation of Registers

In keeping with the goals of simplicity and orthogonality, SUN assembly language performs its data operations *only* in registers. This means that information stored in RAM must be loaded into an available and appropriate register before any operation can be applied. In this chapter we are going to use a very simple allocation strategy, based upon a register ring data structure abstracting the SPARC ® register structure illustrated in Figure 11.2. We will use a single *IRegRingCls* object consisting of a ring of valid integer register numbers. Registers o6 and i6, synonyms for r14 and r30, are reserved for system pointers and so aren't entered into the ring.

A similar *FRegRingCls* object contains the valid floating-point registers. Each of these classes is provided with *get_reg()* member functions, which will check the next available register out and *ret_reg()*, which checks a register back in. The C++ definition and implementation details of *IRegRingCls* and *FRegRingCls* are contained in Appendix C. If all available registers are checked out, a get_reg() message will result in outputting code to spill the oldest register in the ring to a temporary variable.

The strategy for expression evaluation used in this chapter is to assign registers as required for the various operations, but then to return the registers to the available pool as quickly as possible by storing the operation's value in a temporary variable in RAM. Memory and speed resources allow essentially unlimited numbers of temporaries, as described in Section 11.3.5, below. It is possible to dream up Pascal source programs using extensive numbers of parameters in procedure calls, that will force a register spill. Normal programs, particularly those written by students, will not contain expressions of sufficient complexity to exceed the supplies of integer and floating registers.

The code resulting from such a strategy is not very efficient. However, student users or even programmers developing a system are really not that concerned with program speed, especially when such programming can be debugged using an interpreter. The production of high-quality code becomes a more important issue at the later stages of project development. Code profiles can then be run, algorithms adjusted, output code improved, and the generated code can be *optimized*. One effective method for optimizing by improving our register allocation algorithm is described in Chapter 12.

11.3.5   Allocation of Temporaries

A **temporary variable** is a computer-generated identifier to which subexpression values may be assigned during the evaluation of a complex expression. Temporaries are usually entered into the appropriate symbol table by the code generator functions, which then use them to store contents of registers. The symbol tables will then issue assembly language commands for their declaration in the *bss* segment when the user-defined variables are allocated.

Naming conventions for temporaries are highly nonmnemonic, since their use is primarily by compilers. Almost all assemblers expect such identifiers to be of the form

$$Tnnnnn$$

where *nnnnn* is a nonnegative integer falling in some acceptable range. Clashes with user-defined identifiers are avoided by appending an underscore to the beginning of all user-defined variable names.

Emit() functions for binary operations and the object providing available register numbers must all have access to temporary identifiers. It would be possible to keep track of which temporaries, previously created, are no longer being used and so are available for future requests. However, we again choose to take a much simpler route. Since the SPARC ® assembler makes no restriction on the number of such temporaries, we will just generate a new temporary each time a need arises for one. This can be easily accomplished by creating a *TempCls* object, that simply outputs the next *Tnnnnn* when needed. Definition and implementation details for *TempCls* are also described in Appendix C.

11.4 Assembler Templates

11.4.1 Program Node

The following template has been described earlier in Section 11.2.5 and is included here for completeness.

```
        .text
        .global _main

_main:
        save    %sp,-MINWINDOW,%sp
!       writeln(123)
        mov     0x7b,%o0
        call    _Writeln,1
        nop
        ret
        restore %o0, 0, %o0

        .data
#define DW(x)   (((x)+7)&(~0x07))
#define MINFRAME ((16+1+6)*4)
        MINWINDOW = 96 /* DW(MINFRAME) */
        .bss
```

11.4.2 Symbol Table Entries

Symbol table entries representing Pascal declarations such as the following

```
        var i,j: integer;
```

can reserve space for the variables by emitting the following code.

```
        .data
        .align  4
        .common _i,4
        .align  4
        .common _j,4
```

Similarly, space for two `char` variables could be reserved by the following code.

```
        .data
        .common _ch1,1
        .common _ch2,1
```

Double-precision real can be reserved by code like the following.

```
.align  4
.common _x,8
.align  4
.common _y,8
```

Some compilers on SPARC ® machines use the above declaration for single-precision real and take a 16-byte representation for double precision. This can be reasonably implemented, since the architecture includes an extensive collection of 16-byte floating instructions.

User-defined enumerated types are usually stored in a single byte.

```
.common _color,1
```

Arrays are homogeneous data structures, so the allocation of space can be done by just multiplying the size of each component by the number of components.

```
program decArray;
var
    a: array[1..10]of integer;
    b: array[1..10,1..10] of integer;
begin
end.
```

```
.align  4
.common _a,40
.align  4
.common _b,400
```

Accessing a particular component of an array amounts to calculating the distance from the base address. This is usually done using an array mapping function, like the following;

$$add(a[i]) = base + (i - lo) \times L$$

for one-dimensional, or

$$add(a[i,j]) = base + (i - lo_1) \times (hi_2 - lo_2 + 1) \times L + (j - lo_2) \times L$$

for two-dimensional arrays. The usual information that is stored in an array descriptor record in most compilers is already stored in class members in the object-oriented setting. Such records, often called *dope vectors*, usually contain information like array name, element type, element length, ..., most of which already is readily available directly from the objects representing the type and value.

A single block is allocated for Pascal records that is of sufficient size for all the fields. Thus, in the following simple declaration:

```
var r: record
         first: integer;
         second: real
       end
```
space would be allocated as described below.

```
         .align  4
         .common _r,8
```

The size for a record is often rounded up to the word boundary of the largest atomic constituent. For example, a record consisting of an integer and a double-precision real would usually be allocated 16 bytes, rather than 12.

Pointers are addresses, regardless of the derefenced type. On most modern architectures, addresses are 32-bit unsigned integers.

```
type
     PtrType = record
                 first: integer;
                 second: real;
                   end;
var
     p: ^integer;
     q: ^real;
     r: ^PtrType
```

```
         .align  4
         .common _p,4
         .align  4
         .common _q,4
         .align  4
         .common _r,4
```

11.4.3 Block and Statement Sequence Node

There are no templates for blocks and statement sequences. The main thing that the *BlockCls* member function must do is the following.

```
BlockCls emit() (emit.C)

    stmt_seq -> emit();
```

Similarly, the statement sequence object just needs to issue requests for each enclosed statement to emit code for itself.

```
StatementSeqCls emit() (emit.C)

    p = seq_head;
    while (p) {
        p -> emit();
        p = PStatementCls(p -> get_next());
    }
```

11.4.4 Statements

Parse Tree Nodes

Empty statement.   The empty statement emits no code.

Assignment statement.   An assignment statement object requests that the right-side expression emit code that will place the value in a convenient register, such as $\%o0$ or $\%f0$. Then the left-hand side emits code code to load the address of the variable on the left. The single store command is then emitted.

```
!   i := 123;
        mov      0x7b,%o0
        sethi    %hi(_i),%o1
        st       %o0,[%o1+%lo(_i)]
```

If statement.   An *if* statement object requests the boolean expression to emit code for evaluating itself.

```
    if (i< 0) then
        j := -1
```

If the test expression is true, then branch to a first label; otherwise, branch to the bottom label. The code immediately after the first label is obtained by requesting the statement in the *if* body to emit itself.

```
!       if (i< 0) then
            sethi    %hi(_i),%o0
            ld       [%o0+%lo(_i)],%o0
            tst      %o0
            bl       L000001
            nop
            b        L000002
            nop
L000001:
!           j := -1;
            mov      -0x1,%o0
            sethi    %hi(_j),%o1
            st       %o0,[%o1+%lo(_j)]
L000002:
```

Two-way selections are handled similarly. A Pascal *if/else* statement like the following.

```
if (i = j) then
    j := 0
else
    j := 1;
```

could have the following assembly language code for its output.

```
!     if (i = j) then
          sethi    %hi(_i),%o0
          ld       [%o0+%lo(_i)],%o0
          sethi    %hi(_j),%o1
          ld       [%o1+%lo(_j)],%o1
          cmp      %o0,%o1
          be       L000001
          nop
          b        L000002
          nop
L000001:
!         j := 0
          sethi    %hi(_j),%o0
          st       %g0,[%o0+%lo(_j)]
          b        L000003
          nop
L000002:
!         j := 1;
          mov      0x1,%o0
          sethi    %hi(_j),%o1
          st       %o0,[%o1+%lo(_j)]
L000003:
```

- Move the current contents of variable *i* to the first available register.

- Move the contents of *j* to the second.

- Compare the contents of the two registers.

- Branch if equal to the segment of code for the **if** part.

- Otherwise branch to the **else** part.

Case statement. The Pascal *case* statement can be implemented much like an *if/else* statement.

```
case i of
    1: j := 1;
    2: j := 2
end
```

```
!     case i of
        sethi     %hi(_i),%o0
        ld        [%o0+%lo(_i)],%o0
        cmp       %o0,1
        be        L000001
        nop
        cmp       %o0,2
        be        L000002
        nop
        b         L000003
        nop
L000001:
!         1: j := 1;
        mov       0x1,%o0
        sethi     %hi(_j),%o1
        st        %o0,[%o1+%lo(_j)]
        b         L000003
        nop
L000002:
!         2: j := 2
        mov       0x2,%o0
        sethi     %hi(_j),%o1
        st        %o0,[%o1+%lo(_j)]
L000003:
```

Actually, the above code does not quite implement the semantic requirements for *case* as prescribed by Wirth. According to the Pascal standard, it is an **error** for the case index to not appear in the list of case constants. According to the standard, *errors* must be handled in at least one of the following three ways.

1. The documentation must clearly specify that these errors will not be detected.

2. The compiler must print a message specifying that these errors will not be detected.

3. The compiler must report the error when program is being compiled (if it is a static requirement) or being run (if it a dynamic requirement). In the latter case, the program must halt.

The case index requirement is dynamic so if our compiler is designed to behave according to number 3, it will have to generate slightly different code from that displayed above. Most such compilers have a special system routine that issues a warning message and halts. A call to the subroutine should therefore replace the first unconditional branch to L000003. See the paragraph on procedure calls described below for information assembly language instructions used for a call.

For statement.   The following *for* statement is perhaps an oversimplification of a very common application of storing an ith value of something into the jth component of an array.

```
for i := 2 to 5 do j := i
```

In the code below, the start value is loaded into the *for* index. Then the statement making up the *for* body emits its code. Finally, the loop index is incremented by one and compared to the stop value.

```
!       for i := 2 to 5 do
        mov       0x2,%o0
L000001:
        sethi     %hi(_i),%o1
        st        %o0,[%o1+%lo(_i)]
!       j := i
        sethi     %hi(_i),%o0
        ld        [%o1+%lo(_j)],%o1
        sethi     %hi(_j),%o1
        st        %o0,[%o1+%lo(_j)]

        sethi     %hi(_i),%o0
        ld        [%o0+%lo(_i)],%o0
        add       %o0,0x1,%o0
        sethi     %hi(_i),%o1
        st        %o0,[%o1+%lo(_i)]
        cmp       %o0,0x5
        bg        L000002
        nop
        b         L000001
        nop
L000002:
```

It should be noted that even nonoptimizing compilers will often emit much more efficient code than this. In particular, the number of stores and loads of the loop index variable can be decreased dramatically if a particular location of memory is reserved for these values that can be directly accessed by a given register or set of registers.

While and repeat statements. The following segments are a portion of typical *while* and *repeat* statements.

```
while (i < 10) do
    i := i + 1
```

```
repeat
    i := i + 1
until (i = 10)
```

The code below, in the left column, shows the pretest nature of the *while* loop. The first block of assembler code loads the value of the variable i into register %o0 and tests its value. The second block is the usual increment of the loop variable.

For the *repeat* loop (on the right), the statements of the loop body are emitted first, followed by the code for performing the loop condition.

```
!     while (i < 10) do                          !     until (i = 10)
L000001:                                         L000001:
        sethi    %hi(_i),%o0                      !        i := i + 1
        ld       [%o0+%lo(_i)],%o0                        sethi    %hi(_i),%o0
        cmp      %o0,0xa                                  ld       [%o0+%lo(_i)],%o0
        bl       L000002                                  add      %o0,0x1,%o0
        nop                                               sethi    %hi(_i),%o1
        b        L000003                                  st       %o0,[%o1+%lo(_i)]
        nop
L000002:                                                  sethi    %hi(_i),%o0
!        i := i + 1                                       ld       [%o0+%lo(_i)],%o0
        sethi    %hi(_i),%o0                              cmp      %o0,0xa
        ld       [%o0+%lo(_i)],%o0                        be       L000002
        add      %o0,0x1,%o0                              nop
        sethi    %hi(_i),%o1                              b        L000001
        st       %o0,[%o1+%lo(_i)]                        nop
        b        L000001                        L000002:
        nop
L000003:
```

Procedure call.   Let's consider the following simple procedure declaration and call.

```
program stmtProcCall;
var
    i: integer;

procedure Proc(param1,param2: integer);
    var
        i: integer;
    begin
        i := param1 + param2;
        writeln(i);
    end;
begin
    i := 1234;
    Proc(i,i);
    writeln(i)
end.
```

This program contains a single user-defined procedure that contains two value parameters. The assembler code on the next page is the output of our compiler. There are a number of important ideas in this code.

- The format for the actual invocation of the procedure is very simple.

```
        call     _Proc,2
```

The (internal) name of the procedure is used, along with the number of actual parameters, assuming that those values have been stored in the corresponding output registers.

```
              .text
              .global _main

_Proc:
              save      %sp,-MINWINDOW,%sp
!     i := param1 + param2;
              mov       %i0,%o0
              mov       %i1,%o1
              add       %o0,%o1,%o0
              sethi     %hi(_Proc_i),%o1
              st        %o0,[%o1+%lo(_Proc_i)]
!     writeln(i)
              sethi     %hi(_Proc_i),%o0
              ld        [%o0+%lo(_Proc_i)],%o0
              call      _Writeln,1
              nop
              ret
              restore
              .bss
              .align 4
              .common _Proc_i,4
              .text
_main:
              save      %sp,-MINWINDOW,%sp
!     i := 1234
              mov       0x4d2,%o0
              sethi     %hi(_i),%o1
              st        %o0,[%o1+%lo(_i)]
!     Proc(i,i)
              sethi     %hi(_i),%o0
              ld        [%o0+%lo(_i)],%o0
              sethi     %hi(_i),%o1
              ld        [%o1+%lo(_i)],%o1
              call      _Proc,2
              nop
!     writeln(i)
              sethi     %hi(_i),%o0
              ld        [%o0+%lo(_i)],%o0
              call      _Writeln,1
              nop
              ret
              restore %o0, 0, %o0


              .data
#define DW(x)    (((x)+7)&(~0x07))
#define MINFRAME ((16+1+6)*4)
              MINWINDOW = 96 /* DW(MINFRAME) */
              .bss
              .align  4
              .common _i,4
```

- The format for the output code for a procedure is essentially identical to that for the main program.

  - There is code to push the present stack.

  - Each statement then emits its own code.

  - In registers of the procedure are the out registers of the calling code. Local variables have their internal names modified to reflect their level of nesting.

  - The instruction segment is terminated with code that pops the stack and returns to the calling code.

  - Each item in the procedure's symbol then outputs its own declaration code

11.4.5   Expressions

```
Relational operators.
!    if (i < 1) then
        sethi   %hi(_i),%o0
        ld      [%o0+%lo(_i)],%o0
mv      0x1,%o1
        cmp     %o0,%o1
        bl      L000001
        nop
        b       L000002
        nop
L000001:
!       i := 10;
        mov     0xa,%o0
        sethi   %hi(_i),%o1
        st      %o0,[%o1+%lo(_i)]
L000002:
```

It is convenient that the SPARC ® architecture has the same collection of assembly language relational operators as do most higher level languages. In the above code the *LtCls* relational operator node simply emits the following instructions.

```
cmp     %o0,%o1
bl      <next label>
```

The *if* statement node can then output the remainder of the branching structure.

Unary operators.

```
!    test := not test;
        sethi    %hi(_test),%o0
        ldsb     [%o0+%lo(_test)],%o0
        xor      %o0,0x1,%o1
        sethi    %hi(_test),%o2
        stb      %o1,[%o2+%lo(_test)]
!    i := - j
        sethi    %hi(_j),%o0
        ld       [%o0+%lo(_j)],%o0
        sub      %g0,%o0,%o1
        sethi    %hi(_i),%o2
        st       %o1,[%o2+%lo(_i)]
```

A boolean *not* can be achieved by an *xor* with the constant value 1. Code for a unary negative just subtracts the value from zero, which is always stored in the special SPARC ® global register %*g*0.

Additive operators.

```
!    i := i + j;
        sethi    %hi(_j),%o0
        ld       [%o0+%lo(_j)],%o0
        sethi    %hi(_i),%o1
        ld       [%o1+%lo(_i)],%o1
        add      %o0,%o1,%o0
        sethi    %hi(_i),%o1
        st       %o0,[%o1+%lo(_i)]
!    x := x + i;
        sethi    %hi(_i),%o0
        ld       [%o0+%lo(_i)],%f0
        fitod    %f0,%f2
        set      _x,%o1
        ld2      [%o1],%f4
        faddd    %f2,%f4,%f2
        set      _x,%o2
        st2      %f2,[%o2]
```

The parse tree node for the binary plus operator requests that the left operand type object output a command for addition of that type. In the first case the command is the usual integer addition.

```
        add      %o0,%o1,%o0
```

In the second, where an integer value is first being lifted and then added to a double-precision real, the instruction

```
        faddd    %f2,%f4,%f2
```

is a special floating-point operation that exists on most platforms.

In the code, below, the boolean value *true* is implemented as a 1-byte integer value. The Pascal boolean operator *or* just outputs the corresponding assembler instruction.

```
!    test := true;
        mov     0x1,%o0
        sethi   %hi(_test),%o1
        stb     %o0,[%o1+%lo(_test)]
!    test := test or test;
        sethi   %hi(_test),%o0
        ldsb    [%o0+%lo(_test)],%o0
        sethi   %hi(_test),%o1
        ldsb    [%o1+%lo(_test)],%o1
        or      %o0,%o1,%o0
        sethi   %hi(_test),%o1
        stb     %o0,[%o1+%lo(_test)]
```

Multiplicative operators.

```
!    test := test and test;
        sethi   %hi(_test),%o0
        ldsb    [%o0+%lo(_test)],%o0
        sethi   %hi(_test),%o1
        ldsb    [%o1+%lo(_test)],%o1
        and     %o0,%o1,%o1
        sethi   %hi(_test),%o1
        stb     %o0,[%o1+%lo(_test)]
!    i := i * i;
        sethi   %hi(_i),%o0
        ld      [%o0+%lo(_i)],%o0
        sethi   %hi(_i),%o1
        ld      [%o1+%lo(_i)],%o1
        call    .mul,2
        nop
        sethi   %hi(_i),%o1
        st      %o0,[%o1+%lo(_i)]
!    x := x * i;
        sethi   %hi(_i),%o0
        ld      [%o0+%lo(_i)],%f0
        fitod   %f0,%f2
        set     _x,%o1
        ld2     [%o1],%f4
        fmuld   %f2,%f4,%f2
        set     _x,%o2
        st2     %f2,[%o2]
```

In the above code, the assembler instruction *and* has been output by the Pascal *and*
boolean operator. The next collection of assembly language instructions contains a
bit of a surprise. SPARC ® recommends that unless the program must meet very
stringent speed requirements, all integer multiplications be done by a procedure call.
That this is even feasible is a testimony to the efficient design of the architecture,
especially in light of the fact that this particular procedure is also dynamically
loaded on most systems. The last set of instructions again deal with first lifting an
integer value and then multiplying the result with a double-precision real.

Variables.

```
!     i := gcd(12,20)
      mov      0xc,%o0
      mov      0x14,%o1
      call     _gcd,2
      nop
      sethi    %hi(_i),%o1
      st       %o0,[%o1+%lo(_i)]
```

We have already illustrated the code for evaluating variables when they refer to program identifiers. In the code above we illustrate the code for evaluating a function. The call is essentially like that for a Pascal procedure, except that, by convention functions will return their value in the first output register.

Array components.

```
!     arr1[2] := 10;
      mov      0xa,%o0
      sethi    %hi(_arr1+0x4),%o1
      st       %o0,[%o1+%lo(_arr1+0x4)]
!     i := arr3[4,5]
      sethi    %hi(_arr3+0x84),%o0
      ld       [%o0+%lo(_arr3+0x84)],%o0
      sethi    %hi(_i),%o1
      st       %o0,[%o1+%lo(_i)]
```

In the code above, the following declarations are assumed.

```
arr1 : array[1..10] of integer;
arr3 : array[1..10,2..11] of integer;
```

The second collection of assembler instructions shows clearly the use of the array mapping function as an offset from the base address _arr3 of the array.

Fields.

```
      .data
      .align  4
      .common _x,8
      .text
!     x.field1 := 'a';
      mov      0x61,%o0
      sethi    %hi(_x),%o1
      stb      %o0,[%o1+%lo(_x)]
!     x.field2 := 123;
      mov      0x7b,%o0
      sethi    %hi(_x+0x4),%o1
      st       %o0,[%o1+%lo(_x+0x4)]
```

The declaration assumed in the code above is the following.

```
x: record
       field1: integer;
       field2: dreal
   end;
```

Notice the normal practice of rounding the allocation space up to 8 bytes from 5. Then the usual offset table that is used for record fields begins the second field on a normal word boundary, as can be seen from the second and third collections of assembler code.

```
Pointers.

        .data
        .align  4
        .common _p,4
        .align  4
        .common _q,4
!   p^ := 'a';
        sethi   %hi(_p),%o0
        ld      [%o0+%lo(_p)],%o0
        mov     0x61,%o1
        stb     %o1,[%o0]
!   q^[3] := 123
        sethi   %hi(_q),%o0
        ld      [%o0+%lo(_q)],%o0
        mov     0x7b,%o1
        st      %o1,[%o0+0x8]
```

The above code is based on the following declaration.

```
type
        arraytype = array[1..10] of integer;
var
        p: ^char;
        q: ^arraytype;
```

All pointers are 4 bytes, and are just used as addresses into the actual data.

11.5   Exercises

1. Describe the important features of each of the following items.

   (a) IU

   (b) FPU

   (c) IU's registers

   (d) Assembler expressions

   (e) Assembler instructions

   (f) Assembler directives

   (g) .text

(h) .data

(i) delay slot

2. Write a C++ implementation of the *ProgramCls emit()* function, that will output the template described in Section 11.4.1.

3. What kind of assembler code would you produce for a one-way selection structure like the following?

```
        if (i> 0) then
            j := 123
```

4. Consider the following Pascal program.

```
    program exercise;
    var
        i: integer;
    begin
        j := i + 2*i + 3*i + 4*i
    end.
```

(a) Draw a corresponding parse tree.

(b) Write up a corresponding assembly language program. How many registers are active at any one time? Based on this example, make a judgment about the need for a sophisticated register allocation scheme at this point in the compiler construction.

   Hint: You may want to use the sample assembly language program in Section 11.3.1 and try assembling your program if a SPARC ® system is available.

5. Use the regular expressions in Section 11.2.1 to describe a valid SUN-4 ™ assembly language string. Using this information, how would you suggest that a person designate a single character as contrasted to a string of several characters?

6. What is wrong with the following template, which was intended to be output by a nested *for* loop?

```
    !     for i := 2 to 3 do
        mov     0x2,%o0
L000001:
        sethi   %hi(_i),%o1
```

```
        st      %o0,[%o1+%lo(_i)]
!       for j := 4 to 5 do
        mov     0x4,%o0
L000002:
        sethi   %hi(_j),%o1
        st      %o0,[%o1+%lo(_j)]
!           val := i + j
        sethi   %hi(_i),%o0
        ld      [%o0+%lo(_i)],%o0
        sethi   %hi(_j),%o1
        ld      [%o1+%lo(_j)],%o1
        add     %o0,%o1,%o0
        sethi   %hi(_val),%o1
        st      %o0,[%o1+%lo(_val)]

        sethi   %hi(_j),%o0
        ld      [%o0+%lo(_j)],%o0
        add     %o0,0x1,%o0
        sethi   %hi(_j),%o1
        st      %o0,[%o1+%lo(_j)]
        cmp     %o0,0x5
        bg      L000004
        nop
        b       L000002
        nop
L000003:
        sethi   %hi(_i),%o0
        ld      [%o0+%lo(_i)],%o0
        add     %o0,0x1,%o0
        sethi   %hi(_i),%o1
        st      %o0,[%o1+%lo(_i)]
        cmp     %o0,0x3
        bg      L000004
        nop
        b       L000001
        nop
L000004:
```

7. Write templates for the *EqCls* and *GtCls* objects.

8. It is tempting to modify the *IfStmtCls* template to look something like the following. (Put the code inside the jumps to make it more efficient.) Can you suggest reasons why this is not done?

9. What assembly language code would be output for each of the following?

   (a) if i = 3 then j := i * k.
   (b) i := a[5], where *a* is an array of characters.
   (c) a[3].field2 := 123, where *a* is an array of the following record type.

```
        x: record
               field1: integer;
               field2: dreal
           end;
```

Chapter 12

Optimizer

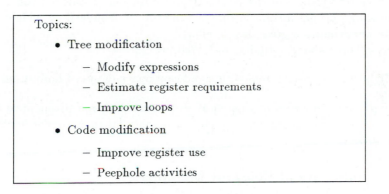

Topics:

- Tree modification
  - Modify expressions
  - Estimate register requirements
  - Improve loops
- Code modification
  - Improve register use
  - Peephole activities

12.1 Introduction

The code production methods of the previous chapter take a fairly conservative approach: Create temporaries for intermediate values of an expression rather than keep them in registers. This approach has the following two results.

- It makes for a simple register allocation algorithm.

- It produces inefficient code.

12.1.1 So Who Needs It?

Code can be inefficient in its use of space or time or both. Some very significant work was done in 1970s on designing languages and compilers specifically for the task of minimizing space requirements for significant applications. Similarly, much work has been done since that time to improve the speed of code generated by compilers.

Recent advances in hardware and software have often rendered such optimization techniques unnecessary. Increased speed of the CPU, RAM, and external memory can make code of rather naive construction execute at more than acceptable levels. Moreover, the increased speed has been accompanied with a significant reduction of prices. Even small PCs are now routinely sporting 8 megs or more of memory.

Today's systems allow for resident programs, that were possible on only the largest of systems 10 or 15 years ago.

Often, time spent improving or replacing an algorithm will produce much better system performance than optimizing code implementing a first algorithm. Even the most sophisticated optimization schemes may produce improved time performance by at most a factor of 0.5. Replacing a $\mathcal{O}(n^2)$ algorithm by one that is $\mathcal{O}(n \log n)$ can make a much more significant change, especially on large quantities of data.

Optimization is a difficult task. Its implementation often requires the use of nontrivial graph-theoretic algorithms. The history of optimization is replete with documented occurrences of the production of erroneous optimized code. Furthermore, making optimized code so that it can still be debugged by widely available tools like *dbx* requires a great deal of effort.

So why worry about optimization? Well, we ...

- Might have to use system with significant space or speed limitations.

- Might want to optimize a hot spot. Understanding optimizing ideas can even help the hand production of quality assembly language replacements of hot spot code.

12.1.2 Summary of Relevant Methods

Even by the mid 1960s, optimizing compilers were able to produce code that was essentially of the same quality as that written by a skilled machine-level (human) programmer. There were several versions of FORTRAN available on the large mainframes of that era that routinely produced *better* code than most programmers could. The 1970s witnessed the remarkable introduction of the minis, computers that often had only 16-bit words and less than 48 K of core memory. Optimization for such a system often meant trying to use the small amount of storage efffectively. And then in the latter part of that decade, we began to see a number of Pascal compilers that produced native object code rather than the P-code emulation that was so popular earlier.

As you read the literature from these efforts, you are struck with the great *diversity* of approaches. Each language and even each compiler contained, in its very design, the sources of much of the bad code. A careful study of the consequences of those design decisions, especially in light of the target machine resources, usually suggested a number of significant improvements that could be made to the code.

Some of the specific techniques have become general optimization principles today.

- Loop optimization. Code generated by loop structures can be optimized by moving loop invariant instructions outside the loop, by eliminating index calculations on inner loops, and by replacing loop body instructions by more efficient operations. used by nearly every modern optimizing compiler. Spotting and removing **dead code** (code that produces results not used later in the program) will also improve performance, especially if the code is in a nested loop structure.

- Improving machine code. Often high-level control structures will translate to curious-looking jump-to-jump code, instructions that branch directly to another (sometimes, unconditional) branch statement.

A very interesting effort at optimization occurred in the mid-1980s. Powell [15] set out to create a compiler outputting good code using optimizations that provided major performance improvements while requiring minimal implementation effort. That he was reasonably successful is evident, since he completed the work singlehandedly in only a matter of months and then made the compiler available to the general public at a very modest cost; certainly it was a test by fire.

In this chapter, we want to focus on some of the major ideas that have come from the Powell compiler. While these ideas are not appropriate for all languages, most modern languages have structures sufficiently close to Modula2 so that the methods are at least relevant. The most important such language feature is the absence of a *goto* instruction. The existence of the *goto* in a language like Pascal can be reasonably ignored, since it cannot be used to enter the middle of any other control structure and also since computational loops are not "supposed" to be programmed using such a structure.

The following are ideas from Powell that we will be discussing.

- Try to predict generated program code structure by information obtained during *parsing*.

- Use registers only for temporaries used during the evaluation of expressions.

The object-oriented approach to compiler construction makes both of these ideas much easier to implement, especially since we have chosen to make the intermediate representation of the program a parse tree of *objects*.

Determining loop bodies is a simple matter for the object representing the loop. Invariant expressions can be discovered by the fact that none of the *VarIdentCls* objects in the expression occur as objects on the left side of an assignment statement in the loop body. These can then be moved out of the body and into the loop header.

Register allocation improvement can also be efficiently implemented in this object-oriented setting using a popular algorithm described in Aho et al. [1] and originally specified in Sethi and Ullman [20], the first half of which is discussed in Section 12.3.1 and the second half in Section 12.3.2, below.

12.2   Modifying Parse Tree

12.2.1   Improving Expressions

Code that evaluates expressions involving only constants can be replace with a single instruction that loads the value of that constant expression into an available register.

This can be easily accomplished by replacing the subtree of objects representing the constant expression by a single object representing the literal value of that expression.

Similarly generated code that calculates standard incrementing instructions such as $i = i + 1$ by register or dynamic library calls can be replaced by target machine equivalents such as the SPARC $^\circledR$assembler's *inc* or *dec* commands. The parse tree can replace a subtree representing such an incrementing expression by a special *IncOpCls* object, that points only to i's *VarFactorCls* object.

12.2.2   Improving Loops

Since our intermediate representation is a parse tree of objects, it is possible to locate loops bodies by the existence of a parent loop object. Invariant expressions can be reasonably detected by the fact that none of the variables in the expression are assigned values in the loop body. These can then be safely moved from the loop body to the set of initializing instructions in the loop header.

12.2.3   Other Methods

There are a number of other methods that can be used to perform code optimization. These methods are often based on the construction of a tree-like structure from the intermediate representation, which is called a **DAG**, or **directed acyclic graph**. Essentially these structures are very much like parse trees, except that a given node may have several parents if each of the parents would have been pointing to essentially the same expression subtree. It would certainly be possible (though not simple) to modify the parse tree structure so that it becomes a DAG. Such activity does not seem to be worth the effort at present.

Subexpression detection. There does not yet appear to be a way to easily produce optimized code from a DAG. Code generated by the methods of Chapter 11 is essentially of the same quality as that produced directly from a DAG.

Next use information. Many rather sophisticated methods of optimization involve the movement of intermediate code from one location in the program to another. Such methods depend heavily of determining when a given variable is next used in the program. Powell's experience was that such efforts are probably not going to pay off in terms of difficulty of programming and corresponding code performance improvement.

Loop structures. DAGs are often used to determine the existence of loops, particularly inner loops. This information can be determined from the language syntax in a *goto*-less language.

12.3 Improving Emitter Algorithms

This section describes the Sethi-Ullman algorithm for minimizing the number of required temporaries by using an special register allocation scheme for registers based upon a labeling of the various nodes in the expression tree.

We will try to explain the algorithm primarily by examining the following un-simplified, though still valid, expression.

$$(a - b) - ((c - d) - (e - f))$$

If we just use the expression tree's *emit()* behaviors described in Chapter 11, we will produce the following code.

```
        sethi   %hi(_a),%o0
        ld      [%o0+%lo(_a)],%o0
        sethi   %hi(_b),%o1
        ld      [%o1+%lo(_b)],%o1
        sub     %o0,%o1,%o2
        sethi   %hi(T0000001),%o3
        st      %o2,[%o3+%lo(T0000001)]
!
        sethi   %hi(_d),%o0
        ld      [%o0+%lo(_d)],%o0
        sethi   %hi(_e),%o1
        ld      [%o1+%lo(_e)],%o1
        sub     %o0,%o1,%o2
        sethi   %hi(T0000002),%o3
        st      %o2,[%o3+%lo(T0000002)]
!
        sethi   %hi(_c),%o0
        ld      [%o0+%lo(_c)],%o0
        sethi   %hi(T0000002),%o1
        ld      [%o1+%lo(T0000002)],%o1
        sub     %o0,%o1,%o2
        sethi   %hi(T0000003),%o3
        st      %o2,[%o3+%lo(T0000003)]
!
        sethi   %hi(T0000001),%o0
        ld      [%o0+%lo(T0000001)],%o0
        sethi   %hi(T0000003),%o1
        ld      [%o1+%lo(T0000003)],%o1
        sub     %o0,%o1,%o2
        sethi   %hi(T0000004),%o3
        st      %o2,[%o3+%lo(T0000004)]
```

Naturally our naive approach to code generation has overused the temporaries, since we are allowing each binary operation to store its information in a separate variable. But even if we modified the algorithm to be more efficient in the use of registers, such a left-to-right approach to the evaluation of the expression would require some temporary storage unless we were assured of unlimited registers. For example, suppose that our target machine contained only four registers %r0 ... %r3. The above code might then be improved as follows.

```
! a - b
        sethi   %hi(_a),%r0
        ld      [%r0+%lo(_a)],%r0
        sethi   %hi(_b),%r1
        ld      [%r1+%lo(_b)],%r1
        sub     %r0,%r1,%r2
! d - e
        sethi   %hi(_d),%r3
        ld      [%r3+%lo(_d)],%r3
        sethi   %hi(_e),%r0
        ld      [%r0+%lo(_e)],%r0
        sub     %r3,%r0,%r1
! spill %r2, so that it can be used.
        sethi   %hi(T0000001),%r3
        st      %r3,[%r2+%lo(T0000001)]
! c - (d - e) ;
        sethi   %hi(_c),%r0
        ld      [%r0+%lo(_c)],%r0
        sub     %r0,%r1,%r2
! (a-b) - (c - (d - e))
        sethi   %hi(T0000001),%r3
        ld      [%r3+%lo(T0000001)],%r3
        sub     %r3,%r2,%r0
```

It is arguable that the %r2 spill in the above code is not really required, and indeed that is true, since %r2 could then be removed from the available register pool. However, only a slightly more complex expression could be devised that would similarly have the effect of removing additional registers until no further operations would be possible.

The key to avoiding register spills like that illustrated above is to try to arrange the evaluation order of subexpressions so that the calculation of immediate children directly precedes the calculation of the node. In this way the results from the calculation of the children can be retained in registers that can then be directly accessed by the parent. This calculation policy essentially just states that we should try to do the evaluation of the most complicated expressions first. Subexpressions requiring more registers should be done before subexpressions using fewer registers.

Obviously, what is needed is some way to associate with each expression node a number-of-registers value. Let's look at a number of examples in the light of SPARC ® assembler and see what kind of labeling we should attach to each node. Since the SPARC ® machines do not allow normal arithmetic or logic operations to access direct memory, the value associated with each identifier leaf in the tree will require one register for commands like the following.

```
        sethi   %hi(_c),%r0
        ld      [%r0+%lo(_c)],%r0
```

Leaves representing literals also need to store the literal value (or the address of the literal value in the case of a string literal) in a register.

For expressions representing a binary operation on two such leaves, we will require no more than the registers needed to store the two values.

```
sethi    %hi(_c),%r0
ld       [%r0+%lo(_c)],%r0
sethi    %hi(_d),%r1
ld       [%r1+%lo(_d)],%r1
sub      %r0,%r1,%r0
```

For an expression like

$$c - (d - e)$$

we still only need two registers, if we are careful about the allocation scheme.

```
sethi    %hi(_d),%r1
ld       [%r1+%lo(_d)],%r1
sethi    %hi(_e),%r0
ld       [%r0+%lo(_e)],%r0
sub      %r1,%r0,%r1
!
sethi    %hi(_c),%r0
ld       [%r0+%lo(_c)],%r0
sub      %r0,%r1,%r0
```

But for an expression like

$$(c - d) - (e - f)$$

having two subexpressions of the same size we will need one additional register to store the value of one subexpression while we are calculating the value of the other.

```
sethi    %hi(_c),%r0
ld       [%r0+%lo(_c)],%r0
sethi    %hi(_d),%r1
ld       [%r1+%lo(_d)],%r1
sub      %r0,%r1,%r0
!
sethi    %hi(_e),%r1
ld       [%r1+%lo(_e)],%r1
sethi    %hi(_f),%r2
ld       [%r2+%lo(_f)],%r2
sub      %r1,%r2,%r1
!
sub      %r0,%r1,%r0
```

The label of a parent of two equal-sized subexpressions must therefore be one greater than the label of either child.

12.3.1   Labeling Expressions: River Algorithm

This first half of the Sethi-Ullman algorithm gets its name from the traditional way rivers are named: If two rivers of the same size meet, the resulting river gets a new name; otherwise the name is taken to be that of the larger river. If two children of the same size meet, the parent gets a new name; otherwise the parent takes the name of the largest child. If two subexpressions take the same number of registers to compute, then the value resulting from a binary operation of the subexpressions can be computed using one additional register used to hold the value from one child while the other subexpression is computed.

Most traditional implementations of such an algorithm would be based upon a post-order tree traversal routine. However, in our object-oriented setting, these number-of-register values can be easily computed by the *constructors* of the various expression nodes during the parsing phase. The *ExprCls* base class can be given a *num_reg* data member and the various derived expression nodes should then exhibit the following register-setting behavior.

Leaves. Parse tree leaves are the various kinds of valid literals and *VarFactorCls* objects representing identifiers. Evaluating a literal amounts to storing the value in a register. Evaluating an identifier, or a string literal, is achieved by loading the corresponding address into a register. In any case, such leaf nodes therefore need to use a new register number. Any leaf object should label itself as a one.

Interior nodes. These nodes are essentially those representing binary operations. Such nodes take as their number-of-registers the larger of the labels of their children, or one greater in the case of children having the same label.

12.3.2   Utilization of Registers: Greedy Algorithm

The second half of the Sethi-Ullman algorithm describes how to utilize registers, based upon the labeling described in Section 12.3.1, above. In this section we discuss how the various *emit()* functions of expression nodes can be modified to make use of the labeling produced during parsing, as described above in Section 12.3.1

The object specifications for leaf nodes are quite simple.

Leaf nodes. The *emit()* function for any integer-valued literal should first obtain the next available register number *nn* as follows nn = IRegRingCls -¿ pop() and then output the instruction

$$\text{mov 0xhhh \%rnn}$$

where hhhh is the hex value for the literal. Similarly, the *emit()* function for a node representing an integer-valued identifier *a* should output the following instructions.

```
sethi    %hi(_a),%rnn
ld       [%rnn+%lo(_e)],%rnn
```

Before examining the actual object specifications necessary for interior nodes, let's examine the following expression.

$$(a - b) - (c - (d - e))$$

Figure 12.1 illustrates this expression's tree labels. By selecting either the left or right subexpression of highest register usage as the first to be calculated, registers spills can be avoided using only three registers, as illustrated in the following code.

```
! (a - b)
        sethi   %hi(_a),%r0
        ld      [%r0+%lo(_a)],%r0
        sethi   %hi(_b),%r1
        ld      [%r1+%lo(_b)],%r1
        sub     %r0,%r1,%r0
! (d - e)
        sethi   %hi(_d),%r2
        ld      [%r2+%lo(_d)],%r2
        sethi   %hi(_e),%r1
        ld      [%r1+%lo(_e)],%r1
        sub     %r2,%r1,%r2
! c - (d - e)
        sethi   %hi(_c),%r1
        ld      [%r1+%lo(_c)],%r1
        sub     %r1,%r2,%r1
! (a - b) - (c - (d - e))
        sub     %r0,%r1,%r0
```

Notice the switching of the order of assigning registers %r1 and %r2 used for the right child $(d - e)$ so that the register allocation in the subtraction in $c - (d - e)$ instruction could proceed in a normal fashion. This switching is accomplished in the following manner. The register allocation object *IntRingRegCls* described in Chapter 11 is provided with four additional member functions, *push()*, *pop()*, *top()*, and *swap*.[1] Then if an expression tree contains an interior node with a larger right child than left, the top two register numbers in the ring are first swapped and then code emitting allowed to proceed as normal. When the code for the right child has been completed, the value is then stored in what would have been the second register. This register is then taken out of the available pool. Code for the left expression is then emitted using the rest of the registers. This now starts with what would have been the first available register. The register containing the value for the right side is then pushed back onto the ring and swapped back into place so that the binary operation will be assigned these two registers in proper order.

Assume that IREGMAX contains the total number of free integer registers.

- **Interior nodes,** *left ≥ right.*

```
if (right_reg < IREGMAX) {
```

---

[1] Actually, *push()* and *pop()* just replace *ret_reg()* and *get_reg()*.

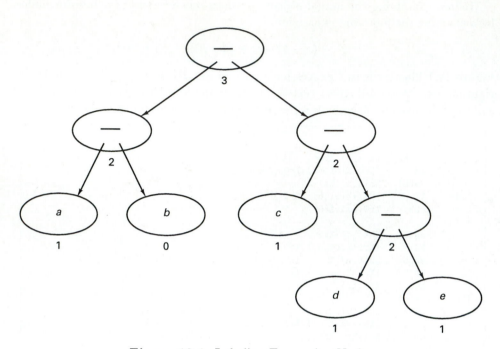

Figure 12.1. Labeling Expression Nodes

```
left -> emit();
reg_num = IRegRingCls -> pop();
right -> emit();
//output code like:
//   sub IRegRingCls ->top(),reg_num,IRegRingCls -> top()
IRegRingCls -> push(reg_num);
```

- **Interior nodes,** *left < right.*

```
if   (left_reg < IREGMAX) {
     IRegRingCls -> swap();   //the top two registers
     right -> emit();
     //take the reg containing the result out of active
     reg_num = IRegRingCls -> pop();
     left -> emit();
     //then output code specific to the particular node, like:
     //   sub IRegRingCls ->top(),reg_num,IRegRingCls -> top()
     IRegRingCls -> push(reg_num);
     IRegRingCls -> swap();
```

- **Interior nodes, both left and right exceed IREGMAX.**

```
left -> emit();
//spill the current contents of the next register.
temp_num =  TempCls -> get_next();
//output code like the following
//   sethi   %hi(Ttemp_num),%rnn (nn is next avail. reg.)
//   st       IRegRingCls -> top(),[%rnn+%lo(T0000001)]
right -> emit();
//output code like
//   sethi   %hi(Ttemp_num),%rnn
//   st       IRegRingCls -> top() %,[%rnn+%lo(T0000001)]
//   sub IRegRingCls ->top(),reg_num,IRegRingCls -> top()
TempCls -> push(temp_num);
```

12.4 Modifying Generated Code

A **peephole optimizer** is a program that examines the output from a compiler
and makes modifications to that code. Often code us run through such an optimizer
several times until the code reaches some invariant form. There are a number of
target machine constructs that peephole optimizers often target. The two most
frequently cited are the following.

- The replacement of trivial machine-level additions with corresponding more
  efficient increment operations

- The replacement of instructions that are branching to another branch instruction with a single branch to the second target

Constructing such a program requires a clear understanding of the precise form
in which the code will be encountered. If one cannot be reasonably sure of the
format, then the recognition of such code patterns becomes very difficult. It is
interesting to note that SUN does not even allow use of their assembler optimizer
package on user-produced assembly language programs.

Replacing Trivial Increments

Most occurrences of trivial increment operations can be spotted at the source level
and appropriate modifications to the parse tree made prior to emitting code. It
can happen, however, that certain language constructs, most notably definite loop
structures can produce code sequences like

```
sethi   %hi(_i),%r0
ld      [%r0+%lo(_i)],%r0
add     %r0,0x1,%r0
```

that can be replaced with the following sequence.

```
sethi    %hi(_i),%r0
ld       [%r0+%lo(_i)],%r0
inc      %r0
```

The use of such *synthetic* instructions can significantly increase performance, if the corresponding hardware synthetic instruction has been implemented. SUN-4 ™ assemblers also recognize instructions that increment by any (small) integer amount. Of course, a full complement (see the SPARC manual [21, page 86]) of corresponding decrement and bit test synthetic instructions are also available.

- *dec*

- *btst*

- *bset*

- ...

Eliminating Jumps to Jumps

Various arrangements of source code selection statements can often create code containing branch or jump statements aimed directly at other branch statements. Even a simple two-way selection can produce code like the following.

```
!    if (i<3) then
        sethi    %hi(_i),%o0
        ld       [%o0+%lo(_i)],%o0
        cmp      %o0,0x3
        bl       L00002
        nop
        b        L00001
        nop
L00002:
!       code for the 'if' part, and then ...
        b        L00003
        nop
L00001:
!       code for the 'else' part, and then ...
L00003:
        b        L00004
        nop
L00004:
!       code for the next instruction
```

A peephole optimizer can replace at least one such jump-to-jump with code like that given below.

```
!       if (i<3) then
        sethi    %hi(_i),%o0
        ld       [%o0+%lo(_i)],%o0
        cmp      %o0,0x3
        bl       L00002
        nop
        b        L00001
        nop
L00002:
!       code for the 'if' part, and then ...
        b        L00004
        nop
L00001:
!       code for the 'else' part, and then ...
L00004:
!       code for the next instruction
```

Multiple passes may be required to rid the code of all such sequences. If the collection of selection statements is contained in a loop, the time savings resulting from the eliminated instructions can be significant.

12.5 Exercises

1. Modify the constructors for *AddOpCls*, ..., so that the tree will replace subtrees of constant expressions with a single object representing the literal value of the constant. Should this activity be done only when a user selects the optimization option?

2. Modify the constructors for *AddOpCls*, ..., so that nodes representing expressions like $i + 1$ are replaced with special *inc* or *dec* nodes if the optimization option has been selected. Define and implement the appropriate classes, *IncOpCls* and *DecOpCls*.

3. Modify the definition of *ExprCls* to include a data member for storing the number-of-registers value. Then make suitable modifications in the constructors of the various derived expression classes to reflect the River Algorithm of Section 12.3.1.

4. Modify the definition and implementation of *IRegRingCls*, FRegRingCls, and TempCls to include the following members required by the river-code generation algorithm.

   - For *TempCls* ...
     (a) A new structure for recording the present list of assigned identifiers for temporary identifiers
     (b) A *TempCls* member function *push(Tid)* that removes *Tid* from the list of currently used temporary identifiers. Modify *next_tmp()* so that it chooses the smallest possible identifier name

- For *IRegRingCls* and *FRegRingCls* ...

  (a) A data member *top*, serving as an entry into the register rings, and simulating the top of a stack containing the available registers in the ring order

  (b) A member function *top()*, that returns the register number currently at the top of the simulated stack

  (c) A member function *pop()*, that returns the present top of the stack and then labels that ring element as no longer available

  (d) A member function *push(reg#)* for the register rings, that returns register reg# to the list of available registers and changes its ring position to precede the previous top register.

  (e) A member function *swap()* that interchanges the ring order of the top two registers on the stack.

5. Consider the following expression.

$$((((a - b) - c) - d) - e)$$

   (a) Construct a parse tree segment corresponding to the expression.

   (b) Label the tree, using the river algorithm.

   (c) Produce corresponding SPARC ® assembler code, using the algorithm in Section 12.3.2.

6. Consider the following expression.

$$(a - b) - (c - (d - e))$$

   (a) Construct a parse tree segment corresponding to the expression.

   (b) Label the tree.

   (c) Produce corresponding SPARC ® assembler code.

   (d) What code is produced if you do not use register swapping in question 6c, directly above?

7. Consider the following expression.

$$(a - (b - (c - (d - e))))$$

   (a) Construct a parse tree segment corresponding to the expression.

   (b) Label the tree.

   (c) Produce corresponding SPARC ® assembler code.

8. Consider the following expression.

$$(a - b) - ((c - d) - (e - f))$$

(a) Construct a parse tree segment corresponding to the expression.

(b) Label the tree.

(c) Produce corresponding SPARC ® assembler code.

9. Consider the expression

$$(a - b) - (c - (d - e))$$

used as an example in Section 12.3.1. One optimizing compiler for the SPARC ® outputs the following code.

```
sethi   %hi(_d),%o0
ld      [%o0+%lo(_d)],%o0
sethi   %hi(_e),%o1
ld      [%o1+%lo(_e)],%o1
sethi   %hi(_c),%o3
ld      [%o3+%lo(_c)],%o3
sethi   %hi(_a),%o5
ld      [%o5+%lo(_a)],%o5
sethi   %hi(_b),%o7
ld      [%o7+%lo(_b)],%o7
sub     %o0,%o1,%o0
sub     %o3,%o0,%o3
sub     %o5,%o7,%o5
sub     %o5,%o3,%o5
```

(a) Verify that this code produces the same output as that listed in Section 12.3.

(b) Devise an algorithm for the production of such optimized code.

Recent work seems to suggest that object-oriented methods do not allow efficient implementation of this kind optimization. Perhaps you may be able to prove otherwise.

10. Modify the various *emit()* functions to output code based upon the ordering algorithm in Section 12.3.2 when the optimize bit has been turned on in the *OptionCls* object's data member.

11. Modify *ForStmtCls* so that it contains a special loop header pointer. Then implement *emit()* so that it will look for invariant instructions in the loop body and move them to the loop header before beginning to emit code.

Appendix A

C++ Digest

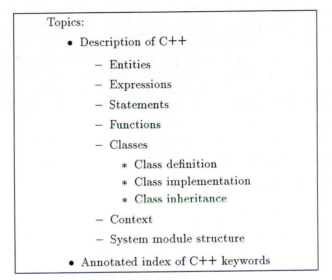

Topics:

- Description of C++
  - Entities
  - Expressions
  - Statements
  - Functions
  - Classes
    * Class definition
    * Class implementation
    * Class inheritance
  - Context
  - System module structure
- Annotated index of C++ keywords

This appendix contains synoptic information about the features of C++ that are used in this text. The discussion should be useful if you need an overview or first introduction to the language. Lippman's excellent text [12] contains a more comprehensive introduction to C++ programming.

If you are fairly knowledgeable about C, you may find the annotated index of C++ keywords helpful (Section A.2). Each keyword entry in the index contains most, if not all, of the following information.

- An official C++ description of the keyword

- General statements of its major applications in this text

- An example of its use

- Entry points into this text for representative applications

The present form of C++ is a result of a reasonably long and well-controlled evolutionary effort at AT&T Bell Laboratories. This effort has been directed by

Bjarne Stroustrup, who in the 1970s, along with a dedicated support team, began the task of bringing many of the object-oriented features of the Simula language into the C programming environment. In 1980, Stroustrup's group produced *C with Classes*, the first language in this development effort. This was closely followed by a first version of C++. Versions 2.0 and following have added nearly all the object-oriented features requested by the rapidly growing C++ user community.

One important design goal throughout this entire project has been the production of efficient executables. C++ has consistently allowed programmers to "eat their cake and have it too", in the sense that execution speed does not have to be sacrificed for the privilege of utilizing object-oriented design methods. To be fair, it should be pointed out that this quest for retaining execution speed has had its down side. Features such as exception handling, that might negatively impact performance have not been added to the language—at least not yet.

C++ translators are available for nearly all computing platforms. Most companies producing workstations provide their own translators, which are based on AT&T's version 2.0 or later. In addition to C++ products for workstation environments, there are several PC C++ programming systems, including convenient editors and debuggers, that can be obtained at very modest cost.

A.1   Description of C++

A.1.1   C++ Entities

The following types can be declared and used in C++.

Logicals.   Like C, C++ does not have an actual logical data type. The usual logical operators

~	Complement
&&	Logical and
&	Bitwise and
||	Logical or
∧	Exclusive or
|	Inclusive or
<<	Left logical shift
>>	Right logical shift

are instead applied to integer expressions, with the value of **false** being represented by 0 and **true** by any nonzero value.

Chars.   The type **char** can be used to represent all characters. Characters are typically stored in 8-bit bytes, since any character can be represented by the usual seven- or eight-bit ASCII representation.

Character literals are represented by using the apostrophe delimiter as in the following examples.

$$'a'$$

$$'1'$$

There are some characters that are either hard to print or are nonprinting and can be very useful in programming. These characters literals are denoted in C++ by the use of an **escape sequence** consisting of the backslash escape symbol and then a single symbol representing the actual character.

Name of Character	Escape Sequence	ASCII Value
null	'\0'	0
backspace	'\b'	8
tab	'\t'	9
newline	'\n'	10
formfeed	'\f'	12
carriage return	'\r'	13
doublequote	'\"'	34
single quote	'\''	39
backslash	'\\'	92

There are no binary or unary operators defined specifically for characters.

All of the usual relational operators

$$=, \ <, \ <=, \ >, \ >=, \ !=$$

are valid.

Ints. There are actually several **integral** types[1] that can be used to store integer values.

- **int** This is the normal type to use for integer storage or operations. Typical implementations use a single 32-bit word for storing each integer.

- **short** If memory is limited, this data type can be used for storing integers of modest size. Integers up to about 32000 can usually be stored as shorts, since most implementations use two 8-bit bytes for their implementation.

- **long** The amount of space allocated for a long integer is implementation dependent. On most systems having 32-bit integers, longs are also implemented in 32 bits, since the maximum integer value is sufficient for almost any large integer problem.

---

[1] Strictly speaking, C++ considers char to also be an integral type, allowing integral binary and unary operators to be performed on the ASCII representation.

- **unsigned** Unsigned integers allow a maximum value of nearly 9×10^{09} by using the normal sign bit for one additional information bit.

Integer literals are represented one of three ways.

Decimal. Any (nonempty) string of decimal digits may be used for the decimal representation of an integer.

Octal. A string of octal digits starting with the zero digit is interpreted as an octal integer literal.

Hexadecimal. A string beginning with the "0x" pair and consisting of hex digits, including "a" – "f," may be used to represent an integer in hexadecimal form.

The usual binary operations associated with integer types in most programming languages also exist in C++.

Operation	Description ...
+	The integer sum of the operands
−	The integer difference of the operands
*	The integer product of the operands
/	The integer quotient of the operands
%	The integer remainder of the operands

The only unary operation for integral literals is the unary minus. The unary increment and decrement operators, ++ and −−, can be applied to variables of any integral type.

The following table describes the precedence and associativity of the various integral operations.

Operators	Associativity
unary − ,++, −−	Right to left
*, /, %	Left to right
+, −	lLft to right

Floats. Two types exist in C++ to handle real numbers.

float. The **float** type usually is assigned 32 bits for storage. This typically allows 1 sign bit, 3 bits for the floating exponent, and the remaining bits left for the usual floating "mantissa." This provides somewhere around 6 or 7 significant decimal digits.

double. There is an increasing amount of scientific programming being done in C and C++ these days. Calculations needing more precision than provided by **float** can use **doubles**. Most C++ implementations allocate 8 bytes, or two 32-bit words, of storage for a double. **Double** floats usually provide 16 significant digit accuracy.

Floating literals can take a number of forms, including the standard decimal form

$$3.14159$$

and exponential forms, such as the following.

$$1.09e5$$

$$3e - 1$$

$$.5$$

Binary operations for floats are, with the exception of the nonexistent remainder operation, denoted in exactly the same way as are integral binary operations.

Operation	Description: Returns ...
+	The floating-point sum of the operands
−	The floating-point difference of operands
*	The floating-point product of the operands
/	The floating-point quotient of the operands

Unary minus is the only unary operation on floats, since the notion of incrementing or decrementing a real variable by a fundamental type unit has no meaning. The same order of precedence and associativity exists for floats as for integers.

Enums. Even though enumerated types are not used in the C++ implementation of the Pascal compiler example of this text, there are many places where the use of such types is indeed a great assistance to the production of readable and accurate code. Enumerated literals are just identifiers, as they are in almost all other programming languages. They are declared in a C++ program with instructions like the following.

```
enum {Mon, Tue, Wed, Thu, Fri};
```

A variable of enumerated type can be declared either by a command like

```
enum Weekday {Mon, Tue, Wed, Thu, Fri};
```

or the following use of typedef and the usual declaration statement.

```
typedef enum {Mon, Tue, Wed, Thu, Fri} DayType;
DayType WeekDay;
```

There are no binary or unary operations on enumerated types.

Subranges. Most of the languages derived from Algol contain a type that specifies the legal range of any of the discrete, scalar types. Somewhat surprisingly, this is not a part of C++ nor of its parent C.

Pointers. Pointer values are memory addresses. Of course, we don't usually have the privilege of specifying literal pointer values. Instead we use the `new` operator to allocate sufficient memory for the object and to return the address of that location. Pointer variables can also be assigned the contents of another pointer variable or the address of an appropriate object.

Pointer variables are declared using the "*" symbol,

```
int  *IntPtr;
```

or

```
TypeName  *PtrToTypeObj;
```

where `TypeName` is some valid type specifier.

The most important operation on pointers is the **dereferencing** operator, *. Note that while the value of $PtrToTypeObj$ is an address, the value of $*PtrToTypeObj$ is the actual object. A related operation on nonpointers is the address operator. If `Obj` is of `TypeObj` then the value of

$$\&Obj$$

is the address of the memory location referenced by `Obj`.

The pointer arithmetic operations of addition and subtraction are possible in C++. If p is a pointer variable pointing to a particular object in memory (like an array element), then

$$p = p + 2$$

increases the address in p by the size of two of the objects to which it was originally pointing. Notice that this is really not a binary operation, since we are "adding" a pointer and an integer. Operations like

$$p = p + p$$

really have no meaning, and so are not valid.

Arrays. An array is a collection of items of a single data type. The individual items are accessed by an index or position number. Array index values start at zero.

Array literals can only be used to initialize an identifier representing an array.

```
int IntArray[] = {0, 1, 2};
```

Multidimensional arrays can be similarly declared.

```
int DoubleArray[4][3] = {
                        {0, 1, 2},
                        {3, 4, 5},
                        {6, 7, 8},
                        {9,10,11}
};
```

There are several things about arrays that tend to cause problems for programmers.

- **No dynamic arrays.** The size of an array must be a constant expression.
- **No range checking on the array index.** Running off the end of an array often makes garbage of other variables or even instructions.
- **No associated array size.** When passing an array as a function argument, the size of the array must also be passed.
- **No array assignment operator.** Assignment of one array to another (even of the same type) requires assignment of the individual array elements. In the event that the elements are themselves arrays, the same rule applies.

Strings. A C++ character string is essentially an array of characters. String literals are specified using the *double quote* symbol.

```
"string"
```

Note that this particular literal consists of the six visible characters plus a terminating null character, $'\backslash 0'$.

There are no C++ string operations or functions, though the usual C string functions defined in the *string.h* include file are available on almost all C++ systems. Character string variables are almost always represented as pointers to a char, since all string manipulation in C++ is done through character pointers. The C++ declaration of such a representation would look like the following.

```
char *Str = "Sample string literal";
```

The primitive nature of C++ string support was sufficient reason for our
building a special StringCls class having the necessary string support for
compiler uses.

Structures. Structures are a means of collecting heterogeneous data into a given
type. For example, a real array and its range bounds could be placed in a
struct by the following declaration.

```
#define MAXSIZE 50
struct  assoc_array {
            int lower,upper;
            float a[MAXSIZE];
}
```

The usual dot notation is available for referencing the individual items or
fields of a struct. So the actual upper limit on `assoc_array` can be referenced
by the following.

assoc_array.upper

One of the most frequent applications of structures is as the underlying type
for a pointer. If p is a pointer to a structure having a field `field1`, then the
notation *$*p.field1$*, though certainly correct, can be replaced by the following,
more informative notation.

p − > field1

Actually, C++ has no `struct` type officially, since structures are really taken
to be an elementary form of the notion of a class (Section A.1.5). However,
structures are available for programming use and can be viewed as C++
equivalent of record structures. At this simplest level, there is no provision
for making a direct assignment of structs.

A.1.2   C++ Expressions

Expressions have types and can be evaluated. The simplest expression is probably
a scalar literal. Its value is itself. The value of an variable is the contents of the
storage location that the variable references.

More complex expressions can be constructed by applying various operations to
other expressions. The operations are typically those specified for the various types
in Section A.1.1. C++ does allow a rather liberal use of mixed types in expressions.
In particular, the various integral types are automatically lifted to floats if required
by the given expression. Similarly, C++ provides a very flexible facility for coercing
the type of a given expression. For example, an assignment

```
Ivar = int(3.14159);
```

will perform the expected truncation. This particular feature of the language is used extensively in the compiler example of this text in connection with coercing the type of a generic pointer to a special type that might have been determined through external or semantic analysis.

It might come as a bit of a surprise that the assignment operator = is actually an expression builder rather than a statement. What this means is that the *expression* $k = 5$ is assigned the value 5 so that it can then be passed on to another expression. This is most often used in initialization of variables such as the following.

$$i = j = k = 5$$

Incidentally, such an expression is not a valid initializer if the variables are also being *declared*. The following is not a valid expression:

$$int \ i = j = k = 5$$

nor can it be made into a valid statement.

In addition to the normal assignment operator =, there are a large number of **compound assignment operators**, two of which are indicated in the following table.

Assignment Operator	Usage	Meaning...
$+=$	$sum += a[i]$	$sum = sum + a[i]$
$-=$	$sum -= a[i]$	$sum = sum - a[i]$

A.1.3   C++ Statements

Statements are the smallest executable unit in a C++ program. All statements are terminated by a semicolon. The statements used most frequently in the compiler example of this text are described below.

Assignment statement. An assignment expression terminated with a semicolon is an assignment statement

Declaration statement. A declaration is a type name followed by a list of identifiers being associated with that type. A declaration statement is a declaration followed by a semicolon.

```
int i, j, k;
```

Declaration statements are the only statements that are valid outside of a function definition.

Compound statement. Any sequence of statements enclosed in a pair of braces is called a compound statement. If there are declaration statement in a compound statement, it is then called a **block**

If statement. The usual selection statements are available in C++ and are illustrated by the following one-way

```
if (i < 3) {
    a[i] = b[i];
}
```

and two-way if statements.

```
if (i < 3) {
    a[i] = b[i];
} else {
    a[i] = c[i];
}
```

These can be extended in the usual manner to a many-way selection.

```
if (i < 3) {
    a[i] = b[i];
} else if (i < 10) {
    a[i] = c[i];
} else {
    a[i] = 0;
}
```

You probably have noticed that the `if` is more of a **control structure** than a statement since it does not require a semicolon terminator. In fact, the particular form of `if` that is illustrated above and also used in this text is a combination of a normal C++ if/else statement and two or more block statements, each of which is also a control structure, rather than a statement. This style of programming has great similarities to structures found in most other Algol-like languages. It also provides some protection from very subtle bugs that can creep into C or C++ programs.

It is an important fact that object-oriented design and implementation features of late binding drastically reduce a programmer's dependence on extensive selections structures such as the many-way `if` and the switch/case statement described below.

Switch/case statement. If multi-way selection is being based on the (discrete) scalar value of a single variable, then the switch/case provides a much more robust control structure. The following example illustrates a typical situation.

```
switch (ch) {
    case 'a': cout << 'A';
```

```
                                  break;
                  case 'b': cout << 'b';
                                  break;
                  default:
                                  cout << endl;
          }
```

The break statement terminates the enclosing switch, so that control will then be transferred to the statement following the switch, if it exists. Break can also be used to similarly terminate a do, for, or while statement.

The peculiar cout item is an output object that sends the object to the right of the output operator << to the output stream. The endl is just a manipulator object that places a newline or end-of-line character in the stream.

While statement. A while statement is a pretest, iterative statement. The following example computes the length of a string.

```
          int len = 0;
          char *tp = String; //Initialized elsewhere.

          while (*tp++) {
                  ++len;
          }
```

The initialization of variables len and tp is typical, since care must be taken to allow entrance into the loop.

Do statement. The do statement produces a posttest iteration. These are often used in interactive programming such as the following.

```
          do {
                  cout << "Input value";
                  cin >> ans;
          } while (! okay(ans)) //Declared elsewhere.
```

For statement. The for statement is commonly used to step through a fixed-length data structure such as an array. A typical example might be

```
          for (int i = 0; i < ARRAYSIZE; i++) {
                  a[i] += i*b[i];
          }
```

where the first expression in the parentheses is an initialization section, the second expression is the control expression and the third controls the incrementing of the array index. It is a bit unfortunate that a variable declared inside the for statement is not local to that statement.

A.1.4   C++ Functions

The only subprogram units in C++ are functions. This means, of course that the calls to all C++ subprograms must occur in expressions rather than in a special procedure call statement.

Function definition consists of two major sections, the function declaration or prototype and the function body.

Function prototype. The function prototype consists of the following three items.

- **Return type.** The return type can be any predefined type or user-defined type other than an array or a function type. And these last two exceptions can be overcome by making the return type a *pointer* type.

- **Name.** The function name is an identifier.

- **Argument list.** An argument list is a (possibly empty,) comma-separated list of declarations, enclosed in parentheses. Since the argument list is often used by the C++ compiler to distinguish one instance of a function from another, it is often called the **signature** of the function.

  The individual variables declared in a function signature are called **formal arguments**, while those used in the calling expression are called **actual arguments**. C++ functions utilize only a pass-by-value protocol for the actual arguments. A copy of the value of the actual arguments is therefore sent passed to the memory allocated for the formal arguments.

  There are two ways to provide a mechanism for a function to modify its arguments.

  - Pointer formal arguments
  - Reference-type formal arguments

The function prototype can occur multiple times in program. It can be placed in an include file and imported into as many modules as necessary to satisfy C++'s *declare before use* rule.

Function body. The function body consists of a compound statement or block. This statement or block must contain a **return statement** to return an expression whose type matches the type of the function.

The sample function below is typed **void**, since its purpose is only to output a sort of last word from the compiler's parser.

```
void yyerror(char *s) {
    if (!s) {
        hard.err("yyerror() LOGIC ERROR!");
    } else {
        soft.err(s);
    }
}
```

Notice the following:

- The message *s* is typed inside the formal argument list as a character string.

- Since the return type is **void**, a **return** statement is not required.

The error objects, **hard** and **soft**, are described in more detail in Appendix C.

The Pascal compiler's main function is given below as another example of a C++ function.

```
int main(int argc, char** argv) {
    cout << " Educational Pascal compiler" << endl;

    PControllerCls ctl = new ControllerCls(argc,argv);
    return 0;
}
```

It takes the usual two UNIX arguments, *argc* and *argv*, which contain any additional switch information given by the user at runtime, creates a controller object for the compiler, that is passed the switch information, and then exits with a 0 to indicate that the compile session terminated normally.

A.1.5 C++ Classes

The object-oriented equivalent of a type is a class. In procedurally oriented languages, a type specifies the values and valid operations of a variable; in object-oriented programming a class describes the values and functions of its instances or objects.

Class Definition

A **class definition** consists of

Class head. The class head consists of the keyword **class**, a class name and the names of any parent classes.

Class body. The class body is enclosed by braces and terminated with a semicolon. It contains the member definitions and specifies visibility issues by using any of the keywords **public**, **private**, **protected**, or **friend**

The following is an example of a class definition.

```
class PTreeCls {
    public:
```

```
                    PTreeCls(PPTreeNodeCls Root);
                    int              execute();
                    int              emit();
                    void             print();
                private:
                    PPTreeNodeCls    root;
            };
```

The datum *root* is called a **member value** of the class and is accessed by exactly the same "." or "− >" mechanisms used by structs. Functions such as *execute(),* *emit()* and *print()* are called **member functions** and are invoked again by using the same "." or "− >" mechanisms. So if *ptree* is made an instance of *PTreeCls* by the definition

`PTreeCls ptree;`

then the member *root* is accessed by referencing ptree.root and the member function *execute()* is invoked by the expression ptree.root(). And if *pt* is a pointer to a *PTreeCls* object that as been created by a declaration like

`PTreeCls *pt;`

then class members like *root* and *execute()* can be accessed by expressions like

```
        pt -> root
```

and

```
        pt -> execute()
```

respectively.

Class Implementation

Class functions are implemented using the scope operator :: as illustrated in the following example.

```
        int PTreeCls :: execute() {
                return root -> execute();
        }
```

Class definitions and class function implementation are often placed in separate files. Section A.1.7 on C++ modules describes the usual conventions for the placement of such information.

Inheritance and Late Binding

The combination of inheritance and late binding greatly reduces a programmer's dependence on traditional multiway selection structures. Inheritance deals with the classification of objects into categories that may have access to the member data or functions of a parent class. Late binding allows the programmer to assign a instance of a subclass or derived class to a parent class variable and then to decide at runtime that object's data or member functions are actually being accessed.

Suppose that we have a base or parent class representing all possible expression nodes in a parse tree.

```
class ExprCls {
  public:
    ExprCls();

    PTypeCls         get_type()
    virtual void     set_type(PTypeCls Type)
    virtual ValueCls *evaluate();
    virtual int      emit();
  protected:
    PTypeCls         type;
};
```

And suppose that we specify that one kind of valid expression is a literal.

```
class LitFactorCls : public ExprCls {
  public:
    LitFactorCls()  {;}
    ValueCls    *evaluate()
    int         emit();
  private:
    ValueCls    *value;
};
```

The following items can then be noted.

- **Syntax for declaring a subclass or derived class.** The first line indicates that a *LitFactorCls* is derived from an *ExprCls*.

- **The derived class redeclares base class functions.** The C++ keyword virtual in the base class declaration of *evaluate()* indicates than any class derived from *ExprCls* has the right to declare its own version of the function.

Now suppose that (a pointer to) a *LitFactorCls* object *lfac* is assigned to a *ExprCls* variable.

$$ExprCls \; * expr \; = \; lfac;$$

At runtime, the call

$$expr \; - > \; evaluate()$$

will select the *evaluate()* function for a *LitFactorCls* objects. If a different kind of expression object had been assigned to *expr*, then that same call would have selected the *evaluate()* function for the new object.

A.1.6   C++ Context

C++ allows for multiple use of the same identifier, if the exact meaning of the identifier can be determined from context. Context is usually determined by one of the following methods.

- **Program signature.** There are often times a programmer wants to solve a particular problem using one of several algorithms that would be chosen from the nature of the data received. C++ provides a mechanism for using the same identifier for these distinct behaviors. A particular call to these functions will be resolved by selecting the function having formal arguments matching the number and type of the actual arguments.

- **Identifier scope.** Every variable has an associated scope that specifies the portion of the program in which it is visible. C++ supports three kinds of scope.

  1. **File scope.** All variables defined in a file, but not redefined in a function within that file, are visible through that file. Variables from other files can be made visible by the use of the `extern` keyword. (See Section A.2.)

  2. **Local scope.** All variables declared either in the formal argument list or main block of a function are called local variables and are visible only within that function block.

  3. **Class scope.** Any identifiers used to specify member data or member functions of a class are taken to be restricted to the scope of that class and therefore access through the normal "." or "− >" mechanisms.

A.1.7   C++ System Module Structure

Groups of classes are called **modules**. The goal is to produce modules that consist of highly similar classes (**cohesive**) that do not extensively communicate with classes in other modules (**uncoupled**).

Logical arrangement. Some grouping is based strictly on the fact that a collection of objects tend to do a lot of work together. Though there may be quite a diversity of uses and behaviors in a module arranged this way, often major problems with module coupling can be solved this way. A good example of this is the symbol table module (Chapter 7), that contains not only the implementation details of symbol tables but also all of the many kinds of items that are stored in the tables.

Common action. Grouping can also be based upon common action or purpose. The collection of all possible parse tree nodes is a large and complex class. In this case there are several subcategories of parse tree nodes such as declaration nodes, expression nodes, statement nodes, and so on. A declaration module could therefore consist of all the parse tree nodes that are produced in declaration activity during the parsing stage. Expression classes are placed in the expression module. Classes representing statement nodes of the parse tree are placed in a statement module.

Often there is a common behavior shared by a large collection of classes. The implementation details of this single member function for the various classes are also often placed into a module. Almost all parse tree nodes have behaviors supporting execution of statements and the emitting of target code. Placing the implementation details for all *execute()* member functions in an interpreter module, and all *emit()* member functions in a code generator module would be examples of this approach to module construction.

Special features. Some modules contain special-purpose items. The error module consists of objects that bear no direct relation to other classes in the compiler and are best encapsulated or separated from other clusters of classes. Objects used by the compiler to provide global information throughout the compiler are also examples of special-purpose modules.

C++ modules most often come in pairs: a **definition** and an **implementation** module, though there are times when one definition module corresponds to a number of (partial) implementation modules.

- **Definition modules.** Definition modules are files having the ".h" extension. These modules contain class definitions and associated constants or data structures.

- **Implementation modules.** Implementation modules are files having a ".c" or ".C" extension, containing code for class constructors and class functions.

A.2   Annotated Index of Keywords

This section contains information on the various C++ keywords. Each C++ keyword entry below consists most, if not all, of the following four items.

> 1. **Description.** Unless otherwise noted, this entry is quoted from an official C++ reference manual, such as Stroustrup [22]
>
> 2. **Applications.** This optional item contains comments about the typical programming uses of the programming construct represented by the keyword. Warnings of programming problems associated with the keyword may also be listed here.
>
> 3. **Example.** This item consists of a representative, though necessarily brief segment of C++ code from the text's compiler example.
>
> 4. **Entry points.** Sections from the text that contain C++ code using the keyword.

break.

- **Description.** The statement

      break;

  causes termination of the smallest enclosing **while**, **do**, **for**, or **switch** statement.

- **Applications.** The number of *break* statements used in a system is inversely proportional to the quality of the object-oriented design or C++ implementation. Its only use in the compiler is in *StringCls* and *ValueCls*. In the former it enables a premature exit from a *for statement*; in the latter it is used in each of the case selectors for a *switch* statement.

- **Example.**

```
for (int x = 1;x <= tmp;x++) {
    // ...
    if (*sp == *c) {
    // ...
    else  {
    // ...
        break;
        }
    }
}
```

- **Entry points.** Sections C.2 and C.4.

case.

- **Description.** In a `switch` statement, the truth condition is implemented as a case label. A case label has the form

    ```
    case <const-expr>:
    ```

    where the constant expression must be of the same type as the switch expression.

- **Applications.** The *case* statement is used to specify the literal values to be selected by a *switch* statement

- **Example.**

    ```
    case '1':
        opt -> set_list();
        continue;
    ```

- **Entry points.** Sections 4.2.3 and C.4.

char.

- **Description.** The fundamental type `char` is large enough to store any member of the computer implementation's character set. If a genuine character from that character set is stored in a character variable, its value is equivalent to the integer code for that character.

- **Applications.** Its primary use is the implementation of strings.

- **Example.**

    ```
    p-> str = new char[64];
    ```

- **Entry points.** Sections 5.2.2, 7.4.2, 9.4.6 and C.2.

class.

- **Description.** A `class` is a type, derived from fundamental and previously defined types by specifying a sequence of data members, member functions, and access restrictions on those members.

- **Example.**

    ```
    class IdentCls : public PTreeNodeCls , public LstSeqBldrCls {
    ```

- **Entry points.** Sections 2.1.3, 7.2.1, and 8.2.

const.

- **Description.** The keyword const may be added to any legal type-specifier. An object of const type cannot be an l-value; that is, a variable of this type cannot be on the left side of an assignment operator.

- **Applications.** One common use of const is the specification of a symbolic constant, especially useful in avoiding the use of magic numbers. Another important use is the specification of a special constructor, that will initialize a new instance of a class from an existing instance, member by member. In the Pascal compiler, we use the #define mechanism for all our symbolic constants. However, there are a number of very important uses of the member-wise initialization constructors.

- **Example.**

```
ValueCls :: ValueCls(const ValueCls& Value) {
    //cout << " Special member-wise constructor" << endl;
```

- **Entry points.** Sections C.1 and C.4.

continue.

- **Description.** The statement causes control to pass to the loop-continuation portion of the smallest enclosing while, do, or for statement. This is essentially a goto statement, whose target is the end of the loop.

- **Applications.** We use the continue statement in place of the more common break in a switch structure inclosed within a loop. That way, the outer loop, then proceeds to the next item in the list.

- **Example.**

```
case 'l':
    opt -> set_list();
    continue;
```

- **Entry point.** Section 4.2.

default.

- **Description.** One of the labels inside a switch statement may have the following form.

```
default:
```

When the switch statement is executed, its expression is evaluated and compared with each case constant. If no case constant matches the expression, and if there is a default label, control then passes to the labeled statement.

- **Applications.** The major application is to provide a more robust switch structure.

- **Example.**

```
default:
    soft.err("Unknown option ");
    soft.err_cont(argv[i]);
    return 0;
```

- **Entry points.** Sections 4.2.3 and C.4.

delete.

- **Description.** The `delete` operator destroys an object that has been created on the free store by the `new` command.

- **Applications.** Modern computers, especially those with virtual memory usually have sufficient memory that objects stored on the heap need not be removed once they have served their purpose. The one exception in the Pascal compiler are the string objects which, because of their wide use, can negatively impact performance if they are left to pasture.

- **Example.**

```
StringCls :: ~StringCls() {
    if (--p->n == 0) {
        delete p->str;
        delete p;
    }
}
```

- **Entry points.** Section C.2.

do.

- **Description.** The `do` statement has the form

```
do <stmt> while ( <expr> );
```

The substatement is executed repeatedly until the value of the expression becomes zero, that is, until the expression is false. This is a posttest iteration.

- **Applications.** This posttest iteration is used to implement a Pascal posttest iteration and a member function for *StringCls*.

- **Example.**

```
int RepeatStmtCls :: execute() {
    do {
        stmt_seq -> execute();
    } while (!(atoi(expr -> evaluate() -> to_char())));
    return 0;
}
```

- **Entry points.** Sections 10.4.2 and C.2.

double.

- **Description.** The type double is a type for allocating sufficient machine resources to support double-precision floating-point storage.

- **Applications.** We use it only to convert from double precision to an internal string representation.

- **Example.**

```
StringCls :: StringCls(double num) {
```

- **Entry point.** Section C.2.

else.

- **Description.** The keyword else may be used in an if statement to provide a two-way selection control structure. As usual, the else ambiguity is resolved by connecting the else to the last encountered "else-less" if.

- **Example.**

```
        if (OptionCls::optimize()) {
    this -> parse_tree -> optimize();
            this -> parse_tree -> emit();
            this -> parse_tree -> peephole();
        } else {
            this -> parse_tree -> emit();
        }
```

- **Entry points.** Sections 4.2, 7.1.1, and many others.

enum.

- **Description.** Enumerations are int types with named constants. The identifiers in an enum-list are declared as constants and may appear wherever constants are required/allowed.

- **Applications.** Enumerated types are far more frequently used in procedurally oriented programming. They are especially useful for labeling complex structs or record structures. We do not use them in the Pascal compiler.

extern.

- **Description.** The extern keyword is use to declare a variable without defining it. It says that elsewhere (in another module) in the program is an actual definition of the variable.

- **Applications.** Sometimes we have a need for an object that can be used widely throughout the program. Such an object can be defined in one module and then accessed in any other module containing this external declaration.

- **Example.**

  ```
  extern StandardTypeCls std_type;
  ```

- **Entry points.** Sections 9.4, C.3 and C.5.

float.

- **Description.** The `float` keyword indicates that a variable is to be allocated sufficient store to support single-precision floating-point representation of real numbers.

- **Example.**

  ```
  float l_val = PExprCls(LVal) -> evaluate() -> to_real();
  ```

- **Entry point.** Section 9.4.4.

for.

- **Description.** The `for` statement has the following form.

  ```
  for (<stmt1> <expr1>; <expr2>) <stmt2>
  ```

  The first statement specifies initialization for the loop. The first expression specifies a test, made before each iteration, such that the loop is exited when the expression becomes 0. The second expression often specifies incrementing that is performed after each iteration. The second statement is the iterated statement.

- **Applications.** This very flexible loop statement is used extensively in the compiler. We try to restrict its use to definite iteration, though many programmers use variants of the statement for almost all their loop structures.

  ```
  for (int i = 0; i<tablesize; i++) {
  ```

- **Entry points.** Sections 4.2, 7.4.2, and many others.

friend.

- **Description.** A friend of a class is a nonmember function that may use the private member names (data and functions) from a class.

- **Applications.** Sometimes normal encapsulation design decisions require overly exhaustive efforts at permitting access to certain kinds of member information. The `friend` specification is a reasonable way to give an entire class access to member data that would normally require various supporting member functions.

- **Example.**

```
class ReadParamLstCls : public PTreeNodeCls {
    public:
        ReadParamLstCls(PPTreeNodeCls ReadParam);
        // ...
        friend class ReadStmtCls;
        friend class ReadlnStmtCls;
    private:
        // ..
```

- **Entry point.** Section 8.2.

goto.

- **Description.** Any statement may be preceded by a label of the following form

      <identifier>:

  that serves to declare the identifier as a label. The only use of a label is a target of a goto statement.

- **Applications.** We do not use goto.

if.

- **Description.** The if statement has one of the two following forms.

        if (<expr>) <stmt>
        if (<expr>) <stmt1> else <stmt2>

  The expression must be of arithmetic or pointer type or a class type for which a conversion to arithmetic/pointer type is defined. If the expression evaluates to nonzero, then the first statement will be executed. If the else keyword is present, then the second statement1 will be executed if the expression evaluates to 0.

- **Applications.** Object-oriented use of selection statements is quite different from that found in procedurally oriented environments. Actions taken, based on the identity of a particular item, are implemented using inheritance, rather than large multiway selection structures.

- **Example.**

```
if (next_location >= (tablesize * 2) / 3) {
    grow();
}
```

- **Entry points.** Sections 4.2, 7.4.2, and many others.

inline.

- **Description.** For extremely small functions, calls designed to allow recursion involve overhead that can significantly degrade performance, even for the highly efficient C++ function call mechanisms. The `inline` keyword is a *request* to the compiler to generate code to place code directly at the location of the function call that will perform the actions of the function. This request may be ignored by the C++ compiler.

- **Applications.** Performance on SPARC ® platforms has been sufficiently fast that no specific `inline` directives have been used in the compiler.

int.

- **Description.** The `int` keyword specifies a type that is allocated a natural machine size, such as a machine word.

- **Applications.** The C++ integer type is the real workhorse of the system. Data members, member functions, local variables, and even static class members are regularly declared to be of this type.

- **Example.**

  ```
  int length = strlen(source_file);
  ```

- **Entry points.** Section 4.2 and many other places.

long.

- **Description.** A `long` integer is usually 32 bits on a 16-bit machine, but still 32 bits on a 32-bit machine.

- **Applications.** Since all internal values are converted to strings, we do not use `long`.

new.

- **Description.** The `new` operator

  ```
  new ( <identifier> )
  ```

  creates an object of the type-name associated with the identifier. The lifetime of an object created by `new` is not restricted to the scope in which it is created. The `new` operator returns a pointer to the object it created.

- **Applications.** The parser is the primary user of `new`. When an instance of a parse tree class is created, an associated class constructor is executed. It not only initializes the created object, but also performs those static semantic checks that are relevant for that portion of the source program.

- **Example.**

```
{PProgramCls pgm = new ProgramCls($2,$5);}
```

- **Entry points.** Section 9.5 and Appendix E.

operator.

- **Description.** The operator keyword allows a programmer to define a member function mapping pairs of the class to itself in terms of conventional infix operations of $+, -, *, \ldots$.

- **Applications.** Rather than having to specify all operations on classes by a function call mechanism, it is possible to define certain member functions as operators.

- **Example.**

```
//assignment operator
StringCls& operator=(Pchar);
StringCls& operator=(StringCls&);
```

- **Entry point.** Section C.2.

overload.

- **Description.** Using the same name for different functions is called **overloading** and is possible in C++. The overload keyword is used as a function specifier

```
overload ( <identifier> )
```

to indicate the identifier represents the name of several functions.

- **Applications.** Often a class is designed primarily to provide normal operations on data for more complex structures. In this case, the new class can extend or overload the old operator definition. We do not use the explicit overload specification for identifiers.

- **Example.**

```
friend int operator==(TypeCls&, TypeCls&)
```

- **Entry point.** Section 9.4.

private.

- **Description.** Members of a class declared `private` can only be used by member functions of that class or friends of that class.

- **Applications.** The primary use of `private` is the encapsulation of data members.

- **Example.**

```
class IdentCls : public PTreeNodeCls , public LstSeqBldrCls {
    // public: ...
    private:
        char *name
};
```

- **Entry point.** Section 8.2.

protected.

- **Description.** Members of a class declared `protected` behave as public members of any derived class and private members for all other classes.

- **Applications.** This allows derived classes to easily access data members of the parent class.

- **Example.**

```
class ExprCls : public PTreeNodeCls, public LstSeqBldrCls {
    // public:...
        protected:
            PTypeCls            type;
            ValueCls            *value;
};
```

- **Entry points.** Sections 8.2.

public.

- **Description.** Members of a class declared `public` can be used by any function. In the example below, the *IdentCls* constructor and member function *get_name*() are examples of such public members.

  There is another use of `public` in this example. A `public` base class allows its public members to be visible to the derived class. A `private` base class will not allow a derived class access to any of its members, not even its `public` ones.

- **Example.**

```
class IdentCls : public PTreeNodeCls , public LstSeqBldrCls {
    public:
        IdentCls();
        IdentCls(char *Name);
        char            *get_name()
                                {return name;}
    // private: ..
};
```

- **Entry points.** Sections 4.1 and 8.2.

register.

- **Description.** `Auto` objects are local to each invocation of a block of code and are discarded upon exit from that block. Objects declared to be of storage class `register` are frequently used objects of storage class `auto`. The `register` keyword just suggests that the compiler should try to store the object in a high-speed register, if possible.

- **Applications.** System performance on SPARC ® platforms has been sufficient that `register` requests have not been used.

return.

- **Description.** The return statement

```
return ;
return  <expression> ;
```

causes a function to return to a caller. The first form can be used only in functions having a `void` return value. The second form returns the expression as the function's value.

- **Example.**

```
class IdentCls : public PTreeNodeCls , public LstSeqBldrCls {
    public:
        // .......
        char            *get_name()
                                {return name;}
    // ...
};
```

short.

- **Description.** The actual size of the `short` integer type is machine dependent. On most 32-bit systems, a short is 2 8-bit bytes.

- **Applications.** The primary use of `shorts` is to conserve space. We have not needed to use this declaration in the Pascal compiler.

sizeof.

- **Description.** The `sizeof` operator yields the size, in bytes, of its operand. A byte is almost always the amount of machine storage required for storage of an object of type `char`.

- **Applications.** The major use of the `sizeof` operator in the compiler example occurs in the scanner. During the development of a compiler, the actual reserved word array tends to grow. Specifying its size would require frequent modifications to the array declaration. Using the array initialization form of declaration and the `sizeof` operator to determine iteration bounds makes for a much smoother development.

- **Example.**

  ```
  #define LEN(x)           (sizeof(x)/sizeof((x)[0]))
  ```

- **Entry point.** Section 5.2.2.

static.

- **Description.** Objects of `static` storage class exist and retain their values throughout the execution of the entire program. A `static` class member acts as a global variable for that class.

- **Applications.** We use classes having static members for the implementation of global objects that provide various services for a wide range of objects. One of the most widely used classes is *StandardTypeCls*, that provides ready access to the actual type objects representing the various Pascal standard types.

- **Example.**

  ```
  class StandardTypeCls {
      //public: ..
      private:
          static PTypeCls        undeclared_type;
          static PTypeCls        integer_type;
          static PTypeCls        real_type;
          static PTypeCls        char_type;
          static PTypeCls        strlit_type;
          static PTypeCls        boolean_type;
  };
  ```

- **Entry points.** Sections 4.1, and 8.2.

switch.

- **Description.** The `switch` statement

  ```
  switch ( <expr> ) <stmt>
  ```

causes control to be transferred to one of several (case-)labeled statements, depending on the value of the expression.

- **Applications.** The number of *switch* statements used in a system is inversely proportional to the quality of the object-oriented design or C++ implementation. Its only use in the compiler is in *ControllerCls* and *ValueCls*. In the former it sets various compiler options; in the latter it determines the behavior of a constructor, a dinosaur required by the limitations of the C++ system available for the Pascal compiler implementation.

- **Example.**

```
switch (kind) {
    case SCALARVAL:
        //To stop aliasing...
        scalar = new StringCls(*(Value.scalar));
        break;
    case ARRAYVAL:
        a_val = Value.a_val;
        break;
    case RECORDVAL:
        r_val = Value.r_val;
        break;
    case POINTERVAL:
        p_val = Value.p_val;
        break;
    case SETVAL:
        s_val = Value.s_val;
        break;
    default:
        hard.err("ValueCls(const&) LOGIC ERROR");
}
```

- **Entry points.** Section 4.2 and C.4.

this.

- **Description.** The this keyword can be thought of as an identifier that contains a pointer to the current instance or object of a given class. If a class has a member function *mbr_fct()* then

$$this-> mmbr\_fct()$$

references that function of the present class.

- **Applications.** The main use of this is to remind the reader or programmer that the particular function is a member of the present class rather than a parent class.

- **Example.**

```
this -> ExprCls::type = l_type;
```

- **Entry points.** Section 9.4 and many other places.

template.

- **Description.** The keyword `template` is expected to be used in future (after 2.0) versions of C++ to support parameterized types.

- **Applications.** This feature was not available in the C++ system used to develop the Pascal compiler.

typedef.

- **Description.** A declaration using the `typedef` declaration specifier

```
typedef <identifier>
```

allows the identifier to be later used as if it was a type keyword.

- **Applications.** Type specification, especially in a compiler project becomes an important, ubiquitous task. An alias for a type, produced by `typedef`, which does not use the C++ dereferencing "*" can greatly simplify expressions.

- **Example.**

```
        typedef class TypeCls *PTypeCls;
// ....
        seq_tail = PTypeCls(seq_tail ->
                    LstSeqBldrCls::append(PTypeCls(Type)));
```

- **Entry points.** Sections 4.1, 9.4, along with many others.

union.

- **Description.** A union is a structure, all of whose members begin at offset 0. At most one member can be stored in a union at any time.

- **Applications.** Object-oriented ideas of inheritance and late binding are often better ways to deal with this kind of data requirement.

- **Example.**

```
        class ValueCls:  public LstSeqBldrCls {
            public:
                ValueCls() {;}
                // ...
            private:
                ValueKind           kind;
                union {
                    StringCls       *scalar;
                    PArrayValCls    a_val;
                    PRecordValCls   r_val;
                    PPointerValCls  p_val;
                    PSetValCls      s_val;
                };
        };
```

- **Entry point.** Section C.4.

unsigned.

- **Description.** Unsigned integers, declared by the keyword **unsigned**, obey the laws of arithmetic modulo 2^n, where n is the number of bits in the normal integer representation.

- **Applications.** Unsigned integers are used primarily where integer precision is helpful. Such an application occurs in the Weinberger hashing algorithm, used in our Pascal compiler.

- **Example.**

    ```
    unsigned int h = 0, g;
    ```

- **Entry point.** Section 7.4.2.

virtual.

- **Description.** A virtual function is specified by prefacing a function declaration by the **virtual** keyword. Only class member functions may be declared as virtual. Classes derived from a base class containing a virtual function may redefine the function for themselves. Then if a base class pointer *bcp* is assigned to an address of a derived object, call

$$bcp- > mmbr\_fct()$$

will be interpreted as a call to the *derived* member function, based upon the particular object to which *bcp* points.

- **Applications.** As noted many times in the text, this idea greatly simplifies implementation details, especially when a large number of objects perform similar tasks.

- **Example.**

    ```
    typedef class PTreeNodeCls *PPTreeNodeCls;
    class PTreeNodeCls {
      public:
            PTreeNodeCls();
            virtual int         emit();
            virtual int         execute();
            virtual int         optimize();
            virtual int         peephole();
            //....
    };
    // ....

            class AssignmentStmtCls : public StatementCls {
              public:
                    AssignmentStmtCls() {;}
                    //...
    ```

```
                      int           execute();
                      int           emit();
                      // ...
    // ...
              while (atoi(expr -> evaluate() -> to_char())) {
                  stmt -> execute();
              }
    };
```

- **Entry point.** Section 9.4.

void.

- **Description.** The keyword void is used to specify that a function does not return a value.

- **Applications.** Most functions that set data member values do not need to return a value.

- **Example.**

```
              class OptionCls {
                public:
                      OptionCls();
                      void          set_no_back_end();
                      void          set_list();
                      void          set_emit();
                      void          set_optimize();
                      void          set_peephole();
                      void          set_format();
                      //....
              };
```

- **Entry points.** Sections 4.1, 7.4.2, and many others.

Appendix B

Finite-State Machines

A **finite-state machine** $\mathcal{M}$ consists of

- A finite set $\mathcal{I}$ of input messages to the machine

- A finite set $\mathcal{O}$ of output messages from the machine

- A finite set $\mathcal{S}$ of machine states

- A next-state function f that tells us which state $f(s, i)$ to go to, given that we are in a present state s and have just received a particular input message i

- An output function g that produces an output message $g(s, i)$ as the machine switches from a state s to state $f(s, i)$

- An initial state s_0

The definition specifies that a finite-state machine consists of the following items.

- Input messages. The set of input messages is usually denoted

$$\{i_1, i_2, \ldots, i_n\}$$

where each i_k represents information coming into the finite-state machine. For the compiler, these messages might be options chosen by the user, or information from various objects about the success or failure of the particular compiler stages as they attempt to convert the source file into the executable module.

419

- Output messages. The set of output messages is usually denoted

$$\{o_1, o_2, \ldots, o_n\}$$

where each o_k represents output from the finite-state machine. A finite-state machine representing the highest level of a compiler might produce output messages requesting various objects to begin their activities; output could also be in the form of error or warning messages sent to the user.

- States. The set of states is similarly denoted

$$\{s_1, s_2, \ldots, s_n\}$$

where each s_k represents a particular state of the finite-state machine.

- Next-state function. Obviously, there must be some rule that the machine uses to determine state changes. If the machine is in state s_i and has just received a message i_j, then the machine's new state is $f(s_i, i_j)$. Here is the Achilles' heel of finite-state machines. The number of domain values (s_i, i_j) is clearly the product of the number of states times the number of input messages, and that can be a very large number, especially if you are the programmer implementing the function $f(s, i)$. Rumbaugh et al. [17, Chapter 5] cites some important work by David Harel that reduces the complexity of the definition of the function f by placing structure on the machine.

- Output function. Note that the output symbols need not be related to the input symbols. In particular there may be different numbers of input and output messages. Implementing the function g can be as difficult as the work involved in implementing the state function f.

Naturally we need a precise way to prescribe the behavior of such a machine. A prose description is often too verbose and rarely sufficiently precise. The specification of finite-state machine behavior is most often done by the use of a transition diagram.

A **transition diagram** for a finite-state machine $\mathcal{M}$ is a directed graph whose vertices are the states $\mathcal{S}$ of $\mathcal{M}$. The directed edges (s_i, s_j) of $\mathcal{T}$ exist whenever there is an input message i causing $\mathcal{M}$ to change from state s_i to state $s_j = f(s_i, i)$.

- Graph: A graph is just a set of vertices or nodes and a set of lines or edges connecting some or all of the vertices. Graphs are often represented as a collection of circles or dots (the nodes) and lines (the edges connecting the nodes).

- Directed graph: A graph is directed if the edges indicate a valid direction of movement from node to node. Arrows are a common representation of the edges in a directed graph.

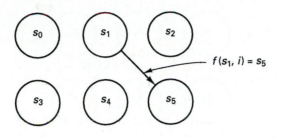

Figure B.1. Partial Transition Diagram

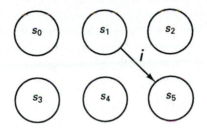

Figure B.2. Labeling Input

- Nodes for transition diagram: Since each possible state of the corresponding finite-state machine is a node of a transition diagram, each state is therefore placed inside a circle.

- Edges for transition diagram: A transition diagram arrow (s_i, s_j) points from state s_i to the state s_j whenever the machine can switch to state s_j on an input message i.

The notation for transition diagrams as shown in Figure B.1, though quite simple, is sufficiently specific to be able to express the state-changing details of a finite-state machine. Since we are interested in transition diagrams specifying system behavior, additional representational facilities need to be devised so that specific input causing the transitions can be placed on the graph. Similarly there must be a way to indicate the corresponding output value during a particular transition between states.

Figure B.2 shows how input messages are noted on transition diagrams. An arrow is drawn from state s_i to state s_j if there is an input message i that sends state s_i to state s_j. The arrow is then labeled by the input as shown in the figure.

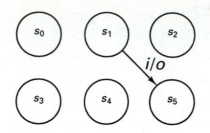

Figure B.3. Input and Output

If an output o occurs during the transition from state s_i to state s_j, then the label of the arrow is modified as shown in Figure B.3. A complete transition diagram for a finite machine would usually be far more complex than that shown in Figures B.1 and B.3, since all the states and all the transitions (together with input and output labels) would be displayed together. Transition diagrams allow us to unambiguously prescribe the behavior of a reasonably complex finite-state machine.

Appendix C

Compiler Utilities

> Topics:
> Class definitions and implementation for ...
> - Linked lists
> - Classes internal strings
> - Error and warning messages
> - Internal values
> - Case and selector values
> - Allocation of registers and temporaries

C.1   Linked-Lists

One of the most widely used object behaviors is that of being able to form a linked-list of objects. In an object-oriented setting, this can be achieved by building a special class that provides the necessary pointer data members and member functions for such activity. Then if a class needs to be able to form itself into a linked-list, the class can be derived from the special list builder class and automatically have whatever functionality it needs.

For example, one of the first classes defined for the parse tree module is *IdentCls*. Grammar productions for Pascal variable declarations like

```
var
     i,j,k: integer;
```

recognize a *list* of variables, each of which is to be typed as integer. The normal way build the tree for such a source program structure is to produce a linked-list of identifier nodes. This is done by specifying that *IdentCls* is derived from the list builder class by the following definition.

```
class IdentCls : public PTreeNodeCls , public LstSeqBldrCls
```

Here, *IdentCls* objects inherit not only the attributes of a parse tree node but also can now form themselves into linked-lists using code such as the following.

```
this -> LstSeqBldrCls::append(PIdentCls(NextIdent)));
```

Other objects needing this list or sequence building ability include the following.

- Symbol tables

- Expressions

- Set member.

- Types

- Statements

- Record variables

- Formal parameters

You may find it instructive to see how client objects make use of the list-building behaviors of these various kinds of objects and where such applications are made.

LstSeqBldrCls Definition. | LstSeqBldrCls constructor (lstbld.h) |

```
 6 typedef class LstSeqBldrCls *PLstSeqBldrCls;
 7 class LstSeqBldrCls {
 8   public:
 9         LstSeqBldrCls();
10         virtual PLstSeqBldrCls  append(PLstSeqBldrCls);
11         virtual PLstSeqBldrCls  prepend(PLstSeqBldrCls);
12         virtual PLstSeqBldrCls  get_next()
13                                         {return next;}
14   private:
15         PLstSeqBldrCls          next;
16 };
17
18 typedef class DLLstCls *PDLLstCls;
19 class DLLstCls { //Doubly linked list
20   public:
21         DLLstCls();
22         virtual PDLLstCls   append(PDLLstCls);
23         virtual PDLLstCls   prepend(PDLLstCls);
24         virtual PDLLstCls   get_prev()
25                         {return prev;}
26         virtual PDLLstCls   get_next()
27                         {return next;}
28   private:
29     PDLLstCls               prev;
30     PDLLstCls               next;
31 };
```

LstSeqBldrCls Implementation. LstSeqBldrCls implementation (lstbld.C)

```
10 LstSeqBldrCls :: LstSeqBldrCls() {
11     //cout << "LstSeqBldrCls()" << endl;
12     next = 0;
13 }
14
15 PLstSeqBldrCls LstSeqBldrCls ::
16                     append(PLstSeqBldrCls ToBeAdded) {
17     //cout << "LstSeqBldrCls::append()" << this << endl;
18     return this -> next = ToBeAdded;
19 }
20
21 PLstSeqBldrCls LstSeqBldrCls ::
22                     prepend(PLstSeqBldrCls ToBeAdded) {
23     //cout << "LstSeqBldrCls::prepend()" << ToBeAdded << endl;
24     ToBeAdded -> next = this;
25     return ToBeAdded;
26 }
27
28 DLLstCls :: DLLstCls() {
29     //cout << "DLLstCls()" << endl;
30     prev = 0;
31     next = 0;
32 }
33
34 DLLstCls :: DLLstCls(const DLLstCls &) {
35     cout << "DLLstCls(const DDlstCls&)" << endl;
36     //Don't want to ever copy pointers when initializing dervied
37     //objects
38     prev = 0;
39     next = 0;
40 }
41
42 PDLLstCls DLLstCls :: append(PDLLstCls DLLst)  {
43     //cout << "DLLstCls::append()" << DLLst << endl;
44     this -> next = DLLst;
45     if (DLLst) {
46         DLLst -> prev = this;
47     }
48     return DLLst;
49 }
50
51 PDLLstCls DLLstCls :: prepend(PDLLstCls DLLst) {
52     //cout << "DLLstCls::prepend()" << DLLst << endl;
53     DLLst -> next = this;
54     this -> prev = DLLst;
55     return DLLst;
56 }
```

C.2   Internal Compiler Strings

Internal strings are used by the compiler for storing almost all internal values, even numeric. The advantage is that the compiler does not then require a particular host machine word size. The listings in this section are a simplification of those used in other compilers, that are subject to such word size limitations. In those settings *StringCls* also is given the ability to perform simple arithmetic on various kinds of numeric strings. These operations are not included here, since the SPARC ® architecture provides sufficient integer and real resources.

StringCls Definition. StringCls definition – part 1 (string.h)

```
11 typedef class StringCls *PStringCls;
12 class StringCls {
13    public:
14          StringCls();
15          StringCls(Pchar s);
16                //Initialize the string to "message" s
17          StringCls(int num);
18                //Convert from integer to (ASCII) string
19          StringCls(double num);
20                //Convert from  real   to (ASCII) string
21          StringCls(StringCls&);
22                // Initialize at assignment (Stroustrup,p.180)
23          ~StringCls();
24
25          int          length();
26
27          int          index(Pchar c);
28          //Find location of null-terminated char string 'c'
29          int          index(StringCls&);
30          //Find location index of StringCls string 'sc'
31          void         set_bit(int BitNum);
32          //Set Bitnum to 'x'
33          void         un_set_bit(int BitNum);
34
35          Pchar        make_char();
36          void         print();
37
38          //assignment operator
39          StringCls& operator=(Pchar);
40          StringCls& operator=(StringCls&);
41
42          //subscript operator
43          char& operator[](int i);
```

The previous listing contains the specification of five constructors and a destructor. Also included is the specification of the usual string operations as well as two special operators.

The second part of the definition contains operators for appending strings, outputting string information, and comparing various strings. The final item is the definition of the actual data structure, taken primarily from Stroustrup's excellent text [22].

```
| StringCls definition – part 2 (string.h) |

46              //append operator
47              friend StringCls operator&(StringCls&, StringCls&);
48              friend StringCls operator&(StringCls&, Pchar);
49              friend StringCls operator&(Pchar, StringCls&);
50
51              //io operators
52              friend ostream& operator<<(ostream&, StringCls&);
53              friend istream& operator>>(istream&, StringCls&);
54
55              //generic relational operators
56              friend int operator==(StringCls&, Pchar);
57              friend int operator==(StringCls&, StringCls&);
58              friend int operator!=(StringCls&, Pchar);
59              friend int operator!=(StringCls&, StringCls&);
60              friend int operator<(StringCls&, StringCls&);
61              friend int operator<=(StringCls&, StringCls&);
62
63      private:
64              struct str_rep {
65                      Pchar str;
66                      int n;
67              };
68              str_rep *p;
69 };
70
```

- *str* points to the leading character in the string.

- *n* counts the number of times that the string is currently being accessed. If this number is larger than one, then the class destructor does nothing.

StringCls Implementation. The first listing contains the implementation of the five nontrivial *StringCls* constructors. The first just constructs an empty string, the next one translates a C++ string into an internal string. The following two constructors convert numerical values into string objects containing a string version of the numbers. The final constructor is called whenever one string object is used to initialize and create a new string object. Notice the allocation of space and the use of *strcpy* to eliminate aliasing.

```
StringCls 'constructors' (string.C)

21 StringCls :: StringCls() {
22          p = new str_rep;
23          p -> str = 0;
24          p -> n = 1;
25 }
26
27 StringCls :: StringCls(Pchar s) {
28          p = new str_rep;
29          p -> str = new char[ strlen(s) + 1];
30          strcpy(p->str,s);
31          p -> n = 1;
32 }
33
34 StringCls :: StringCls(int num) { //integer to string
35          p = new str_rep;
36          p-> str = new char[64];
37          sprintf(p -> str,"%d",num);
38          p-> n = 1;
39 }
40
41 StringCls :: StringCls(double num) { //real to string
42          p = new str_rep;
43          p-> str = new char[64];
44          sprintf(p -> str,"%f",num);
45          p-> n = 1;
46 }
47
48 StringCls :: StringCls(StringCls& s) {
49          //s.p->n++;
50          //p = s.p;
51          p = new str_rep;
52          int len = strlen(s.p->str);
53          p -> str = new char[len];
54          strcpy(p -> str, s.p->str);
55 }
56
57 StringCls :: ~StringCls() {
58          if (--p->n == 0) {
59                  delete p->str;
60                  delete p;
61          }
62 }
```

The final item in the listing above is a **destructor**. It keeps track of the number of references to the string object still pending and only removes the string if it is no longer needed.

The next two listings contain the implementation of the *StringCls* member functions.

```
┌─────────────────────────────────────────────────────────────┐
│ StringCls member functions – part 1 (string.C)              │
│                                                              │
│  66 void error(Pchar Message) {                              │
│  67            //string's own error message                  │
│  68         cerr << Message << endl;                         │
│  69         exit(1);                                         │
│  70 }                                                        │
│  71                                                          │
│  72 int StringCls :: length() {                             │
│  73                 return strlen(p -> str);                │
│  74 }                                                        │
│  75                                                          │
│  76 int StringCls :: index(Pchar c) {                       │
│  77     //cout << "StringCls::index()" << endl;             │
│  78     int count = 0;                                       │
│  79     Pchar sp = p->str;                                   │
│  80     int tmp = strlen(c);                                 │
│  81     int tmp2 = strlen(sp);                               │
│  82     do {                                                 │
│  83        for (int x = 1;x <= tmp;x++) {                    │
│  84            int tmpcount = count;                         │
│  85            if (*sp == *c) {                              │
│  86                if ( x == tmp) return tmpcount;          │
│  87                sp++;                                     │
│  88                c++;                                      │
│  89                }                                         │
│  90            else  {                                       │
│  91                for (int y = 1; y < x;y++) {              │
│  92                        sp--;                             │
│  93                        c--;                              │
│  94                        }                                 │
│  95                break;                                    │
│  96                }                                         │
│  97            }                                             │
│  98        sp++;                                             │
│  99        count++;                                          │
│ 100     } while (count < tmp2);                              │
│ 101     return(NULL);                                        │
│ 102 }                                                        │
│ 103                                                          │
│ 104 int StringCls::index(StringCls& sc) {                   │
│ 105         //cout << "StringCls :: index(StringCls)" << endl; │
│ 106         Pchar c = sc.make_char();                       │
│ 107         return StringCls::index(c);                     │
│ 108 }                                                        │
└─────────────────────────────────────────────────────────────┘
```

The first *index()* returns the location (if any) where the incoming *c* matches *this* string. The second *index()* does the same for an actual object, rather than just a pointer to a character.

```
    StringCls member functions – part 2 (string.C)

111 void StringCls :: set_bit(int BitNum) {
112     //cout << "set_bit() " << endl;
113     if (this -> length() < BitNum) {
114         error("Attempt to change string beyond boundary");
115     } else {
116         Pchar q = p -> str;
117         for (int i=0; i < BitNum; i++) q++;
118         *q = 'x';
119     }
120 }
121
122 void StringCls :: un_set_bit(int BitNum) {
123     //cout << "un_set_bit() " << endl;
124     if (this -> length() < BitNum) {
125         error("Attempt to change string beyond boundary");
126     } else {
127         Pchar q = p -> str;
128         for (int i=0; i < BitNum; i++) q++;
129         *q = '-';
130     }
131 }
132
133 Pchar StringCls :: make_char() {
134 //cout << "StringCls :: make_char -- p  " << p << endl;
135     return p->str;
136 }
137
138 void StringCls :: print() {
139         if (strlen(p->str) == 0) {
140             cout << "''";
141         } else {
142             cout << "'";
143             cout << p->str;
144             cout << "'";
145         }
146 }
```

StringCls assignment operators (string.C)

```
150 StringCls& StringCls :: operator=(Pchar s) {
151         if (p->n > 1) {
152                 p->n--;
153                 p = new str_rep;
154         } else if (p->n == 1) {
155                 delete p->str;
156         }
157         p->str = new char[strlen(s) + 1];
158         strcpy(p->str,s);
159         p->n = 1;
160         return *this;
161 }
162
163 StringCls& StringCls :: operator=(StringCls& s) {
164         s.p->n++;
165         if (--p->n == 0) {
166                 delete p->str;
167                 delete p;
168         }
169         p = s.p;
170         return *this;
171 }
```

StringCls subscript and append operators (string.C)

```
175 char& StringCls :: operator[](int i) {
176         if (i < 0 || strlen(p->str) < i) {
177                 error("index out of range");
178         }
179         return p->str[i];
180 }
181
182 StringCls operator&(StringCls& arg1, StringCls& arg2) {
183     Pchar tmp1 = arg1.make_char();
184     Pchar tmp2 = arg2.make_char();
185     Pchar tmp = new char[strlen(tmp1) + strlen(tmp2) + 1];
186     strcpy(tmp,tmp1);
187     strcat(tmp,tmp2);
188     StringCls concat = tmp;
189     return concat;
190 }
191
192 StringCls operator&(StringCls& arg1, Pchar arg2) {
193     Pchar tmp1 = arg1.make_char();
194     Pchar tmp2 = arg2;
195     Pchar tmp = new char[strlen(tmp1) + strlen(tmp2) + 1];
196     strcpy(tmp,tmp1);
197     strcat(tmp,tmp2);
198     StringCls concat = tmp;
199     return concat;
200 }
201
202 StringCls operator&(Pchar arg1, StringCls& arg2) {
203     Pchar tmp1 = arg1;
204     Pchar tmp2 = arg2.make_char();
205     Pchar tmp = new char[strlen(tmp1) + strlen(tmp2) + 1];
206     strcpy(tmp,tmp1);
207     strcat(tmp,tmp2);
208     StringCls concat = tmp;
209     return concat;
210 }
```

StringCls input/output operators (string.C)

```
214 ostream& operator<<(ostream& s, StringCls& x) {
215         return s <<  x.p->str ;
216 }
217
218 istream& operator>>(istream& s, StringCls& x) {
219         char buf[256];
220         s >> buf;
221         x = buf;
222         cout << "echo: " << x << "\n";
223         return s;
224 }
```

StringCls relational operators – part 1(string.C)

```
314 int operator<=(StringCls& x, StringCls& y) {
315     //cout << "StringCls " << x << " <= " << y << "\n";
316
317     Pchar x_c = new char[(strlen(x.make_char()))+1];
318     x_c = x.make_char();
319
320     Pchar y_c = new char[(strlen(y.make_char()))+1];
321     y_c = y.make_char();
322
323     //First, determine the signs
324     int x_is_pos, y_is_pos, both_positive;
325     if (*x_c == '-') {
326         x_is_pos = 0;
327         x_c++;
328     } else if (x_is_pos = *x_c == '+') {
329         x_c++;
330     } else {
331         x_is_pos = 1;
332     }
333
334     if (*y_c == '-') {
335         y_is_pos = 0;
336         y_c++;
337     } else if (y_is_pos = *y_c == '+') {
338         y_c++;
339     } else {
340         y_is_pos = 1;
341     }
```

```
    ┌─────────────────────────────────────────────────────────────┐
    │ StringCls relational operators – part 2(string.C)           │
    └─────────────────────────────────────────────────────────────┘

344      //Go for an easy answer, if possible
345      if ((!x_is_pos)&&(y_is_pos)) {
346          return 1;
347      } else if ((x_is_pos)&&(!y_is_pos)) {
348          return 0;
349      } else {
350          both_positive = x_is_pos; //==y_is_pos, to
351      }
352
353      //in case real, find decimal, otherwise go to the end
354      Pchar x_p,y_p;
355      for (x_p=x_c;(*x_p != '\0')&&(*x_p != '.');x_p++);
356      for (y_p=y_c;(*y_p != '\0')&&(*y_p != '.');y_p++);
357      //now back to the beginning
358      while( (x_p != x_c)&&(y_p != y_c) ) {
359          x_p--;
360          y_p--;
361      }
362      if (x_p != x_c) {          // x_c > y_c
363          return (both_positive)? 0: 1;
364      } else if (y_p != y_c) { // x_c < y_c
365          return (both_positive)? 1: 0;
366      } else {
367          int more_x = 1;
368          int more_y = 1;
369          while ( more_x && more_y &&
370            (*x_p == *y_p)) {
371              more_x = *++x_p != '\0';
372              more_y = *++y_p != '\0';
373          };
374          if (!more_x && !more_y) {       //x_c == y_c
375             return 1;
376          } else if (more_x && !more_y) { // x_c > y_c
377             return (both_positive)? 0 : 1;
378          } else if (!more_x && more_y) { // x_c < y_c
379             return (both_positive)? 1 : 0;
380          } else {
381             return (both_positive)?
382                             *x_p <= *y_p : *x_p > *y_p;
383          }
384      }
385
386 }
387 /* end-relational-opr */
```

C.3   Error Handling

ErrorCls Definition. | ErrorCls definition (error.h) |

```
 6 const int MAXERR = 5;
 7 typedef char* Pchar;
 8 typedef class ErrorCls *PErrorCls;
 9 class ErrorCls   {
10    protected:
11         void          send_hdr();
12         void          send_msg(Pchar Msg);
13         virtual void  msg_continued(Pchar ContMsg);
14         static int    num_errors;
15         void          terminate_compile();
16         int           too_many_errors();
17 };
18
19 class WarningCls : public ErrorCls {
20    public:
21         void          warn(Pchar Msg);
22         void          warn_cont(Pchar CMsg)
23                    {msg_continued(CMsg);}
24 };
25 extern WarningCls just;
26
27 class SoftErrorCls : public ErrorCls {
28    public:
29         void          hdr();
30         void          err(Pchar Msg);
31         void          err_cont(Pchar CMsg)
32                    {msg_continued(CMsg);}
33 };
34 extern SoftErrorCls soft;
35
36 class RuntimeErrorCls : public ErrorCls {
37    public:
38         void          err(Pchar Msg);
39         void          err_cont(Pchar CMsg)
40                    {msg_continued(CMsg);}
41 };
42 extern RuntimeErrorCls runtime;
43
44 class HardErrorCls : public ErrorCls {
45    public:
46         void          err(Pchar Msg);
47         void          err_cont(Pchar CMsg)
48                    {msg_continued(CMsg);}
49 };
50 extern HardErrorCls hard;
51
```

There are increasingly stronger levels of actions taken as the error category moves from top to bottom of the previous listing.

- Warnings only output a message.

- Soft errors are associated with syntax and static semantic problems. Error messages are sent to the user and the compiler then suppresses any back-end activity.

- Run-time errors are violations of dynamic semantic specifications that occur during program interpreting. Messages are sent and then all interpreting is terminated.

- Hard errors are internal errors, most often generated by design problems that are producing nil pointers. These errors terminate the execution of the compiler after printing a message.

ErrorCls Implementation. The first listing defines global variables that are made available to the rest of the compiler through the C++ *extern* specification.

```
ErrorCls globals (error.C)

13 /* ************************************************* */
14            //Global variable definitions
15 WarningCls just;
16 SoftErrorCls soft;
17 RuntimeErrorCls runtime;
18 HardErrorCls hard;
19
20 /* ************************************************* */
```

- A client could issue a warning by using code like the following.

```
just.warn("Variable used but not set");
```

- A syntax error could be issued as follows.

```
soft.err("Declaration error -- missing semicolon?");
```

- A semantic error could be issued as follows.

```
runtime.err("Execution terminated -- array out of bounds");
```

- A compiler design error should immediately terminate the execution of the system.
```
hard.err("SomeCls :: fct -- LOGIC ERROR!");
```

The next listing contains implementation details for the base class member functions, that are inherited by the four derived error classes. The first three are used in the outputting of the error messages. *Terminate_compile()* is called by *HardErrorCls* to halt the program.

```
ErrorCls member functions (error.C)

23 extern int line_no;
24 void ErrorCls::send_hdr() {
25     cout << endl << endl << "[error #" << ++num_errors
26                     << " , Line " << line_no << "]      ";
27 }
28
29 void ErrorCls::send_msg(Pchar Msg) {
30     cout << endl << "   ->" << Msg << "<-" << endl;
31 }
32
33 void ErrorCls :: msg_continued(Pchar ContMsg) {
34     cout <<  "          " << ContMsg << endl;
35 }
36
37 int ErrorCls :: too_many_errors() {
38     //cout << "ErrorCls::too_many_errors" << endl;
39     return (num_errors > MAXERR);
40 }
41
42 void ErrorCls :: terminate_compile() {
43     //cout << "ErrorCls::terminate_compile()" << endl;
44     cout << endl <<
45        "Too many errors, cannot recover...Sorry" << endl << endl;
46     exit(1);
47 }
```

- *Num_errors* is a static member of *ErrorCls*.

- *Line_no* is a global, defined by the scanner.

- *Too_many_errors()* simply returns true if the number of errors during the compilation process exceeds a system wide constant value.

- *Terminate_compile()* halts execution of the system by calling the *exit()* function from a standard library. Your system should have a similar, if not identical, function.

```
Warning member function (error.C)

50 void WarningCls :: warn(Pchar Msg) {
51     //cout << "WarningCls::warn()" << endl;
52     cout << "Warning -> ";
53     ErrorCls::msg_continued(Msg);
54 }
```

SoftErrorCls member functions (error.C)

```
57 void SoftErrorCls :: hdr() {
58     ErrorCls::send_hdr();
59 }
60
61 void SoftErrorCls :: err(Pchar Msg) {
62     //cout << "SoftErrorCls::err()" << endl;
63     //++ErrorCls::num_errors;
64     ErrorCls::send_hdr();
65     ErrorCls::send_msg(Msg);
66     if (ErrorCls::too_many_errors()) {
67         ErrorCls::terminate_compile();
68     }
69     POptionCls opt = new OptionCls;
70     opt -> set_no_back_end();
71 }
```

RunTimeCls and HardErrorCls member functions (error.C)

```
74 void RuntimeErrorCls :: err(Pchar Msg) {
75     cout << "RuntimeErrorCls::error() " << endl;
76     ErrorCls::send_msg(Msg);
77     exit(1);
78     //May want to set a global variable
79     //  and not exit the interpreter.
80 }
81
82 void HardErrorCls :: err(Pchar Msg) {
83     //cout << "HardErrorCls::error() " << endl;
84     ErrorCls::send_msg(Msg);
85     exit(1);
86 }
```

C.4   Internal Compiler Values

ValueCls Definition. | ValueCls definition – part 1(value.h) |

```
12 typedef class ComponentCls *PComponentCls;
13 class ComponentCls: public LstSeqBldrCls {
14    public:
15          ComponentCls(int IndexVal, ValueCls *CompVal);
16          int                 get_ival()
17                              {return i_val;}
18          ValueCls           *get_comp_val()
19                              {return comp_val;}
20          void                set_value(ValueCls *Value);
21
22          void                print();
23    private:
24          int                 i_val;  // in case of chars, it's ord
25          ValueCls           *comp_val;
26 };
28
29 typedef class ArrayValCls *PArrayValCls;
30 class ArrayValCls {
31    public:
32          ArrayValCls(TypeCls *IndexType, TypeCls* CompType);
33          ValueCls           *get_component(int Index);
34          void                set_component(int Index,
35                                          ValueCls *Value);
36          void                print();
37    private:
38          ComponentCls       *head;
39          ComponentCls       *tail;
40 };
42
43 typedef class RecordValCls *PRecordValCls;
44 class RecordValCls {
45    public:
46          RecordValCls();
47          void print();
48    private:
49 };
51
52 typedef class PointerValCls *PPointerValCls;
53 class PointerValCls {
54    public:
55          PointerValCls();
56          void print();
57    private:
58 };
```

The listing, above, describes the various kinds of values out of which a *ValueCls* is constructed. In particular, array values are constructed from component objects.

The listing below, then defines the member structure for *ValueCls*. This is the only use of a C++ union in the compiler. Its presence is required by the lack of certain C++ language features in version 2.0 and earlier.

```
(value.h)

 97 typedef enum {
 98         SCALARVAL, ARRAYVAL, RECORDVAL, POINTERVAL, SETVAL
 99 } ValueKind;
100
101 typedef class ValueCls *PValueCls;
102 class ValueCls:  public LstSeqBldrCls {
103    public:
104         ValueCls() {;}
105         ValueCls(char*);
106         ValueCls(int);
107         ValueCls(float);
108         ValueCls(PArrayValCls AVal);
109         ValueCls(PSetValCls SVal);
110         ValueCls(const ValueCls& Value);
111
112         char             *to_char();
113
114         int              to_integer();
115
116         float            to_real();
117
118         PValueCls        get_component(int Index);
119         void             set_component(int Index,
120                                   PValueCls Value);
121
122         void             print(int Width);
123
124         void             print()
125                             {print(1);}
126
127         friend ostream& operator<<(ostream&, ValueCls&);
128    private:
129         ValueKind        kind;
130         union {
131            StringCls      *scalar;
132            PArrayValCls   a_val;
133             PRecordValCls  r_val;
134            PPointerValCls p_val;
135            PSetValCls     s_val;
136         };
137 };
```

ValueCls Implementation.   ComponentCls implementation(value.C)

```
17 ComponentCls :: ComponentCls(int IndexVal, PValueCls CompVal) {
18     //cout << "ComponentCls()" << endl;
19     i_val = IndexVal;
20     comp_val = CompVal;
21 }
22
23 void ComponentCls :: set_value(PValueCls Value) {
24     cout << "ComponentCls::set_value()" << Value << endl;
25     comp_val = Value;
26 }
27
28 void ComponentCls :: print() {
29     //cout << "ComponentCls::print()" ;
30     cout << "[" << i_val << "," ;
31     comp_val -> print();
32     cout << "]" ;
33 }
```

ArrayValCls – part 1 (value.C)

```
36 ArrayValCls :: ArrayValCls(PTypeCls IndexType, PTypeCls CompType) {
37     //cout << "ArrayValCls()" << endl;
38     if (!IndexType || ! CompType) {
39         hard.err("ArrayValCls() LOGIC ERROR");
40     }
41     int min_ord = IndexType -> get_min_ord();
42     int max_ord = IndexType -> get_max_ord();
43
44     this -> head =
45         this -> tail =
46             new ComponentCls(min_ord++,CompType -> make_value());
47     for (int i=min_ord; i <= max_ord; i++) {
48         this -> tail =
49             PComponentCls(this -> tail -> append(
50                 new ComponentCls(i,CompType -> make_value())));
51     }
52 }
```

ArrayValCls – part 2 (value.C)

```
55 PValueCls ArrayValCls :: get_component(int Index) {
56     //cout << "ArrayValCls::get_component()" << Index << endl;
57     PComponentCls p = this -> head;
58     while (p) {
59         if (p -> get_ival() == Index) {
60             return p -> get_comp_val();
61         }
62         p = PComponentCls(p -> get_next());
63     }
64     return new ValueCls(0);
65 }
66
67 void ArrayValCls :: set_component(int Index, PValueCls Value) {
68     //cout << "ArrayValCls::set_component()" << endl;
69     PComponentCls p = this -> head;
70     while (p) {
71         if (p -> get_ival() == Index) {
72             p -> set_value(Value);
73         }
74         p = PComponentCls(p -> get_next());
75     }
76 }
```

Set member class (value.C)

```
109 MemberCls :: MemberCls(PExprCls StartExpr, PExprCls StopExpr) {
110     cout << "MemberCls(expr,expr)" << endl;
111
112     if (!StopExpr) {
113         StopExpr = StartExpr; //Single elt.
114     }
115     elt_type = StartExpr -> get_type();
116     if (!(elt_type -> is_ordinal())) {
117         soft.err("Sets require ordinal types");
118     } else if ((StartExpr -> is_var()) ||
119                (StopExpr  -> is_var())) {
120         soft.err("Sets require constant member values");
121     } else {
122         PStringCls start =
123             new StringCls(StartExpr -> evaluate() -> to_char());
124         PStringCls stop  =
125             new StringCls(StopExpr  -> evaluate() -> to_char());
126         PClosedIntervalCls intvl =
127             new ClosedIntervalCls(start,stop,elt_type);
128         elt_lst = new FSigmaCls(intvl);
129     }
130 }
```

SetValCls (value.C)

```
133 SetValCls :: SetValCls(PTypeCls EltType) {
134     cout << "SetValCls" << endl;
135     elt_type = EltType;
136     elt_lst = new FSigmaCls(elt_type); // empty
137 }
138
139 SetValCls :: SetValCls(PSetMemberLstCls SetMemberLst) {
140     cout << "SetValCls(Expr)" << endl;
141     if (!SetMemberLst) {
142         elt_type = 0; //empty set is untyped in Pascal
143         elt_lst = 0;
144     } else {
145         PSetMemberCls p = SetMemberLst -> get_seq_head();
146         elt_type = p -> get_start_elt() -> get_type();
147         while (p) {
148             PMemberCls member =
149                 new MemberCls(p -> get_start_elt(),
150                               p -> get_stop_elt());
151             if (!elt_lst) {
152                 this -> elt_lst =  member -> elt_lst;
153             } else {
154                 this -> elt_lst =
155                     this -> elt_lst -> join(member -> elt_lst);
156             }
157             p = PSetMemberCls(p -> get_next());
158         }
159     }
160 }
```

ValueCls – normal constructors (value.C)

```
162
163 ValueCls :: ValueCls(char *Val) {
164     //cout << "ValueCls(char*) " << endl;
165     kind = SCALARVAL;
166     scalar = new StringCls(Val);
167 }
168
169 ValueCls :: ValueCls(int Val) {
170     //cout << "ValueCls(int) " << endl;
171     kind = SCALARVAL;
172     scalar = new StringCls(Val);
173 }
174
175 ValueCls :: ValueCls(float Val) {
176     //cout << "ValueCls(float) " << endl;
177     kind = SCALARVAL;
178     scalar = new StringCls(Val);
179 }
180
181 ValueCls :: ValueCls(PArrayValCls AVal) {
182     //cout << "ValueCls(AVal)" << endl;
183     if (!AVal) {
184         hard.err("ValueCls(AVal) LOGIC ERROR");
185     }
186     kind = ARRAYVAL;
187     a_val = AVal;
188 }
189
190 ValueCls :: ValueCls(PSetValCls SVal) {
191     cout << "ValueCls(SVal)" << endl;
192     if (!SVal) {
193         hard.err("ValueCls(SVal) LOGIC ERROR");
194     }
195     kind = SETVAL;
196     s_val = SVal;
197 }
```

ValueCls – initializing constructor (value.C)

```
199
200 ValueCls :: ValueCls(const ValueCls& Value) {
201     //cout << " Special constructor ValueCls& Value " << endl;
202     if (!&Value) {
203         hard.err("ValueCls(const&) LOGIC ERROR");
204     }
205     kind = Value.kind;
206     switch (kind) {
207         case SCALARVAL:
208             //To stop aliasing...
209             scalar = new StringCls(*(Value.scalar));
210             break;
211         case ARRAYVAL:
212             a_val = Value.a_val;
213             break;
214         case RECORDVAL:
215             r_val = Value.r_val;
216             break;
217         case POINTERVAL:
218             p_val = Value.p_val;
219             break;
220         case SETVAL:
221             s_val = Value.s_val;
222             break;
223         default:
224             hard.err("ValueCls(const&) LOGIC ERROR");
225     }
226 }
```

(value.C)

```
237 int ValueCls :: to_integer() {
238     //cout << "ValueCls::to_integer()" << endl;
239     if (kind != SCALARVAL) {
240         hard.err("ValueCls::to_integer() -- LOGIC ERROR");
241     }
242     return atoi(scalar -> make_char());
243 }
244
245 float ValueCls :: to_real() {
246     //cout << "ValueCls::to_real()" << endl;
247     if (kind != SCALARVAL) {
248         hard.err("ValueCls::to_integer() -- LOGIC ERROR");
249     }
250     return atof(scalar -> make_char());
251 }
252
253 PValueCls ValueCls :: get_component(int Index) {
254     //cout << "ValueCls::get_component" << Index << endl;
255     if (! (this -> kind == ARRAYVAL)) {
256         hard.err("ValueCls::get_component() LOGIC ERROR");
257     }
258     return a_val -> get_component(Index);
259
260 }
261
262 void ValueCls :: print(int Width) {
263     //cout << "ValueCls::print()" << endl;
264     if (this -> kind == SCALARVAL) {
265         cout.width(Width);
266         cout << *scalar ;
267     } else if (this -> kind == ARRAYVAL) {
268         a_val -> print();
269     } else if (this -> kind == RECORDVAL) {
270         r_val -> print();
271     } else {
272         p_val -> print();
273     }
274 }
275
276 ostream& operator<<(ostream& s, ValueCls& x) {
277     if (x.kind == SCALARVAL) {
278         return s << *PStringCls(&x)  ;
279     } else {
280         return s << "ValueCls: " << x.kind << *PStringCls(&x)  ;
281     }
282 }
284
```

C.5   Case and Field Selector Values

One of the more painstaking tasks in dealing with source programs is that of checking constants for the following properties.

- Distinct specification

- Range specification

- Completeness of specification

In languages like Modula-2 there may even be a syntax that specifies a range, like 2..5. In an object-oriented setting, such detail is often encapsulated into a class, especially if messy and detailed computation can be hidden by such an effort. The specification for case statements in most languages is a good candidate for this kind of activity.

The main idea behind the design and implementation of this class is that any specification of this kind can be viewed as essentially a union of closed intervals. A Pascal case label list like $2, 4$ is just the union of the two intervals $[2, 2]$ and $[4, 4]$. A list like $2, 4, 5, 6, 8$ is just

$$[2, 2] \cup [4, 6] \cup [8, 8].$$

Moreover, issues about the existence of labels not yet specified can be easily described by examining the set complement of the set representing the union of all labels that have been declared.

The most general set needed for this kind of activity is one that is a union of closed intervals. Borrowing (and perhaps abusing) from mathematical topology, a notion of F_σ sets, that are countable unions of closed sets, we have called the class of sets we shall be using *FSigmaCls*.

FSigmaCls Definition.   Since the intersection of two closed intervals is a (possibly empty) closed interval, *ClosedIntervalCls* has a member function *meet()*. There is no *join()* function for obvious reasons.

```
┌─────────────────────────────────┐
│ FSigmaCls definition (fsigma.C) │
└─────────────────────────────────┘

15 typedef class ClosedIntervalCls *PClosedIntervalCls;
16 class ClosedIntervalCls {
17    public:
18         ClosedIntervalCls(PStringCls Start,
19                                 PStringCls Stop,
20                                      PTypeCls UType);
21         PClosedIntervalCls      meet(PClosedIntervalCls);
22         void                    print();
23    friend class FSigmaCls;
24    friend int operator<=(ClosedIntervalCls&, ClosedIntervalCls&);
25    friend int operator<=(FSigmaCls&, FSigmaCls&);
26    private:
27         PTypeCls                univ_type;
28         PStringCls              start;
29         PStringCls              stop;
30         PClosedIntervalCls      next;
31 };
32
33 typedef class FSigmaCls *PFSigmaCls;
34 class FSigmaCls {
35    public:
36         FSigmaCls(PTypeCls t);  //null set
37
38         FSigmaCls(PClosedIntervalCls x);
39
40         PFSigmaCls              join(PFSigmaCls x);
41         PFSigmaCls              meet(PFSigmaCls x);
42         PFSigmaCls              complement();
43         void                    print();
44         void                    test_cls();
45    friend int operator==(FSigmaCls&, FSigmaCls&);
46    friend int operator<=(FSigmaCls&, FSigmaCls&);
47    friend int operator<(FSigmaCls&, FSigmaCls&);
48    private:
49         PTypeCls                univ_type;
50         PClosedIntervalCls      head;
51 };
52
```

FSigmaCls contains the usual collection of set operations as well as three of the relational operations often associated with sets.

FSigmaCls Implementation. The constructor first sets the element type. This completely specifies the universal set.

```
  ClosedIntervalCls constructors (fsigma.C)

  24 ClosedIntervalCls :: ClosedIntervalCls(PStringCls Start,
  25                                         PStringCls Stop,
  26                                         PTypeCls UType) {
  27     cout << "ClosedIntervalCls::" << endl;
  28     if (UType) {
  29         univ_type = UType;
  30     } else {
  31         univ_type = std_type.integer();
  32     }
  33     if (Start == 0) { //Empty interval
  34         start = stop = 0;
  35     } else {
  36         start = new StringCls(*Start);
  37         stop  = new StringCls(*Stop);
  38     }
  39     next  = 0;
  40 }
```

Then the upper and lower bounds of the closed interval are set. Note that the empty interval is specified by nil pointers.

It remains to implement our workhorse for this class, the member function *meet()*, that calculates the intersection of various configurations of closed intervals. As noted above, we are trying to encapsulate the tedious bookkeeping associated with various ranges of discrete values. The following implementation determines the intersection for the following conditions.

- If the first interval overlaps (to the left) the second interval

- If the first interval contains the second interval

- If the second interval contains the first interval

- If the first interval overlaps (to the right) the second interval

ClosedIntervalCls member functions (fsigma.C)

```
44          ClosedIntervalCls :: meet(PClosedIntervalCls x) {
45      //cout << "ClosedIntervalCls::meet()" << endl;
46      if ((*start <= *x -> start)&&(*x -> start <= *stop)).{
47          StringCls min_stop;
48          if (*stop <= *x -> stop) {
49              min_stop =  *stop;
50          } else {
51              min_stop =  *x -> stop;
52          }
53          return
54              new ClosedIntervalCls(x->start,&min_stop,univ_type);
55      } else if ((*start <= *x -> stop )&&
56                  (*x -> stop  <= *stop))  {
57          StringCls max_start;
58          if (*start <= *x -> start) {
59              max_start = *x -> start;
60          } else {
61              max_start = *start;
62          }
63          return
64              new ClosedIntervalCls(&max_start,x->stop,univ_type);
65      } else if ((*x -> start <= *start)&&
66                  (*start <= *x -> stop))  {
67           StringCls min_stop;
68          if (*stop <= *x -> stop) {
69              min_stop =  *stop;
70          } else {
71              min_stop =  *x -> stop;
72          }
73          return
74              new ClosedIntervalCls(start,&min_stop,univ_type);
75      } else if ((*x -> start <= *stop )&&
76                  (*stop  <= *x -> stop))  {
77          StringCls max_start;
78          if (*start <= *x -> start) {
79              max_start = *x -> start;
80          } else {
81              max_start = *start;
82          }
83          return
84              new ClosedIntervalCls(&max_start,stop,univ_type);
85      } else {
86              return 0;
87          }
88 }
```

```
┌─────────────────────────────────────────────────────────────────────┐
│ FSigmaCls constructors (fsigma.C)                                     │
│                                                                       │
│  92 FSigmaCls :: FSigmaCls(PTypeCls UType) {                          │
│  93         cout << "FSigmaCls::(null set)" << endl;                  │
│  94         univ_type = UType;                                        │
│  95         head = 0;                                                 │
│  96 }                                                                 │
│  97                                                                   │
│  98 FSigmaCls :: FSigmaCls(PClosedIntervalCls x) {                    │
│  99         cout << "FSigmaCls::(non-empty)" << endl;                 │
│ 100         head = x;                                                 │
│ 101         if (!x) {                                                 │
│ 102                 hard.err("FSigmaCls:: LOGIC ERROR");              │
│ 103         }                                                         │
│ 104         univ_type = x -> univ_type;                              │
│ 105 }                                                                 │
└─────────────────────────────────────────────────────────────────────┘
```

```
┌─────────────────────────────────────────────────────────────────────┐
│ FSigmaCls operations – part 1 (fsigma.C)                              │
│                                                                       │
│ 116 PFSigmaCls FSigmaCls :: join(PFSigmaCls x) {                      │
│ 117         //cout << "FSigmaCls::join() " << endl;                   │
│ 118         return ((this -> complement()) ->                         │
│ 119                 meet(x -> complement())) -> complement();         │
│ 120 }                                                                 │
│ 121                                                                   │
│ 122 PFSigmaCls FSigmaCls :: meet(PFSigmaCls x) {                      │
│ 123         //cout << "FSigmaCls::meet() " << endl;                   │
│ 124         PClosedIntervalCls p = this -> head;                      │
│ 125         PClosedIntervalCls ret_head = 0;                          │
│ 126         PClosedIntervalCls q = x -> head;                         │
│ 127         while (p && q) {                                          │
│ 128                 PClosedIntervalCls current;                       │
│ 129                 PClosedIntervalCls r;                             │
│ 130                 if (r = p -> meet(q)) {                           │
│ 131                         if (!ret_head) {                          │
│ 132                                 ret_head = current = r;           │
│ 133                           } else {                                │
│ 134                                 current = current -> next = r;    │
│ 135                         }                                         │
│ 136                 }                                                 │
│ 137                 if (*p -> stop < *q -> stop) {                    │
│ 138                         p = p -> next;                            │
│ 139                 } else {                                          │
│ 140                         q = q -> next;                            │
│ 141                 }                                                 │
│ 142         }                                                         │
│ 143         if (!ret_head) {                                          │
│ 144                 return new FSigmaCls(univ_type);                  │
│ 145         } else {                                                  │
│ 146                 return new FSigmaCls(ret_head);                   │
│ 147         }                                                         │
│ 148 }                                                                 │
└─────────────────────────────────────────────────────────────────────┘
```

```
     FSigmaCls operations – part 2 (fsigma.C)

150 PFSigmaCls FSigmaCls :: complement() {
151     //cout << "FSigmaCls::complement() " << endl;
152     PClosedIntervalCls p,q;
153     int done = 0;
154
155     PClosedIntervalCls new_head = 0;
156
157     int loword  = 0;
158     PStringCls low = new StringCls(loword);
159     int i = loword;
160     PStringCls str_i = new StringCls(i);
161
162     int highord = univ_type -> get_max_ord();
163     PStringCls high = new StringCls(highord);
164
165     PClosedIntervalCls universe =
166         new ClosedIntervalCls(low,high,univ_type);
167
168     p = this -> head;
169     if (!p) {
170         return new FSigmaCls(universe);
171     }
172     if ((*p->start == *low) && (*p->stop == *high)) {
173         return new FSigmaCls(univ_type); //Empty set
174     }
175     while (p) {
176         int p_start = atoi(p -> start ->make_char());
177         if (i < p_start) {
178             int j =  p_start - 1;
179             PStringCls str_j = new StringCls(j);
180             if (!new_head) {
181               new_head = q =
182                 new ClosedIntervalCls(str_i,str_j,univ_type);
183             } else {
184               q = q -> next =
185                 new ClosedIntervalCls(str_i,str_j,univ_type);
186             }
187         }
188         if (*p -> stop < *high) {
189                 i = atoi(p -> stop -> make_char()) + 1;
190                 str_i = new StringCls(i);
191         } else {
192                 done = 1;
193         }
194         p = p -> next;
195     }
```

FSigmaCls operations – part 3 (fsigma.C)

```
197        if (!done) { //there's more
198            if (!new_head) {
199                new_head = q =
200                    new ClosedIntervalCls(str_i,high,univ_type);
201            } else {
202                q = q -> next =
203                    new ClosedIntervalCls(str_i,high,univ_type);
204            }
205        }
206        if (!new_head) {
207            return new FSigmaCls(univ_type);
208        } else {
209            return new FSigmaCls(new_head);
210        }
211 }
```

FSigmaCls relational operators (fsigma.C)

```
228 int operator==(FSigmaCls& a, FSigmaCls&b) {
229        //cout << "a == b" << endl;
230        return ((a <= b) && (b <= a));
231 }
232
233 int operator<=(FSigmaCls& a, FSigmaCls& b) {
234        //cout << "a <= b (FSigmaCls)" << endl;
235        int contained = 1;
236        PClosedIntervalCls x = a.head;
237        while (x && contained) {
238                contained = 0;
239                PClosedIntervalCls y = b.head;
240                while (y && !contained) {
241                        contained = contained || (*x <= *y);
242                        y = y -> next;
243                }
244                x = x -> next;
245        }
246        return contained;
247 }
248
249 int operator<(FSigmaCls& a, FSigmaCls& b) {
250        //cout << "a < b" << endl;
251        return (a <= b) && (!(b <= a));
252 }
```

Appendix D

Testing the Compiler

```
┌─────────────────────────────────────────┐
│ Topics:                                 │
│   ● Knuth debugging strategy            │
│   ● Schreiner regression tool           │
└─────────────────────────────────────────┘
```

There are few things in life that provide the satisfaction afforded by observing a creation of our own mind and hands that is actually working! Of course, once the original euphoria of success has subsided to more rational levels of consciousness, we are immediately reminded of our own limitations and lack of perfection. There always are subprojects that we haven't quite finished. More importantly there are almost always system behaviors that we had not intended. We euphuistically call them *features*, assuming that we will have time in the future to determine their root causes. And if we are lucky, perhaps we will be called to another new project before we have to thoroughly test and rework our creation. After all, software maintenance is a *perfect* place for entry-level programmers.

Of all the areas of computer science, testing is probably the subject most avoided by undergraduate students and instructors, alike. Our usual course structure rewards the student for getting the program running but precious little class time is spent on testing strategies and almost no marks are given for actually finding program errors.

One of the most significant discussions of program testing and verification can be found in Knuth's description of his efforts in the construction and testing of the TEX publishing system. He makes the point that while programmers declare a program to be debugged when large applications can be run successfully, most large applications tend to use only about 50 percent of of the system. Only when some unusual use is made of the system is a part of the other half of the system exercised, and this part may be riddled with errors! He also notes that formal correctness proofs of systems are at least as suspect of errors as the system they are designed to test.

That leaves us with a difficult problem. We can't *prove* that our system is correct and we can't just run lots of (even large) ordinary applications. About all that is left is to produce applications designed to test all possible sections of code, and doing this takes a lot of effort, as well as a fair amount of computational support.

Knuth T_EX debugging strategy. Knuth has, since 1960, successfully used the following strategy on a number of compilers, assemblers, and simulators that he has produced.

- Keep as many errors as possible out of the system by use of informal program verification proofs. The careful construction and use of loop invariants is the major tool for keeping out program errors as the code is being written.

- Construct a fiendish test file that attempts to trip up the program:

    - Make the data as *different* as possible from normal data used by the program.

    - Choose data to produce boundary conditions for all function arguments.

    - Choose data that will guarantee executing all major paths through the system. Then run a profiler and see which sections are still not being executed. Try to guarantee that at least 99 percent of all code has been executed and verified as accurate.

- Run the fiendish test, using a system profiler to note any sections of code not being exercised. Supplement the test to test these sections as well.

- Carefully hand check all the output from these test to find erroneous system behavior.

- Continue to profile and to add instructions until you are satisfied that all portions of the code have been exercised.

Naturally, this is not pleasant work. Sitting at a desk and poring over stacks of computer output takes a lot of time; it also takes a lot of effort. But the method has been so successful for Knuth that he dares anyone to find a bug in his programs and even offers to pay $10.20 for each bug found![1]

There is a way to reduce some of the labor involved in creating the fiendish test and in monitoring the output. First, just construct test data while the particular segment of code is being written, or as near to that time as is possible. Then the *new* information can be carefully checked when it is produced the first time, and all subsequent tests can be checked against the approved output using a simple *diff* program. We discuss one possible way for implementing this such backward compatibility testing in the following section.

Schreiner regression tool. In biology, **regression** is reversion to an earlier or simpler form of life; in psychoanalysis it means reversion to an earlier behavior pattern. In programming, it just means that system behavior not related to a particular program modification should remain unchanged from previous patterns.

---

[1] Only two bugs have ever been found in his 1960 compiler, and he later discovered testing information on one of those bugs in the results of his test. He had failed to notice its presence in the test output.

As noted in earlier chapters, object-oriented methods amount essentially to the construction of an immature, but correctly functioning system first, that is then slowly worked into the mature system. It is crucial that the entire compiler continue to function properly during this maturation process. The system's future development must depend upon the verifiable integrity of the system's present state. Clearly what is needed is a way to be sure that when changes are introduced into the compiler, things that used to work still do! The usual method of testing the upward integrity of a system is called **regression testing**. The main feature of this method is that it gives us a *systematic* way of comparing the system's response to fixed input data before and after system modifications.

```
Tool for regression testing

 1 # shell script for trying to trip the embryonic pascal compiler
 2 #        ideas taken from Schreiner
 3
 4 BaseDirectory=epc
 5 InDirectory=$BaseDirectory/Test/in_files
 6 OutDirectory=$BaseDirectory/Test/out_files
 7
 8 if test ! -d $OutDirectory
 9 then    mkdir $OutDirectory
10 fi
11
12 for i in $InDirectory/*
13 do   file=`basename $i`
14      echo $file
15      $BaseDirectory/epc -l $i > $OutDirectory/\&$file
16      if test -r $OutDirectory/$file
17      then if cmp -s $OutDirectory/\&$file $OutDirectory/$file
18           then    echo "$file unchanged"
19                   rm $OutDirectory/\&$file
20           else    echo "$file CHANGED  <new   >old"
21                   diff $OutDirectory/\&$file $OutDirectory/$file
22                   mv $OutDirectory/$file $OutDirectory/$file{_old}
23                   mv $OutDirectory/\&$file $OutDirectory/$file
24           fi
25      else echo "$file created"
26           mv $OutDirectory/\&$file $OutDirectory/$file
27      fi
28 done
29 echo "epc checking complete ..."
30 exit 0
```

One of the nicest tools for regression testing that we know about is the above shell script, slightly modified from its original form in Schreiner and Friedman [18]. To use the script make a testing directory with *in_file* and *out_file* subdirectories. Then place fiendish test files in *in_files* and execute the script that feeds the files to the compiler and stores the output from the compiler into corresponding files in *out_files*. The script then compares the new files with output files from the previous test. If there is a difference, the user receives a reasonably adequate report of the discrepancies. This form of testing should begin as soon as the compiler is capable of outputting information.

Pascal Grammar

This appendix contains a working grammar for the Pascal compiler of this text, including error recovery productions as prescribed by Schreiner and Friedman [18] and added semantic actions described in Chapter 9.

```
 1 Program:
 2      PROGRAMTK Ident External_files SCTK Block DOTTK
 3          {PProgramCls pgm = new ProgramCls($2,$5);}
 4    | PROGRAMTK Ident error Block DOTTK
 5          {soft.err("Programm Header Error -- expecting semicolon");}
 6    | error
 7          {soft.err("Syntax error -- cannot recover, sorry");}
 8    | PROGRAMTK error
 9          {soft.err("Program Header Error");}
10    | PROGRAMTK Ident External_files SCTK Block DOTTK error
11          {soft.err("Missing end dot");}
12      ;
13      External_files : /*empty*/
14          | LPARENTK  Ident_lst RPARENTK
15          | error
16              {soft.err("Header error -- expecting left paren");}
17          | LPARENTK  Ident_lst error
18              {soft.err("Header error -- expecting right paren");}
19      ;
20      Block:
21          Label_dec_part
22          Const_def_part
23          Type_def_part
24          Var_dec_part
25          Proc_fun_dec_part
26          Statement_part
27            {$$ = new BlockCls($6);}
28          | error
29          {soft.err("Block error");}
30      ;

33 Label_dec_part:  /* empty */
34      | LABELTK Label_lst SCTK
35      | LABELTK error
36          {soft.err("Label error -- possibly missing semicolon");}
37      ;
```

459

```
38
39    Label_lst: Label
40        | Label_lst COMMATK Label
41            {yyerrok;}
42        | error
43            {soft.err("Error in list of labels");}
44        | Label_lst error
45            {soft.err("Expecting comma in label list");}
46        | Label_lst error Label
47            {yyerrok;
48             soft.err("Expecting comma in label list");}
49        | Label_lst COMMATK error
50            {soft.err("Error after comma in label list");}
51        ;
52
53        Label: UNSIGNEDINTTK    /* 0 <= value <= 9999 */
54            ;


57 Const_def_part: /* empty */
58     | CONSTTK Const_def_lst SCTK
59     | CONSTTK error
60         {soft.err("Constant error -- possibly missing semicolon");}
61     | CONSTTK Const_def_lst  error
62         {soft.err("Constant error -- possibly missing semicolon");}
63     ;
64     Const_def_lst: Const_def
65         | Const_def_lst SCTK Const_def
66             {yyerrok;}
67         | error
68             {soft.err("Error in constant definition");}
69         | Const_def_lst error Const_def
70             {yyerrok;
71              soft.err("Expecting semicolon in const definition list");}
72         | Const_def_lst error
73             {soft.err("Error in constant definition");}
74         ;
75     Const_def: Ident EQTK Constant
76             {new ConstDefCls($1,$3);}
77         | Ident error
78             {soft.err("Expecting '=' ");}
79         ;
80        Constant: Unsigned_number
81            {$$ = new LitFactorCls($1);}
82          | PLUSTK Unsigned_number
83            {$$ = new LitFactorCls($2);}
84          | PLUSTK error
85            {soft.err("Expecting number ");
86             PLiteralCls lit = new LiteralCls(0);
87             $$ = new LitFactorCls(lit);}
88          | MINUSTK Unsigned_number
89            {PLitFactorCls lit = new LitFactorCls($2);
90             $$ = new UMinusCls(lit);}
91          | MINUSTK error
92            {soft.err("Expecting number ");
93             PLiteralCls lit = new LiteralCls(0);
```

```
 94                       $$ = new LitFactorCls(lit);}
 95             | Ident    /*check that it is constant*/
 96                 {PVarFuncDesignatorCls vfd =
 97                             new VarFuncDesignatorCls($1,0);
 98                 $$ = vfd -> get_factor();}
 99             | PLUSTK Ident
100                 {PVarFuncDesignatorCls vfd =
101                             new VarFuncDesignatorCls($2,0);
102                 $$ = vfd -> get_factor();}
103             | MINUSTK Ident
104                 {PVarFuncDesignatorCls vfd =
105                             new VarFuncDesignatorCls($2,0);
106                 PExprCls vf = PExprCls(vfd -> get_factor());
107                 $$ = new UMinusCls(vf);}
108             | STRINGTK       /*type is char if len=1*/
109                 {PLiteralCls lit = new LiteralCls(0);
110                  $$ = new LitFactorCls(lit);}
111             | BADSTRINGTK
112                 {soft.err("Wrong string delimiters");
113                  cout << "just saw bad string" << endl;
114                  PLiteralCls lit = new LiteralCls(0);
115                  $$ = new LitFactorCls(lit);}
116             ;
117      Unsigned_number: UNSIGNEDINTTK
118                 {$$ = new LiteralCls(std_type.integer());}
119              | UNSIGNEDREALTK
120                 {$$ = new LiteralCls(std_type.real());}
121             ;


124 Type_def_part: /* empty */
125     | TYPETK Type_def_lst SCTK
126     | TYPETK error
127         {soft.err("Type error -- possibly missing semicolon");}
128     | TYPETK Type_def_lst  error
129         {soft.err("Type error -- possibly missing semicolon");}
130     ;
131     Type_def_lst: Type_def
132         | Type_def_lst SCTK Type_def
133             {yyerrok;}
134         | error
135           {soft.err("Error in type definition");}
136         | Type_def_lst error Type_def
137           {yyerrok;
138            soft.err("Expecting semicolon in type definition list");}
139         | Type_def_lst SCTK error
140             {soft.err("Error in type definition");}
141         ;
142     Type_def: Ident EQTK Type
143             {new TypeDefCls($1,$3);}
144         | Ident error
145             {soft.err("Expecting '=' ");}
146         | Ident EQTK error
147             {soft.err("Type definition error");}
148         ;
149           Type: Simple_type
```

```
150                     | PACKEDTK Struct_type
151                     | Struct_type
152                     | UPARROWTK IDENTIFIERTK   /*forward reference */
153                     ;
154             Simple_type: LPARENTK Ident_lst RPARENTK
155                     {$$ = new EnumTypeCls($2);}
156                 | Constant DDTK Constant
157                     {$$ = new SubrangeTypeCls($1,$3);}
158                 | error DDTK
159                    {soft.err("Subrange error");}
160                 | Constant DDTK error
161                    {soft.err("Subrange error");}
162                 | Ident
163                    {PSpecifiedTypeCls st =
164                              new SpecifiedTypeCls($1);
165                  $$ = st -> get_type();}
166                 ;
167             Struct_type: ARRAYTK
168                 LBRACKTK Index_t_lst RBRACKTK OFTK Type
169                    {$$ = new ArrayTypeCls($3,$6);}
170                 | ARRAYTK error
171                    {soft.err("Array type error ");}
172                 | ARRAYTK LBRACKTK error
173                    {soft.err("Array index type error");}
174                 | RECORDTK /*a scope*/ Field_lst ENDTK
175
176                 | RECORDTK  error ENDTK
177                    {soft.err("Record error");}
178                 | SETTK OFTK Simple_type
179                    {$$ = new SetTypeCls($3);}
180                 | SETTK error
181                    {soft.err("Set error");}
182                 | FILETK OFTK Type
183
184                 | FILETK error
185                    {soft.err("File error");}
186                 ;

188             Index_t_lst: Simple_type
189                    {$$ = new TypeLstCls($1);}
190                 | Index_t_lst COMMATK Simple_type
191                    {$$ = PTypeLstCls($1) -> append($3);}
192                 | Index_t_lst error
193                    {soft.err("Error in index list");}
194                 ;

196             Field_lst: Fixed_part Variant_part
197                 ;
198             Fixed_part: Field
199                  | Fixed_part SCTK Field
200                 /*
201                 | error Field
202                    {soft.err("Error in record");}
203                 */
204                 ;
205             Field: /*empty*/
```

```
206                             | Ident_lst COLONTK Type
207                             | Ident_lst EQTK error
208                                 {soft.err("expecting colon");}
209                             ;
210                 Variant_part: /* empty */
211                     | CASETK Ident OFTK Variant_seq
212                     | CASETK Ident COLONTK
213                         Ident OFTK Variant_seq
214                     | CASETK error
215                         {soft.err("Variant error");}
216                             ;
217                 Variant_seq: Variant
218                     | Variant_seq SCTK Variant
219                     ;
220                     Variant: /*empty*/
221                     |Case_label_lst COLONTK
222                             LPARENTK Field_lst RPARENTK
223                             ;

226 Var_dec_part: /* empty */
227     | VARTK Var_dec_lst SCTK
228     | VARTK error
229         {soft.err("Declaration error -- missing semicolon?");}
230     | VARTK Var_dec_lst error
231         {soft.err("Declaration error -- missing semicolon?");}
232     ;
233     Var_dec_lst: Var_dec
234         | Var_dec_lst SCTK Var_dec
235             {yyerrok;}
236         | error
237             {soft.err("Error in variable declaration");}
238         | Var_dec_lst error Var_dec
239             {soft.err("Expecting semicolon");}
240         | Var_dec_lst SCTK error
241             {soft.err("Error in variable declaration");}
242         ;
243     Var_dec: Ident_lst COLONTK Type
244             {new VarDecCls($1,$3);}
245         | Ident_lst COLONTK error
246             {soft.err("Variable declaration error");}
247         ;

250 Proc_fun_dec_part: /* empty */
251     |Proc_or_fun_dec_seq
252     ;
253    Proc_or_fun_dec_seq: Proc_or_fun_dec
254     | Proc_or_fun_dec error
255         {soft.err("Procedure/Function  error");}
256     | Proc_or_fun_dec_seq /* SCTKs already there */ Proc_or_fun_dec
257     ;
258     Proc_or_fun_dec:
259         Proc_heading SCTK
260             {$$ = new ProcDecCls($1);}
261             Body SCTK   /*check if forward or fwd refd*/
262             {$$ = PProcDecCls($3) -> finish($4);}
263         |  Proc_heading error SCTK
```

```
264                 {soft.err("Procedure error");}
265         |  Func_heading SCTK /*also func heading may be -type*/
266            {$$ = new FuncDecCls($1);}
267            Body SCTK /*also func heading may be -type*/
268            {$$ = PFuncDecCls($3) -> finish($4);}
269         |  Func_heading error SCTK
270            {soft.err("Function error");}
271         ;

273     Proc_heading: PROCEDURETK
274                    {$$ = new ProcHeadCls;}
275               Ident Formal_param_stuff
276                    {$$ = PProcHeadCls($2) -> finish($3,$4);}
277         ;
278         /* result determined in block */
279         ;
280     Body: Block
281         | FORWARDTK
282            {$$ = 0;}
283         ;

285     Func_heading: FUNCTIONTK
286                    {$$ = new FuncHeadCls;}
287               Ident Function_form
288                    {$$ = PFuncHeadCls($2) -> finish($3,$4);}
289         ;
290         Function_form: /*empty*/     /*if forward referenced*/
291                 {$$ = 0;}
292            | Formal_param_stuff COLONTK Ident
293               {PSpecifiedTypeCls st =  new SpecifiedTypeCls($3);
294                $$  = new FuncFormCls($1,st -> get_type());}
295            | Formal_param_stuff COLONTK error
296               {soft.err("Function error -- is function type missing?");
297                $$ = new FuncFormCls($1,std_type.undeclared());}
298         ;
300         Formal_param_stuff: /*empty*/
301                 {$$ = 0;}
302            | LPARENTK Formal_p_sect_lst RPARENTK
303               {$$ = new FParamStuffCls($2);}
304         ;
305         Formal_p_sect_lst: Formal_p_sect
306               {$$ = new FParamSecLstCls($1);}
307            | Formal_p_sect_lst SCTK Formal_p_sect
308              {yyerrok;
309               $$ = PFParamSecLstCls($1) -> append($3);}
310            | error
311              {soft.err("Error formal params");
312               $$ = new FParamSecLstCls;}
313            | Formal_p_sect_lst SCTK error
314              {soft.err("Error after semicolon in formal params");
315               $$ = new FParamSecLstCls;}
316            ;
318            Formal_p_sect: Param_group
319                 {$$ = new ValParamGrpCls($1);}
320               | VARTK Param_group
321                 {$$ = new VarParamGrpCls($2);}
322               | Proc_heading
```

```
323                              {$$ = new ProcParamCls($1);}
324                          | Func_heading
325                              {$$ = new FuncParamCls($1);}
326                          ;
327              Param_group: Ident_lst COLONTK Paramtype
328                          {$$ = new ParamGrpCls($1,$3);}
329                      | Ident_lst EQTK error
330                          {soft.err("Expecting colon");
331                          $$ = new ParamGrpCls($1,
332                                      std_type.undeclared());}
333                          ;
335              Paramtype: Ident
336                      {PSpecifiedTypeCls it =
337                              new SpecifiedTypeCls($1);
338                      $$ = it -> get_type();}
339                      | ARRAYTK
340                          LBRACKTK Index_spec_seq RBRACKTK
341                                              OFTK Paramtype
342                      | PACKEDTK
343                          ARRAYTK LBRACKTK Index_spec RBRACKTK
344                                              OFTK Ident
345                      ;
346              Index_spec_seq: Index_spec
347                      | Index_spec_seq SCTK Index_spec
348                      ;
349                  Index_spec:
350                          Ident DDTK Ident COLONTK Ident
351                              ;


354 Statement_part: Compound_stmt
355     /*
356     | Compound_stmt error
357         {soft.err("Statement error");}
358         */
359         ;
360     Compound_stmt: BEGINTK Statement_seq ENDTK
361             {$$ = $2;}
362         ;
363         Statement_seq: Statement
364             {$$ = new StatementSeqCls($1);}
365         | Statement_seq SCTK Statement
366             {yyerrok;
367             $$ = PStatementSeqCls($1) -> append($3);}
368         | error
369             {soft.err("Statement error");
370             $$ = new ErrStmtCls();}
371         | Statement_seq SCTK error
372             {soft.err("Statement error");
373             $$ = $1;}
374         ;
375         Statement: /*empty*/
376             {$$ = new EmptyStmtCls;}
377         | Assignment
378
379         | IFTK Expr THENTK Statement
```

```
380                     {$$ = new IfStmtCls($2,$4,0);}
381             | IFTK Expr THENTK Statement
382               ELSETK Statement  /*1  shift/reduce conflict*/
383                     {$$ = new IfStmtCls($2,$4,$6);}
384             | ELSETK error /* 6 shift/reduce conflicts */
385           {soft.err("Possibly terminated if with a ';'?");
386                     $$ = new ElseStmtCls($2);}
387             | CASETK Expr OFTK Case_lst ENDTK
388                     {$$ = new CaseStmtCls($2,$4);}
389             | CASETK Expr OFTK Case_lst error
390                     {$$ = new CaseStmtCls($2,$4);
391                      soft.err("Case statement error");}
392             | FORTK Ident ASGTK Expr Dir Expr DOTK Statement
393                     {$$ = new ForStmtCls($2,$4,$5,$6,$8);}
394             | FORTK Ident ASGTK error
395                     {$$ = new ForStmtCls($1,0,0,0,0);
396                      soft.err("For statement error");}
397              | FORTK Ident error
398                     {$$ = new ErrStmtCls();
399                      soft.err("For statement error -- '=' for ':=?");}
400             | WHILETK Expr DOTK Statement
401                     {$$ = new WhileStmtCls($2,$4);}
402             | WHILETK error
403                     {$$ = new ErrStmtCls();
404                      soft.err("While statement error");}
405             | REPEATTK Statement_seq UNTILTK Expr
406                     {$$ = new RepeatStmtCls($2,$4);}
407             | WITHTK Rec_var_lst DOTK Statement
408                     {$$ = new WithStmtCls($2,$4);}
409             | WITHTK error
410                     {$$ = new ErrStmtCls();
411                      soft.err("With statement error");}
412             | ReadStmt
413             | WriteStmt
414             | Procedure_call
415             | Label COLONTK Statement
416                     {$$ = $3; /* temporarily */}
417             | Compound_stmt
418             | GOTOTK Label
419             ;
420     Dir: TOTK
421                     {$$ = new DirectionCls(1);}
422             | DOWNTOTK
423                     {$$ = new DirectionCls(0);}
424             ;
425
426     Rec_var_lst: Record_var
427                     {$$ = new RecVarLstCls($1);}
428             | Rec_var_lst COMMATK Record_var
429                     {$$ = PRecVarLstCls($1) -> append($3);}
430             ;


433     Assignment: Variable ASGTK Expr
434                     {$$ = new AssignmentStmtCls($1,$3);}
435             | Variable EQTK error
```

```
436                          {soft.err("Use ':=' for assignment");}
437                  /* must test for fn_ident */
438                  ;


441          Procedure_call: Ident Actual_param_stuff
442          {$$ = new ProcCallCls($1,$2);}
443          ;
444          Actual_param_stuff:  /*empty*/
445                  {$$ = 0;}
446              | LPARENTK RPARENTK
447                  {$$ = 0;}
448              | LPARENTK Actual_param_lst RPARENTK
449                  {$$ = $2;}
450              | LPARENTK Actual_param_lst error
451                  {soft.err("Actual parameter error");}
452          ;
453          Actual_param_lst: Actual_param
454                  {$$ = new ActualParamLstCls($1);}
455              | Actual_param_lst COMMATK Actual_param
456                  {$$ = PActualParamLstCls($1) ->
457                                          append($3);}
458              ;
459              Actual_param: Expr
460                  {$$ = new ActualParamCls($1);}
461              /* a Variable or a proc/fn id */


464          Case_lst: Case_lst_elem
465              {$$ = new CaseLstCls($1);}
466          | Case_lst SCTK Case_lst_elem
467              {$$ = PCaseLstCls($1) -> append($3);}
468          ;
469          Case_lst_elem: /*empty*/
470              {$$ = new CaseEltCls(0,0);}
471          | Case_label_lst COLONTK Statement
472              {$$ = new CaseEltCls($1,$3);}
473          ;
474          Case_label_lst: Case_label
475              {$$ = new CaseLabelLstCls($1);}
476          | Case_label_lst COMMATK Case_label
477              {$$ = PCaseLabelLstCls($1) -> append($3);}
478          ;
479          Case_label: Constant
480              {$$ = new CaseLabelCls($1);}
481              ;


483          ReadStmt: READTK
484              {PReadParamCls rp = new ReadParamCls(0);
485               $$ = new ReadStmtCls(rp);}
486          | READTK
487              LPARENTK Read_params_lst RPARENTK
488              {$$ = new ReadStmtCls($3);}
489          | READLNTK
490              {PReadParamCls rp = new ReadParamCls(0);
491               $$ = new ReadlnStmtCls(rp);}
492          | READLNTK
```

```
493                          LPARENTK Read_params_lst RPARENTK
494                          {$$ = new ReadlnStmtCls($3);}
495                    ;
496               Read_params_lst:  Read_params
497                      {$$ = new ReadParamLstCls($1);}
498                    | Read_params_lst COMMATK Read_params
499                      {$$ = PReadParamLstCls($1) -> append($3);}
500                    ;
501               Read_params: Expr
502                      {$$ = new ReadParamCls($1);}
503                        ;
504          WriteStmt: WRITETK
505                    LPARENTK Write_params_lst RPARENTK
506                    {$$ = new WriteStmtCls($3);}
507               | WRITELNTK
508                 {PWriteParamCls wp = new WriteParamCls(0,0,0);
509                  $$ = new WritelnStmtCls(wp);}
510               | WRITELNTK
511                    LPARENTK Write_params_lst RPARENTK
512                    {$$ = new WritelnStmtCls($3);}
513               ;
514               Write_params_lst:  Write_params
515                      {$$ = new WriteParamLstCls($1);}
516                    | Write_params_lst COMMATK Write_params
517                      {$$ = PWriteParamLstCls($1) -> append($3);}
518                    ;
519               Write_params: Expr
520                      {$$ = new WriteParamCls($1,0,0);}
521                    | Expr COLONTK Expr
522                      /* integer */
523                      {$$ = new WriteParamCls($1,$3,0);}
524                    | Expr COLONTK Expr COLONTK Expr
525                      /* real */
526                      {$$ = new WriteParamCls($1,$3,$5);}
527                        ;


530 Expr_lst: Expr
531         {$$ = new ExprLstCls($1);}
532     | Expr_lst COMMATK Expr
533         {yyerrok;
534          $$ = PExprLstCls($1) -> append($3);}
535     | error
536         {soft.err("Error in Epression list");}
537     /*
538     | Expr_lst error
539         {soft.err("Error in Epression list -- expecting comma");}
540      */
541     | Expr_lst COMMATK error
542         {soft.err("Error after comma in  Epression list");}
543     ;
544     Expr: Simple_expr
545         | Simple_expr Relational_op Simple_expr
546            {$$ = PRelOpCls($2) -> make_tree($1,$3);}
547         | Simple_expr Relational_op error
548            {soft.err("Expression error");}
```

```
549          | error  /* this causes 6 reduce/reduce conflicts! */
550              {soft.err("Expression error");}
551          ;
552      Relational_op: EQTK
553              {$$ = new EqCls;}
554          | LTTK
555              {$$ = new LtCls;}
556          | GTTK
557              {$$ = new GtCls;}
558          | LETK
559              {$$ = new LeCls;}
560          | GETK
561              {$$ = new GeCls;}
562          | NETK
563              {$$ = new NeCls;}
564          | INTK
565              {$$ = new InCls;} .
566          ;


568      Simple_expr: Term
569          | PLUSTK Term
570              {$$ = $2;}
571          | MINUSTK Term
572              {$$ = new UMinusCls($2);}
573          | Simple_expr Add_op Term
574              {$$ = PAddOpCls($2) -> make_tree($1,$3);}
575          | Simple_expr Add_op error
576              {soft.err("Simple Expression error");}
577          ;
578      Add_op: PLUSTK
579              {$$ = new PlusCls;}
580          | MINUSTK
581              {$$ = new MinusCls;}
582          | ORTK
583              {$$ = new OrCls;}
584          ;


586          Term: Factor
587          | Term Mul_op Factor
588              {$$ = PMulOpCls($2) -> make_tree($1,$3);}
589          ;
590          Mul_op: ASTERTK
591              {$$ = new TimesCls;}
592          | SLASHTK
593              {$$ = new DivideCls;}
594          | DIVTK
595              {$$ = new DivCls;}
596          | MODTK
597              {$$ = new ModCls;}
598          | ANDTK
599              {$$ = new AndCls;}
600          ;


602          Factor: Unsigned_lit
603          | Variable
```

```
604                         | Set
605                         | NOTTK Factor
606                             {$$ = new UNotCls($2);}
607                         | LPARENTK Expr RPARENTK
608                             {$$ = $2;}
609                           ;
610                         Unsigned_lit: Unsigned_number
611                                 {$$ = new LitFactorCls($1);}
612                             | STRINGTK       /* type is char if len=1 */
613                                 {PLiteralCls lit = new LiteralCls(0);
614                                  $$ = new LitFactorCls(lit);}
615                             | BADSTRINGTK
616                                 {soft.err("Wrong string delimiters");
617                                  PLiteralCls lit = new LiteralCls(0);
618                                  $$ = new LitFactorCls(lit);}
619                             | NILTK
620                               ;
621                         Set: LBRACKTK Member_stuff RBRACKTK
622                                 {$$ = new SetFactorCls($2);}
623                               ;
624                         Member_stuff: /*empty*/
625                                     {$$ = 0;}
626                             | Member_lst
627                               ;
628                         Member_lst: Member
629                                 {$$ = new SetMemberLstCls($1);}
630                             | Member_lst COMMATK Member
631                                 {$$ = PSetMemberLstCls($1) ->
632                                                    append($3);}
633                               ;
634                         Member: Expr
635                                 {$$ = new SetMemberCls($1,0);}
636                             | Expr DDTK Expr
637                                 {$$ = new SetMemberCls($1,$3);}
638                               ;


642 Variable: Ident Actual_param_stuff
643         /* could be a const, variable or  fn_call*/
644         {PVarFuncDesignatorCls vfd = new VarFuncDesignatorCls($1,$2);
645          $$ = vfd -> get_factor();}
646     | Variable LBRACKTK Expr_lst RBRACKTK
647         {$$ = new ArrayDesigCls($1,$3);}
648     | Variable DOTTK Ident
649         {$$ = new FieldDesigCls($1,$3);}
650     | Variable UPARROWTK
651         {$$ = new DereferenceCls($1);}
652       ;
653 Ident_lst: Ident
654         {$$ = new IdentLstCls($1);}
655     | Ident_lst COMMATK Ident
656         {yyerrok;
657          $$ = PIdentLstCls($1) -> append($3);}
658     | Ident_lst error
659         {soft.err("Expecting comma in Ident list");
660          $$ = $1;}
```

```
661      | Ident_lst COMMATK error
662          {soft.err("Error after comma in Ident list");
663           $$ = $1;}
664      ;
665      Ident: IDENTIFIERTK
666          {$$ = new IdentCls();}
667          ;
668  Record_var: Variable
669      {$$ = new RecVarCls($1);}
670      ;
```

Bibliography

[1] Alfred V. Aho, Ravi Sethi, and Jeffery D. Ullman. *Compilers, Principles, Techniques, and Tools*. Addison-Wesley, Reading, MA, 1986.

[2] J. W. Backus. The IBM Speedcoding system. *Journal of ACM*, 1:4–6, 1954.

[3] Grady Booch. *Object Oriented Design with Applications*. Benjamin/Cummings, Redwood City, CA, 1991.

[4] Daniel I. A. Cohen. *Introduction to Computer Theory*. Wiley, New York, 1986.

[5] Doug Cooper. *Condensed Pascal*. Norton, New York, 1987.

[6] Neill Graham. *Learning C++*. McGraw-Hill, New York, 1991.

[7] Jim Holmes. *Building Your Own Compiler with C++*. Prentice Hall, Englewood Cliffs, NJ, 1995. A compiler project, coordinated with *Object-Oriented Compiler Construction*.

[8] Allan I. Holub. *Compiler Design in C*. Prentice Hall, Englewood Cliffs, NJ, 1990.

[9] John E Hopcroft and Jeffrey D. Ullman. *Introduction to Automata theory, Languages, and Computation*. Addison-Wesley, Reading, MA, 1979.

[10] Brian W. Kernighan and Dennis M. Ritchie. *The C Programming Language*. Prentice Hall, Englewood Cliffs, NJ, second edition, 1988.

[11] Donald E. Knuth. *The Art of Computer Programming: Sorting and searching*, volume 3. Addison-Wesley, Reading, MA, 1973.

[12] Stanley B. Lippman. *C++ Primer*. Addison-Wesley, Reading, MA, 1989.

[13] P. D. Mosses. *Action Semantics*. Cambridge University Press, Cambridge, England, 1991.

[14] Peter D. Mosses and David A. Watt. Pascal action semantics—towards a denotational description of ISO Standard Pascal using abstract semantic algebras. Technical report, Aarhus University, Denmark, 1986. A revised version is in process.

[15] M. L. Powell. A portable optimizing compiler for Modula-2. *ACM SIGPLAN Notices*, 19(6):310–318, 1984.

[16] Terrance W. Pratt. *Programming Languages, Design and Implementation.* Prentice Hall, Englewood Cliffs, NJ, 1984.

[17] James Rumbaugh, Michael Blaha, William Premerlani, Frederick Eddy, and William Lorensen. *Object-Oriented Modeling and Design.* Prentice Hall, Englewood Cliffs, NJ, 1991.

[18] Axel T. Schreiner and H. George Friedman, Jr. *Introduction to Compiler Construction with UNIX.* Prentice Hall, Englewood Cliffs, NJ, 1985.

[19] Robert W. Sebesta. *Concepts of Programming Languages.* Benjamin/Cummings, Redwood City, CA, 1989.

[20] R. Sethi and J. D. Ullman. The generation of optimal code for arithmetic expressions. *Journal of ACM*, 17(4):715–728, 1970.

[21] SPARC International, Inc. *The SPARC Architecture Manual.* Prentice Hall, Englewood Cliffs, NJ, 1992.

[22] Bjarne Stroustrup. *The C++ Programming Language.* Addison-Wesley, Reading, MA, 1987.

[23] *SUN4 Assembly Language Reference Manual*, 1988.

[24] David A. Watt. *Programming Language Semantics.* Prentice Hall, Englewood Cliffs, NJ, 1991.

[25] W. M. Wulf, R. K. Johnsson, C. B. Weinstock, S. O. Hobbs, and C. M. Geschke. *The Design of an Optimizing Compiler.* American Elsevier, New York, 1975.

Index